MODERN INDUSTRY
AND THE AFRICAN

PUBLISHERS NOTE

This Enquiry was made in 1932 under the auspices of the Department of Social and Industrial Research of the International Missionary Council and does not represent the contemporary research of that organisation.

The Carnegie Corporation of New York and the Phelps-Stokes Fund contributed to this study and made possible its original publication.

MODERN INDUSTRY
AND THE AFRICAN

*An Enquiry into the Effect of the Copper Mines
of Central Africa upon Native Society and
the Work of the Christian Missions*

J. MERLE DAVIS

Chairman of the Commission of Enquiry and Editor of the Report

SECOND EDITION

with a new introduction by

ROBERT I. ROTBERG

FRANK CASS & CO. LTD.

1967

Published by
FRANK CASS AND COMPANY LIMITED
67 Great Russell Street, London W.C.1
by arrangement with Macmillan & Co. Ltd.

First edition   1933
Second edition   1967

Printed in Holland by
N.V. Grafische Industrie Haarlem

MEMBERS OF THE COMMISSION
OF ENQUIRY

J. MERLE DAVIS, *Chairman.*
> Director, Department of Social and Industrial Research, Geneva.

CHARLES W. COULTER, Ph.D.
> Professor of Sociology, Ohio Wesleyan University.

LEO MARQUARD.
> History Master, Grey College School, Bloemfontein.

RAY E. PHILLIPS.
> Missionary and Welfare Worker, Johannesburg.

E. A. G. ROBINSON.
> Fellow of Sidney Sussex College and Lecturer in Economics in the University of Cambridge.

MABEL SHAW, O.B.E.
> Principal, Livingstone Memorial Girls' School, Mbereshi.

INTRODUCTION
TO THE SECOND EDITION
by
ROBERT I. ROTBERG

Modern Industry and the African was originally written as a Christian response to the problems posed for the future of African society and missionary policy by the creation in Central Africa of a vast industrial complex based on the mining of copper. From at least the eighteenth century, the inhabitants of Zambia (formerly Northern Rhodesia) and Katanga exported smelted copper in the form of bangles or crosses to ports on both the Atlantic and Indian Ocean coasts of Africa. For utilitarian purposes as well, they made extensive use of what were essentially surface outcroppings of ore, naturally remaining unaware of the vast deposits that lay underground and were subsequently to provide Europe with many of the necessities of war and peace. David Livingstone and numerous other nineteenth century explorers realized the potential of this region, however, and directed the attention thither of entrepreneurs.[1] Both King Leopold II's Congo Independent State and Cecil Rhodes' British South Africa Company coveted it, and attempted by diplomatic and military means to bring the entire mineral-rich plateau within its own sphere of influence. But, in 1891, the Independent State and the Company divided the plateau, with its underlying lode of copper bearing ore, among themselves. The northern part of this region became a part of Katanga and the Congo

[1] David Livingstone (ed. Horace Waller), *Last Journals* (London, 1874), II, 120; Verney Lovett Cameron, *Across Africa* (London, 1877), 298, 353, 358, 475.

while the southern section—now known as the Copperbelt
—passed successively under the administrative aegis of
Northeastern, Northwestern, and Northern Rhodesia.[1]

In Northwestern Rhodesia, itinerant prospectors were
soon active. Between 1895 and 1899, Britons discovered
large ore bodies in the Hook of the Kafue region and at
Kansanshi, near Solwezi. The copper concentrate found
there proved insufficiently rich, however, to justify large-
scale mining. During the next decade, government officials
and prospectors located a number of more promising
outcrops of ore, many of which together provided the
economic base upon which later developed the urban
conditions that are the primary concern of this book.
Farther south, the Broken Hill lead, zinc, and vanadium
mine began operations in 1906, when the railway from
Cape Town and Livingstone extended its tracks there. In
1909 the railway reached the site of modern Ndola on the
Copperbelt, and, in 1910, Elisabethville, the Katangan
mining center. It permitted the import of coal and
machines and the economic export of concentrates that
had previously been carried on the heads of Africans. But
the Rhodesian surface ores were oxidized and of poor
quality compared to those of similar composition that had
been found in Katanga. The former therefore remained
unexploited until 1923, when a rising world demand encouraged British and American financiers carefully to
investigate the potential value of the Copperbelt deposits.
Soon thereafter, an American mining engineer demonstrated that a zone of sulphide copper lay at moderate
depths below the surface ore bodies and the ground-water
level, and others invented the so-called flotation method
of concentration which permitted its profitable exploitation.[2] Together, these discoveries radically altered the
economic future of Northern Rhodesia.

[1] In 1911, the amalgamation of Northwestern and Northeastern
Rhodesia created Northern Rhodesia.
[2] In Katanga, the otherwise richer deposits of copper remained
oxidized to the lowest depth mined. See *Infra*, 142.

The Copperbelt experienced its first boom in 1929/30 and the mines recruited white and black labour from all over southern Africa. The British and American-financed companies that had leased the subsoil rights of the Copperbelt soon constructed new towns, sunk shafts underground, and, in 1930, employed about thirty thousand Africans. But the world-wide slump in demand soon affected Northern Rhodesia; during the early years of the Depression several of the mines shut down and the others retrenched their labour, thus adding to the unease already experienced by Africans largely unaccustomed either to industrial or to urban life. Nevertheless, the Rhodesian companies weathered the crisis more successfully than their competitors, emerging as low-cost producers dependent upon abundant supplies of unskilled labour and ores that proved technically easy to treat.

The mining companies stood *in loco parentis* to their African employees. With the assistance of organizations established for the purpose, they initially attracted prospective workers from the rural areas of Northern Rhodesia and Nyasaland and provided transportation between their homes and the mines. They also conveyed families and, at the conclusion of a contracted period, repatriated to their villages those Africans who wanted to leave the urban areas. While two of the three major copper producers also attempted to encourage the growth of a stable resident working force, the management of the Nkana mine feared "detribalization"—i.e., sophistication—if Africans should remain on the mines for more than two consecutive years. Adopting the South African practice, this mine preferred to employ single men. The other concerns saw virtue in family life and supplied some of the social services believed to be conducive to urban adjustment.[1] On all of the mines, Africans lived either with their families in small huts supplied by a company, or individually in communal barracks. The "bachelors" at Nkana were served by a

---

[1] Compared to the need, however, the contribution of the mining companies to educational development was negligible.

common kitchen; elsewhere families and single men all
received weekly rations of maize meal, meat, salt, and
vegetables from the commissaries of their respective
employers. They attended their own medical clinics, saw
free movies, usually of an instructional variety, shopped
at their own stores and market stalls, and looked to their
companies for every conceivable kind of service and
support. "Considered as labour camps," a later report
opined, "the conditions in the compounds of these mines
[were] good in many ways."[1]

But Africans greeted such paternalism uneasily. They
believed themselves to be badly paid, particularly in
comparison to the wages received by the whites with
whom they worked. African miners drew compensation at
an average rate of 23/- a month, out of which they purchased all of the necessities demanded by urban conditions. Africans disliked the supposedly inferior houses to
which they were assigned, and complained of primitive
sanitary arrangements. In their eyes, conditions of
employment, particularly underground, were considerably
less than ideal. More than anything else, however, Africans
resident on the Copperbelt resented being constantly confronted with virulent expressions of white prejudice.
Whites insulted Africans openly and erected a *de facto*
colour bar which effectively prevented the promotion of
Africans to better paying positions of responsibility. At
the same time, they encouraged Africans in practice to
perform the "skilled" work for which they themselves
received handsome remuneration. The management at
Nkana, an official wrote, simply wanted "to get two
shillings worth of work for one shilling's wage out of the
'bloody nigger'."[2] The mine managements and the white
miners, many of whom had earlier lived in South Africa,
together compelled Africans individually and collectively

---

[1] A. W. Pim and S. Milligan, *Report of the Commission Appointed to
Enquire into The Financial and Economic Position of Northern Rhodesia*,
col. no. 145 (1938), 41.

[2] Sec/Lab/16: R. S. W. Dickenson to Harold Francis Cartmel-
Robinson, 6 October 1933, Lusaka archives.

to appreciate the extent of their inferiority. "I have the impression," a British official reflected, "that the attitude of the Europeans to natives at Nkana is neither politic nor in the best interests of the Mine."[1] The social malaise on the Copperbelt thus expressed a discontent generated as much by instances of discrimination as by sharply felt grievances of a narrowly economic kind.

The incorporation of rurally-experienced Africans into a growing white-dominated urban complex presented a concatenation of immediate and potential areas of social concern. In large, if the general nature of most of the resultant problems were obvious and capable of a rough and ready description, their precise analysis and prescriptive solution remained unknown. Neither the government of the Protectorate of Northern Rhodesia—since 1924 a direct responsibility of the Colonial Office— nor any of the missionary societies had, before 1933, come to terms with the needs of the Copperbelt. The government, although it exercised an administrative oversight on the Copperbelt and in the rural areas from which much of the labour force was recruited, generally interfered little in the day to day operations of the mining companies. Its revenues, being restricted, limited the extent of its initiative on social matters. Furthermore, many governmental officials preferred for the most part to concern themselves with the more easily understood affairs of village Africa. Whenever they tried to cope with township matters, their natural sympathy for the interests of the white farming and business community led them to overlook and obscure the African aspect.

In social welfare matters, the government looked to the missionary societies for assistance. In the rural areas, missionaries had, from the very earliest days of the

---

[1] *Ibid.*, Cartmel-Robinson to Dickenson, 11 October 1933. For additional detail and further references for much of the foregoing, see Robert I. Rotberg, *The Rise of Nationalism in Central Africa: The Making of Malawi and Zambia*, 1873–1964 (Cambridge, Mass., 1965), 156–161. For their help with parts of this essay, the author gratefully wishes to acknowledge Frederic Mosher and Trevor Coombe.

Company's rule, provided social services of the kind needed on the Copperbelt. In the years between 1882 and 1921, thirteen Protestant and Catholic missionary groups had occupied various sections of the territory. Each had started schools; a few had employed doctors and constructed hospitals.[1] The government had even begun to subsidize many of their activities. But because the area of the Copperbelt had, before payable ores were discovered, been sparsely populated, a small Baptist denomination only had settled there. And after the boom of the 1920s, only one other society, the Italian-based Roman Catholic Order of Franciscan Fathers Minor (Conventual) entered the region. Thus in 1932, one Baptist (A. J. Cross) and a few Franciscans ministered to the myriad needs of the large African population of the Copperbelt. Four other European ministers—two Congregationalists, an Anglican, and a Methodist—lived on the Copperbelt but concerned themselves almost exclusively with the spiritual needs of the white population.[2] (Curiously, *Modern Industry* gives only a brief mention to the already flourishing, exclusively African, Union Church of the Copperbelt. It had been established in 1925 by African Christians employed on the Copperbelt.)

It is with such considerations in mind that Dr. Joseph H. Oldham, the then secretary of the International Missionary Council, on behalf of British missionary societies having an interest in Africa, in 1930 proposed that the Department of Social and Industrial Research and Counsel of the International Missionary Council should "undertake a thorough field study of the effect of modern industry, and particularly that of the great copper mines of the Belgian Congo and Northern Rhodesia, upon African

---

[1] See Robert I. Rotberg, *Christian Missionaries and the Creation of Northern Rhodesia*, 1882–1924 (Princeton and London, 1965).

[2] J. Merle Davis to Frederick P. Keppel (President of the Carnegie Corporation of New York), 12 January 1932, Carnegie Corporation files used and cited with permission; *Infra*, 296–297; John V. Taylor and Dorothea A. Lehmann, *Christians of the Copperbelt: The Growth of the Church in Northern Rhodesia* (London, 1961), 34–37.

tribal society."[1] The Department of Social and Industrial Research and Counsel had opened in Geneva earlier in the same year. In inspiration, it stemmed largely from speeches by Professor R. H. Tawney and Harold Grimshaw to the second International Missionary Council meeting, which had been held in Jerusalem in 1928. Tawney stressed the inadequacy of a world-wide missionary programme which failed to take account of economic and social factors in the development of self-supporting and enduring Christian churches; strongly endorsing this criticism, Grimshaw, then the director of the Native Labour Section of the International Labour Office, urged the International Missionary Council to open a research bureau which could help his own organization maintain its oversight of conditions of employment in the underdeveloped areas of the world.[2]

Oldham and Dr. John R. Mott, the chairman of both the Council and the World's Alliance of Young Men's Christian Associations, accepted the challenge and proved instrumental in the establishment of a Department of Social and Industrial Research. Mott also recruited the Research Department's first director, the Rev. Mr. John Merle Davis. To this new work Davis brought a wide range of administrative, research, and practical experience overseas. The son of a Congregational missionary educator who founded an important university in Japan, Davis grew up in the church-centered town of Oberlin, Ohio, and later attended its famed liberal arts college. There, neglecting his studies, he became a mainstay of the powerful college football team, pole vaulted, high jumped, threw the hammer, put the shot, and won medals in pentathlon competitions. After attending classes at the Oberlin

---

[1] John Merle Davis, *An Autobiography* (nd, np, but Tokyo, 1959), 128. For Oldham's interest in and influence upon African events, see George Bennett, "Paramountcy to Partnership: J. H. Oldham and Africa", *Africa*, xxx (1960), 356–361; Robert G. Gregory, *Sidney Webb and East Africa* (Berkeley, 1962), 27–43 ff.

[2] Proceedings of the Jerusalem meeting, *The Christian Mission in Relation to Industrial Problems* (New York, 1928), V, 63, 119, 123–131.

seminary, Davis taught in a boys preparatory school, worked for the Young Men's Christian Association in New York, explored most of Western Europe, and then decided to resume the study of theology. At the Hartford Theological Seminary he concentrated particularly on the mastery of church history, and later returned to Europe to pursue this academic interest at the Universities of Göttingen, Leipzig, and Munich. It was at this point in his career that Dr. Mott, who had known Davis' father, persuaded the younger Davis to forswear a life of academia and, instead—like so many other Oberlinians—to accept the call of missionary service overseas.

In early 1906, Davis became the first secretary of a newly opened Young Men's Christian Association in Nagasaki. He subsequently occupied a similar position in Tokyo, where, from 1916 to 1918, he undertook a pioneering social and economic study which led to an awakening of Protestant and Buddhist interest in the social welfare of Japanese slum dwellers.

In 1923, after he had settled in California, Davis became the administrative director of a West Coast race relations survey with which Dr. Mott was connected, and two years later moved on to become executive secretary of the first Pan-Pacific Conference in Honolulu, which was sponsored by the International Association of Young Men's Christian Associations. This conference expressed the concern of American and Asian university and church leaders with the deterioration of race relations in the Pacific Ocean basin and led to the formation of the influential Institute of Pacific Relations; Davis became its general secretary and, as its most energetic promoter, travelled extensively throughout Oceania, Southeast Asia, Europe, and the Soviet Union during the next few years.[1] Thus, when Dr. Mott urged him to direct the International Missionary Council's proposed Research Department and, having moved to Geneva, when Dr. Oldham requested a

[1] Biographical information is derived from Davis, *Autobiography*, 4–125.

study of conditions of African industrial life, Davis was alive to the intrinsic importance of both suggestions and fully aware of the larger context of race relations in which the specific study and his more general directorship set.

"After millenniums of comparatively quiet and unrestricted, undirected life," Davis wrote from the Victoria Falls in 1931 at the beginning of his preliminary survey of southern African conditions, "the Bantu race has taken a tremendous plunge and is pouring into a restricted channel hemmed in by forces it has not known before and which it cannot cope with. It has to surge forward between these walls at a speed it has never experienced and whither it knows not. Let us hope that as with the Zambezi, there lies before it a normal river bed into which it can expand and find its way in due course to the sea. But I suppose the component elements of this people's life are being shattered irrevocably apart, and will, as the particles of water, have to find new forms and alignments in the life that is ahead."[1] Subsequent conversations with officials of the Northern Rhodesia government and the managers of the Copperbelt mining companies only deepened Davis' conviction that the new conditions of urban life in emerging Africa merited a full-scale research project of unprecedented scope. The government seemed out of touch with the events that it was expected to direct, the mine managements generally unconcerned, and the missions hesitant. In terms of pure research, the field was obviously virgin. Moreover, like Oldham, who hoped that one of the results of the study would be an intensification of missionary activity on the Copperbelt, Davis was impressed by the extent to which the missionaries, if they grasped the nettle of urban opportunity, might in default of governmental initiative lay the foundations of a new, deeply religious civilization on the Copperbelt. He wrote

[1] Davis to Mott, 20 September 1931, files of the International Missionary Council, New York, quoted with permission. The author wishes gratefully to acknowledge the assistance that he received from Misses Pauline Heppe and Beryl Saunders of the World Council of Churches.

excitedly to Mott: "I have been profoundly impressed from the day I landed in South Africa with the tremendous responsibilities and opportunity of Christian missions in Southern Africa. I have experienced nothing to compare with it in any other part of the world. While in some parts of Asia missions have been wondering just what their job might be, in Africa they have had placed in their hands the greater part of the task of recreating the life of the race, of rebuilding the Black Man's world and adjusting him to his new surroundings. It is a staggering task, literally dumped upon missions by the government concerned. The leaders . . . frankly say that were it not for the missionary program of educational, industrial, and religious work they would find themselves in an untenable position."[1]

As a result of his preliminary survey of conditions, Davis recommended a detailed examination of the three-fold impact of governmental policy, industrial life, and the missionary endeavour upon the emergence of Northern Rhodesia's African population.[2] With financial support from the Carnegie Corporation of New York and the Phelps-Stokes Fund, Davis enlisted the services of Leo Marquard, then a lecturer in history at the Grey College School in Bloemfontein, the Orange Free State, and later the managing director of the Oxford University Press in Cape Town;[3] Edward Austin Gossage Robinson, then a fellow of Sidney Sussex College, economics lecturer at the University of Cambridge, and consultant economist to the Gaekwar of Gwalior, India (his father was Dean of Winchester Cathedral) and later Professor of Economics at Cambridge; Charles W. Coulter, a professor of sociology at Ohio

---

[1] *Ibid.*

[2] Davis to Keppel, 9 May 1932, Carnegie Corporation files.

[3] Marquard remembers that he was asked to join the Commission as a result of a chance meeting with Davis in 1931. "I was doing some research work on Native administration in various London libraries, and . . . I think he selected me because he wanted someone who was thoroughly familiar with southern Africa and who had made a study of administrative questions". Marquard to the author, *in litt.*, 16 September 1965.

Wesleyan University who had taught in China and the Union of South Africa and served as a member of a Chicago race relations survey and the South African "Poor White" commission of 1930: Mabel Shaw, a pioneer women's educationist with the London Missionary Society in Northern Rhodesia; and the Rev. Mr. Ray Edmund Phillips, an American Congregational missionary who had —together with the Rev. Frederick Bridgman, Davis' brother-in-law—for many years operated a flourishing social welfare centre for Africans in Johannesburg. Phillips subsequently became the principal of the Jan Hofmeyr School of Social Work, also in Johannesburg.[1]

Although each contributed to the work of the commission of inquiry and played an equal part in its deliberations, neither Miss Shaw, who had already published four books about her work, nor Phillips, who had described the urban conditions of Johannesburg in *The Bantu Are Coming: Phases of South Africa's Race Problem* (London, 1930), wrote any part of the final report that follows this introduction.[2]

In July, 1932, Davis and his team crossed the Zambezi River and commenced their study of Northern Rhodesia. After holding discussions in Livingstone with officials of the government, they spent a week on the Copperbelt and two weeks in Katanga. From Elisabethville they drove across the Luapula River into Northeastern Rhodesia, where they spent three weeks in what Davis called "the wilds." From Fort Rosebery, *via* ten mission stations and the various administrative centers, they reached

---

[1] Phillips to the author, *in litt.*, 27 October 1965. In 1931, Professor John Coatman of the London School of Economics and Professor Rexford Tugwell, then of Columbia University, had both agreed to serve with Davis in Africa. (Davis to Keppel, 20 February and 12 May 1931, Carnegie Corporation files.) When the expanded inquiry was organized, presumably neither were available.

[2] Miss Shaw had published *Children of the Chief* (London, 1921), *Dawn in Africa* (London, 1927), *Treasure of Darkness* (London, 1930), and *God's Candlelights* (London, 1932). See also Rotberg, *Christian Missionaries*, 125. Phillips later wrote *The Bantu in the City: A Study of Cultural Adjustment on the Witwatersrand* (Lovedale, 1938).

Abercorn before returning to the Copperbelt *via* Chinsali and Mpika. "This 2,000 mile tour," Davis wrote, "formed the heart of our work. It gave us an admirable opportunity to study native society in the recruitment areas of the deep interior . . . ."[1] For the next two weeks the members of the Commission once again investigated conditions in Ndola, and on the Roan Antelope and Nkana mines. They talked at length to managers, civic leaders, provincial and district officers, persons responsible for the social welfare of Africans, missionaries, white miners, and a variety of African employees. Later Coulter, Phillips, and Davis visited the Broken Hill mine and Mazabuka, in Northern Rhodesia. Minus Miss Shaw, the whole group continued their researches in Southern Rhodesia, and Marquard, Robinson, and Davis drove from Johannesburg to Cape Town *via* Basutoland, the Transkei, and the Ciskei. The report that follows contains the sum of their divers impressions and comparisons.

At the time of its publication, *Modern Industry and the African* represented a progressive, essentially liberal approach to the development of the Copperbelt of Northern Rhodesia and the response thereto of the Christian Church. It expressed the authors' very real fears that urbanization would irreparably damage the foundations of indigenous life and demonstrated their implicit faith in the virtues of a past "golden age" of rural social stability. They sought to soften the hammer blows of detribalization and, at the very least, to improve the conditions under which such blows would be received. Davis and his colleagues thus urged the essentially rurally-based Church to accept the Copperbelt as its most critical challenge. "The profound social changes which the copper belt is causing in the structure of Bantu society," they concluded, "constitute an obligation and a necessity on the part of missions to consider the problem of social welfare as an important

---

[1] Davis to Keppel, 17 November 1932, Carnegie Corporation files. For the trip see also Davis, *Autobiography*, 157–159.

field for study and for cultivation."[1] In addition to recommending that the Protestant churches in the interests of efficiency should pool their efforts on the Copperbelt (the United Missions in the Copperbelt, the forerunner of the United Church of Central Africa in Rhodesia, was established in 1936), they encouraged missionaries to make a number of specific alterations of approach in order to keep abreast of contemporary developments, to strive for improvements in racial understanding—to secure an estimate of the Black man "on the basis of individual quality and achievement rather than on the basis of his racial group alone",[2] and even suggested that the various societies themselves should accord to Africans a larger degree of responsibility and leadership than hitherto in the affairs of the Church and mission-run schools.[3] Of the seventy-five recommendations that comprised the final chapter of *Modern Industry*, most implicitly recognized the extent to which the missionary bodies active in Northern Rhodesia had either remained unaware of or refused to concern themselves with problems of social change. The recommendations collectively may be regarded as a blueprint for Christian action; had missionaires paid it more than lip service, many of their subsequent difficulties of adjustment might have been avoided.

The report is more than a document of particular interest to students of missionary strategy. Two of its sections, on economics and government, contain data and analysis of very great value to the historian of colonial Central Africa. Except possibly in technical journals, Robinson's summary of the opening-up of the Copperbelt has only very recently been superseded by Richard Hall, *Zambia* (London 1965), chapter eight.[4] His chapter on methods of recruitment of labour, and their organization on

---

[1] *Infra*, 376.
[2] *Infra*, 379.
[3] *Infra*, 384.
[4] Lewis H. Gann, "The Northern Rhodesian Copper Industry and the World of Copper; 1923–1952", *The Rhodes-Livingstone Journal*, xviii (1955), 1–7, is in part derivative of Robinson.

the mines, remains the best of its kind. And his chapter on
the consequences of industrialisation reflected a broad
understanding of the problems of economic growth in the
context of a developing society. When acted upon, two
among many of his specific recommendations—that the
Government should provide a unit of currency smaller
than a threepenny piece (the ubiquitous "tickey") and
establish produce markets—significantly encouraged the
participation of Africans in the Protectorate's money
economy. Marquard, in his discussion of the government
of Northern Rhodesia, reached a number of complementary conclusions. He drew attention to the lack of any
means by which urban Africans might express their
grievances (the Copperbelt riots of 1935 and 1940 under-
lined this deficiency), deplored the likely consequences of
increasing settler control of urban and territorial affairs,
and prophesied that the political destiny of Northern
Rhodesia lay with territories to the east (Nyasaland and
Tanganyika) and not, as "amalgamationists" preferred,
with those to the south. His description of the legislature,
the executive, and the judiciary of Northern Rhodesia is
still valuable. His chapter on indirect rule, however,
idealized a theory that, for the reasons which he himself
noted, proved incapable of translation into reality.

In writing their different sections, Robinson, Marquard,
Coulter, and Davis, were all aware of the extent to which
the poison of racial prejudice had already infected urban
Rhodesia. Coulter outlined six problem areas that have
since become the familiar terrain of subsequent students of
race relations, and realized that African grievances had a
basis in fact. "Few of the inconsistencies of European
civilisation," he wrote, "have escaped the rapier-like
thrusts of a people who see our faults and failings with the
same clearness as we see theirs."[1] Davis, aware that the
urban experience had already begun to produce English-
speaking, assimilated Africans of some sophistication,
wisely warned missionaries not to scorn these seemingly

[1] *Infra*, 98.

"cheeky" Copperbelt hybrids. "A new criticism born of disillusionment of the White man now shows in [the African's] dealings with Europeans. He has begun to discern, discriminate and question, and these uncomfortable faculties are turned upon all White men, including the missionary. "Fortunate," Davis continued, "is the missionary who sees in this mental and spiritual awakening the birth of a new man, and who can successfully readjust his attitude of mind, assumptions and his message to the needs of this prodigy that has been created on the copper belt."[1]

Dispassionate in their analysis and largely free from any semblance of bias, the authors of *Modern Industry*, with the exception of Coulter, also betrayed few traces of ethnocentricity. In the main, their argument was soundly constructed. Unfortunately, however, Coulter, Marquard, and Davis occasionally accepted common knowledge as fact and sometimes repeated historical cliches that had no basis in reality. Chapter II, "The Historical Background," which Marquard culled from the then available sources, contains several inaccuracies; the data on pages 19–21 are exceptionally untrustworthy. In keeping with the style of the times, it also deals exclusively with the events of the European occupation, remaining unaware of contributions by Africans. Davis' Chapter XVIII—"The Missionary Occupation of the Copperbelt"—also exhibits errors of omission and commission. The sequence and many of the dates are wrong. Nevertheless, if the sumaries of past events are questionable, the modern reader may accept the description of the then contemporary dilemma both with confidence and with wonder at the extent to which the authors proved prescient.

The publication of *Modern Industry* focused the attention of the government, missionary societies, and anthropologists upon the problems of Copperbelt life and the transition thereto from the rural, more traditional, existence hitherto enjoyed by the vast majority of

[1] *Infra*, 291.

Rhodesian Africans. It is difficult to assess the precise impact that *Modern Industry* alone may have made, however, because although the missionary societies, the government, and the mining companies all attempted to improve the provision of social services to Africans resident on the Copperbelt, and eventually satisfied many of the recommendations embodied in the report, the riots of 1935 probably had a catalytic effect much greater than that of the book.[1] If Davis and his colleagues provided the intellectual framework within which sympathetic administrators could understand the riots, the disturbances themselves engendered the necessary sense of immediacy.[2]

[1] For the riots, see Rotberg, *Nationalism*, 161–168. The missions had, however, already begun the consultations that led in 1936 to the formation of the United Missions in the Copperbelt. Dr. John Mott again played a significant role in this development. For details, see Taylor and Lehmann, *Christians of the Copperbelt*, 37–40ff.

[2] After publishing *Modern Industry and the African in* 1933, Davis managed to encourage the Carnegie Corporation to underwrite and the British Colonial Office to sponsor the so-called Bantu Educational Cinema Experiment, which from 1934 to 1937 pioneered the showing of instructional films to Africans resident in Tanganyika, Kenya, and Uganda. Thereafter, as the director of the International Missionary Council's Research Department, he travelled throughout Asia in preparation for the third World Missions conference of the Council, which was held in a suburb of Madras, southern India, in 1938. There Davis presented an important report on the economic and social basis—the so-called Fourth Dimension—of the Church in non-Western areas. A series of studies of the role of the Church in Central and Southern America followed. After World War II, he and others persuaded the Carnegie Corporation and the British Colonial Office to support a study of African marriage and family life that had originally been mooted at the Madras conference. (Arthur Phillips [ed.], *A Survey of African Marriage and Family Life* [London, 1953].) Having retired in 1949, Davis became a Fellow of the Institute of Economic Studies of the University of California, Berkeley. He maintained an active interest in a variety of projects until his death on 15 March 1960. In addition to the present volume and a number of unsigned reports, he wrote *Davis, Soldier Missionary: A Biography of Rev. Jerome D. Davis, D.D.* [his father] (Boston, 1916); *Some Observations on China* (n.p., c. 1926); *The Institute of Pacific Relations* (Worcester, Mass., 1926); *Notes from a Pacific Circuit: Report Letters of J. Merle Davis to President Ray Lyman Wilbur* (Honolulu, 1927); *The Economic Basis of the Church* [Volume V of the Proceedings of the Madras meeting of the International Missionary Council] (New York, 1939); *The Economic and*

These events, and the very growth in size and importance of the Copperbelt also set in train a series of related
studies that deepened the excavation that had been
originally examined in *Modern Industry*. In 1940 and 1941,
Godfrey Wilson, the first director of the recently established Rhodes–Livingstone Institute for Social Research,
published, in two parts, *The Economics of Detribalization
in Northern Rhodesia* (Livingstone). It presented data
gathered from the African employees of the Broken Hill
mine, and with respect to the need for the development of
agriculture and secondary industries, came to conclusions
similar to those advanced in *Modern Industry* by Robinson.
After World War II, the Copperbelt naturally attracted
the attention of other sociologists and anthropologists. In
1950, Clyde Mitchell began a survey of social conditions
on the Copperbelt; he has since published a number of
articles and *African Urbanization in Ndola and Luanshya*
(Lusaka, 1954). A. L. Epstein, who collaborated with
Mitchell, published *Politics in an Urban African Community* (Manchester, 1958). William Watson, who studied
one of the groups that had traditionally sent men to the
mines, wrote *Tribal Cohesion in a Money Economy*
(Manchester, 1958). Hortense Powdermaker, who did her
field investigation primarily in Luanshya in 1953/4 and
was interested in the influence of mass media upon
attitude formation, published *Copper Town: Changing
Africa; The Human Situation on the Rhodesian Copperbelt*
(New York, 1962). Of these and the many other studies

Social Environment of the Younger Churches (London, 1939); The
Economic Basis of the Evangelical Church in Mexico (London, 1940);
The Church in Puerto Rico's Dilemma (New York, 1942); The Cuban
Church in A Sugar Economy (New York, 1942); The Evangelical Church
in the River Plate Republics (New York, 1943); How the Church Grows
in Brazil: A Study of the Economic and Social Basis of the Evangelical
Church in Brazil (New York, 1943); and New Buildings on Old Foundations: A Handbook on Stabilizing the Young Churches in Their Environment (New York, 1945), his major work. For a brief memorial note,
see Fred Field Goodsell, "Serenity Amid Labour: Observations Concerning the Life and Work of John Merle Davis, 1875–1960," The
International Review of Missions, xlix (1960), 443–445.

published or now in progress, however, Taylor and Lehmann's *Christians of the Copperbelt*, sponsored as it was by the International Missionary Council, is the only one that deals at any length with the relations of the Church to the conditions of modern economic life. Within its pages may be found the fullest assessment of the role of the missionary movement in the shaping of the urban environment of modern Zambia.

Robert I. Rotberg

Harvard University,
31 December 1965.

FOREWORD
TO THE FIRST EDITION

AN enquiry into the impact of the copper-mines of Central Africa upon Bantu society and the work of missions was undertaken in 1932 by the Department of Social and Industrial Research of the International Missionary Council. This bureau was opened at Geneva in 1930 to provide the means of studying those social and economic developments in various parts of the world that are affecting Christian missions with the desire to create an informed public opinion with regard to such developments and to assist the Church in making needful adjustments to them.

The investment of Western capital in African industries has made the Native dependent upon the demand of world markets for the products of his labour and the resources of his continent. Alien influences such as wage economy, European law and Christian teachings are shaking the foundations of Bantu life.

Missions are deeply concerned with the changes these influences are bringing. The fibre and form of the Christian community and the healthy growth of the Church are dependent upon the new social and economic values and standards that are appearing. In view of these changes, in which direction shall the Church lend its influence, where put the emphasis of its activities and toward what goal direct the life of the people?

The copper belt of Northern Rhodesia was chosen as the chief field of study because its mines are among the latest that have been opened in Africa, and have been developed with a vigour and on a scale that have attracted a large Native working population. Moreover, the position of these mines between those of the Belgian Congo and the Union of South Africa with their widely contrasted labour policies gives Northern Rhodesia an opportunity to profit from the older experience of its neighbours.

The enquiry envisages the impact of European civilisation upon the African Native as a whole and undertakes to analyse the position of Christian missions in this impact in all its relationships. With this in view the problem was approached from four angles, viz. Sociology, Economics, Government and Religion.

1. To understand the effect of new influences upon human society calls for a clear picture of that society; its background, environment, the natural forces and human contacts that have shaped it, its way of life, values, beliefs, controls and the institutions it has evolved.

2. Underlying the whole enquiry are the economic forces operating in the Territory. A forecast of the probable demand of the copper-mines for Native labour is attempted and the effect of the mines upon Native industries, agriculture, markets and future centres of population is described.

3. The administration of the Territory, its policies for the development of the country and its people is next studied, together with the programme of Indirect Rule and the political stabilisation of the Bantu tribes.

4. The concluding section deals with the position of missions in relation to the new order; the implications for the Church of the new economic forces in the Territory; the implications of the administrative system and the interplay of these factors and of Christian teachings upon Native social, cultural, political and economic institutions. It finally points out certain changes in mission policy and methods that these developments suggest to the Church for more effectively realising its aim in this part of Africa.

A preliminary visit to the copper belt of Central Africa was made by the director of the Geneva Department in

1931. The problem was examined in its local setting; sources of co-operation were discovered and the most effective lines on which an enquiry could be undertaken were determined. The generous financial assistance of the Carnegie Corporation made it possible to secure the services of an international Commission equipped to study the various aspects of the problem.

The Commission was led by Mr. J. Merle Davis, the Director of the Department of Social and Industrial Research of Geneva. Associated with him were Dr. Charles W. Coulter, Professor of Sociology of Ohio Wesleyan University; Mr. E. A. G. Robinson, Fellow of Sidney Sussex College and Lecturer in Economics in the University of Cambridge; Mr. L. Marquard, History Master at the Grey College School, Bloemfontein; Miss Mabel Shaw, O.B.E., Principal of Livingstone Memorial Girls' Boarding School, of the London Missionary Society, Mbereshi, Northern Rhodesia; and Rev. Ray E. Phillips of the American Board of Commissioners for Foreign Missions and Social Worker under the Transvaal Chamber of Mines, Johannesburg.

The Commission spent from July until December 1932 in Africa. After consultation with advisers at the Cape and in the Transvaal the members proceeded to Livingstone, the capital of Northern Rhodesia, where Government officials supplied them with every possible facility for their work. Visits were made to the Rhodesian and Katanga copper-fields and to the Native labour recruitment areas, missions and administrative posts of the North-Eastern section of Northern Rhodesia. This was followed by a two-weeks tour of Southern Rhodesia and four weeks of study of the mining and recruitment areas in the Union of South Africa, including the Rand, Basutoland and the Transkeian and Ciskeian Native territories. The use of their own motor-cars enabled the Commission to visit many of the remote areas from which labour is drawn, thus supplementing their studies of conditions in the mines and settlements along the railway lines. The final two weeks on the continent were devoted to the organising of the Commission's findings at Cape Town.

In a project of the scope of this enquiry it is impossible to mention the names of the large number of persons whose assistance has made possible its successful conclusion. The Commission wishes especially to record its deep appreciation of the kindness of the late Governor of Northern Rhodesia, His Excellency Sir James Maxwell, and the hospitality with which they were received in Livingstone. The courtesy of the Head of the Northern Rhodesian Government was reflected by every branch of the service in the Protectorate.

Special acknowledgment is due to the officials of the Roan Antelope and Nkana mines for their hospitality and the invaluable co-operation of their staffs; to Col. A. Stephenson, Director of the Native Labour Association of Northern Rhodesia; and to Rev. H. C. Nutter, Welfare Director of the Nkana mine. Particular mention should be made of the courtesy extended to the Commission by His Excellency Governor E. Heenen of Katanga, and by Dr. L. Mottoulle, Director of Welfare Activities of the Union Minière.

Among the many missionaries who assisted the Commission should be named Rev. A. J. Cross of Ndola and Rev. E. I. Everett of Elisabethville, who aided in the study of conditions in their districts. A lively sense of indebtedness is felt to Mr. J. D. Rheinallt Jones of the Institute of Race Relations of South Africa, to Bishop Karney and Mrs. F. B. Bridgman of Johannesburg, to Principal H. R. Raikes of the University of the Witwatersrand, and to Professors S. Herbert Frankel, C. M. Doke, (Mrs.) R. F. A. Hoernle and W. M. MacMillan for help and invaluable counsel.

Gratitude is due to Professors Eric Walker of Cape Town, Edgar H. Brookes of Pretoria, J. F. W. Grosskopf and R. W. Willcox of Stellenbosch, for assistance in counsel and in criticism of manuscript; to Lord Lugard, Mr. F. E. Melland, Rev. Edwin W. Smith of London,

Dr. Otto Iserland, Rev. H. Junod and Dr. J. B. Condliffe of Geneva, and Dr. John Reisner and Dr. Thomas Jesse Jones of New York, for their criticism of the plan of the report and the manuscript.

Particularly does the editor wish to thank Mr. C. H. Weaver of the International Labour Office for valued counsel and help in assembling material, Monsieur Henri Anet of Brussels for assisting in contacts with the Belgian Colonial Office, Rev. Emory Ross of Leopoldville for guidance in Katanga, and Dr. J. H. Oldham of the International Missionary Council for the stimulus he gave to the inception of the enquiry and for assistance at many stages of its development. Finally, the editor voices his indebtedness to Dr. John R. Mott of New York and Mr. William Paton of London, who have worked untiringly for the creating of the department, and have given most generously of their counsel in this its first field project.

J. MERLE DAVIS
1933

CONTENTS

PART THREE

THE ECONOMIC PROBLEM

E. A. G. Robinson

Part Four

THE PROBLEM OF GOVERNMENT
Leo Marquard

PART FIVE

THE PROBLEM FOR MISSIONS

J. Merle Davis

PART ONE

INTRODUCTION

MAP OF
AFRICA
SHOWING
RELATIVE POSITION
OF
NORTHERN RHODESIA

CHAPTER I

THE CHANGING POSITION OF MISSIONS IN AFRICA

THERE are certain aspects of the position of Christian missions in Africa that differentiate their task from that of missions in many of the non-Christian areas of the world. Missions in Central Africa deal with backward races who are in a different cultural cycle from the peoples of Asia, Europe or America. The universal communalism of Bantu tribal life gave small room for individual progress. An aristocracy or leisure class was not evolved, nor feudal courts in which the arts or crafts could be encouraged. For these and other reasons it has come about that these peoples possess neither a culture, arts nor handicrafts which attract the European. The Bantu have no written language, records or literature, either philosophic, historical or religious. Their rich oral tradition and a wealth of fable shed no light upon their background. With the exception of the ruins of Great Zimbabwe and contemporary irrigation works in Southern Rhodesia, ruins which are by many attributed to foreign invaders, they possess no monuments nor enduring witness of material achievement.[1] The African of the areas of this study stands before the modern world with empty hands and with little apparent contribution to offer to world culture. The riches of his primitive culture, like the mineral wealth of his continent, have long been overlooked by the European, and like that mineral wealth will yield themselves only to persistent and skilled search.

Added to the poverty of his life is the helplessness of the African when faced with the advance of European civilisa-

[1] "Great Zimbabwe", *R.G.S. Journal*, February 1891, p. 105; Keane, *The Gold of Ophir*, p. 6; J. T. Bent, *The Ruined Cities of Mashonaland*, 1892; Petermann, Geographical Communications, Supplement, p. 37.

1

tion. In contrast with the Asiatic peoples who possess governments and social institutions to which the individual may look for protection, the African Native is powerless and without resource. He is a pawn to be moved about the African chess-board by the Powers who control his continent. In difficulty he must look to alien Governments interpreting alien codes of justice whose decisions he has no alternative but to accept.

However, the African has proved that he can withstand the shock of Western civilisation. In this respect he is in a favoured position as compared with the primitive races of other regions. The American Indian, the Polynesian and the Australian have given way or all but disappeared before the White invader. On the contrary, the last fifty years of the Western occupation of Africa has been attended with expanding numbers and, on the whole, increasing health and prosperity for the African. The Bantu refuses to wilt and die before the European. He possesses a toughness of fibre, an adaptability to new conditions, a joyousness in life, that the shock of Western culture has not broken. This is a factor of immense import for the human societies that are evolving in Africa. It is also a fact that lends peculiar hope and importance to the missionary enterprise in that continent.

In Asia to-day missions are asking what they can do to strengthen the life of advanced peoples. In Africa the missionary is faced with the same question but finds a very different answer. The culture of the African is in danger of being submerged by European civilisation. African society requires a complete reconstruction in which the missionary must help the Native to make a multitude of readjustments.

The task of modern African missions is not only to create a new social and spiritual order. That were difficult enough. The growth of Anthropology, Ethnology, Sociology and Linguistics has opened avenues into hitherto obscure recesses of the African mind and has revealed values, concepts, controls, sanctions and motivations that must be reckoned with by the Christian message. To explore these areas, sift their elements and evaluate them in the light of Christ's teachings is the obligation of the modern mission. These inner values are the stuff from which African society is built, and the missionary must select those which fundamentally undergird Native life and build them into the Christian structure.

This is a more difficult and delicate undertaking than to condemn the old building, tear it entirely down and build anew. The task of the modern missionary in creating a new social and spiritual structure for Bantu society is like that of the engineer who rebuilt the railway bridge over the Niagara River gorge so that it might withstand the strains of increased traffic. With consummate care girder after girder was replaced with materials of new design, without interrupting the international traffic passing over the bridge. Gradually a new structure emerged, but one that rested on the former foundations and utilised some of the piers of the original bridge.

The evolution of Japanese feudal society and its integration with Western individualism illustrates how a synthesis of the new and the old culture can be achieved. The kinship obligations of old Japan have been guarded in the new age of individualistic competition by the forming of family corporations in which the immediate relatives are stockholders and the directors are chosen from the family circle. The Christian family has continued to function on the feudal pattern, accepting the code of wide family obligations without dislocation from the national social structure. The Christian Japanese, too, has adjusted himself to Shinto Emperor worship by an attitude and practice not incompatible with his loyalty to God. In these ways the foundation has been laid for an indigenous Christian life in Japan that would not have been possible had the decks been swept clear by the entire substitution of European social and ethical forms.

An inherited handicap of African missions is the historic rôle of the Black man as slave and servitor to the White.

Colour prejudice, with its accompanying assumption of superiority, is a lasting entail from the centuries of contact of Europe and America with Africa. It is inherent in every approach of European civilisation to Africa and tends to limit the possibility of building a social order in which Native and European can meet with mutual respect and justice. Christian service itself is no guarantee of freedom from the treatment of the Native as a being of an inferior order. The arrogance and harshness of the European in dealing with the slow, blundering Native may be understood, if not excused, but least of all is it excusable in the missionary. The modern missionary is dealing with an African who is demonstrating his great latent and actual capacities and increasingly commands respect.

The growing number of mission societies has altered the position of missions in Northern Rhodesia during the last three decades. We are not here concerned with the reasons for this increase nor its relation to the total need of the territory. It is of interest because this multiplication of Christian sects complicates the task of the Church in the new field of the copper belt and railway zone.

The movement of the population to these areas at once opens the question of mission co-operation. Missions working for widely scattered rural populations need hardly be aware of the presence of missions of other denominations in adjoining areas. However, with the free passing to and fro of the people, and the large concentration of Native population at the mines, there arises a need for a new Christian comity between the missions and an adequate plan for uniting their ministry to the Christians in these districts.

The Native movement to the copper belt gives an impetus to the forming of Separatist Bantu Churches. If the Bantu is discontented in his home church, if there are rules which are irksome, or if he has been disciplined for moral laxity, it is easy to gather a few friends and form a so-called "Church" freed from these limitations. The presence of many other Christians temporarily away from the tutelage of mission churches, and the liberty given to religious work at the mines, accelerate the growth of these Separatist groups.

The coming of the European colonist into the areas of his endeavour is a further problem for the modern missionary in Central Africa. This factor, so disturbing to the work of missions in various lands, has until recently been absent from the Northern Rhodesian field. European immigrants in many cases have aims which are fundamentally at variance with those of missions. The exploitation for their own benefit of the country and the people leads them to fear and oppose programmes, whether governmental or missionary, directed toward the development of the native, the protection of his rights, and efforts to prepare him for any rôle above that of a hewer of wood and drawer of water. Not a few of the European settlers are men and women of the highest integrity and generosity in their treatment of Natives. But the presence of representatives of Christian countries whose lives do not bear out the teaching of the missionaries, and whose treatment of the Native is an affront to his self-respect and ideas of justice, creates a major difficulty for the young Church in Central Africa.

In these territories European civilisation, urged on by both its acquisitive and humanitarian instincts, is in peril of reaching a stalemate in its programme for the Native. Its left hand takes away what its right hand gives. The Christian Church in this new situation is called to turn its energies upon itself and purify the civilisation that is extending to Africa. The White man must have a change of heart if the Black man and Black woman are to find it possible to become and remain Christians.

Thus the modern missionary in Africa may find that he exercises a disturbing economic, social and political influence in the territory of his endeavours. His efforts on behalf of Native education and Native amenities may clash with the interests and alleged rights of the European population. The liberating and energising philosophy of

life implicit in his teaching produces a type of Christian
Native who seems to the White settler impertinent, dis-
honest and spoiled. The trained Native craftsman produced by the mission school appears a potential threat to
the supremacy of the White worker. The modern mission
must increasingly reckon with such opposition from their
own countrymen and women. In early days this was
negligible or non-existent: to-day this White public opinion
cannot be ignored, and the missions should study the
problem of resolutely meeting it.[1]

The early missionaries to Central Africa found themselves in the midst of Native peoples without formal
Government protection, obligations or sanctions. After
establishing himself in the confidence of the local chief the
missionary was a law unto himself. He not infrequently
found himself, as with Livingstone, Coillard and Moffat,
in the rôle of a representative of his Government in
negotiating with Native potentates. His station tended to
become a place of refuge, influence and of new conceptions
of justice and of right and wrong. This was partly because
of his own personal qualities and partly from the representative character of his position. He was looked upon
by the Native not only as a teacher of a new way of life
but as an agent and forerunner of the distant Government
that was demanding territorial and mineral rights. This
pioneer phase of missionary activity entirely passed with
the occupation of Central Africa by the European Powers.
The missionary to-day finds himself freed from the semi-
political rôle of his predecessor. He carries on under a
responsible, beneficent and, in the main, sympathetic
Government which is in complete control of the territory
and the people for whom he is working. This is a significant
change for African missions. By it they have been divested
of an unspiritual and complicating function which con-

[1] The Missions' Exhibit organised by the Transvaal Missionary
Council in 1931 in Johannesburg proved an admirable means of convey-
ing to many thousands of visitors a knowledge of what missions are
doing and the relation of their work to the advancement of the whole
community.

fused the real motive of missions. Furthermore, it was an activity which tended to distract both the attention of missionary and people from the spiritual objectives of the enterprise.

On the other hand, the presence of a strong Government and the promulgation of Native policies are new factors of the utmost importance to which missions must make adjustments. Such adjustments are not always easy to make. Government policies relating to Native laws and customs, education and the authority of chiefs may readily embarrass mission programmes, teachings and attitudes that were developed in the previous era.

Missions in this part of Africa enjoy the immense advantage of working in territories controlled by Christian Governments which, on the whole, are committed to the policy of upbuilding Native society. Furthermore, these Governments recognise the place of religion in the task of administering Native peoples and, in the main, give strong support to Christian missions. The Government of Northern Rhodesia is instructed to promote to the utmost of its power religion and education among the Natives, and in every possible way encourages mission work as a means of achieving this end.[1] The importance of such a Government policy for the position of Christian missions is difficult to over-estimate and can probably best be understood by one who has attempted Christian work in lands where the missionary is tolerated merely, and his educational activities are subjected to strict limitations in respect to religious teaching.

Governments early decided to utilise the advantageous position of missions. Their numerous stations, the intimate knowledge of language and people of many of the missionaries, the confidence of the Natives in them, their invaluable fund of experience, their high average of intelligence and devotion, and their exposition of the best of European civilisation constitute a well-adapted agency for implementing Government Native policies. Missions, on the other

[1] Vide *Northern Rhodesia Govt. Gazzette*, par. 23, No. 211 of 1/4/1924.

hand, recognise that the stability of the economic and
political order in which they operate, and the advancement
of that order, are dependent upon Government, and find
that Government counsel, encouragement and support of
their educational and practical activities are a source of
strength.

Governments have shown their confidence in missions
by placing upon them the major load of Native education.
In addition to the spiritual task, missions have been entrusted with both the tool which moulds the African in
his adjustments to the modern world and the key which
opens his mind to the storehouse of European culture.
This heavy responsibility puts the missionary into a position of commanding influence.

Gradually a relationship, some aspects of which are like
a partnership, is evolving between missions and Governments in Central Africa. While the relationship lends itself
to a certain amount of friction and misunderstanding, both
parties have much to gain by it, and the possibilities of the
advancement of Native interests thereby are very great.

The rapid growth of the territories in which missions are
operating has placed the missionary in new and exacting
relationships. In the early days the missionary might be
the only university man in his district. To-day he deals
with Government officials who have been trained at Oxford
and Cambridge Universities. The great industries have
placed men of first-class mental and technical qualifications in his field. Many of the colonists are people of
superior culture and academic attainments.

The missionary's task is related to all of these groups,
and his success in carrying out his programme for Native
society will not a little depend upon his preparation for
dealing with them.

The secular enterprises in Central Africa are demanding
the highest possible qualifications for the leadership of
their interests. The spiritual enterprise is under the same
necessity if it is to measure up to the difficult task with
which it is entrusted.

As in mediaeval Europe the influence of the Church and State were supplemented by the rise of the Third Estate, so in modern Africa a third major influence has been added to that of missions and government. It is this Third Estate, represented by great industrial enterprises, which has introduced the most sweeping changes in the position of modern missions in Central Africa, and provides the main theme of this report. Heretofore the influences of the outer world broke in in desultory fashion upon the Native community and missions. The occasional contacts of trader, traveller and administrator could be to a certain extent buffered and interpreted by the missionary to the Christian society he was fostering. Now, however, that the outside world itself has come to Africa and the people are exposed to the complex of forces political, economic, social and moral that is modern life, they are making their own interpretation of the White man's culture. The human material with which missions deal is changing so rapidly that their old methods are inadequate. Modern missions faced with the sophisticated Native who has "seen the world" on the mines are much in the position of the hen that hatched a brood of ducklings.

Thus probably the chief factor in the changing position of missions in Central Africa is the changed African. For decades his education has proceeded in a wide variety of ways. Every contact with the outer world, whether through labour contract, trader, official or missionary, has opened his mind and made him aware of the presence of a new order of life.

The African is on the move. He is cutting his moorings and is headed for an unknown port. A static mission or a static educational policy will not overtake him. The progress of the Native is forcing the pace for the missionary enterprise to a degree where it can with difficulty plan its course. This calls for alertness, sensitiveness of imagination and the ability to adapt methods to a fluid situation.

The discovery of precious metals in Central Africa, the creating of vast corporations and the investment of huge

sums for their exploitation which has called out thousands
of Natives from their villages to supply labour for these
enterprises, now presents a question which missions and
Governments must answer. "To what end and with what
purpose are we training and developing these peoples
and shaping their destinies?" "What rôle is the African
being prepared to play in his own continent and on the
world stage?" Is the Black man to be considered an em-
barrassing inheritance of a prehistoric past, handed on to
the White man by Africa along with its wild animals,
insect pests and other obstacles to progress? Is he to be
segregated into reserves and restricted with every possible
bar to freedom of action and development? Is the African
to be treated as one of the natural resources of the country,
a valuable concomitant of its mineral wealth, whose
energies are to be conserved so as to be an efficient tool
for the production of European wealth? Or is the Black
man temporarily a ward in the hands of Europe, whose
interests are to be administered as a trust until he is able
to enter into his inheritance?

During this period of tutelage and transition what is the
nature of those social, economic and religious institutions
by which he may be enabled to span the gulf between
savagery and civilisation. Can the Church assist the Native
in that perilous crossing and present the Gospel of Christ
in such terms and with such methods as will meet his
deepest needs? The ensuing chapters attempt to throw
light upon these problems. They portray the stage on
which this Central African drama is being enacted, the
chief forces at work with their nature and direction, and
some of the results and possibilities of their interplay.

CHAPTER II

THE process, now slow now hurried, by which the Bantu tribes of Southern and Central Africa were brought into contact with Western civilisation; by which vast areas of Africa came to be controlled by European administration; by which the mineral and agricultural resources of these areas were exploited by European energy and capital with the aid of Bantu labour; and by which Christianity accepted the challenge of, and began the long struggle with, the force of heathendom, forms an essential background for an understanding of the problems set forth in this report. From North, South, East and West came men of Africa, of the East and of Europe, driven forward by the desire for trade or plunder, led on by stories of fabulous wealth in the interior, forced to trek by the relentless pressure of their neighbours, urged by the spirit of discovery, exploration and colonisation, or compelled by a burning desire to spread their religious faith. They brought with them their own customs, beliefs, superstitions and laws, their hopes and their fears; and the interaction of the forces thus let loose, sometimes in coalition and at other times in opposition, produced the complex pattern that is Africa to-day.

Up till the end of the fifteenth century it was the East which, both in religion and trade, impinged on Africa. The Arabs indeed confined their immediate attention to the East Coast, but the results of their slave-raids were felt far in the interior, where restless movements of the Bantu tribes culminated in a southward drive which brought them to the banks of the Fish River in the Cape Colony. As the fifteenth century drew to a close the Portuguese explorers rounded the Cape of Storms and within two

11

decades had turned the flank of Islam and established themselves on the East Coast of Africa. Later in the century, in 1560, Father Gonzalo da Silviera landed at Sofala as the first missionary to Southern Africa, and shortly afterwards he baptized a local chief named Gamba and four hundred of his followers.[1] Some years later the Dominican Fathers settled at Mozambique, which they used as a base of operations; but in spite of this, and in spite also of journeys of exploration into the interior, neither the Portuguese Government nor the Roman Catholic Church obtained any real hold on or influence over the interior.

Portuguese control of the spice trade with the East lasted during the greater part of the sixteenth century, and then Holland, England and France began to take a hand in the game. By 1652 Jan van Riebeeck had established a refreshment station for the Dutch East India Company at the well-watered Cape of Good Hope and the process had begun by which South and Central Africa were to come under European control.

By the end of the seventeenth century the station at the Cape was becoming a colony, and though the Company realised what was happening, they did not relish this development. Governor Simon van der Stel brought out settlers, including French Huguenots, who were to exercise a powerful influence on the settlement, and when, in 1699, he retired, the first steps toward the northward spread of Western civilisation had been taken. His son carried on the experiment in colonisation until his recall in 1706, after which all serious efforts in that direction ceased until, in 1820, the British settlers arrived.

During the eighteenth century the advance guard of the thinly-spread Dutch population penetrated farther and farther north and east, establishing large cattle-farms widely separated from each other and from the Govern-

---

[1] This chief was supposed by the Portuguese to be the Monomotapa, the legendary chief over all Southern Africa, and they gave him the title of Emperor.

ment at Cape Town. By 1779 this frontier civilisation had come into contact with the Bantu on the banks of the Fish River and there ensued, for the next hundred years, a bitter struggle for land which ended in the defeat of the Bantu and which brought in its train dissension in the ranks of the European conquerors. But before this struggle was concluded the Napoleonic Wars in Europe had caused Great Britain first to occupy the Cape in the interests of William of Orange, a fugitive in England, and then to negotiate its transfer to the British Crown. From 1806, the date of the final occupation of the Cape by Great Britain, events moved more rapidly than during the spacious and leisurely days of the East India Company. The British Government took its administrative duties more seriously than the parsimonious Company, with its financial responsibility of paying big dividends to share-holders in Holland, had been able to do. Further, the in-fluence of French revolutionary and evangelical ideas made itself felt in England, and the nineteenth-century reforms found their counterpart in colonial policy.

The story of the nineteenth-century expansion of Euro-pean settlement in South Africa, of the undaunted courage of the Dutch trekkers who founded the two Boer Re-publics of the North, and of the establishment and rapid northward march of the mission societies, must be sought elsewhere.[1] We must pick up the thread at the point where the founder of the Rhodesias appears on the scene of South African history.

As a young man of twenty at the new diamond diggings, Rhodes was dreaming of the extension of the British Empire in Africa and realising that he required wealth and political power to make his dreams come true. In less than twenty years he had acquired a firm hold on the diamonds of Kimberley and had, in 1881, entered the Cape

[1] *Vide* Walker, *A History of South Africa*, and, for the whole subject of missions in Southern Africa, J. du Plessis, *A History of Christian Missions in South Africa* and *The Evangelisation of Pagan Africa*.

Parliament. In carrying through the amalgamation of the keenly conflicting mining interests at Kimberley he had, to the undisguised surprise of his financial partners, stipulated that profits from de Beers could be used in the development of the North. By the time Rhodes was ready the scramble for Africa had begun, and Germany, Portugal and the Transvaal were all anxious to secure a share of the spoils in Central Africa. By co-operating with the Afrikander party at the Cape, by urging the Cape to look to the hinterland for new markets and for a legitimate sphere of expansion, and by making Great Britain realise that her rivals would outstrip her unless she shook off her lethargy, Rhodes succeeded in inducing the British Government and the Cape Colony between them to take control of Bechuanaland, partly by annexation and partly by the declaration of a Protectorate. This step prevented Germany or the Transvaal from cutting off the line of British expansion to the north, and having acquired the "neck of the bottle", Rhodes now planned a farther advance.

Gold had been discovered in 1886 on the Witwatersrand, and there had long been rumours of more gold north of Bechuanaland and the Transvaal in the country ruled by Lobengula, the son of Mziligazi. Hearing that the Transvaal Boers were contemplating a move in that direction, Rhodes persuaded the High Commissioner to send John Moffat, who had been appointed Assistant Commissioner in Bechuanaland in 1887, on a mission to Lobengula. In 1888 this son of Robert Moffat of the London Missionary Society negotiated a treaty with Mziligazi, his father's old friend and protector, by which Lobengula agreed to make no concessions to anyone else without the consent of Britain. This was all that Rhodes could hope for at the moment. As it was, the treaty brought forth strong protests from Portugal and from the Transvaal, who produced previous but unconvincing treaties in proof of their claims to the territory in question. But the British Government stood by its action and refused to listen to complaints or counter-claims. So Rhodes sent his

friends Rudd, Maguire and Thompson to negotiate a concession from Lobengula. Other concession-hunters flocked
to Bulawayo, and for many weary months the air was
thick with intrigue of the rival aspirants. By infinite
patience and by a judicious use of the Queen's representatives the agents of Rhodes succeeded in getting the Rudd
Concession. The King, Lobengula, was undoubtedly an
able man and probably realised quite clearly that the
advance of the Europeans would not be denied; but he had
to conciliate his followers, who were all in favour of ex-
terminating the White man. Able as he was, he became
more and more confused and disturbed by the insistence
of the concession-hunters in pleading for permission to dig
for gold, and it was when he was at last sure that the
British Government was behind Rhodes that he granted
the mineral concession in return for 1000 Martini-Henry
rifles, 100,000 rounds of ammunition, £1200 a year and a
steamboat on the Zambesi.

In 1889 Rhodes, having amalgamated most of the competing interests to form the British South Africa Company,
pressed for and obtained a Charter for the Company.

By the Charter the Company was empowered to make
full use of concessions so far obtained and of any that
might be obtained in the future, subject to the consent of
the Secretary of State; it was to remain British in character; it was instructed to keep the peace and maintain
order, and empowered to make ordinances to that effect;
it was to regulate and control the sale of liquor, refrain
from undue interference with the customs and beliefs of
the inhabitants and allow freedom of religious worship; in
the administration regard was to be had for Native law and
custom; no monopoly of trade might be set up, but railways,
banks, telegraphs and similar works were not to be considered subject to this rule. Further, the Company was
empowered, subject to the control of the Secretary of
State, to do most things that a Government may do,
though the High Commissioner at the Cape was to have
such control as he would have over a Protectorate. The

Crown reserved the right to revoke the Charter and to amend it after twenty-five years and, thereafter, at the end of every decade.

There were no limits to Rhodes' imperial ambitions. These included the acquisition for Great Britain of all Native territories in South and Central Africa that had not yet actually been occupied by another European Power. By 1884 the Powers of Europe had begun to feel uneasy about Africa as a source of friction, and the Berlin Conference met on November 15 of that year to draw up rules for the scramble for Africa. The results of the Conference were summed up in a General Act of 1885, by which the Powers agreed, among other things, that future acquisitions of territory would immediately be notified to the other signatory Powers so that counter-claims might be lodged. Occupation must in future be effective, which meant that the occupying Power would have to point to mission stations, Government offices, traders and settlers as proof of the validity of its title. But it was recognised that occupation could not always be immediately effective, so a new phrase was added to international language and "Spheres of Influence" were recognised by the General Act. It was a large "Sphere of Influence" which Rhodes wanted for his Charter; for, implicit in his scheme was the extension of railway and telegraphic communication from the Cape to Cairo which would give Britain uninterrupted control; and for such vast plans a Charter which closely defined boundaries would not suit his purpose. So the Charter was left vague in the matter of boundary lines, and the sphere of operations was to be "immediately north of British Bechuanaland, and to the north and west of the South African Republic, and to the west of the Portuguese Dominions".[1]

After the granting of the Rudd Concession and the Charter, Lobengula began to be tortured by doubts judiciously fostered by Rhodes' defeated opponents, and it required all Jameson's tact and fluency to keep him to his

[1] *Vide* Charter of B.S.A.C., etc. (C—8773), 1898.

bargain and give them "a hole to dig in". Rhodes himself
was anxious to push forward the occupation of Mashonaland because, whatever value concessions might have,
actual occupation was the strongest argument. Accordingly
two hundred pioneers of all classes were recruited and,
guided by Selous the hunter and protected by the Bechuanaland police, they waited for the High Commissioner's word
to proceed. The word given, the pioneers moved up and,
carefully skirting Matabeleland, where Lobengula was becoming increasingly nervous of the situation, they planted
the Company's flag at Salisbury on September 12, 1890.

Meanwhile Rhodes had sent his emissaries to East
Africa, to the Katanga and to Barotseland, to make use
of the wide field allowed by the Charter by coming to
terms with the ruling chiefs and obtaining concessions.

Between 1859 and 1873 Livingstone had discovered and
explored the regions lying between the Great Lakes of
Nyasa, Tanganyika, Mweru and Bangweulu, and in 1875
his challenge had been accepted by the Scottish missionaries who set out for Lake Nyasa. Three years later came
settlers and traders, and the Moir brothers formed the
African Lakes Company to trade in conjunction with the
missions. This Company helped to open up the country by
building the Stevenson Road from Lake Tanganyika to
Lake Nyasa; but its long struggle against Arab slavers
exhausted its funds, and in 1890 Rhodes, thinking in terms
of effective occupation, came to the rescue with an offer
to absorb the Company. The final absorption by the
Chartered Company took place in 1893, and to this day
the African Lakes Corporation, as it was then called, has
pursued a prosperous course and "Mandala" stores are
known throughout the country, though all connection
with missionary endeavour has long since ceased. In 1883
the first British Consul arrived in what is to-day Nyasaland,
and from 1885 successful efforts were made to destroy the
Arab slave-trade. More missionaries and settlers came, and
the discovery that Chinde was a river entrance to the

interior placed Nyasaland and what is now North-East Rhodesia in communication with the sea. In 1890 an agreement with Germany defined the boundary between British and German territory, and in 1891 the Anglo-Portuguese Convention settled the boundaries of Portuguese East Africa. These boundaries, like all those drawn at the time, were based on very inadequate geographical knowledge and were defined in terms of latitude and longitude, with the result that political boundaries cut across cultural and economic areas. In 1891 a Protectorate was declared over Nyasaland, and by arrangement with the Foreign Office the British South Africa Company was given an extended field of operations in what is now North-East Rhodesia, where Rhodes' agents, with the assistance of the British Consul, Sir H. Johnston, had secured numerous treaties with Native chiefs. For the time being the powers of government were vested in the Commissioner for Nyasaland, to whom the Company paid £10,000 a year for administrative expenses; but by 1894 the Company itself was ready to take over the administration of North-Eastern Rhodesia.

In the North-West Rhodes failed to secure the Katanga. In 1876, as a result of the explorations of Livingstone, Stanley and others, King Leopold II. of Belgium had formed the International Association for the Exploration and Civilisation of Africa, and two years later Stanley was sent out by the King to make treaties and establish stations. He spent four successful years there, and the Association became less international and more Belgian in character. By the time the Powers met at the Berlin Conference, Leopold had transformed the Congo into a Free State, with himself as the head, and had secured international recognition. It is not certain whether the boundaries of the Congo as stated in the General Act of the Berlin Conference included the valuable Katanga, but there was sufficient doubt to encourage Rhodes to strain every nerve to secure the country. Only a series of mishaps to his agents prevented them from obtaining a treaty with the powerful Chief Msiri, and in

1891 an Englishman, Stairs, acting for the Katanga Company, took possession of the country for the Congo Free State. The new boundary was recognised by Britain in 1894, and thus the minerals of the Katanga passed to Leopold and, in 1908, with the rest of the Congo Free State, to Belgium.

On the other hand, the mission to Barotseland met with ultimate success. The Barotse had brought under their sway numerous surrounding tribes in the Zambesi valley and received annual tribute from them under a well-developed system of administration. After an abortive attempt in 1879 Coillard had, five years later, established a mission station for the Paris Evangelical Missionary Society. Under his influence the Paramount Chief Lewanika began to hanker after a British Protectorate. Lewanika had heard that Khama's country in Bechuanaland was protected by the Queen, and on sending to him for information, received reassuring reports. Rhodes' messengers came at the right moment, and in June 1890 the Company obtained a concession for mining and commercial rights, while Lewanika was admitted to the protection of the Crown, saving certain extensive constitutional rights for himself and his people. After much delay which nearly lost Britain the country, a Resident was sent in 1897 to organise the administration, a task in which he received the enlightened co-operation of the Paramount and his Chiefs.

South of the Zambesi, events had not gone smoothly since the occupation. Transport difficulties (the cost from the Cape Colony ports was £70 per ton), floods and the absence of gold in paying quantities made the lot of the pioneers a hard one. Moreover, it soon became apparent that the Matabele were thoroughly dissatisfied with the occupation and with what they considered unwarrantable interference with their hereditary right to harry the Mashona. Whoever precipitated the war—and the evidence is strong that Jameson and his settlers were convinced that

a war was necessary and were anxious to have it over—
the root causes were land and gold. Lobengula probably
did not want to fight, but he found it impossible to restrain
his men, and in 1893, over a trivial question of the theft
of telegraph wire, war broke out. The settlers, with Imperial assistance, were more successful than anyone had
dared hope. Bulawayo was occupied and Lobengula fled
north to die, leaving a leaderless people who sued for peace.
Jameson had recruited his men by promises of land in the
conquered territory, a system which was common enough
in South Africa, but which sounded strange to the sensitive
English ears of the 'nineties. He now began marking out
farms, and Rhodes, with his characteristic sense of the
dramatic, built a house on the site of the old royal kraal
at Bulawayo. But the Matabele, though subdued, were not
conquered, and indifferent administration produced a rebellion in 1896 after the abortive and ill-conceived Jameson
Raid on the Transvaal. First the Matabele and then the
Mashona rose and killed most of the Européans on isolated
farms and stations. After a while the Matabele were driven
into the hills, and Rhodes, realising the costliness and
length of a campaign in these circumstances, went to visit
the Chiefs in the Matopos,[1] to listen to grievances and to
discuss terms of peace. With wonderful patience and skill,
and a fearless disregard for personal safety, he brought the
Matabele round to a less warlike frame of mind and a peace
was concluded which has lasted till the present time.

Space forbids a discussion on the rights and wrongs of
the occupation of Southern Rhodesia by the Chartered
Company. It is a subject about which much has been
written, and it is sufficient to say that, thus far, no full
and truly impartial account of the occupation and of the
Matabele War and Rebellion has been published.[2] The
main facts are readily ascertainable, but the inner political
history is still a matter of controversy.

[1] A labyrinth of rocky hills and valleys in the south-western part of
Southern Rhodesia well suited for fortification and defence.

[2] *Vide* Walker, *A History of South Africa*, for an impartial but not a
full account.

The discovery of minerals at Kimberley and on the Witwatersrand gave an impetus to railway and telegraph construction. By 1893 Cape Town was in direct railway communication with Johannesburg, and in 1897 the first train was run from Cape Town, through Bechuanaland, to Bulawayo. By 1902 Salisbury was linked by rail to Beira on the east coast, and the line from Bulawayo was pushed forward to reach Wankie and its coal in 1903, and the Victoria Falls in 1904. From there it continued through Livingstone to join, some ten years later, with the railways of the Congo, thus connecting the copper belt with the South.

Though economic development assisted the missionaries in their task, and though political events often hindered them, they neither waited for the one nor were unduly put out by the other, and the last half of the nineteenth century witnessed a rapid expansion of mission work. The Dutch Reformed Church of South Africa established missions in the Zoutpansberg, in Mashonaland and, in 1882, in Nyasaland. The fruits of this latter mission were reaped fifty years later when a Native Church sent its own Bantu missionaries from Nyasaland into Portuguese territory. New missionary societies such as the Swiss Romande and the Scandinavian societies came into the field, and the Anglican Church also awoke to its responsibilities. As early as 1859 an effort was made to establish a station at Linyanti, about a hundred miles west of the present Livingstone, among the Makololo, but after suffering incredible hardships the party abandoned the attempt. A station was established in Matabeleland, and after the death of the terrible Mzili-gazi in 1868 Hope Fountain, near Bulawayo, was opened. The Coillards in Barotseland and the Moffats in Bechuanaland were statesmen-missionaries in the highest sense of the word and showed how effective mission work could be when backed by intelligent chiefs. In the North-East the London Missionary Society, the Universities Mission, the White Fathers, the Scottish Missions and others penetrated from the east coast and left their indelible mark on the country. It is an impressive record, and the invaluable part played by missions in the opening up of Central Africa should never be forgotten.

The whole territory which had been brought under the British flag by the activities of Rhodes was, in 1895, officially given the name of Rhodesia. South of the Zambesi it was called Southern Rhodesia, and various Orders-in-Council and agreements with the Government made provision for the administration of Southern Rhodesia along lines which, while giving the Imperial Government effective control, left the Company with the main responsibilities. An Administrator, an Executive Council and a Legislative Council on which the Company had an official majority were instituted; Magistrates' Courts and a High Court, with appeal to the Supreme Court at the Cape, administered the law of the Cape (which included Roman-Dutch civil law) and such ordinances and regulations as were made from time to time. A Secretary for Native Affairs and Native and Assistant Native Commissioners applied Native law and custom wherever possible under regulations laid down by the High Commissioner at the Cape. Imperial control was maintained by subjecting all the important appointments and all legislation to the approval of the British Government; by safeguarding, in advance, against legislation discriminating between Europeans and Natives, and against interference with the rights of the Company, and by direct representation in the person of a Resident Commissioner appointed and paid by the British Government.

In 1911 a new Order-in-Council gave the elected members a majority on the Legislative Council, and the demand grew for responsible government or, at least, the status of a Crown Colony. Ever since the pioneering days had come to an end settlers in Southern Rhodesia had complained that the Company looked after its own interests and neglected those of the colonists. It was the old case of a clash between the commercial interests of the Company and the political interests of the colonists, and the settlers could hardly be expected to see the point of view of the shareholders. Every attempt on the part of the Company to get the legislature to assume responsibility, by way of a national debt, for past administrative deficits met with a steady refusal. In 1914 the first twenty-five years of the Charter had expired, but revision had to be postponed owing to the outbreak of the Great War. By 1924 the Privy Council judgment on the question of the ownership of land had been delivered [1] and the outstanding financial disputes between the Company, the British Government and the Legislative Assembly had been settled; so the Company withdrew and Southern Rhodesia became a responsibly governed colony. Legislation affecting mining and railways, and that which discriminated between European and Bantu, was reserved for the approval of the Secretary of State, and the Company retained large interests in the country. Till 1964 the half of all sales of Crown land goes to the Company, and, in addition, it draws mining royalties, though its right to do so is likely to be challenged in the courts in the near future. Since the Matabele Rebellion there has been a steady flow of settlers to the country. The gold export in 1905 was one and a half million pounds; four years later it was over two and a half million pounds, and Southern Rhodesia ranked fourth among gold-producing countries. Gold and coal-mining, agriculture, railway development, banking and commerce have all made progress, and Southern Rhodesia has become, in many ways, a South African State. As regards her politics, her legal system and, largely, her economics, her destiny would appear to be linked with that of the Union of South Africa, though she has so far refused all invitations to become a fifth province of her southern neighbour.

North of the Zambesi a different kind of development took place.[2] Prior to 1899 the whole of the present territory

---

[1] Vide *Papers connected with the Case before the Privy Council on Land in Southern Rhodesia*, 14 pts., 1918.

[2] *Vide* Gouldsbury and Sheane, *The Great Plateau of Northern*

of Northern Rhodesia was vaguely included in the Charter, but it was only in that year and the next that provision was made for its administration. The Barotseland–North-Western Rhodesia Order-in-Council of 1899 and the North-Eastern Rhodesia Order-in-Council of 1900 defined, respectively, the western and eastern portions of the present territory. By the first of these Orders the High Commissioner at the Cape appointed an Administrator, a judge, magistrates and other officials, for North-Western Rhodesia, all on recommendation by the Company, and legislated for the territory by proclamation, being bound to take the opinion of the Company into account. The British Government kept control by retaining the right to disallow proclamations. No revenue might be raised without the consent of the Company. While Native law and custom, in so far as they did not conflict with natural justice or public morality, were recognised, the laws of England were to apply to the territory. Barotseland was in a peculiar position owing to the treaties with Lewanika, and special provision was made for its administration along lines which left far more power in the hands of the Chief and his Council than was done in other parts of the country.

The North-Eastern Rhodesia Order was more elaborate than the North-Western and provided for the appointment by the Company, subject to the approval of the Secretary of State, of an Administrator and a Council consisting of the senior judge and three other members. The Administrator and his Council legislated by regulations subject to approval by the Secretary of State, and the Commissioner of the British Central Africa Protectorate (Nyasaland) could make Queen's Regulations if he consulted the Company before doing so. No revenue might be raised without the Company's consent; there might be no discriminating legislation without the consent of the Secretary of State except in the matter of the sale of

Rhodesia, and Hole, *The Making of Rhodesia*, for the earlier history of Northern Rhodesia.

arms, ammunition and liquor ; Natives might acquire, hold, encumber and dispose of land on the same terms as Europeans, but there were safeguards to protect the Native in his sale of land; Native law and custom was to be applied to civil cases between Natives, and the courts could appoint assessors to advise on Native custom; polygamous marriages were recognised. Finally, provision was made for a High Court, for magistrates, for a Secretary of Native Affairs and for Native Commissioners with judicial powers.

It will be noticed that the two territories were administered separately and that, while North - Western Rhodesia came under the High Commissioner at the Cape, North-Eastern Rhodesia came under the Commissioner of Nyasaland, and it is important to note that the present territory of Northern Rhodesia was occupied from two directions, from the south and from the east. A glance at the map will show the physical reason for this double approach. The later development of mining and railways in the West has accentuated the influence from the South, but it is well to remember that a large part of the present territory of Northern Rhodesia was for many years almost solely under influences from the East Coast and, in particular, from Nyasaland. The effect of Nyasaland missions alone on Northern Rhodesia is profound. One has only to see the number of Nyasaland-trained Africans who to-day occupy good positions in Government service both in Northern Rhodesia and in the Congo to realise how strong was the stream that flowed from the East Coast.

In 1911 the two territories were amalgamated by an Order-in-Council which followed closely the model of the North-Eastern Rhodesia Order-in-Council of 1900, except that the whole territory of Northern Rhodesia, as it was now called, fell within the province of the High Commissioner at the Cape. In 1917 an Advisory Council of five elected members was instituted, and in 1924, the same year that Southern Rhodesia became a responsibly governed colony, Northern Rhodesia ceased to be administered by the Company and became a Protectorate of the British Crown.

Except for the railway area Northern Rhodesia was not in the same close touch with European civilisation in the South as was Southern Rhodesia; European settlement was, and is, comparatively sparse, and the Company had fewer problems of a racial kind to settle. Its chief task was to maintain order among the tribes and to suppress such pagan practices as were not consonant with European conceptions of morality and natural justice. Human sacrifice at the burial or succession of a Chief could no longer be permitted; the Babemba had to be prevented from exacting tribute of fish, hoes and spears from the neighbouring tribes; Chiefs had to be compelled to surrender their customary rights of tribute in labour and kind from their subjects; slavery had to be suppressed. Native Commissioners toured their districts to collect taxes (they used to be called Collectors in the early days), to do census work and to hold court. The difficulties in the way of building up a sound administration were great. Transport was in its infancy; disputes over chieftainship had to be decided by men who were not always aware of the intricacies of Bantu succession law; political boundaries divided tribes, and the Paramount might be in one territory while most of his subjects were in another. Above all, the prevention of war and raids tended to break up tribal organisation. Codrington, the Deputy Administrator, reported from the North-East as early as 1900 that the power of the Chiefs was nominal and that "every village is more or less a republic".[1] The old-time large defensive villages made way for small scattered villages, thus adding to the difficulties of control. Emigration to the mines of the South and, later, to the copper-mines in Katanga and North-Western Rhodesia brought its own peculiar difficulties. Unfortunately, the Company's policy of breaking down the power of the over-mighty, and failing to support the authority of the lesser, Chiefs tended to hasten the decay of one of

[1] Vide *British South Africa Company Report, 1898–1900*, p. 71.

the most powerful institutions upon which a system of
Native Administration may be built. It is true that in
1908, and again in 1916, attempts were made to associate
the Chiefs and headmen with the Administration. Regulations in those years provided for the appointment, dismissal and punishment of Chiefs, headmen and messengers
and prescribed their duties, which were principally the
prevention, suppression and reporting of crime. The Chiefs
had no real judicial or administrative or legislative authority, and the very small subsidies they received were inadequate to compensate for the loss of prestige and of
customary rights. Authority passed, in effect, into the
hands of the officials, although in practice Chiefs still
arbitrated unofficially in a great number of civil cases. In
Barotseland the powers of the Chief were preserved by the
original agreements with Lewanika, and the officials operated much more through the Chiefs than they did elsewhere.

From 1894, when the Company first began to assume
responsibility for the government of the territory, until
1924, when it handed over the reins, a system of administration was patiently built up, a system that had its faults,
and that necessarily, since the country never paid its way,
failed to achieve some of the objects which any Government must set itself to achieve; nevertheless, a system
which brought peace where there had been war, which
abolished slavery and took long strides towards humanis-
ing the more barbarous of the Native customs. If the
Company did not conquer, it fought relentlessly against
witchcraft. To the best of its ability it assisted education
and missionary effort, and, finally, it set a standard of
honest administration, of official integrity and of justice
which formed an excellent foundation on which the new
administration might successfully build.

PART TWO

THE SOCIOLOGICAL PROBLEM

CHARLES W. COULTER

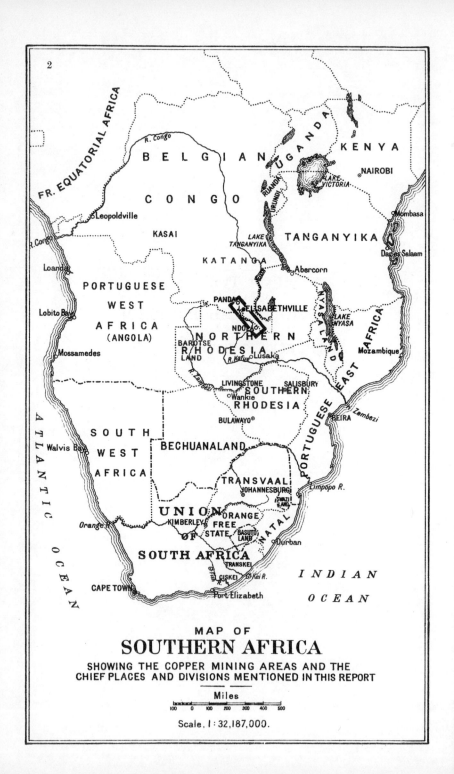

2

R. Congo

FR. EQUATORIAL AFRICA

BELGIAN

CONGO

UGANDA

KENYA

NAIROBI

RUANDA
URUNDI

LAKE
VICTORIA

Leopoldville

KASAI

R. Congo

LAKE
TANGANYIKA

TANGANYIKA

Mombasa

Loanda

KATANGA

Abercorn

Dar es Salaam

PORTUGUESE

WEST

Lobito Bay

AFRICA

(ANGOLA)

PANDA

ELISABETHVILLE

NDOLA

NORTHERN

RHODESIA

LAKE
NYASA

PORTUGUESE EAST AFRICA

Mossamedes

BAROTSE
LAND

R. Kafue

Lusaka

Mozambique

R. Zambesi

LIVINGSTONE

SALISBURY

SOUTHERN

Wankie

RHODESIA

BULAWAYO

BEIRA

Zambezi

SOUTH

Walvis Bay

WEST

BECHUANALAND

AFRICA

TRANSVAAL

Orange R.

ATLANTIC OCEAN

UNION

KIMBERLEY

OF

ORANGE
FREE
STATE

JOHANNESBURG

SWAZI
LAND

Limpopo R.

BASUTO
LAND

NATAL

Durban

SOUTH AFRICA

TRANSKEL

CAPE TOWN

CISKEI

Kei R.

Port Elizabeth

INDIAN

OCEAN

MAP OF

SOUTHERN AFRICA

SHOWING THE COPPER MINING AREAS AND THE
CHIEF PLACES AND DIVISIONS MENTIONED IN THIS REPORT

Miles

100   0   100   200   300   400   500

Scale, 1 : 32,187,000.

CHAPTER III

ENVIRONMENT AND SOCIAL CONDITIONING OF THE RHODESIAN NATIVE

THE LAND

WHATEVER the Native's organisation, administration or level of cultural attainment, he is and must, for many years, continue to be a child of the soil. Land is the primary conditioning factor and sets negative limits of variation to all cultural advance. It is true that much can be done to change a hostile, infertile and obstinate environment, but this does not occur until the pressure of population or the strategy of the geographical position demands it. It is a well-recognised fact that the dykes of Holland came into being partly to protect the rich lowlands, partly because the pressure of population demanded them, but mainly because the available rich land had already been occupied. Here, as elsewhere, the law of marginal returns controlled. The operation of the principle is so universally verifiable that it might be stated as a law that the more primitive the group the more directly is it influenced by natural conditions, geographic, hydrographic and climatic. Hence the necessity for some consideration of the physical character of the areas from which the mining recruits of Northern Rhodesia come.

The territory of this British Protectorate comprises an area computed to be 288,400 square miles, which, with the exception of the river valleys, consists of a table-land varying from 3000 to 4500 feet in height, though in the north-eastern portion the altitude is considerably higher. It may be conveniently divided on the basis of the physical conditions determining its density of population into five main sections:

(a) The great north-eastern plateau watered by a net-

31

work of tributaries of the Luapula and other feeders of the Congo, containing Lake Bangweulu and forming on the east a watershed for the minor streams flowing into the Luangwa. It is a fertile area with salubrious climate, showing a fine correlation between the density of population and the areas in which sleeping sickness is least prevalent, and also a thinning out of population in the fly-infested sections of the south and east.

(b) The south-eastern section of Northern Rhodesia, mainly about the Luangwa valley, itself a tributary of the Zambesi, shading off to the boundaries of Nyasaland and Portuguese East Africa, with an increasing density of population in the fly-free areas around Fort Jameson of 7·5 persons and in the border country of Petauke of 6·9 per square mile.

(c) The southern half of the high central plateau containing the railway corridor, spreading like a fan from Livingstone to touch Luangwa on the east, including the fertile Kafue valley with its tributary system, and losing itself in the fly-infested Kasempa flat lands to the west. The land is largely open veld, the industry cattle-raising, and the density of population south of Mazabuka 7·6 per square mile.

(d) The northern half of the plateau touching Barotseland and Angola on the west and the Belgian border on the north, and merging into the north-eastern section. It is a heavy bushveld country interspersed by agricultural land indifferently worked, and thins in the north-west to a population of 1·6 per square mile, the smallest in the entire Protectorate.

(e) The Barotse Reserve—a broken section indented by the innumerable confluents of the Upper Zambesi, entirely free from the tsetse-fly, and, logically enough, showing a population density as high as 25·4, which is greater than that of any other section of the colony.

These five sections form fairly distinct culture-areas with linguistic groupings, social customs and adjusted modes of self-support, in spite of the fact that there had been many tribal migrations before the incursion of European culture. The differences in environment may also be indirectly responsible for the not unfounded popular opinion that certain tribal groups are more intelligent, adaptable, tractable and teachable than others. In a word, the race group characters have been modified by environment.

That density of population is closely correlated with the character of the land may be seen from the fact that in the Luangwa district mainly occupied by a cattle-raising people it required from two acres of land (in the Kafue flats) to twenty acres (on the less watered plateau) to support a unit of the population; and in two-thirds of the Baluba territory containing a traditional pastoral people it is impossible for cattle to be raised at all. In the Baila country in less than a decade cattle have been decimated 30 per cent by the invasion of the tsetse-fly, entailing not only a change in culture but a slowing-up of the population increase which is taking place in surrounding areas.

POPULATION

The total Native population of Northern Rhodesia in 1931 was 1,295,081, as compared with 13,846 Whites of that same year [1]—roughly 94 Natives for every White person in the colony. The question of the limitation of the Natives by the White minority to spacious reserves in territories now most densely populated need not concern us here, as it will be treated later.[2] One fact, however, must not be overlooked, as it has a significant bearing on the entire study, viz. that the Native population is unequally distributed within the territory. Moreover, the Ndola district, in which mining operations are now carried on, is one of the sparsely settled areas with a population density

---

[1] Report of Census, 1931. Figures are as accurate as the census methods will permit.

[2] See below, Chapter XIII. pp. 235-6.

of only 2·2 per square mile, and the mines are almost equi-distant from the four main centres of population.

It is significant that the total number of Natives for the Protectorate has increased 32·9 per cent during the decade ending 1931.[1] A number of factors are responsible for this phenomenal growth, all of which are connected with the superimposition of European civilisation, increased oppor-tunities of wage labour, improved sanitation, hygienic and medical attention, making for a safeguarded effective birth-rate, the cessation of tribal wars, provision against recurring famine, and Governmental improvement of justice. Should the conditions favouring this effective Native fecundity continue at the same rate we might reasonably expect the population to double in from thirty-five to forty years. This increase goes on in spite of a child mortality within the first two years of birth variously estimated at from 33 to 60 per cent.[2] The figures must be tentative as no accurate method has yet been used for gathering Native vital statistics. Births are not registered, and many deaths doubtless occur which are not reported.

Another point of primary importance in considering any problem of cultural change is the mobility of population. Other factors being constant, though they seldom are, movements of population with the accompanying contacts shatter provincialism, build up a body of new life modes and methods, break through the crust of established custom, increase susceptibility to change and thus facilitate social progress. Until the present century the population of the vast Central African territory of which Northern Rhodesia is a part, on the whole, has been immobile.

---

[1] Report of the Native Commissioner for 1931.. Population figures are as accurately estimated as is possible under the methods in use for collecting vital statistics.

[2] There is reason to believe that this rate is gradually decreasing. The Secretary for Native Affairs of Northern Rhodesia writes: "Sta-tistics collected in villages in each district show that the infant death-rate for the past few years is: 1928—47 per cent; 1929—38 per cent; 1930—34 per cent; 1931—33·7 per cent. A steady decline is shown if the statistics gathered by the District Officers are to be relied upon: there is no reason to doubt they are gathered with care."

Tribal customs have favoured neither individual nor group migration. Through unnumbered generations tribal custom was conventional and slow of modification. Dialectic differences, tribal hostilities and chieftainship prerogatives have confined each group within definite boundary limits, thus restricting the adoption of new methods, diminishing breadth of outlook and making for credulity and stagnation.

It is true that isolation of peoples in Central Africa was not complete through this period. Frequent intertribal wars and the rudiments of trade had doubtless set the pattern which was to be delineated more fully later by contact with the culture of the White man.

Since the opening of construction and development work in the copper-mines at Ndola within the past five years the contacts of Whites and Natives have increased enormously both in kind and extent. An average of 20,961 men were employed in the nine Northern Rhodesian mines operating in 1931.[1] Considering the Native servants of the White population, together with the wives and children, this means a total of well over 40,000 temporary expatriates who were brought into close juxtaposition with the Whites by the mining industry alone.

These 20,961 men who were working on the Northern Rhodesian mines, many of them with their wives and families, formed only about one-fifth of the Natives of the territory who were in the employment of Europeans. So that it would be safe to say that the Natives in contact with Whites during 1931 totalled well over 150,000, or a little beyond one-tenth of the Native population.[2]

A final consideration in regard to population is that of Native health. With the exception of malaria and sleeping

[1] Cf. Economics section, Chapter IX.: Table showing number of Natives employed on all mines at the end of each month, 1927–32.

[2] Male Natives recruited in Northern Rhodesia for work outside the territory for 1931 totalled 1762, those working independently outside the territory are estimated at 29,181, and the average number of Natives employed within the territory (estimate) for all purposes 79,165, making a total of 110,108. *Annual Report upon Native Affairs, 1931*, p. 25.

sickness (trypanosomiasis), regarding which there is some question, few of the diseases most disastrous to the Rhodesia Native are indigenous to Africa. Among the most prevalent are malaria and sleeping sickness, which are endemic in vast sections of the population; pneumonia and other chest diseases, which are most fatal; smallpox and influenza, which tend to be epidemic; some venereal infection, which, but for the malarial antidote, might conceivably become the most terrible scourge of the region; dysentery and the minor affections, which are sporadic and show no greater incidence than in a White community. The shifting sleeping sickness areas are carefully charted by the Government and every effort is made to keep the Native, whatever his natural immunity, out of the affected sections. As might be expected in a tropical climate, malarial infection carried by the anopheles mosquito abounds throughout the colony. Where it is most virulent children are infected in infancy and, though death from this cause is uncommon, the entire population suffers from a depleted vitality occasioned by the disease. This probably accounts for the significant correlation between the regions where malaria is most prevalent and the phenomenal death-rate from pneumonia and other chest diseases in these areas. Filth diseases are reduced or eliminated as hygienic conditions are improved. We are informed that in one of the mining compounds in the Ndola district cases of tropical ulcer now never occur unless brought in from the outside, and this finds confirmation in the older mining compounds of Southern Rhodesia, where medical inspection is rigid.

GROUP ORGANISATION FOR SELF-MAINTENANCE

Group methods of self-maintenance differ widely as between African peoples with a cattle-raising economy and those whose subsistence comes directly from the land through agriculture, although both groups practise hunting and fishing to obtain occasional supplies of meat. As has been pointed out, the chief group occupation shows a fine adaptation to the land, climate and other environing conditions in the territory occupied. On this occupational base is elaborated the tribe's organisation, habitudes and ethics—in a word, its culture.

Cattle-raising was formerly far more widespread in Rhodesia than it has been since the present wide diffusion of the tsetse-fly. It is rare to find agricultural tribes which have no traces of pastoral tradition. At present only five groups are mainly cattle-raisers, viz. the Barotse, Baila and related Batonga, Angoni, Wenamunga and Mambwe.[1] These tribes are found in the areas showing least of the cattle scourge. All other groups in Rhodesia are exclusively or mainly agricultural.

Native methods of cattle-raising and care are still in a very primitive stage. Selective breeding is almost unknown. The cattle get so little care that only the hardiest survive. Yet with all their imperfections these cattle are suited to the conditions of those who use them and the land in which they and their forerunners have lived. There is little inclination to adopt the cattle and methods of Europeans. Native ways are traditional, and the care of their cattle is limited by their ignorance. Here and there, however, one finds a Native who has got beyond tribal methods and is living on individualistic lines. Although 78 per cent of all cattle in the Protectorate is produced by Natives, they are so dirty that the milk products can scarcely be used by Europeans. The Choma Creamery Company in Namwala, which is typical, flatly refuses to accept the cream from Native cattle unless it is produced under European supervision. Cattle-raising figures so little in the maintenance economy of the groups employed on the mines and is so rapidly giving place to agriculture that we may confine our attention to a brief description of the latter industry.

Before describing a typical agricultural village in Rhodesia, three basic contrasts between the life of the African

[1] See tribal map in Appendix.

and the European should be emphasised. First, it must be borne in mind that Native life is carried on in a village community. Isolated huts and farms familiar to the European do not exist. Every village cultivates the land adjacent to the village settlement. Again, a large number of village enterprises are communal or are carried out by a complicated system of kinship obligations. Men, women and grown children had recognised duties to perform under a well-established sex and social division of labour which has crystallised through the years. In the villages remote from contact with civilisation a man would not think of doing a woman's work nor the woman of carrying the responsibility which the group recognises as belonging to the man. The logic of such division of labour is more apparent the longer one lives among these people.

Dr. Doke has characterised the sex division of labour among the Lambas thus: "The sign of the man is the axe and the spear, and the sign of the woman is the hoe. This, to a great extent, determines the division of labour between the sexes. Hoe-work is women's work, though men may take a hoe to assist them. Axe-work is primarily men's work, though here again women may use an axe to assist them. A woman would not use a spear."[1] In villages where contacts with Europeans have been closer, and especially where a majority of the men have been recruited for labour on the mines and thus are away through the planting and harvesting period, tribal conventions have bowed to expediency.

A further contrast lies in the fact that property in the European sense exists only in relation to one's tools, weapons, implements, ornaments, utensils and, in some measure, to his hut. He may enjoy the usufruct of land and herds, but he has no claim to them in fee-simple and no right to transmit to posterity by will. The title to land is technically vested in the Chief as representative of the tribe, and this ownership is supernaturally sanctioned.

These and similar basic concepts have been integrated

[1] C. M. Doke, *The Lambas of Northern Rhodesia*, p. 96.

into a balanced tribal organisation through the centuries and have made for cohesiveness and ease of control. Their modification by White influence, particularly in the villages near European settlements, and by tribesmen who have returned after periods of White employment, creates a series of social problems which, as will be indicated later, are fraught with grave consequences to the future of European and Native alike.

Tribal organisation, methods and dialects in Northern Rhodesia differ widely. Maps hitherto available include as many as sixty-nine different tribes resident in the Territory.[1] There is little doubt that more careful future findings on the interrelations between them will show but a few main groups. Of these listed tribes the most important are the Babemba (110,659), Achewa (75,108), Angoni (50,652), Awisa (41,706), in the eastern districts; the Barotse (55,123), Batonga (45,445), Balenje (39,580), Balovale (58,853), Bakaonde (33,642), Baila (21,632), in the western districts; and the Ansenga (64,546) and Alunda (55,445), which are resident in both eastern and western districts.[2] There are said to be fifty distinct Native dialects in use, of which the Chiwemba and Chinyanja are the educational and administrative media in the eastern districts, and Chitonga and Sikololo in the western.

In view of the differences between this large number of tribes a brief description of typical agricultural methods and organisations cannot be correct in detail for every group, although in general they are built over a fairly constant social pattern. An average village may contain between twenty and a hundred huts. The Government, for convenience in administration, now requires that it domicile at least ten tax-paying males. The village of the Paramount Chief of the tribe is usually considerably larger. The village of Kasembe, Paramount Chief of the Lunda, numbers more than 2000 huts. So it will be seen that communal gardens sufficient to support a village population

---

[1] As listed in the *Annual Report upon Native Affairs, 1931*, p. 49.
[2] See tribal map in Appendix.

may be quite extensive, especially as the land is superficially worked, usually without ploughing. In some cases
the gardens extend for twenty miles around a Native
village, necessitating that the men build temporary huts
for occupation through the burning, planting and reaping
seasons.

When a new village is to be constructed a site is selected
by the headman with the sanction of the Chief, and with a
canny view to the fertility of the land, proximity of water-
supply and the distance the village is to be moved. The
location of the cattle kraal, communal buildings and
residence of the tribesmen are determined by custom, and
the construction is carried out with expedition and due
propitiation of the local spirits.

The ordinary method of working the land around a
village is first to select a likely patch of ground and, if
millet is to be grown, to chop the trees four feet from
the ground, or only the branches if the trees are large,
within a radius of twenty to thirty yards. After they are
thoroughly dried they are burned and, with the coming
of the rains, the grain is planted in the ash. It may require
as many as twenty of such patches to supply food for a
single family. A fence may be built around each patch or
around the series of family gardens. Owing to the method
of soil preparation little hoeing and weeding is needed, and
this little is done by the women. After three, or at most
four, successive harvests the site is abandoned and a new
village is constructed on virgin soil. A variation of this
method is employed in the growing of sorghum, and a still
further modification in producing cassava. In the former
case the trees are felled in rows; the ash-loosened earth is
dug into heaps, making it possible for the plot to be
worked for four years, after which the village moves on.
The method of growing cassava, a ground tuber introduced by the Portuguese and now forming a staple food
for Natives in a large section of Northern Rhodesia, differs
further still. The ground is hoed into rounded heaps, all
weeds and débris being carefully buried within the mounds.

Slips broken from the mature plants in the old patch are set out in these mounds. They are carefully tended until the third year, when they are sufficiently matured to yield. Owing to the time required for maturation and the fact that the tubers cannot be stored indefinitely without deterioration, it is customary to cultivate three fields of varying age each year. There has also grown up a system of fallowing the worn-out garden, resting the land and providing a natural weed fertiliser, which has ensured a permanency of from five to ten years for the village site. Cassava villages have the advantage of requiring the construction of no fences, outside of the Abercorn Territory, which is infested by elephants, as the plants and tubers are not molested by other animals. In addition to a stabilised main food product the system favours a varied dietary of maize, beans, sweet potatoes, monkey nuts, cucumbers and pumpkins, which can be grown in the cassava mounds without duplicating the labour of weeding. The system has also ensured cassava-growing groups against the hunger months [1] so common in other sections of the Protectorate.

Another type of permanent garden is met with on the river flats, particularly in the Zambesi and Luangwa valleys, where by reason of natural irrigation and annual hoeing the land can be worked for many years, and the moving of villages does not occur.

Such systems entail an immense amount of labour for returns so inadequate that many villages have food for only part of the year and the supply has to be supplemented by wild roots, herbs, leaves and other forest products gathered by the women to tide over the settlement until the following harvest. It is difficult indeed to induce the Native to change his methods of agriculture. To his mind they are adequate. Nothing could be more firmly

---

[1] In certain sections of Northern Rhodesia, due to thriftlessness and periodic food shortage, the Natives are entirely without cereal food and have to subsist on the wild products of the bush and field until the following harvest. This period varies from one to three months.

entrenched in his traditions or more intricately intertwined with his religious beliefs and social practices. Thus
his living standards are pitiably low and the surplus product for sale or trade is negligible or nil. It seems never
to occur to the Native that the soil of the cattle kraal might
be used to fertilise the garden, or that the ubiquitous ant-
heap provides rich salts for the fertilisation of the land.
Yet he continually uses the abandoned kraal sites for the
growing of pumpkins and other plants requiring much
humus for successful production. The semi-nomadic method
of periodically abandoning villages characteristic of the
people in large sections of the country discourages the
construction of stable dwellings, planting of fruit-trees and
such permanent improvements of the landscape as are met
with in other parts of the world.

Until recently the wants of the Native have been few
indeed. His dietary was narrow—a staple grain product,
maize, millet or cassava, the ground meal of which, after
careful preparation, was cooked into a thick porridge;
a relish of wild herbs, roots or leaves, gathered by the
housewife and supplemented in season by pumpkins, yams,
cucumbers, potatoes, sorghum, ground nuts and the natural
fruits of the tropical bush. Meat, at long intervals, provided a welcome change and, for the tribes on the streams,
fresh or dried fish.

His clothing shows some changes; the former nakedness
or bark cloth garments have given place to a medley of
gaudy trade cotton garments covering the body indifferently from shoulder to knee, and the blanket where the
nights are cold. This has been slightly supplemented in
recent years by nondescript cast-off wearing apparel and
cheap factory-made clothing brought in by returning mine
and domestic workers.[1] From this it will be seen that
the equipment of the Native, particularly in the sections
remote from the centres of White civilisation, is casual
and well integrated into the traditional civilisation. Ambi-

---

[1] *Vide* Appendix B for itemised list of purchased articles in the kits
of three typical workers returning from the mines of the copper belt.

tion to succeed in the European system of wage-earning slumbers, and the fires of desire and emulation burn low.

SOCIAL ORGANISATION

The kinship and tribal organisation of the Bantu shows a richness of elaboration curiously at variance with the poverty and simplicity of physical equipment, conveniences and comforts of Native life. To understand the authority of the habits and customs in Native tribal organisation one must remember that the Native lives in three distinct but interrelated environments: the physical, the social, and the imaginary—including the magical and religious. That the inhabitants on the last-named plane cannot be seen in no sense robs them of reality. "A cloud of witnesses around holds them in full survey", and—what is more significant—these unseen witnesses are ancestors who themselves observed identical rules and usages. They are pleased by unvarying conformity to ancient *mores*, and distressed or angered by the new and unfamiliar. Thus for a mortal to change approved group custom is dangerous not only to the individual but to his group; for innovation here is an offence against the unseen host.

The belief in the ethereal persistence of the dead thus makes for grave hesitation about introducing change into tribal or kinship organisation. Notions of goblinism are inextricably intertwined with traditional procedures, crystallising them and coercing the group to conform to them. This is not to say, however, that changes in tribal customs do not take place. Change may be necessary to ensure the very persistence of the group, but it is never to be lightly undertaken. It must always be carried through with due propitiation of the unseen host, which acts as an effective brake on the rapidity with which the modification of existing custom may take place. So that, in addition to the natural conservatism of familiarity, characterising all societies, there is an added reason for the Native inertia and reluctance to accept even patently advantageous changes in custom and group organisation. Especially is this true of the older men and women of the group.

The organisation of Native life is entirely tribal. Everyone has his place in the life of the tribe. This place is usually determined by birth or at most by well-recognised variation limits set by birth. The highest controlling authority of the tribe is the Chief. His office is hereditary, the succession in all matrilineal groups passing through the female line to the nearest male. So that the Chief is succeeded by his brother, i.e. next younger son of the same mother, failing this by the eldest son of his sister by the same mother, and so on down to the son of his elder sister's daughter, or the son of his next younger sister. This is technically called matrilineal succession. In other groups, particularly in the South and West, succession is patrilineal, the office going directly from the father to son. Among still other groups such as the Baila the Chiefs are elected.

In a few cases the tribal head is a woman. This occurs only in matrilineal groups and under rules of heredity which are conventional but rather obscure. Where it does occur, polygamous marriage is permitted to her. An official at Livingstone cited three such cases of polyandry, all women of rank, one of whom now has four husbands.

The Chief has numerous rights and privileges, but he has recognised duties as well. Beside the honour, which is no empty thing in itself, the following prerogatives traditionally belong to him: a definite part of all ivory, large game such as the eland, honey, the skin of certain animals, the feathers of certain birds, presents of sorts from any of his people who have been away, and labour in his gardens. For many years it has been the policy of the Government to pay the Chief a small subsidy in return for which he performed certain police functions and unofficially settled most civil disputes among his subjects. The Government has discouraged customary labour for the Chief, in some cases slightly augmenting the subsidy by way of compensation.[1]

On the other hand, the Chief is responsible for civil and minor criminal jurisdiction. It is customary for him also to provide strangers with food, apportion the land among his headmen, allot new land and authorise the removal of villages. In some tribes he is responsible for granting permission to carry on a "beer drink" and distributing Native intoxicants. He is usually polygynous or, to be exact, juridically monogamous, having one status wife and others enjoying less prestige. The Paramount Chief of the Lunda until recently had forty wives, although the number is now smaller. On the other hand, Chitimukulu, the Paramount of all the Babemba, technically has three, although his subjects assert that "his wives are as numerous as the ants on an ant-hill". The Chief may be subject to a Paramount Chief, and under him, if the territory is large and populous, to a group Chief who may live in a village some miles distant. The marks of subjection, though in the former militaristic society very important, are now largely honorary, involving a periodic gift of respect. Both Paramount and local Chiefs have about them councils of elders whose advice is sought before any important step is taken involving either justice or the welfare of the tribe as a whole. Each village in the local Chief's domain has a headman whose business it is to look after all interests of the village, agricultural, legal and customary, and he is held rigidly responsible to the Chief. He serves without remuneration beyond the honour incident to the position.

Whatever may be said for or against the tribe as a primitive form of governmental control, it must be recognised as a successful expedient for the integration of community life; everybody was domiciled, fed and clothed according to the standards of the group, crime was rare, prostitution, orphanage and pauperism were altogether unknown. In the commune everybody was conventionally

[1] For fuller description of the administrative powers of the Chief see section on Government.

assigned to a definite position, each recognised the status and family position of the other, and so the life of the tribe flowed along the consistent, even tenor of its way.

Indeed, the very virtue of tribal organisation, with its integrated solidarity and mutual dependence, became its gravest fault. The fear of calamity was eclipsed by group dependence. The incentive to thrift was reduced to a minimum. Foresight, the most dynamic force in advanced society, was smothered in group responsibility for individual need. Thus the Native was an easy prey to famine, pestilence, tyranny and exploitation, which, with the background of a meagre military equipment and training, rendered him powerless when opposed by the older individualistic civilisations.

Within the tribe there exists a number of kin groups, the adults in which are related to each other in a special way, and the grouping is marked by a totemic recognition of relationship to some animal. Totemism is weak among Rhodesian Natives. Totems serve, however, to demarcate groups within which marriage cannot and must not take place, so that their chief value is as a guarantee that marriage shall be endogamous within the tribe but exogamous with reference to the clan or kin group. Inside the clan, as marked by the totem, is the father-mother-children family.

The marriage relation among a majority of the tribes is both matrilineal as to descent and matrilocal as to place of residence. Under this system the husband builds his hut in the village of his wife and her people, and the care of the children is largely taken over by the maternal grandmother. The children take the wife's name and consider themselves part of the mother's kin. Such a system makes for a highly integrated group relationship. The individual is considered but a unit of the group. Group life, group efficiency and group control take precedence over individual ideas, enterprise or authority.

While, as has been indicated, plural marriage has been allowed only to women of rank, plural marriages for men are common. It is conservatively estimated that 20 per cent of the Native male population of Northern Rhodesia is polygynous. Some wives are inherited and others purely nominal. It was one of the traditional ways of caring for all women in the group, especially where there existed a wide disparity between the number of men and women. Though this disparity is diminishing, the 1931 census shows 369,882 adult males to 446,302 adult females.

Where a man has more than one wife, each has a separate hut for herself and her children. While domestic infelicity does occur, it is curbed by the traditional tribal system which defines status, rights and duties. We cannot be sure how far polygamy actually flourished before the present decade, as the Native had reason for hiding the fact. Before the Native Amendment Ordinance of 1929 abolishing the tax on plural wives, many polygamous marriages were concealed to avoid the tax. Those in closest touch with the Natives think the system is gradually breaking down. It is certain that with the cessation of intertribal wars, the growing dependence of the family on the earnings of the father, and the safeguarding of the life of the bread-winner, the numbers of the sexes will tend to equalise and polygyny to disappear.

The training of children during the period from infancy to parenthood is largely designed to acquaint them with these kinship, marital and tribal obligations. The male initiation ceremonies, phenomena mainly of patrilineal groups, with their long educational preparation, taking place before the boy reaches the age of puberty and conducted by the men, are observed not alone to induct the boy into the man group and to harden him for the tasks of adulthood, but to impress upon him his tribal obligations. Nothing less would cause parents to suffer through the years without complaint so rigorous an initiation régime that sometimes the exposure results in the death of the child. Similarly also the mysteries imparted by the women to the damsel before marriage are calculated to prepare her to share the obligations of kinship and maturity with the adult members of the tribe. Bantu usage abounds in evidences of this group solidarity which is greater than the interest, or indeed than the life, of the individual. Even in the case of the exposure or drowning of the child whose upper teeth appear before the lower, though it must tear the heart of the fond parents, the sad rite is carried through not for the sake of the parents or of their other children, but because failure to destroy the little life will bring grave injury or, it may be, death to someone else in the village.[1] Another case in point is the present given by the groom to the parents of the bride, called in the North "Mpango" and in the South "Lobolo".[2] This system is toughly wrought into the very fabric of Native life in Central and South Africa. A woman does not feel that she is married until the property transfer has been made. It ensures conventional good conduct on the part of both husband and wife. Undoubtedly it serves also to stabilise group relations. The marriage takes place between individuals, but it is the concern of the parental families and totem groups that it should be permanent. The value of the gift varies as between tribes. In Northern Rhodesia it has never been as high as among cattle-raising Natives of the Union. Since the coming of the White the Lobolo payment in both territories tends to be made in money. Its significance lies in its guarantee of the permanency of the relations and in the legitimisation of the children, and as such it is an important factor in group cohesion.

RELIGION

Native religion can scarcely be described as a thing in itself, as it has connections with and ramifies into every

---

[1] At Morgenster mission of the Dutch Reformed Church in Southern Rhodesia a small orphanage is maintained for the children who would in the ordinary course of events surreptitiously disappear under the tribal usage requiring the death of twins of unlike sex and those whose upper teeth appear before the lower. Eight such children are in the orphanage at the present time.

[2] In the North among matrilocal peoples the gift is of minor value, as the groom goes to live in the village of the bride and must supplement the formal marriage gift by a period of service to her parents.

phase of primitive life. In some particulars, as for example the recognition of conventional relationships between the inhabitants of the unseen world, it differs markedly from our own. Among most Rhodesian tribes three classes of inhabitants of the unseen world can be identified, although minor differences in belief concerning them and some minor elaborations are traceable in different groups. One usually finds (a) a supreme being, (b) a group of beneficent *eidola* or disembodied souls, and (c) a group of *daimons* or spirits. The latter may be subdivided into two classes: the ancestral spirits of those who have died violent deaths, who have been injured in life or committed suicide, and a much larger class of land spirits which are attached to certain streams or tracts of land and are responsible for the fertility of the soil and the rainfall. These land spirits, usually of former Chiefs, subtly complicate all land-tenure disputes and inhibit changes in agricultural methods.

The one and supreme god is Lesa, whether known by that name or some derivative or correlative. Lesa dwells in heaven, is the creator of all things, including goblins and demons, and will ultimately come to gather all the dead unto himself. Lesa is high and lifted up beyond the reach of men. Thus, except in the direst extremity and as a last resort, there is no worship of him, neither offerings, priests nor prayers. All things are in his hands and mortals can but accept his acts with stoical fortitude.

Quite different is it with the many spirits by which the unseen environment is peopled. The simplest of these resemble the *eidola* of the Greeks—disembodied souls of the dead awaiting final discharge to the abode of the spirits. During this period the Bantu wraith is to be fêted and propitiated—especially is it necessary in the case of the disembodied soul of the chief or other influential tribesmen. Neglect is not merely disrespectful but dangerous, hence the care with which worshipful rites are observed. These wraiths may be responsible for otherwise inexplicable or difficult phenomena: the dream, the vision, the whirlwind or, more rarely, strange cases of possession. They are usually reincarnated in new-born children.

The ethereal beings in the third class are more significant. They resemble the Greek *daimonia*: powerful spirit beings which may be either beneficent or malevolent. They are capricious, vindictive and work in subtle ways against the health, happiness, safety and even the life of mortals. On the other hand, they may be guardian spirits and avengers. In rare cases they inhabit the madman or the idiot.

Particularly are some of them guardians of the moral and ethical rules and rights of the tribe, and swift and summary is their avenging punishment for the infraction of the group taboos. Thus much of the religious life of the Native is taken up in the propitiatory cult of these inhabitants of darkness. And it is on this belief that the trade of the witch-doctor thrives. By his art he is thought to be able to identify the *daimon*, to deal with and effectively ward off evil, to guarantee prosperity and ensure happiness.

Religious beliefs and practices thus are part of the group's equipment to carry on its struggle for existence. Every act of individual life, every economy of group life, bears the solidifying effect of the sanction of the unseen world. Organisation and ethical controls are of one piece in the visible and invisible spheres of life. It was against this crystallised, fear-ridden Native system, this well-balanced culture with its inadequate premises, its provincialism, its ineffectiveness from a world standpoint, its conservatism and stagnation, that the progressive and advanced European culture came with irreconcilable clash, the results of which we shall presently estimate.

CHAPTER IV

INFLUENCES DRAWING WORKERS TO THE MINES

OPPOSED to the well-integrated system briefly characterised in the preceding chapter, within the past two decades
has come the copper-mining industry, one of the finest
fruits of science and engineering which the White culture
has yet produced. Mr. Letcher does not overstate the importance of these changes in the opening paragraph of his
history of *South Central Africa*: "In no other area of the
world has there been, during the present century, such a
transformation or such an intensive application of scientific
knowledge to so large a region previously so primitive and
so little known as in the territories which contain the
watershed of the Congo and Zambesi Rivers and the
states geographically or politically associated with or linked
to this area".[1]

As one is conducted through the buildings housing the
surface machinery of a Northern Rhodesian mine one is
struck with the interminable elaboration of electric, hy-
draulic, compressed air and mechanical devices. The richest
products of European knowledge and American enterprise
are harnessed together in imposing combinations that
Africa's apparently inexhaustible resources may be speedily
extracted to further enhance the wealth of the world.

One realises that the physical equipment is but the concrete evidence of the technical knowledge and skill of
highly trained Europeans and Americans who have braved
the tropical climate and brought their ideas, systems,
standards and culture into the rough mining territory,
still abounding in wild game and in bacteria of strange,
untamed diseases more dangerous still.

[1] Owen Letcher, *South Central Africa*, p. 16 (African Publications,
Johannesburg, 1932).

The White man discovered that one of his main advantages in African mining lay in the presence of a vast cheap Native labour supply, although the Natives had to be acclimatised and accustomed to the work in order that the White man might successfully compete in placing the metals on the markets of the world. Native efficiency meant dividends, wealth and security. Moreover, White and Native interests were economically reciprocal in this great new mining venture. If any tribal solidarity opposed the White man's purpose it had to be broken down just as the difficulties of the physical environment had to be met and reduced. So a mining industry of mutual interest became a tremendous engine for social disintegration.

We may now proceed to an examination of the forces which have brought the Natives to the mines. One can say that there were three correlated sets of factors favouring Native participation in mining labour and contributing to the breakdown of his inertia, isolation, lack of ambition and contentment with the traditional life. There are also some minor and subsidiary considerations. The play of these main factors has changed Native psychological attitudes and created a set of poignant problems which White and Native alike at present find it difficult, if not impossible, to solve.

The first set of factors relates to the Native's familiarity with mines and mining labour; the second to his desire for foreign goods, and the third to the increasing necessity for money to discharge his growing obligations, some of which had formerly been paid in kind. These must ever be kept in mind if one would understand the recent industrialisation of Native life.

The Native's familiarity with the conditions of mine labour is perhaps the strongest influence attracting him to the copper-mines. This influence was not lacking in Northern Rhodesia. The mining of copper had been carried on in an indifferent and desultory fashion by Natives through many centuries. Ingots of copper 99 per cent pure

produced by Northern Rhodesian Natives have been recovered from ancient workings, the age of which it is
difficult to place. There is some evidence in support of the
theory that the extractive industry flourished for more
than a millennium in Southern Rhodesia.[1] So there has
been a certain amount of familiarity with surface mining
and some knowledge of ores from the beginning of, if not
before, Bantu occupation.

Natives from the Abercorn and Kasama districts of
Northern Rhodesia were employed in some of the smaller
gold-mines near Salisbury as early as 1906. They were
recruited as an experiment, but proved themselves so
useful, adaptable and trustworthy that on their return
to their Native villages they were commissioned to bring
back others like themselves.

The opening of the Katanga copper-mines in 1911 marks
another epoch. Then for the first time Native labour from
Northern Rhodesia was extensively used in industry. Although employment figures differentiating Rhodesian and
Congo labour are available only from 1920, they show that
in that year 5747 Rhodesian Natives were working for the
Union Minière,[2] i.e. 47·8 per cent of their entire Native
force. This number rose to 6006 or 56·1 per cent the following year, since which time there has been a gradual reduction until, by agreement between the Governments concerned, recruitment for Katanga mines in Rhodesia stopped
July 31, 1931. After 1923 the workers were permitted to
bring their wives and families with them into Katanga,
and the records indicate that 20 per cent of them did so.
These workers came long distances, many from Barotse-

---

[1] The Owanda skeleton exhumed from an old mine working in
Owanda, S. Rhodesia, now on display in the Bulawayo Museum, indicates that copper was taken from this spot by negroid people at least
1000 years ago. It has been suggested by Professor Raymond Dart that
certain S. Rhodesian mines were operated by pre-Bantu groups as early
as 3000 B.C. (*Sunday Times*, Johannesburg, August 21, 1932), but the
evidence is far from conclusive.

[2] The principal mining corporation in the Belgian Congo, which since
its formation in 1905 has been responsible for developing the rich
mineral resources of Katanga Province.

land and the Balovale country in the south-west, and many more from the highlands adjoining the Tanganyika border.

It is to be remembered also that until December 27, 1927, all Katanga contracts were for six months' duration, after which period of service the Native was free to go home. He might return to the mines later if he so desired. The labour turnover under these conditions was tremendous. No sooner was the Native sufficiently trained to be an asset than he was off for a protracted period, and to secure his return the recruiting process had to be repeated. Gradual recognition of this situation caused the Union Minière belatedly to establish a three-year contract in 1927. The short contract system both in Katanga and in the southern colonies, however, had already familiarised the inhabitants even of remote villages in the eastern, central and western sections of the colony with conditions on the mines: the Native knew the rigour of the work, the conditions of labour, the wages, the White man's ways and not a few of his weaknesses. So that the coming of the White man to open mines in the Rhodesian copper belt was neither an unwelcome nor unfamiliar invasion.

Thus the process of familiarisation with the White man's ways, methods and paraphernalia of civilisation was gradual and casual through a long period, but for the past two decades it has been speeded up by the Native's intensive contact with mining operations. Out of the familiarity born of contact with White civilisation came a phenomenal increase in desire not alone for the utensils, but for other material conveniences of the White man's civilisation as well. Like Eve, his wife had eaten of the tree of knowledge of good and evil and knew that they both were naked. The desire for trinkets and the White man's cast-off finery gave place to a conscious desire for blankets, showy clothes, the European knife and axe, the mirror, mouth-organ, gramophone, sewing-machine and bicycle. It was natural that sugar, tea, rice, cigarettes and even tinned food should follow close upon the heels of the former. He had little or no substantial surplus product to exchange with the European for them. These things could be procured by money only, and money came as wages. Thus the multiplication and growing complexity of Native desires not only induced him to work for wages, but caused him to return to such labour again and again. The impelling force was not the doctrine of the dignity of labour, but the painful necessity to secure those things which satisfied increasing needs.

Some of the most significant urges to human activity are socially incited, and chief among them is the desire for prestige and recognition. The African Native, by reason of his very social organisation, places a high premium on the admiration of other members of his group. Personal possessions added to his prestige. The fact that he had adventured into the White man's world brought him prestige. His ability to give presents to his Chief and members of his family on his return increased his prestige. It was recently stated by a competent person that "in some tribes the fact of a man having travelled and worked 'abroad' gives him a status not vastly inferior to that acquired some years ago by the fact that he had killed an enemy or a lion".[1] The keen edge of exhaustion, indignity, illness or even discharge were minimised in the glamorous reiteration of the exploits of his long absence. So that what was at first an individual adventure soon built itself into a social custom to which men were not only willing but anxious to conform. The Chief recognised the returned worker by granting him a partial exemption from customary services and payment. Moreover, it was a great lark for the Native to go out for a period of service. He could see the world at little expense and satisfy his desire for new experience and adventure. The conservative wives of workers gradually followed their husbands to the mines and brought home with them the tangible evidence of their exile. In fact this experience extended even to unmarried women,

[1] Quoted from a personal letter written by Col. A. Stephenson, Director of the Native Recruiting Association for the copper belt of Northern Rhodesia.

precarious though the adventure has proved. In a White Fathers Mission at Rosa, far from the main road in the North-East section, a young woman was brought forward who had been at Livingstone, and the fathers explained that her experience in the White man's world had given her an enviable reputation among the women of the group. Such cases, however, are rare and are usually discouraged by the Chief and elders.

This is not to say that the worker had intimately come into contact with the higher culture, nor that his condition had been substantially improved. From the White man's standpoint he was but a cog in the machine, to be safeguarded in physical and mental health because he was a necessary tool to the extraction of metal. But incidentally the human machine suffered a psychological modification. Its desires improved, its wants became poignantly conscious and a new world of interest was born.

The third set of factors inducing Natives to come to the mines can scarcely be classified as attractive, but rather as compulsive. Need for money provided the incentive for labour. The Government required a tax from all Natives, varying by districts (outside Barotseland, which has a special rate of 8s. 6d.), from 10s. to 12s. 6d. per adult male. This governmental pressure for money in the majority of cases could be met only by the wages of labour. Wages could be procured in the mines and settlements, in domestic service and, for a few, on European farms, and the pay was highest in the mines. Tax payment could not be escaped, hence the compulsion to work.

Then also there were dues required by his own customs. Formerly these obligations had been discharged by gifts and labour, but under the new money economy payment was required in cash. The marriage payment by the groom to the parents of the bride, referred to above, was formerly a conventionalised transfer of cattle or goods, now it has become increasingly the equivalent in money. The fees for medical attention, for education and for initiation into age rank, not to speak of the possible penalties for the infraction of law, must be provided for in cash. Indeed, even the contribution necessary for the support of his new religion was customarily paid in money to maintain his standing and his self-respect. In this complex set of influences it is difficult to determine which had most power in pushing the Native into the mining job. The tax collector, the shopkeeper, the missionary, have all contributed to the same end.

Still another compulsive factor was present before the recent depression which reduced the demand for labour on the mines. The parts of Rhodesia yielding the best labour supply were systematically recruited by agents of the mines. Every legitimate inducement was brought to bear on the able-bodied men to persuade them to labour for the mines. In the early years of recruitment Chiefs were given presents for their co-operation. Premiums from blankets to bicycles found their way into the hands of the men. Sometimes this recruitment was carried on by private agents, sometimes by associations of employers, both of whom worked under governmental regulations. The system in the past has been susceptible of grave abuses, and although necessary to secure the requisite labour supply, has been a cause of mutual misunderstanding and recrimination between White and Native. No governmental regulation could eliminate its susceptibility to tricks, petty bribery, cash advances, presents and premiums. This is not the place to deal with the legal terms of the contract, which will be discussed later.[1]

In some regions, particularly among the Babemba, so effectually did the above factors combine in their attraction and compulsion that in 1931 an army of 60 per cent of the able-bodied males between fifteen and forty-five were away from their villages—a majority of them on the mines—to the disruption of agriculture, the unusual burdening of women and the disorganisation of tribal life. Perhaps to a limited degree also the conditions of freedom from restraint, health and recreation at the mining centres

[1] See below, Chapter X. pp. 161-2.

were an attraction. In talking to Natives throughout Northern Rhodesia and those in closest touch with them, this factor assumes less importance than might be theoretically supposed. It is true that the health of the Native on the mine is safeguarded. The doctor and the hospital are at hand, but African Natives have little thought of misfortune until it is upon them. Living conditions are more elaborate than in the Native kraal, but they are attracted by the familiar, not the unfamiliar. Recreations, the cinema and team games do appeal to them, but the appeal represents the vague desire for new experience and forms only a minor contributory factor in the uprooting process.

CHAPTER V

CONDITIONS IN INDUSTRIAL CENTRES

THE world depression belatedly but acutely affected the demand for Native labour in the Northern Rhodesian mines. At the end of 1931 only Roan Antelope, Nkana and Broken Hill were employing more than a clean-up and watchman force. The other six mines[1] were closed. The causes and extent of this labour market slump are treated elsewhere.[2] There was considerable disappointment and suffering of the Native population entailed by this necessary retrenchment in labour. The Native population in large sections of the country was dependent on mine labour for the provision of ready money necessary for the payment of taxes and the satisfaction of multiplying wants. Thus the sudden cessation of mining operations left them confused and not a little resentful.

Moreover, a part of the labour force was already sufficiently emancipated from the obligations and attractions of the Native villages to find themselves more at home in a settlement near the mines or in a town location. Some had married wives of a foreign tribe and could not go back. Others had failed to fulfil their kinship obligations or were in disgrace at home and preferred not to return. These latter became squatters near White settlements or semi-detribalised inhabitants of town locations, eking out a precarious existence by casual labour for Europeans.

During the year also the working force on the two operating mines had been cut in half. As in European industry, this labour situation permitted the mines to make a careful selection of its workers, retaining only the more

---

[1] The nine mines in 1931 were Broken Hill (lead and zinc), Luiri Gold-fields, Bwana Mkubwa, Kasanshi, Nchanga, Nkana, Roan Antelope, Chambishi, Mufulira (the last-named seven mines produce copper).

[2] See below, Chapter IX. pp. 143-50.

efficient and best adapted Natives. Hence it is only fair to say that this survey of Native life in the mining location shows it at its best and of the town location at, or near, its worst.

Perhaps the best method óf evaluating the factors conditioning Native life both in mines and town locations is by picturing that life as an observer sees it. The mine labourer may be either recruited from the Native village, in which case he is definitely contracted for a specified term of service, or he may present himself at the mine and, if desirable on the grounds of physical fitness, secure employment on a monthly basis. The men formerly recruited comprise 50 per cent of the present labour force, the volunteers 50 per cent.[1] After the recruited man's contract period is over, if his record is satisfactory, he is kept at work on a monthly basis.

Recruitment, now almost at a standstill, has been carried on in the following manner. The Native Labour Association, established in March 1930, under the direction of Colonel A. Stephenson, undertook to secure sufficient labour for all mines and to supply them as and when requisitioned. In 1931 it had twenty seven agents stationed at strategic points throughout the most desirable labour-yielding territory. It is the business of the local White agent to pass the word as to the number of workers needed, to look them over with reference to physical fitness, explain to them the conditions of the contract, and send the most promising by motor transport to the distribution depôt at Bwana Mkubwa. Here the terms of the twelve months' contract and the stipulated pay are again explained to them, and the contract is signed before the District Commissioner. Then follows a period of rest and examination lasting from five to seven days. Rigid medical tests are made, particularly for weakness of eyes, heart,

[1] The proportion in normal times has been 30 per cent recruited and 70 per cent voluntary. Naturally, in a time of labour retrenchment the monthly labour was first to be discharged, leaving a considerably higher proportion of recruited boys who still had some legal claim upon the company.

lungs, tropical ulcers and venereal disease. The examination satisfactorily passed, the Native's preference as to the place in which he desires to labour is consulted, and where possible in harmony with this preference he is recontracted to the mine, whither he is immediately sent by rail; rejected men being repatriated to the home village. At the mine he is again examined by the medical official in charge. The men failing to qualify here are repatriated at the expense of the Native Labour Association and the contract is cancelled. The recruits chosen are now employed at light work for an acclimatisation period not exceeding a month, assigned to underground or surface work, given some instruction about explosives, the names of the tools to be handled, the machinery to be used, drilling operations and the conditions of the labour. They are then assigned to a White boss or "ganger" and started on their long period of service.

Any recruited worker may bring his wife and young children with him or, if he should come alone, at any time, on request, he may have them brought to him at the mine's expense. Statistics of mine labour compiled on the copper belt indicate that the married worker is more efficient, healthier, more contented and remains longer than the single Native.[1] The reasons for this difference are many. Single men find it easier to go from place to place. Their habits of life are less stable. They are less willing to work on contract, and are more at the beck and call of Chief, headmen or relatives at home. They are more easily stampeded by villagers returning home. To which must be added the fact that married men's houses are kept cleaner, food is cooked more regularly and more in the traditional manner, not to speak of the social advantages real or fancied accruing to wife and family.

All Natives are housed in a mining location, which is divided into quarters for single men and those for married

[1] At the Roan Antelope, with a force of 1839, the married men employed remain an average of 20·25 months; the single men 9·79 months. At Nkana, with a total strength of 2727, the average stay for married men is 12·9 months and single men 8·6 months.

workers and their families. There is a wide diversity in the type of hut used for this purpose. One finds in the same location round huts twelve feet in diameter constructed of Kimberley brick with thatched roofs; huts fourteen feet square with cement floors, brick walls and corrugated iron roofs; and long end-to-end houses containing separate living-quarters, with approximately the same cubic air space for several families. There is as yet no unanimity as to the best type of hut. Under ideal conditions huts are built in rows, with a window and always with doors fitted for padlocking, and separated by at least fifteen feet. The single men's section of the location is cleaned by children detailed for that purpose. That of the married men must be swept by the family, the refuse buried and the quarters made ready for periodic inspection.

The furnishing of the huts varies with individual taste and financial ability. It is common to find in the quarters of an unmarried man the Spartan simplicity of an iron bed, washing utensils, a tin trunk and chair; in the married man's hut the added embellishment of bright calico hangings, a lantern, cooking and toilet accessories, cheap pictures and the feminine accretion of trinkets.

The legal food ration of meal, meat and vegetables is issued once a week to the wife of the married man, on the presentation of monthly food checks, the amount varying with the size of his family. It is cooked in front of the hut in clear weather, and during the rainy season in a lean-to or small cooking kitchen attached to the hut. The wife and children augment the food issue by the purchase of small quantities of dried fish, the collection of snared birds, mice, frogs, flying ants or locusts, the leaves of the pumpkin, sweet potato, certain varieties of wild spinach and grasses, gathered from neighbouring fields and woods. These are cooked into a stew called *munane* or *ndiwo*. Into this common pot the ball of dough, resembling hard-cooked porridge, is dipped by each member of the family before it is eaten. Well-prepared *munane* is highly prized by all Natives, and its absence is a matter of keen regret and disappointment to unmarried men. Roughly 30 per cent of all mine-workers are married men, and the proportion is steadily increasing.

The eating arrangements for single men differ slightly as between the mines. In Nkana they are fed at a common kitchen. At the Roan Antelope food is issued to them as to married men. Some of the young men have adopted the questionable expedient of clubbing together and hiring a woman to cook for them, paying her the princely salary of 2s. 6d. a month. Those less fortunate, in addition to doing their own washing and cleaning, find it necessary to cook their food after the day's work is over. The majority, however, in groups of two or three living in the same hut, about sunset prepare their hurried and somewhat haphazard meal lacking the relish they so much enjoy.[1]

All employees about to go underground are given bread and coffee. The former they usually carry with them down the shaft to serve as a light lunch sometime during the eight-hour shift.

When not at work the Native loafs about his hut or keeps up an incessant chatter with other men of similar shift hours. As will be shown later, he has no desire and little encouragement to spend his off-hours in either constructive, recreational or other self-improvement occupation. His rather drab life flows on through the weeks of his engagement.

After his contract is fulfilled or if a voluntary labourer he decides to go back to his Native village; he gathers up his belongings into bundles capable of being carried on his head and in his arms and starts on his long journey, sometimes of several days, homewards. If he has been working on contract his employers are responsible for his transportation, provisioning and safe conduct to his Native village.

---

[1] In the older mining fields like the Globe and Phoenix gold-mine at Queque in Southern Rhodesia some of the single men employ youths at 5s. a month to cook, wash and keep their huts in order, passing on a portion of their own rations of food in part payment. The system has spread also to some of the married men whose wives refuse to do the menial service and force their husbands to employ boys for that purpose.

The amount and variety of articles in his kit as he starts on the homeward journey shows a surprising range of necessity and taste. European clothes, lengths of calico and silk, cooking and eating kits, blankets, mirrors, shaving equipment, cutlery, trinkets for presents to his Chief, kin and friends, occasionally a gramophone or hand-operating sewing-machine and, more rarely still, the much-prized bicycle. Not infrequently he has spent all but a very small portion of his entire earnings. Three typical lists of articles taken from the carefully examined baggage of seventy-three Nkana repatriots about to start for home are given in Appendix B.

The rapidity and completeness with which these things disappear among relations and friends immediately on the return to the Native kraal under the communistic tribal system is most surprising.

Native wages differ for various types of work. While at both mines the average cash wage for all adult employees is 12·124d. per day, the wages run from 5d. a day at the beginning, for surface work, to 11d., and underground from 10d. to 21d., though a highly skilled carpenter can make 40d. a day.

No fine can legally be assessed against the worker for inefficiency, laziness or obstreperousness, as is the case in the Union Minière in Katanga, where, though the fines are small and go to support welfare work, the fining system is extensively used. At the Roan Antelope there is, however, an indirect means of control through the bonus system. The underground labourer, if he misses no shift and is satisfactory to his White gang-boss, is given a bonus of 1s. 3d. a week. In addition, if he wears the boots provided and his coat to and from work he may collect an extra bonus of 9d. each week, i.e. it is possible for him to procure an added income of 4d. a day. On the other hand, if he is unsatisfactory and his gang-boss fails to recommend him, the omission acts as an effective fine. This has resulted in the growth of loyalty, regularity and efficiency.

To the casual observer these cash wages paid to Natives

seem pitiably small in comparison with wages paid to Whites. They tell, however, only half the story. The employer stands in a double relation to the worker. When wages are paid his obligations are only partly discharged. He is also *in loco parentis* to the boy and must provide free food, medical care, housing, recreation and a completeness of supervision equal to that maintained toward a dependent child. These obligations increase real wages tremendously. The cost of such services must be added to the wage of every worker however small or large his pay. A cash wage of 5d. paid to the new surface worker may be augmented by 17d. as service liability. So that actually he may be receiving the equivalent of 22d. a day. At the Nkana the average cash wage throughout the entire mine is 12·12d. per day, but the service wage is 11·64d. At the Roan Antelope, because of the more extensive welfare activities, the service cost is considerably higher. While the average wage is identical, 12·12d., the average service cost is· 16·56d.[1] In the Union Minière the service cost is higher still, and the added welfare charge is claimed to have more than commensurately increased the efficiency of the worker. The average wage throughout the company's vast workings is eleven francs per day, the service cost fifteen francs a day per man, making an effective average wage of twenty-six francs a day per worker, or 16·5d., 22·5d. and 39d. respectively in English currency.

As might naturally be expected, the welfare services differ widely as between the mines. To the far-seeing management wisdom dictates a liberal welfare policy with some assurance of commensurate future dividends. To the management with myopic vision it is a needless and unjustifiable expenditure of company funds, which should be reduced to the legal and customary minimum. Here more than elsewhere the influence of civilisation through the mines can be beneficial to Native life. In this connection

---

[1] The items included: food, 7·68; hospital, 1·68; welfare, 0·24; recreation and repatriation, 0·96; citrus farm expenses, 0·12; location maintenance, 0·6; and operation, 5·28.

Rhodesia may have something to learn from the long experience of the Union Minière in Haut Katanga.

The average death-rate of Natives in all Northern Rhodesian mines in 1931, according to the reports compiled in the office of the Secretary for Native Affairs, was 25·03 per 1000 Native employees.[1] Nkana lost through death thirty-nine per 1000, Roan Antelope seventeen. The difference has been variously explained as due to an unfortunately selected group of recruits, to the difficulty of acclimatisation, to a faulty system of reporting illness, now corrected, to the fact that the Nkana camp is flat and the floors of the huts damp for a part of the year, increasing the incidence of pneumonia and influenza. Whatever the cause, the discrepancy is considerable, and though conditions have been improved[2] they are still far from ideal. On the copper belt across the border in the Belgian Congo amid similar conditions and with a similar labour force, but with much greater attention to the human phase of the problem, the wastage of human life was 8·01 per 1000 Natives.

The difference is not explicable on the basis of inferior medical provision, as the hospital staff and equipment for

[1]

	Average No. of Employees.	Deaths.	Rate per 1000.
Broken Hill . . .	1217	15	12·3
Bwana Mkubwa . .	667	14	21
Luiri Goldfields . .	621	31	49
Kansanshi . . .	445	20	45
Nchanga	2176	53	24·4
Nkana	5499	214	39
Roan Antelope . .	6823	99	17
Chambishi . . .	702	6	8·5
Mufulira	2811	54	19·2

Special Mortality Table compiled by the Secretary for Native Affairs for 1931 at Livingstone.

[2] The death-rate at Nkana for the first eight months of 1932 was at the annual rate of 18·5 per 1000, that at the Roan Antelope 8·5, although it must be remembered that the most critical months were yet to come. That the Roan Antelope has made considerable progress in reducing the death-rate is evident in the comparative death-rates of the last four years: 25·97 in 1928, 28·05 in 1929, 31·8 in 1930, and 17 in 1931.

research and Native care at both Nkana and the Roan
Antelope leave little to be desired. The medical examination on reaching the mines is searching and thorough. Few
detectable physical weaknesses or diseases escape the
watchful eyes of three medical examiners detailed for this
purpose. It' must be attributable in some measure to de-
fects in conditions under which the men are cared for, but
more, perhaps, to the very short period the Northern
Rhodesian mines have been operating. The mortality
rate is always highest in the development period and
tends to fall with the age of the mines. Thus with the
greater age of the mines and the longer stabilisation of the
workers the death-rate from this cause falls significantly.
The Katanga mines, with a history of twenty-one years,
have gradually reduced their death-rate to 8·01. The gold-
mines on the Rand, with the added phthisis risk, have
stabilised their mortality rate at approximately twelve
per 1000 workers. With the passing years we should expect
a gradual decrease in the mortality rate in the Ndola
district as well.

Pulmonary diseases most frequent and fatal to the
Native seem to be aggravated by the presence of men
from different sections coming together for the first time
in large groups. Dr. A. J. Orenstein, Head of the Department of Sanitation of the Rand Mines Limited, after long
experience in the Rand gold-mines, questions the popular
impression that it is a matter of susceptibility of certain
tribes. His observations show that the incidence of the
disease varies directly with the size of the group and the
recentness of its assembling irrespective of the sections
from which the recruits come.[1]

The Native moved from the habitat to which he is
peculiarly adjusted needs intelligent and special care. He
is particularly susceptible to pneumonia, bronchitis, influenza and spinal meningitis. His lack of immunity to

[1] " Tuberculosis in South African Natives, with special reference to
the Disease among the Mine Labourers on the Witwatersrand" (Publications of the South African Institute for Medical Research, vol. v.
No. xxx. p. 22 ff., also pp. 349-50).

recently introduced diseases makes him their easy prey. There is little doubt that his natural defence against disease has been reduced by repeated attacks of malaria from earliest childhood to maturity.[1] His dietary is far from balanced or satisfactory for increasing his resistance. Nor is it increased by his mode of life in the Native hut, where a fire is lighted in the centre of the floor, the door closed and the smoke permitted to find exit through the heavily thatched roof. Breathing such vitiated air, the overworked lungs are in no condition to withstand the onslaught of bacteria. His habit of rising in the cold morning (for the nights on the tropical plateau can be particularly cold) and wandering about half clad imposes further strain on an already weakened physique.

In the light of these conditions it is surprising, not that the Native labourer so easily succumbs to new diseases as he changes habitat, but that he manifests such vital resistance to them. This fact, however, does not relieve his White employer from the responsibility of giving him every possible assistance in his fight for life and health in the new environment.

The underground conditions at the mines, with the rapid changes of temperature and the fatigue incidental to the work, are also a strain on Native vitality. At both Nkana and Roan Antelope we were informed that the mortality rate of Native women and children was considerably less than that of the men, in spite of the frequent hazard of maternity. Accurate statistics as a check on this point, however, were not available.

The health, comfort and contentment of the married workers is affected also by the health and happiness of their wives and children. Family health conditions on each of the mine locations might be considerably improved by the employment of a full-time location nurse. Natives have an antipathy to hospitals and are entirely ignorant of

---

[1] Dr. P. H. Ward, chief medical officer of the Northern Rhodesia Government, gives this as the predisposing cause of certain enumerated chest diseases.

prenatal care and modern hygiene as applied to confinement and child nurture. Native medicines are extensively
used, though in advanced or serious illness they seek
ministrations at the Native hospital. Mining policy now
seems to be "If a Native woman is in serious enough
trouble she will come in for treatment", oblivious of the
fact that the contentment, regularity and efficiency of the
Native worker depends largely on the health, welfare and
happiness of his wife and children.

The accident rate both minor (less than fourteen days'
confinement) and major for underground workers is rapidly
decreasing, and the compensation for partial and total disability seems adequate. The Northern Rhodesian law
governing Native compensation sets the minimum and
maximum, leaving the adjustment of individual claims
between these limits to the fairness of the mine management. In cases of total disability the adjustment is decided
by the location manager, ratified by the management and
submitted to the District Officer for approval. If approved
it becomes legal, if not it is referred back and a further
adjustment is effected. Should this fail to satisfy the
Native he may seek redress through appeal to the higher
courts. Compensation is paid in a lump sum, which is a
convenient though somewhat questionable method. It is
the practice of the Katanga mines, for reasons which are
obvious, to pay the indemnity in monthly instalments
through life or the term of disability.

In Northern Rhodesia Native compensation is adjusted
on the basis of wages received, although minor increments
are added by the mine administration in consideration of
the impairment of the worker's probable future earning
power, number and age of dependents and the possibility
of his doing light work, though partially incapacitated, on
the mine property and thus remaining on the pay-roll.

In education, little has been done at either mine. The
work seems to be particularly discouraging. At Nkana a
day school for children on mine property with three teachers
has a registration of two hundred and an average attendance

of fifty. A night school for adults with two Native teachers and a White supervisor has an attendance of seventy. At the Roan Antelope the educational difficulties are similar. With a registration of forty-five the average attendance at the day school for children is thirty, and the experiment of holding night classes for adults had to be abandoned from lack of Native interest.

In every conference with Natives, uneducated as well as educated, Native ambition for education was stressed. Though they are aware of its significance they easily tire of the grind necessary for its achievement. Supervisors at both mines say Native parents will not compel their children to attend schools, and there the matter rests. This policy is curiously at variance with that of the Katanga mining interests, which insist that every child of school age shall not only attend school every day, but shall be given training in the crafts as well as in academic subjects, and shall be fed with other location children under controlled conditions at a common school kitchen.

It would be difficult to over-estimate the value to children on Northern Rhodesia mining locations if the schools were conducted on modern lines and with modern educational methods. In the light of the experience of those who have been working in this field, however, it would be necessary to make attendance obligatory for all children of school age and the wilful infraction of the rule a cause for disciplining the adults in the family responsible for their care.

The educational policy is closely connected with the policy of stabilisation and deliberate detribalisation of Native workers. As long as the present indeterminate period of labour and the early return of the worker and his family to the Native territory continues there is some cogency in the argument that it is scarcely worth while to force the educational issue. The mines have a right to say that the general education of the Bantu is the responsibility of Government, for it should not be necessary for the industry to have to carry the added burden. The

Congo Belge has frankly faced the problem and embarked on a policy of detribalisation. Everything possible is being done to keep the Native workers on the mine property indefinitely, to educate their children, safeguard their marriages in the interests of selective breeding and care for them in old age. The mines are willing to carry the responsibility because of the improvement of their industrial efficiency. It is a long-time policy with factors which are worthy of careful consideration.

Naturally, any comparison of the length of service as a measurement of the degree of Native detribalisation between mines must be made on the background of the comparative lengths of time the mines have been operating. Detribalising tendencies, however, are evident in the newer mines.

The average length of service of the Native on the Rhodesian copper belt is slightly over one year. At Nkana less than half remain beyond the third year.[1]

The length of stay, which is the closest comparable index to detribalisation, seems to increase rapidly with the age of the mine. Broken Hill, with a mining population of 748 and a mining history of twenty-six years, shows a higher distribution of workers who have had continuous residence in the mining location.[2] The Wankie Colliery Company

[1]

Nkana.			Roan Antelope.		
Time.	No.	Per Cent.	Time.	No.	Per Cent.
Under 1 year .	1862	68·28	Under 1 year .	1248	67·86
Between 1 and 2 years	782	28·68	Between 1 and 2 years	439	23·87
Between 2 and 3 years	65	2·38	Between 2 and 3 years	82	4·46
Between 3 and 4 years	13	0·48	Between 3 and 4 years	36	1·96
Over 4 years .	5	0·18	Over 4 years	34	1·85
Present total strength	2727	100·00	Present total strength	1839	100·00

[2] The Rhodesia Broken Hill Development Company, Ltd., submits the following figures for labour on its mines. The large proportion of

at Wankie over the border in Southern Rhodesia has had
an unbroken mining history since 1904. Although its staff
of Native workers was reduced from 4975 in 1929 to 1900
in 1932, it still shows 852 of its workers continuously resident in the location for more than three years, and 252
who have been away from their Native kraals for more
than ten years.[1]

It must be remembered that many of those who leave
return to their old jobs after an average fourteen months'
holiday. The Native territories are thus a reservoir for the
absorption of those who are out of work, have been discharged or are broken in health, and the small group whose
vital energy has been expended in the copper-mines. The
continuance of this casual labour policy means that Native
groups or Government must ultimately be responsible for
human mine wastage.

The Director of Recreation finds it difficult to interest
the Native in recreation. The latter will attend a moving
picture exhibit[2] and is measurably enthusiastic about
football, but otherwise indoor and outdoor sports and
games have no continuous attraction for him. The Roan

old hands as against new casual labourers has probably been increased
during the recent period of severe retrenchment.

Period of Service.	No. of Natives.	Percentage.
Under 1 year	210	28·07
Between 1 and 2 years . . .	168	22·46
,, 2 ,, 3 ,, . . .	44	5·88
,, 3 ,, 4 ,, . . .	59	7·89
,, 4 ,, 5 ,, . . .	61	8·16
,, 5 ,, 7 ,, . . .	55	7·35
,, 7 ,, 8 ,, . . .	19	2·54
,, 8 ,, 9 ,, . . .	27	3·61
,, 9 ,, 10 ,, . . .	34	4·55
Over 10 years	71	9·49
Strength .	748	100·00

[1] At the Wankie Collieries 85 per cent of all workers have been with
the company for more than three years, 30 per cent for more than ten
years, and eight men for more than twenty-five years continuous
service.

[2] Roan Antelope has bi-weekly showings to an average of 1000
Natives. Nkana is now in process of installing a moving picture machine.

Antelope has a welfare club-house with games, writing
facilities, newspapers, a gramophone and a dry canteen,
but the average daily attendance is less than a score.
Also, an experiment has been made in the organisation
of a Pathfinders group of thirty boys. Although small, it
has created real enthusiasm by organising, equipping and
providing with uniforms a drum corps of twenty-four
boys. At this mine there is also a well-equipped playground for the use of the younger children.

Thirteen stores are rented on the Roan Antelope location to Europeans and Indians who staff them with Native
clerks. They are open two days a week only. The average
income of each is estimated at £25 a month.

There has recently grown up a flourishing mail order
business with the J. D. Williams and Oxendale Companies in
England, which do a monthly business of £60 with Natives
at Roan Antelope and a proportional amount at Nkana.
It is increasingly popular for a number of workers to club
together, pooling their orders to escape the carrying charge.

This seems to be a defensive policy, as throughout
Northern Rhodesia the prices charged Natives by White
and Indian storekeepers are ethically unjustifiable. It is
true the Native buys smaller quantities than does the
White, and perhaps on staple products, because of the
added inconvenience, he might reasonably be charged a
slightly higher price. That prices are usually in multiples
of the 3d. or "tickie", which is a high monetary unit in
comparison with the wages of the Native, further contributes to a higher price for small articles. It is true also
that the shopkeeper must carry a large stock of goods and
his turnover is slow, but there can be no justification of
a double price system which includes articles usually
purchased singly. The Native is building up a sense of
values, and when he discovers he can purchase by mail
order for 15s. a blanket manufactured by the same firm
of the same weight and material as that offered for sale
by the local merchant at 45s., one cannot blame him for
the overseas purchase. Complaints of this sort on the part

of Natives are universal throughout the Protectorate, and a careful check reveals the reasonable grounds of the resentment. It is a short-sighted mercantile policy and will act as a boomerang on the Rhodesian trader.

The Nkana mine has not encouraged the establishment of any beer-hall, either on or near the mine property. In lieu of it the company periodically grants a licence to each family to make eight gallons of Native beer. The permission rotates through the location, so that everyone has opportunity to celebrate in Native fashion once in from eight to twelve weeks. The beer-making process, however, goes on surreptitiously irrespective of the licence. Native beer is manufactured from millet and maize, and while the alcoholic content is small, the drink is quite heady.

The reverse system is in vogue at Roan Antelope. A Government beer-hall is within easy walking distance of the mine location, where beer-making is strictly prohibited. A close check reveals that the Roan Antelope workers spend 1s. 5d. of their total wages, i.e. £600 a month, in the Native beer-hall.

In spite of the current expenditure of these childlike people the seeds of thrift have germinated. Information from Barclay's Bank at Nkana shows that between 10 and 15 per cent of the Natives employed already have accounts with them. It is customary for the worker with an account to lay by about 10s. a month, which, by the time he leaves, gives him a savings account averaging over £6. The newer accounts are small, but a few of the older employees have accounts exceeding £50. Every inducement is held out to have them treat the account as savings, and withdrawals are discouraged even to requiring the location manager to be present when they are made.

The Roan Antelope mine has introduced a promising innovation in its agricultural plot assignment. Any Native employee may obtain on request an acre plot of land near the compound to be used for gardening purposes. If his family has a surplus of vegetables and cereals they may be disposed of to the mine at current market prices. These plots last year yielded between 40,000 and 50,000 lb. of produce in excess of the personal needs of the workers. This produce was purchased by the mine and provided a satisfactory means of supplementing the family exchequer.

There seems to be little difference between tribal groups so far as preference of work is concerned. Many boys, irrespective of tribal affiliation, prefer surface to underground work in spite of the higher wages paid for the latter work. Some prefer location police duty, others service as hospital orderlies. The least desirable task on the location, viz. that of sanitation, is readily undertaken by two tribal groups, the Baila and Bakaonde.

The mines follow the policy of paying little attention to tribal lines in the selection of work gangs, though in housing them tribal preferences are observed as far as possible. It is on Sunday afternoons, as the men wander aimlessly about the location, that one finds them falling into tribal groups for the casual performance of their several Native dances. Occasionally also when the Chief or perhaps the Paramount of a tribe visits the location tribal lines are clearly demarcated.

Mine administrations in the past have readily extended the courtesy of their locations to Chiefs desiring to visit their people, and the invitations have frequently been accepted. A few of the designing Chiefs have left an unenviable reputation behind them for exploitation. Timing their visits or extending them over the pay day, they have extracted considerable tribute in the form of gifts from their various subjects. In the visit of one Paramount the tribute is said to have totalled over £150, so that invitations are now extended with greater discrimination.

The mine location also domiciles some of the houseboys and other domestic servants of Europeans living on the property. They form a considerable army. At Nkana, where all must live on the location, there are 522 of these domestic servants, 50 per cent of whom are married. They look after a White population of 450 men, 270 women and 480 children. At the Roan Antelope the domestics number

453 for a total mine population of 351 men, 236 women
and 265 children.

Crime is comparatively rare.[1] Due to careful policing
methods, few cases have to be carried to the District
Commissioner's office. Wise location managers unofficially
work closely with the District Commissioner in the prevention of crime. The four main offences are thieving,
embezzlement of funds entrusted to a Native by his friends
or kin, wife-beating and an occasional case of witchcraft.
Juvenile delinquency manifests itself sporadically and
usually as a gang phenomenon. At one mine nine children,
ranging from ten to twelve years, were brought to the
location manager on the suspicion that they had been
stealing chickens and selling them to a European butcher.
This is the kind of boyish prank which frequently develops
into more serious offences. After an investigation by the
manager and a confession by the boys, they were remanded
to their parents for a thorough spanking, which successfully put an end to the petty thieving in that quarter.

In spite of unquestionably better food and hygienic
conditions, it cannot be said that family life in the
mine locations is on a higher plane than in the Native
village. The reverse is the case. The individual is away
from tribal restraints and close kinship supervision; women
and children have little to do. The freedom of camp life
emancipates from the tyranny of Native custom. Husbands
are working unvarying eight-hour shifts, and under such
circumstances it would be surprising to find no marital
infidelity. To make the situation more serious, it is possible
for a Native with a wife in his home village to bring a
woman into the location as his wife, live with her until
he starts for home or is tired of her, and pass her on to

---

[1] List of crimes for 1931 secured from the local magistrate and
checked by the location manager at the Roan Antelope follows:

Murder	.	.	.	.	2	Larceny (all types)	.	.	61
Rape	.	.	.	.	2	Assault	.	.	.	47
Indecent assault	.	.	.	20	Arson	.	.	.	3
Incest	.	.	.	.	1	Forgery	.	.	.	9
Housebreaking and burglary				6	Uttering	.	.	.	2

another man. This serial wifehood is common. One welfare worker cited two women still in the location who had changed hands four and five times respectively. Detection is difficult, and location managers find it discreet, unless serious family trouble should develop, not to inquire too closely into the marital relationships of their wards. The mine is not primarily interested in Native morals, but in a contented and efficient labour force. Moreover, prostitution for money flourishes in spite of the vigilance of the management. A location manager told us that unattached women were constantly introduced as sisters or sisters-in-law and permitted to remain as visitors for a time in spite of the suspicion. They plied their trade as prostitutes, venereal infection was thus introduced and the doctor indicated that it ran through sections of the camp before it could be detected and the culprit ejected. Inquiry in Native villages revealed that the infection was brought to the Native territories and these women were known. How this rate of infection compares with that of former years it is difficult to say, as figures for former years are not available.

One of the most promising methods of easing White-Native adjustments, as well as mobilising Native opinion to combat disorder and secure co-operation in reducing incipient misunderstandings, is the establishment of the Native Council. At the Roan Antelope this semi-official advisory group is composed of the twenty-two outstanding elders irrespective of tribal affiliation on the location. It functions as a contact group between White officials and Natives keeping either side informed about the other. By this means information regarding changes in laws or regulations are diffused throughout the entire camp. Any general dissatisfaction is made known to the management while yet in the incipient stage.

Religious ministrations for Natives are not neglected on these mine locations. At the Roan Antelope representatives of one Roman Catholic, one Mohammedan, one Anglican and two Protestant mission societies hold Sunday services. At Nkana a resident clergyman attached to the welfare department of the mine holds regular meetings for the Native congregation. Religious activities and problems involved will be treated more fully in the section on missions.

MUNICIPAL LOCATIONS AND NATIVE TOWNSHIP SETTLEMENTS

Every White settlement of any size has its segregated Native quarters. These are usually a mile or more from the business section, and where possible across a railway, stream, a flat or other natural barrier forming a strip of no-man's-land. In Livingstone and Ndola they are called municipal locations and are directly under the management of a committee of the Town Council. In all other White settlements in the Protectorate the locations are under the supervision of the Native Commissioner of the district and are called township locations. In most towns the inhabitants of the Native locations considerably outnumber the Whites.

Like Topsy they "just growed" until they became large enough or menacing enough to command White attention. Then a location manager was appointed to safeguard the interests of the Natives in the interests of the Whites. All workers, male and female, domestic and others, who have not been definitely requisitioned in writing to live on the premises of their employers, are domiciled in the locations. As will be readily recognised, the Native settlements differ slightly as between towns. An examination of many of them shows that they are strikingly similar, so that a brief description of one with necessary contrasts will give a fairly accurate picture of the problems of all.

The Ndola municipal location houses 4100 Natives. Its high-water mark was 5200 in 1929. It lies on the edge of an extensive swamp and by a stream which is almost dry before the November rains begin. The municipality has been to considerable expense in draining this mosquito-breeding stronghold for the protection of both White and Native. Seventeen hundred conical mud and wattle huts with thatched roofs and earth floors of varying diameters have been built by successive families of Natives. There is no order of arrangement other than their twelve-feet separation from each other. Stooping to enter a low narrow door, one finds himself in a dark, unventilated interior. Some of the smoke from the central fire issues through the grass roof and *en route* leaves the wall and ceiling ebonised by oily soot. The little family or group of single men squat about the fire, for the place is innocent of furnishings beyond the sleeping-mats and cheap knick-knacks which one finds in a Native kraal.

Here are herded together Babemba, Balamba, Angoni, Atonga and Baila families, from two to five persons in a single hut. A plot of ground large enough for the erection of three huts with right to drinking water is rented by the Native for half-a-crown a month; or the hut built by a former resident may be taken over at a similar rental. All shop-boys, artisans, craftsmen, and all domestics, in excess of one for each White family, are crowded together in this strange Native village.

Labour opportunities are few and precarious in these days of retrenchment. If the Native should belong to the jobless tenth he borrows rent money under the free-masonry of tribal obligation, tightens his belt and lives on the surplus mealie porridge of those who are more fortunate than he. Failing to secure the rent, he is ejected from the location. If completely destitute he and his family are rationed by the manager and started on foot to the distant Native kraal.

The average wage of unskilled labour in this location is 15s. a month, but if more skilled the workman may obtain as much as 30s. In addition to this, his employer furnishes a daily ration of mealie meal for food. Firewood is purchased or gathered from the neighbouring bush. In case of illness he is looked after in the Native hospital at the expense of his employer or of the town.

The sewage and hygienic system of the location is communal. Fifty pits behind grass screens are gradually filled in, and although inspected daily they are so horrific that, in spite of the risk of arrest, the surrounding land is fouled with night soil. Water for drinking and cooking is obtainable from six water-taps in a corner of the location, but the Natives wash their clothes and bathe in the neighbouring stream. The old huts gradually become infested with mice and vermin. When "the huts bite" and the families refuse to live longer in them they are torn down and new ones constructed. A squad of boys is employed to keep the spaces between the huts free of rubbish, and a fire-furrow around the location kills the grass and ensures against an errant spark which, in the windy season, might easily destroy the entire settlement.

For single boys and transients who do no cooking, food of sorts may be obtained at a municipal restaurant operated by a Greek, and two Native eating-houses, which, in spite of a weekly inspection, leave much to be desired even from a Native standpoint. The ubiquitous house-fly abounds. Its numbers are not decreased by the Native custom of cutting into strips the meat he is able to procure and hanging it in the sun to dry. These strips soon become so covered with flies that it is difficult to see the meat at all. So menacing has the custom become that at one of the mining locations[1] across the Southern border only cooked meat is issued to married and single men alike.

Approximately 30 per cent of the location residents are married and live in quarters separated from those of the single boys. Sex associations are casual. It was estimated that at least a hundred and fifty workers were living with women other than their wives, the periods of co-habitation lasting from weeks into years. These temporary wives are turned over to others or abandoned. Little notice is taken by the management unless inter-family friction should develop.

From a careful comparison of the locations situated near

[1] Globe and Phoenix Gold Mine at Queque, Southern Rhodesia.

Native villages with those at greater distance, it would seem that the farther afield the Native has to go to secure work, the greater the tendency to enter into these temporary marital unions. It is difficult for him to take his wife and family long distances.[1] There is reluctance on the part of her kin to let her go. He tends to remain longer in the more remote location; the frequency of contact with his people is reduced; fewer of his own tribal group are about him to act as a check upon his aberrant conduct; tribal sanctions grow less insistent; the urge for the consolations of female society increases, and the vague social pattern of the new environment permits of easy emancipation from former marital customs. That such promiscuity is more common than it was a few years ago is the impartial opinion of Government officials. "In some districts there were more cases of adultery coming before the Native courts than usual, and it was presumed that the absence of males at work was the cause, but this is impossible to prove."[2] The men from Northern Rhodesia working in the towns of Southern Rhodesia and the Union are partial to these temporary unions, a fact which tends to protract their stay. Word filtering through from the more remote locations to the home kraals weakens the family bonds here and renders the kraal wife an easy prey to the temptations of illicit unions.[3]

[1] In Salisbury location the proportion of married Natives varies with the distance from their homes. Males here are 2356, females 679. The proportion of those from Nyasaland is 750 males to 72 females, and from Northern Rhodesia 146 to 58, while from Southern Rhodesia the ratio is 1024 to 426.

[2] Answer to a question on the accuracy of statements in the *Northern Rhodesia Government Report for 1930* submitted to the Acting-Governor and referred for written reply to the Secretary for Native Affairs, November 7, 1932.

[3] A careful study of the marital situation in the Umtali location (S. Rhodesia) made jointly by Government and town officials disclosed 91 unions of males and females. Two had been celebrated under the auspices of the Christian Church, 12 were civil marriages performed by the Native Commissioner, 13 men had brought wives from other territories, the sanction to which unions was questionable. The remaining 64 unions were distinctly irregular, i.e. unions in which *lobola* had not been transferred nor any other sanction of tribal custom followed. In the

Prostitution for money flourishes also,[1] with its inevitable accompaniment, venereal disease. Natives are reluctant to present themselves for examination and treatment, especially in the less acute but more insidious of the two venereal infections. In spite of this reluctance the Native clinic on the Ndola location, open only two hours a day, clears an average of twelve cases in a month. The visiting doctor and nurse in charge insist that their work would be greatly facilitated if a close watch were kept on houseboys, nurse-girls and other employees by their White employers and the results made known immediately to the medical authorities. Self-interest on the part of Europeans should dictate the wisdom of a united effort to stamp out the disease among the Natives. The presence of the infected servant in the house of the White and his close juxtaposition with young children make him a menace to the health of the White community. There seems to be no unanimity in Europe or America as to the most effective control of these diseases. Expedients range from compulsory registration with penalties for failure to report and free clinical treatment to prophylactic treatment and popular education.

The increasing menace of venereal infection in urban native settlements is closely connected with the problem in the rural areas. That it is widespread is evident even from the inadequate figures submitted by the Director of Medical and Sanitary Services for the Territory.[2] These

latter the woman had no claim recognised by law or custom on her husband nor ,he on her.

[1] In an attempt to clean up the town location at Bulawayo in 1931 thirteen girls, who were avowedly plying their trade as prostitutes, were ejected, but the numbers who escaped detection in this clandestine trade, so difficult of verification, must have been considerable.

[2] The report on actual cases of venereal disease submitted by the Director of Medical and Sanitary Services in Livingstone for all medical districts for 1931 follows:

Broken Hill Mine	.	.	8	Nchanga Mine .	.	. 16
Bwana Mkubwa Mine		.	9	Livingstone	.	. 116
Roan Antelope Mine .		.	23	Mazabuka	.	. 137
Mufulira Mine .		.	32	Broken Hill (town)	.	. 88
Nkana Mine	.	.	28	Bwana Mkubwa (town)	.	108
Abercorn .	.	.	136	Fort Jameson .	.	. 65

figures by no means cover the Territory, as large areas are
entirely without medical attention. Their value lies rather
in their indication of the number of cases passing through
the hands of accredited and strategically placed medical
officers in a single year.

The wide discrepancy of these figures seems to be due
to the varying interest and thoroughness of the overworked medical officers in charge. The average number of
cases for the medical districts reporting in 1931 was 139·7,
but from the one district in which the medical officer had
made a special study of venereal infections the number
reported was 1237, or an incidence of nearly ten times that
of the average. There is no reason to assume that the
Mongu district is proportionally more venereal than the
others, but that the intense interest of the physician in
this medical speciality had brought a larger number of
cases into the open.

The similar wide difference in the incidence of venereal
disease as reported by mission hospitals is probably attributable to the same cause. An old-established medical
mission service with the confidence of the Natives of the
surrounding district may reveal an amazing proportion of
venereal to other cases, and a newer station in a contiguous territory a much more modest ratio. Of the out-
patients of the Dutch Reformed mission at Morgenster
in Southern Rhodesia, with a wonderfully well-organised
medical department and the confidence of a wide clientèle,
the nurse in charge indicates that 75 per cent of all cases
presenting themselves are treated for venereal disease.

The interpenetration and interdependence of urban locations and Native villages is so close that a correlated
attempt to reduce this menace (which is everywhere
thought to be increasing, though no reliable figures are
available for comparison) will require a vigilant and con-

Footnote continued—

Mongu	.	.	.	. 1237	Lusaka	. . .	. 508
Balovale	.		.	. 85	Chitambo Mission	.	. 15
Choma	.	.	.	. 40	Sesheke	. .	. 101
Kasama	.	.	.	. 28	Fort Rosebery	. .	. 136

sistently planned if not indeed a militant onslaught by medical and governmental authorities in rural as well as urban areas.

One of the most popular centres of location life at Ndola is the Native beer-hall, a commodious brick building furnished with benches and tables, municipally operated and supervised by the location manager. Beer is brewed in one end of the building and sold to men and women indiscriminately in the large common room between three and six o'clock in the afternoon. The beverage must be consumed on the property except in cases of special permission. The retail price is 6d. a quart, and the monthly profit exceeding £100 is said to be devoted exclusively to "Native amenities", including the support of the medical clinic, recreations and a common meeting-room in the beer-hall when requested. Usage governing the appropriation of beer-hall profits differs widely as between towns.[1]

Limited space in this report precludes a discussion of the merits of Native beer. That it is antiscorbutic, has some food value, and in Native territories has a social significance which is intricately bound up with the traditional customs of the tribe, is unquestionable. But in urban Native locations where it is commercially manufactured, sold at a high profit, produces revelling and sordidness and elicits frequent complaints from White employers that their house-boys are tardy, irregular and a nuisance because of drunkenness, municipal or governmental participation in the debauchery of the Native is open to grave question. That the beer-hall is a focal point of prostitution because of lowered moral resistance is the general opinion of impartial observers.

The free Government school in the Ndola location ex-

---

[1] Livingstone, with a Native population of 2100 as against Ndola's 4100, reports a net monthly profit of £85, and this fund has a yet wider application. Bulawayo, in Southern Rhodesia, with a location population of 6000, reports a monthly profit of well over £300, which is frankly applied to the rebuilding of location huts as well as the subsidising of welfare work. In fact eight of the nine mission churches on the Bulawayo location receive a subsidy from the beer-hall profits to carry on their Christian work.

periences the same difficulties as do those on the mines.
In spite of an excellent teacher and a modern pedagogical
method, out of 960 children the daily pupil average is 56.
In the light of this deadening apathy to educational opportunity the reiteration *ad nauseam* of Native interest in
education means little. One finds children of school age
running loose over the location and the neighbouring town,
picking up an odd penny by caddying on the golf-course
or ganging together in minor devilment to get some fun
out of a barren and unnatural life, while the parents
blithely side-step responsibility by saying: "I can't make
my children attend school. They do as they like." Compulsory attendance would provide the child with the
modicum of the education necessary to safeguard his
maturity, not to speak of keeping him out of mischief for
a part of the day.

The evening classes show a slightly better attendance.
Sixty-five adults attend the night school. While their alertness is slightly dulled by age and the physical exhaustion
of the day's work, they seem over-anxious to make amends
for the lost opportunities of youth. Though the motive is
avowedly a commercial interest in English, incidentally
they increase their fitness for a larger participation in the
White man's world.

The recreational situation on the urban location is also
analogous to that on the mining location. A football field
which is used for match games on Sundays, a large open
concourse for Native dances or other amusements and the
beer-hall for approved meetings comprise the recreational
facilities. Sport for the sake of sport is a concept which is
foreign to the Native. Even members of the football team
sometimes flatly refuse to play unless paid for the labour.
As a substitute for payment members of teams playing in
the Sunday afternoon game put up 1s. each and the 22s.
purse is divided among the members of the winning team.

The night school students take small interest in the
indoor equipment which has been provided in the school
building at the Ndola location. As one watches the crowds

aimlessly wandering about the central concourse one wonders if an energetic recreational director could not teach these children of Nature to play, as with some pains we habituate the children of civilisation to the joy of sport.

The picture of urban Native life is not all shadow. Some commendable beginnings have been made in Native welfare. A new model location within the Ndola location has been constructed for Government clerks and others able to pay a higher rental. It domiciles the Native aristocrats and solves the housing problem for them, while at the same time it creates a class problem of equal dimensions. A child-welfare clinic and little dispensary have been set up with the part-time services of a doctor and a nurse. So insistent and numerous, however, are the pathological cases that practically no time is given to prenatal or post-natal care. Children are born in the Native huts. Mothers are attended by friends and, unless serious trouble should develop, no professional attention is paid and no safeguards volunteered in the way of feeding or child-care.

Unconnected with the Ndola location and yet having a bearing upon its inhabitants is the Native township ten miles away, set up by the District Commissioner. This township is divided into sixty-nine twelve-acre plots of fertile land. Each plot is rented to a Native who has saved enough to build his own hut and pay a rental of 5s. 5d. a month. It is possible for an enterprising Native and his family to make £3 a month growing vegetables, poultry and eggs, selling them on the location or in the town. Fifty men, some of them still working in the town, are already resident on these garden plots.

Nor have the Natives of long residence in the location at Ndola become entirely oblivious to the need of co-operative welfare activity. Fifty-two of the most economically and educationally favoured have formed a local Native Welfare Organisation similar to those at Lusaka, Broken Hill, Livingstone and the Roan Antelope mine. Its leaders in three of these centres indicated that its purpose was frankly to safeguard the rights and interests of the Natives of Northern Rhodesia. The organisation holds monthly meetings and operates as a safety-valve for Native discontent, which usually results in memorials to the District Commissioner or Secretary for Native Affairs. Its programmes sound trivial to the European and indicate the local concrete operation of the Native mind.[1]

The association leaders stoutly refuse to consider merging its identity into a joint council, although they welcome White visitors to their monthly meetings.

From the foregoing description, which has omitted some of the sordid details not readily capable of verification, there can be little doubt that the influence of the urban location is socially disintegrative. The Native feels it vaguely and speaks of it sadly. He is disillusioned and confused. Neither in his work, his temporary home, nor elsewhere has he come into contact with the constructive influences which are the dynamic of the higher civilisation. Inadvertently he has been robbed of the traditional customs, ideals and sanctions of tribal life. He has touched but the superficialities of this great new civilisation which is so rapidly changing his world. Perhaps it is for this reason that, as he returns to the Native kraal, he carries with him few of those forces which make for reintegration and easily slumps back into the life of the Native village, not infrequently finding refuge and security in the very practices from which he had been partially emancipated.

[1] Conference with Native officials of the associations in Ndola, Livingstone and Roan Antelope mine indicated a rather heterogeneous programme of which the following items are typical : the tangible recognition by the Whites of different classes of Natives; the cleaning up of the local location (by outside help); the safeguard of the quality of meat issued as rations to Natives; the reduction of pedlars' monthly licences, which in some locations run as high as 2s. 6d. for a stand six feet square; the provision of Native Government schools; the encouragement of sport (rather vaguely stated).

CHAPTER VI

SOCIAL TENSIONS AND PROBLEMS

To even the casual observer there appears to be a vast gulf between White and Black in Northern Rhodesia. Though they are living in close juxtaposition they are in and of two separate worlds. On the White side there is an obvious feeling of superiority. The European has introduced his own civilisation, taking over little or nothing of Native methods of life. His standards are high in education, health, hygiene, industrial efficiency, living, art, music, recreation, food requirements and in thrift.

If the Natives are quick to conform to these standards they are rewarded with the White man's recognition and admiration. A few of the more generous Europeans, mostly those of long residence in the colony, respect the Native for what he is, recognise the integrity of his social life and accommodate their standards of judgment to the values discoverable there. But in the main, if conformation to the European pattern is slow or impossible, the attitude is one of pity, exploitation or contempt. By reason of the backwardness of his culture the Native has found it hard to compete with the White invader, and harder still to adopt the new culture or harmonise it with his own. This continuous disability has farther increased the social distance between him and the White man. Thus it became easy for him to accept the White man's definition of his inferior status and satisfactorily to rationalise his position. So that through the earlier stages of the contact, before the opening of the present century, the White man and his ways were measurably sacrosanct. The changes in Native civilisation which took place were incidental and mainly resulted from unconscious imitation.

With the opening of the mines in Southern Rhodesia in

1906, in Katanga in 1911 and later at Ndola, and especially as a result of the Native's participation in the activities of the Great War, the pressure of the higher civilisation became more acute. He conceived the social distance as susceptible of bridging and his imitation of the European became conscious. It was in this latter period that the Native discovered that the White man had feet of clay. Resentment, irks and grievances against White injustice, real or fancied, gradually replaced his blind admiration. Occasionally these complaints were overtly expressed. More frequently they were masked by a smiling face and an exaggeratedly polite demeanour, or were studiously repressed only to be aired among his own people in the kraal, township or location. As Dr. R. S. Moton, president of Tuskegee Institute, has pointed out, the Black is a master in the art of dissimulation.[1] Under his stoical acceptance of an unpleasant situation, his inarticulateness, blind obedience and apparent apathy, there may slumber attitudes of bitterest resentment awaiting only a propitious occasion to manifest themselves in acts disproportionately rebellious or disastrous.

That the Rhodesian Native harbours grievances against the White man is unquestioned in spite of his recognition of the values to be gained from the adoption of elements of the White man's culture, and that these grievances are expressed most vigorously by semi-detribalised individuals longest in contact with the Whites is equally well known. Northern Rhodesia is in much the same situation as the Union of South Africa was two and a half decades ago, and might well be safeguarded against repressive White policies dictated by fear of Native competition which have resulted in such riots as those at Port Elizabeth in 1920, Bloemfontein in 1925 and Durban in 1929, the White civilian reactions to which deepened the rift between the races. These risings were initiated, not by tribes as in the Kaffir wars and rebellions which took place from 1779 to 1896, but by semi-detribalised Natives living

[1] R. S. Moton, *What the Negro Thinks*, p. 63 ff.

in towns, and were the explosive outbreak of accumulated grievances which had had little or no opportunity of expression. A generous conciliatory Native policy and a suitable institution for their expression would have acted as a Native safety-valve and avoided the explosive and disastrous outbreaks.

In any study of the forces tending to destroy the cohesion of Native social organisation and those facilitating the integration of group life on a new plane, not to speak of the forces favouring better co-operation, an honest consideration of these grievances is essential. That they exist in the mind of the Native and are considered by him to be genuine is far more important than that they may be incapable of justification.

The situation has not changed since 1924, when Professor Brookes wrote: "It has often been observed that little things seem to count for more with Natives than big ones. It is not so much unjust or unwise systems as tactless administration which causes trouble, boorishness, incivility, tactlessness, carelessness for Native susceptibilities, unnecessary complications of officialdom: these have done more to rouse ill-feeling between Black and White than land acts, exclusion from political rights or any other legislation."[1]

Such grievances, if they may be dignified by that name, fall into three classes: those which are real and measurably remediable; that large group which is patently the result of misunderstanding; and those which are bound up with difficult world problems of a biological, economic or social character and are thus incapable of local reduction.

It should be noted that some of the resentments against White men are vague, imperfectly phrased, in fact almost inarticulate indications of group feeling. They are symptomatic of basic maladjustments. When one follows them down to their roots one discovers large fundamental problems which it would be moral cowardice to evade. The

[1] Edgar H. Brookes, *The History of Native Policy in South Africa from 1830 to the Present Day* (1924).

quack treats symptoms, the conscientious physician seeks out the deep-seated and often stubborn causes and essays their reduction honestly, however long the treatment.

It is our purpose to list briefly the most typical of these complaints as they have been expressed by various Natives with whom we have spoken and in the replies to a request for life-histories sent to a carefully selected group of 400 Natives, representing thirty separate tribes. These included ministers, teachers, journalists, professional people, college students, Government and other clerks, shopkeepers and workmen.[1] The majority of the written replies were from Natives in the Union of South Africa and are coloured by their experience there where there has been longer contact with Europeans. Furthermore, they are the reactions of the better educated individuals and reveal more boldness in the expression of grievances. The replies range over Northern and Southern Rhodesia as well. Northern Rhodesian Natives are less articulate and less educationally advanced. But it must not be forgotten that the irritations of Natives in the territories to the south are known by many in the north, where the beginnings of these same tensions are already noticeable though they may be still in the incipient stage.

AFRICAN TENSIONS

Tension between differing racial groups in the same environment and the menace of overt conflict is not peculiar to Africa. Dr. Firth generalised the observation on the basis of his experience with the Maori in New Zealand.[2] "Close connection between free peoples of dif-

---

[1] The method of the accompanying questionnaire (see Appendix C) is not statistical but that of securing case evidence. It was designed to discover the attitudes of the Natives growing out of their relations with Europeans and the grounds for those attitudes in the life experience and social conditioning of the individual. It will be noted that provision has been made for an adequate check on individual tribal custom as well as bias and the factors which have conditioned it in the earlier part of the questionnaire.

[2] R. Firth, *Primitive Economics of the New Zealand Maori*, p. 443 *et seq.*

ferent cultural type, especially if they are in partial occupation of the same territory, is liable to produce grave social
tension. The degree to which this will occur varies according to the relative number of the peoples concerned, their
disposition, their primary economic pursuits, their efficiency in the material arts and the like. But the difference
in the customs and beliefs is bound to engender some suspicion and mistrust, while the divergence in their social
aims is a certain cause of friction. Continuous adjustment, even if only of a minor nature and in personal
relations, is necessary to preserve friendly intercourse.
Sometimes this is maintained at comparatively small
cost, at others the strain becomes too severe and war is
the result."

An accommodation relation of the White and Black
races built over mutual resentments like dynamite needs
but a jar to set off an explosion entirely incommensurate
with the causes involved. So that the reduction of tensions
before they crystallise into hatred and conflict is the
primary responsibility of Whites and Blacks alike.

Certain of the following resentments as expressed to us
are readily reducible if the will to reduce them is present.
No attempt here is made to meet the recriminations, as
their roots will be examined under "problems" later, and
the line of their reduction is obvious. A charge which
occurred in every conference and in all but a single life-
history is that the White man has no respect for the
Native, no real friendship for him; that he regards him as
inferior and "treats him like a dog". The following ex-
cerpts will indicate the intensity of the feeling:

White men are unkind to their servants. They only care for
them as long as they are an asset. They do not care how they
are fed or housed. If they own a horse the animal receives much
more sympathy than their servants, for often they visit the
stable to see how it is housed and fed. This teaches us that the
humanity of the European is very shallow although his education is very deep.[1]

---

[1] From the life-history of a Basuto teacher.

A White man will expect you to address him as Mr., but he dare not return the compliment. A White man expects you to greet him first if you are Black, even if he knows you very well, but if you are wise you don't greet him at all if he is among his own White friends. If you do you'll be terribly disappointed, because he will either pretend not to know you or will evade you and look the other way.[1]

"What incentive", he inquires, "is there to self-improvement according to the White man's standard? The skilled labourer by reason of his classification by the European receives a wage little above the raw recruit. It is paid on the basis of colour, not efficiency."

My education has been a disappointment to me. Although I hold a certificate such as is possessed by a White man, yet I am not paid at the same rate, and, further, a half-caste is paid better than myself or any of my group qualified in that way. The average White man in his dealings with my group is unable to understand that there are those of my race who are already his equals, and thus in his treatment of the Black man he becomes impatient, unfair and lacks an understanding of him.[2]

Such expressions of disability as this give point to Dr. Leubuscher's observation that nowhere in the world is there such a vast difference between White skilled and Native labour.[3]

In Ndola the Natives complained bitterly that when the depression came they had been discharged by the town in spite of their long employment in the service department, that their places had been filled by poor Whites at more than double the wages: "Because", they insisted, "we are supposed to have a place among our kin in a Native village. Many of us have been away for years; our villages have moved; we have no hut or garden."

Unfairness in the administration of justice is a common grievance. The argument runs: "The White man is often

---

[1] From the life-history of a Gamopedi.
[2] Life-history of a Basuto.
[3] "Diese Struktur ermöglicht eine Spannung zwischen den Löhnen der relativ kleinen Zahl gelernter Arbeiter und den Löhnen der Masse der ungelernten Arbeiter, wie sie in gleichem Ausmass nirgends in der Welt zu finden ist" (Dr. Charlotte Leubuscher, *Der südafrikanische Eingeborene als Industriearbeiter und als Stadtbewohner*, p. 54).

unfair where a case at law involves one of us and a White man. If found guilty the White man is never punished as severely as we are. Moreover, we are compelled to conform to a changing law which we do not understand. Even the White man's moral standards are vague and confusing to us. The *Boma*[1] official says: 'I'm not concerned about polygamy, marry as many wives as you can support', but the missionary insists that our ancient custom of polygamy is wrong. Who are we to believe and whose standard should we follow?"

Nor does the White settler and trader escape castigation for the rise of a miscegenate population. The complaint is that the White employer misleads his woman employee, the trader and hunter leave a trail of coloured children unwanted by their parents and preventing the subsequent marriage of the young mother, in some cases driving her into a life of prostitution. "We do not cohabit with White women", he insists. "Why should White men mislead our daughters? The difficulty of controlling our daughters is increased by the rewards in money with which the White man tempts them. Your large schools yield concrete evidence of these deliberate moral wrongs; indeed, it is no uncommon thing to find the Black-White progeny of officials charged with Government administration. How can we maintain the integrity of family life while this thing is going on?"

From the Union mainly comes the feeling of political disability. "Every Native is directly taxed but has no representation in Government. You have poor Whites and poor people, 76·5 per cent[2] of whom pay no direct tax at

---

[1] This is a widely used native word in Central Africa signifying "The Government".

[2] The report of the Poor White Commission shows 22 per cent Poor Whites in the Union (measurably pauperised people), 34 per cent so poor that they cannot maintain an adequate standard of living or provide their children with proper food, clothing and shelter, 41 per cent who are in average circumstances and 3 per cent well-to-do. The non-taxpayers comprise the 22 per cent plus the 34 per cent, plus half the 41 per cent, i.e. 76 per cent of the entire White population. Such facts are commonly known in the Union of South Africa.

all, and yet they vote and have a voice in governing themselves." It is a long distance between the Union and
Northern Rhodesia, but one finds in the latter territory
the incipient beginnings of political-mindedness, requiring
only an incident to precipitate it into overt expression,
as evidenced in the near-riots in November 1932 at
Livingstone, Lusaka and Ndola.

Other irritations are directly due to misunderstandings,
a mutual lack of knowledge of the psychology, language
and code of the other. "We do not know what the European
law is until we are punished for its infraction. Customary
law is talked over in our Native villages, but some White
officials say, 'It is the law; there is no discussion'." [1]

"For many years before the coming of the White man
our specialists smelted iron and wrought it into implements
for us. We grew cotton and wove it into cloth. Now both
industries are denied us. What right has the White man to
prevent us carrying on the industry of our fathers? Look
at our smelters everywhere idle and abandoned." This
seemed strange and unwarranted to the investigator, so
inquiry was made at the local *Boma*. The official assured
us that the statement was ludicrous and absurd; that
smelting and iron-working had everywhere been encouraged. To prove the statement he called in his uniformed
head man and put the question: "Do your people say you
are prohibited from smelting iron?" The man's reply was
an unequivocal affirmation. It transpired that a single
case of discouragement of the industry some years before
had been responsible for the widely current statement that
the smelting of metals was a thing entirely taboo. From
which it will be seen how easily an erroneous idea due to
misunderstanding can circulate through a widely distributed group.

The cotton prohibition was, we discovered, rooted in
fact. White farmers who had been experimenting with
cotton-growing had found it impossible to continue while
Natives on contiguous land allowed pests to multiply and

---

[1] From the life-history of a Zulu native.

refused to burn the stubble after the picking season was over.

In the field of mission education vast appreciation is expressed. This, however, is not without penetrating reservations:

My White teachers received from me prompt and absolute obedience from fear of being taken as impudent, and disobedient. By-and-by I began to find out that the White man will keep his foot on you so long as you don't tell him he is giving you any pain, and if you do tell him he will pretend he does not know he is hurting you. . . . I often wonder if the African who does not know anything about the White man is not happier than I am. He does not see the failings of the White man. He does not feel the slights because he does not know him as I do. I am disappointed with my education when I consider the energy and time and patience I spent to get it . . . and yet after all these years of labour and hard work I am offered a salary which is anything but adequate. As an enlightened man I am supposed to live a clean, decent, hygienic life, eating a variety of foods suitable and wholesome, wearing neat, fairly attractive clothes and living in a furnished home. . . . But the White man in this country, including a great number of good missionaries, is out for White superiority. They know that the best way of keeping the African under subjection is by keeping him poor.[1]

Occasionally resentment is felt because the education received by the Native is not suited to his needs:

My education does not enable me to stand by myself . . . (missionary education) has not much bearing on the life of my people. There is not much of real life in it. It is abstract, does not fit one for living and does not give enough scope for one's own initiative . . . the missionary is content to save the souls of men, but he has no apparent interest in their material needs, economic and social.[2]

Even the White man's heaven does not escape a mild censure, and at the same time the censure itself displays a pitiful inferiority complex. In a group of thirty-five

---

[1] Life-history of an educated Bemba of Northern Rhodesia.
[2] Life-history of a Shoshon in the Bechuana Protectorate (slightly edited as to construction).

Natives to whom the writer spoke one man asked: "Why is God White and the Devil Black? Our people say that Heaven is for White men. How can it be heaven to the White men if the Black men should be there?"

On the other hand, there is a set of criticisms some of which we are forced to share with the Native in spite of our knowledge that the forces are inevitable in their operation. The White man has to adjust himself to the same world situation against which the Native complains. "The European", he says, "gave us work, accustomed us to it, and now he has taken it away. There is no other source of revenue open to us even to pay our taxes than that paid us for labour at the mines." Childlike, he does not realise that thousands of people in all countries are unemployed to-day, that it is a world-market situation and the mineral and other exports of Rhodesia are involved in this world situation. "But", he persists, "our people are discharged and replaced by Whites at higher wages." He seems oblivious to the fact that if the White community does not look after its unemployed it must support them, and the Native, despite the inconvenience, has a home and a tribal right to share the last pot of mealies with his kin.

Similarly he charges: "The White man has created a civilisation for me I cannot pay for".

The White man speaks of better living, better housing and such like—all these need money. Where is it? We die in hundreds because we try to keep up with civilisation. Venereal diseases were not known among my people; to-day they are numerous. Clinics and doctors are needed. The White man's civilisation is expensive. It needs money. We cannot go back now. We want to go forward.[1]

It is the wail of the impoverished millions, the labourers of every land, as it is only for the few that human wants do not outstrip financial ability to satisfy them.

"The European has prevented us moving freely from country to country. He charges us duty on what we bring back with us: was it not all our country?"

[1] Life-history of a Fingo native, one of a family of twelve.

Some say: "We cannot hunt game in our own country. We cannot have a high-power rifle without paying an impossible tax. Why should we be taxed to kill the game so sorely needed as food, especially as it ranges in our own door-yard?" Such laws are but the modern counterpart of primitive totemic regulations which have ever protected against wholesale slaughtering of animals. Game laws and customs tariffs are recognised in every land and always occasion local hardships. Few of the inconsistencies of European civilisation have escaped the rapier-like thrusts of a people who see our faults and failings with the same clearness as we see theirs.

Basic Social Problems

We shall now turn to an examination of a series of correlated basic problems in which these resentments have their roots, not to offer a solution, which we shall deliberately avoid here, but to present the factors of which they are composed.

A. *The Land Problem*

It seems anomalous that there should be a land question[1] in a tropical Protectorate with a population density including European Whites of only 4·66 persons per square mile in comparison with countries showing a density of over 600. Yet Mr. F. H. Melland, sometime magistrate of Kasempa District in Northern Rhodesia, insists: "There is one great problem in South Central Africa, viz. the Land Problem. The others are mostly connected with or subsidiary to it."

As has been indicated, land here is far from uniform in its supporting power. Vast stretches of open veld are arid, unwatered and unproductive. Vaster stretches still are far from railways or urban markets and connected with civil-

---

[1] The details of the land question will be treated in the Economics section. It is our purpose here to indicate how it becomes a human problem ramifying through all Native-White consideration.

isation by winding roads, little more than trails through
scrubby woodland. When cleared and watered the land is
abundantly fruitful. Without water it yields but a precarious existence. Pests abound and are harboured by
well-meaning but mistaken Natives. It is unsuited, so far
as is now known, for the production of any plantation
crop—just as it is for small-scale English country-gentle-
man farming. With prices of agricultural products on the
world market as they are, and have been since the World
War, the Protectorate cannot attract large-scale investment and nothing less will suffice. "The day of middle-
scale individualist farming is past. It would become
subsistence farming of the poor White plattveld type."[1]
So that as long as cheap land is available elsewhere this
Territory to any large extent must remain below the
margin of desirability.

But European farmers are already on the land with an
average holding of 4000 acres each, and Native fears of
larger occupation are not entirely groundless. Until his
tenure was threatened the Native was indifferent to
ownership or alienation of land. There was abundance of it
for him. He so little understood soils that in many localities the light land was cultivated and a contiguous section
of heavy but fertile soil remained unworked. It was into
this situation that the Europeans and South Africans
came with their knowledge of soil-chemistry, machinery,
capital and technical methods. But the settlers brought
with them also, or quickly acquired, something more
open to question, viz. the general attitude of the South
African toward the Native.

This attitude included some gratuitous assumptions, to
wit—that Natives were more prolific than Whites; that
they were measurably immune from the diseases of the
districts; that they were a menace to national security;
that they were potential competitors who, if given the
White man's advantages, might presently repossess the

[1] W. M. Macmillan, "The Development of Africa", *Political Quarterly*,
vol. iii. No. iv. p. 552 ff.

land, and that with a little skill and education they become "cheeky" and difficult to control. They must be
segregated in separate areas or reserves and kept there,
except to fulfil the demand for labour by the White man.
These reserves should be arranged in a manner to leave
free large tracts of good land available to markets for
White purchase and occupation. Natives on these latter
tracts should gradually be moved into the reserved
territory.

It was readily conceded that the reserves in Northern
Rhodesia should be proportionally larger than those in the
Union, for the untenable Reserve situation in the Transkei
and Ciskei was an offence to the sense of justice even of
those who for the sake of expediency upheld it. Nevertheless the Reserve policy characterising the Union should be
followed with slight variation in Northern Rhodesia.

Conditions in Northern Rhodesia are, however, so different from those in the Union of South Africa that to
follow slavishly the policy of the latter would be dangerous.
Further reference to the question of reserves is made in a
later chapter.

B. *Native Agricultural Methods*

Closely connected with the land question is the problem
of improvement of Native agricultural methods. There are
four obvious ways of supporting an increasing population:
extending the area occupied, increasing the productivity of
the area already occupied, sending a part of the population
out of the area to work, or artificially limiting population
growth by a widespread knowledge and encouragement of
birth-control. Of these, the first is wasteful and a challenge
to White supremacy; the third is limited, precarious and of
questionable ultimate value; and the fourth, at the present
stage of Native culture, is impossible, as a large family of
children is regarded as a positive insurance. The love for
and moral pressure to beget children is extremely strong.

The second method only offers any hope of ultimate

solution so far as Northern Rhodesia is concerned. The improvement of the wasteful agricultural methods already described alone can provide for an adequate subsistence economy, avoid the recurring hunger months in large sections of the Territory, and supply a surplus for local trade and the satisfaction of modest but growing wants.

Northern Rhodesia at present must purchase all its manufactured articles on the world market as there are no local factories. Unless it is to be considered a mining territory and nothing more, the wages of mine labour cannot possibly satisfy the potential market for overseas manufactured articles. It must export raw products to pay for its imported goods, but it has no export raw products to pay for them. It has no export crop beyond tobacco, and the amount of this commodity exported is considerably less than the amount of foreign tobacco brought into the country. To increase export, then, it must improve agricultural methods.

Maize, sorghum, cassava, beans and monkey-nuts could be grown on the area now under cultivation in quantities vastly exceeding the amount produced at present. Crop rotation, seed selection, deep ploughing, adequate fertilising and weathering for market are understood only in a small fraction of the Protectorate. It is regrettable that at this time the funds for the extension of Government experimentation and demonstration in connection with missions and in the Department of Agriculture should be cut to the bone.[1]

The encouragement of cattle-breeding for meat export in the agricultural areas has been suggested as a necessary expedient for agricultural development. This is especially necessary as the fly is gradually controlled and there takes place an improvement in quality and a limitation of the quantity of cattle in these areas. There is needed a long-time plan of Government experimentation in these vast

---

[1] Especially is this true at a time when in other countries maize is being grown not only for cattle food but is being experimented with industrially in the production of power, alcohol, dry ice, etc.

areas. Coffee is successfully produced in the Lake districts, but as yet on a small scale because certain aspects have yet to be proved. Cotton, it has been demonstrated, can be grown in the Abercorn district but quite uneconomically at present prices. The mulberry for the feeding of silk-worms is indigenous and grows luxuriantly over vast stretches of the country. Under experimentation silk might be made an export crop, while sericulture has possibilities of indefinite local Native employment, although the Native seems quite unsuited for it at the present time. The establishment of a maize control board such as that recently appointed in Southern Rhodesia, the improvement of roads, the extension of railway lines, and the systematic creation of overseas markets, have been suggested as ways of increasing the potential producing power of the Territory.

A forward-looking national policy requires enterprise and foresight in a time of depression to prepare for future days of expansion, and an uninterrupted teaching of the people to help themselves. A concerted and long-sighted missionary agricultural programme would stimulate the entire society to co-operative effort along this line.

C. *Absentee Labour*

One of the main obstacles to Native agricultural development is the absence of a large proportion of the able-bodied men in the local mines and farms and in the mines in other territories. Many Northern Rhodesian workers live outside the Protectorate. The Native inspector of the Katanga Province reports 5698 registered men from Northern Rhodesia resident there in 1931, to which must be added approximately half that number who are unregistered. Southern Rhodesia reports a minimum of 8431 registered Northern Rhodesian workers in the mines alone, a figure which it is estimated would have to be doubled to include the Northern Rhodesian adult males in that colony. No definite figures are available for the Union, but Rhodesian Natives are found from Johannesburg and Kimberley all

the way to Cape Town. The number of men away from the
Native kraals are reported by the Rhodesian officials for
1931 as 110,108, which, with the unregistered workers,
would exceed 150,000, or one-tenth of the total population.[1]

Were these absentee agriculturalists distributed uni-
formly throughout the Territory the situation would be
serious enough. If the able-bodied males constitute one-
fifth of the Native population, as the Katanga officials
estimate, this means that 110,108 out of a total in Northern
Rhodesia of 259,016, or nearly half the able-bodied male
population, are periodically away from home. But the
workers are not drawn evenly from all sections of the
Territory. In the North-Eastern and Eastern districts,
because of the character of the workers, they are much
more in demand, in fact so considerably that in certain
villages we visited every adult male had been "at the
front".

That this entails on vast sections deleterious effects
there can be no doubt. The preparation for planting is left
in the unaccustomed hands of women and children. Tree-
cutting is man's work; women, except in dire necessity,
never engage in it. Cassava must be planted in plots seri-
ally for three years in order to have a continual supply. The
absence of the planter for a year means that two years of
the staple food supply has been cut off. Preparation of the
wooded land and planting is neglected, or the gardens are
so reduced in size as to be insufficient to meet the needs of
the family, and famine periods are extended or the worker
on his return must turn over his wages and luggage for
food.

Other factors contribute to the food shortage in certain
territories. The Native lives very near to the margin of
need. Irregular rains, bad seasons and a greater demand
for foodstuffs by prospectors, geologists, travellers and missionaries have sometimes plunged him into a temporary
famine.

The moral life of the tribe also suffers from the absence

[1] See footnote, p. 35.

of the men. Group integrity is broken down; parental control relaxed; marital fidelity, both of the husband in his abnormal surroundings and the wife in the Native kraal, passes into license with the forming of new unions, and thus the necessary tyranny of Native marital custom is assailed. Moral sanctions have in them a large religious element. This latter under conditions of constant moral infraction falls into disrepute.

In any discussion of the more spectacular process of stabilisation of workers on the mine, stabilisation of normal group life in the kraal cannot be minimised or forgotten. If the Native villages are to be regarded as reservoirs of cheap labour which can be drawn off in any desirable quantity and poured back when no longer needed, which can be used as an asylum for the unwanted or broken human wreckage, the consequences of the system ought to be frankly faced. It is striking inconsistency to encourage tribal integrity on the one hand under the system of indirect rule[1] (for without tribal integrity no chief can successfully function) and on the other hand to encourage its disruption by the present chaotic economic system. Dr. Brookes goes to the extreme of unequivocally advocating the desirability of eliminating the Native from industrial work altogether and confining his labour to the farm. "Such employment", he urges, "is more suited to his natural economic condition and less likely to break up families and disintegrate Bantu social life."[2] The South African Union has met the problem by ignoring it, and suffered such consequences as are experienced in the Transkei, where Natives are forced to go to the mines at Johannesburg in order to secure wages to keep their families from starving. If for any reason the Rand mines should close, many of the inhabitants of these sections would be a public charge. Katanga has met the problem in another way. The entire province has been divided into sections, and the policy has been followed of drawing from

---

[1] Discussed in the section on Government Administration.
[2] E. H. Brookes, *The History of Native Policy in South Africa*, p. 324.

each section by recruitment only the number of able-bodied males which the section can afford to lose. In a village of 400 people it has been computed there will be 96 able-bodied males, 304 adult females, incompetents and children. It is considered that in such a village 88 males are required to maintain the social and economic equilibrium. So that from six to eight able-bodied men only may be recruited for service on the mines. They are carefully acclimatised on the mining location; their children are educated under a compulsory system and everything is done to detribalise them and keep them permanently there. The system has been in operation too short a time to reach definite conclusions as to its value. It has its dangers, particularly as regards what is to become of the children of industrialised Natives as they mature. It can at least be said that if the policy is carried through consistently as planned the deleterious effects on the Native territories would be very largely reduced.

D. *Education*

The educational problems are bound up with the policy of stabilisation. No educational system can function with anything approximating 100 per cent efficiency unless it can define the aim and purpose of what it is doing. If the Native is to be a peasant the system will be modified to that end; if he is to be in industrial or commercial work the system must be motivated by that fact.

There seem to be two contrasted schools of thought as to Native development which have a bearing on the type of education he shall receive. One group thinks and speaks of him only as a wage-earner—a labour force to be exploited. He is to be a serf dependent on the goodwill of his employer. There should be no technical education, no contact with the world of new ideas, no modern methods deliberately provided for him. The less he is educated the more amenable will he be to the White man's will. Some who hold this view go to the length of saying that the opening-up of the railways is an unprovoked threat to an unspoiled cheap labour supply.

The other school insists that he shall be a skilled producer of his own exportable produce: under direction he may be taught to grow coffee, cotton, ground-nuts and other crops for ready market or to produce stock for export. This would make him independent of the work-seeking habit, or at least the latter would be subservient to the former. The Native when consulted has but one stock answer. He wants the same education for his children that White children receive.

The European's view of the Native's function in future Rhodesian society, however, will determine the type of Native educational policy. Some indication of the timidity with which Government agricultural education is carried on (outside Barotseland) lies in the fact that there is but one Government institution for the teaching of scientific agricultural methods to Natives, viz. the agricultural school at Mazabuka. At the end of the 1931 session eight students were in residence, and the director concludes his report with the pessimistic remark: [1] "Until the department again is in a position to embark on a definite scheme of agricultural extension work in Native reserves it is doubtful if employment could be found for any considerable number of Native assistants".

Agricultural demonstration, the value of which is obvious in parts of Southern Rhodesia, is not even contemplated for immediate trial by the northern territory. "There is now no intention that they should be sent to the villages as agricultural demonstrators as it is considered doubtful whether sufficient knowledge has been acquired in regard to local African agriculture, soil and climate to warrant the adoption of any definite method of agricultural demonstration in the absence of adequate European supervision." [2] In the face of this confession, the Govern-

[1] Northern Rhodesia *Annual Report upon Native Education, 1931*, p. 16.
[2] *Ibid.* p. 16.

ment agricultural education carried on with small Government grants-in-aid would not even be a motion toward the most essential type of education for the Protectorate. This in spite of the fact that the Protectorate is mainly agricultural and that every able-bodied Native over eighteen years of age must pay an annual tax. Naturally those interested in Native development inquire on exactly what Native purposes this tax has been expended, or if indeed the Europeans of Northern Rhodesia are not becoming the Black man's burden.

It is the "policy of the Government to help missions with grants to do the bulk of the elementary school work and to train teachers and to share with missions as it becomes necessary and possible the higher education and vocational training of Natives".[1]

The Government schools at Mazabuka, Ndola and in Barotseland have a total enrolment of 600 students in addition to the mission schools, which have 73 teachers in training and a primary school enrolment of 24,000 boys and 25,393 girls. Many of these students are in bush schools,[2] others in mission boarding-schools, in one of which the girls are encouraged to remain as long as twelve years. Thus a significant beginning of primary and normal education has been made.

That it should be extended goes without saying: that it might well be supplemented by compulsory education in the mine and town locations where mission or Government equipment is available should be equally obvious. Otherwise the younger urban generation, without right to land, alienated from the soil, without moral standards of either White or Black, will become wanderers, inclined to crime, a prey to the agitator and a menace to good order and prosperity. But education for its own sake is not enough. It must prepare the student for the kind of life he is subsequently to lead.

---

[1] *Annual Report upon Native Education, 1931*, p. 7.
[2] A small school usually at a mission outpost and in charge of a Native infrequently doing more than sub-standard work.

Technical education is carried on solely by the missionary societies with Government grants-in-aid. This is largely
in the building trades: carpentering, furniture-building,
brick-making, masonry and related crafts. For such skilled
workmen the Native territories offer at present a limited
field, and little return on the educational investment. No
mechanical training has yet been attempted nor any preparation for work on the mines. Until a definite policy with
reference to the future and function of the Native is determined and long-time plans are elaborated and consistently
adhered to, there can be no hope of progress in this direction. Here again the experience of Katanga is suggestive.
We attended a school for engine-drivers in the railway
service which differed in no essential particular from
schools for European and American firemen and drivers.
Educational facilities are provided for railway repair-men,
mechanics and medical assistants. We found children
being technically educated in the schools by the Government to prepare them for intelligent participation in the
mechanical and industrial arts. His Excellency Governor
E. Heenan stated the Katanga policy to the Commission:
"It is the policy of the Government to assist the Native
to rise as high as he can go and as rapidly". It should
not be concluded from the statement of this idealistic
policy that there is no colour bar in Katanga or that in
practice the Native is pushed into the professions or
highly skilled occupations. There is a wide hiatus between
ultimate ideal and present practice. The invisible colour
bar is effective. Bantu seldom advance beyond the semi-
skilled occupations. Some are kept on routine jobs
throughout the entire period of their employment. But
the policy promises no disability to gradual advancement
as the Native is prepared for it.

Nothing of this sort can happen in Northern Rhodesia
until there is some consensus as to the purposes for which
the Native is to be educated. Dr. Oldham states the same
urgent need for a united educational policy from the
standpoint of missions:

If Christian missions are to achieve their distinctive purpose and at the same time to co-operate, as they must do, with Government in education, they must know clearly what they want. If they have not a clear policy of their own they will either have to accept one dictated by Government or withdraw from the educational field altogether. . . .[1]

The important task of fitting education to educational needs has been consistently carried on by some of the Government subsidised missions. We attended a refresher class of the Church of Scotland Mission at Chitambo. Teachers were here for a short period of intensive training. In building school desks they were using European chisels; the mission superintendent took them all away and insisted that each teacher sharpen the small end of his Native axe and use it as a chisel. "You'll not have chisels when you have to build your school in the bush", was his comment. Similarly at Morgenster Mission in Southern Rhodesia the Dutch Reformed missionary not only insisted on the use of Native tools but on the making of the things which the Native could use in his kraal: the cart and ox yoke, simple furniture and a carpentry adapted to the Native methods of house construction. Here the ideal was the acquainting of the student with patterns easily transferred to his Native habitat and the development of pride in achievement, in other words the creation of effective craftsmen rather than indifferent hired labourers. One could wish it were so in some of the missions where students were engaged in building large station churches and homes for Europeans, or in manufacturing tiles and burned brick, training which will not be applied for many years to come, if ever, to uses in the Native kraals.

In addition to agricultural, academic and technical education there is another unexplored factor in the problem, viz. special education for Chieftainship, particularly as the Chiefs are expected to function in a co-operative Governmental way. Only two schools exist in South Central

[1] J. H. Oldham and B. D. Gibson, *The Remaking of Man in Africa*, p. 16.

Africa for this purpose: one in Nyasaland, the other in Natal. Of the latter Dr. Malherbe writes: "In Zululand a special training institution has been established for the training of sons of Chiefs. . . . While the usual instruction is given in scholastic subjects the boys are trained with a view to fitting them for the posts they will have to fill as Chiefs, how to administer laws, etc., in a just and proper manner in accordance with the tradition of their people. They receive some training in agriculture, and are acquainted with progressive measures which are needed for the advancement of an agricultural and pastoral people. At present sixty students are attending this institution. Results have still to show the value of this type of training when the alumni assume office as Native Chiefs or Indunas."[1] Whether an aspirant to the Chieftainship is educated at such a school or at institutions like Lovedale and Fort Hare with later training in a Governmental office, the fact remains that such education is a *sine qua non* if he is to co-operate with Government officials and to keep his people on the highway of progress.

The Chief's education is especially pertinent during this transitional period when his younger tribesmen are returning from the "front" with attitudes menacing to authority and subversive to established order. Even the Native children who have been educated in mission schools lose their respect for a Chief who has no understanding of the White man's culture.

The influence and value to the territory of an educated, wise and progressive Chief can scarcely be over-estimated. That fact is evident in the case of Linchwe, the Chief of the Bakhatla in Bechuanaland Protectorate, who made it an absolute rule that his tribe should have a three years' supply of grain in storage before any should be sold. The rule has been observed by his son Isang Pelone, a young man of some education and culture, who has added to it

---

[1] E. G. Malherbe, "Native Education in the Union of South Africa", article contributed to the *Year Book of Education, 1932*, edited by Lord Eustace Percy. (Evans Bros., London.)

the requirement that his people use sorghum as a subsistence crop for home consumption and that they grow maize
for export.[1] Miss Hodgson gives us the negative side of this
picture:[2] "Everywhere else in the Territory the shadow of
starvation hovers now high now low but never quite out
of sight, and never perhaps since the establishment of
British protection has it come so low as it is to-day when
external circumstances are closing all the old avenues of
economic effort".

For any educational policy to be effective in a tribe it
must have the co-operation of the Chief. If by reason of his
ignorance he is shorn of respect, influence and control the
best ally of the educational agency is weakened. This fact
is abundantly evident in the experience of the Union of
South Africa. The District Agricultural Union, a body
of White farmers around Potgietersrust in Northern
Transvaal, recently met with the Chiefs of the district to
work out jointly a scheme of farm apprenticeship training.
It was agreed that qualified young Natives should receive
an attractive monthly wage after finishing the three years'
apprenticeship. The scheme promised to benefit both
Black and White. All were enthusiastic about it. The
Chiefs returned to recruit their subjects, but their prestige
and control had so waned that they could not provide
even a handful of Native apprentices to carry out the
project.

The educational problem could be considerably reduced
were the European employers honestly to face their obligations to their servants.

Perhaps it is too soon to expect any considerable number
of White women to be genuinely interested in the welfare
of the wives of their servant boys living in the mine or
town location. Formerly it was not popular for the
European and American woman to extend any but professional assistance to the poor. Now with a recognition

[1] Reported by Mrs. R. F. A. Hoernle, Professor of Anthropology at
the University of the Witwatersrand, Johannesburg.
[2] Margaret N. Hodgson and W. G. Ballenger, *Britain in South Africa*,
pp. 45-46.

of their humanitarian responsibility the friendly visitor plan has commended itself to those who have leisure for voluntary welfare work. The plan has incipient beginnings in the Union. "There has been a remarkable growth in recent years in the number of European voluntary social workers, most of whom have been drawn into the work by missionary organisations which have developed an extensive network of social agencies . . . at Grahamstown Mrs. J. E. H. Mylne (wife of the honorary secretary of the Joint Council) has succeeded in gathering together fifty or sixty of the women of the location whom she has taught to spin and knit, so also a number of women and girls in domestic service who spend their 'afternoons out' together pleasurably engaged in these occupations."[1] The plan as applied to Northern Rhodesia would involve spending a morning or two a week in intimate contact with the mothers of future Africa, giving to them some of the values of our civilisation.

Either the Northern Rhodesian White man will educate the Native to something like his own standard, or his own will fall toward the level of the Black. Two cultures cannot continue side by side without each mutually influencing the other.

Acculturation through race contact is reciprocal, and it is only as the higher civilisation deliberately and purposefully promulgates its standards that the resulting civilisation shows progress.

E. *Fear of Native Competition*

Another set of correlated problems group themselves about the possibility and methods of reducing the fear on the part of the European of Native economic competition. This fear complex lurks in the background of every discussion of race relations in Africa. The wide disparity between the numbers of Black and White lends poignancy to it; the increase of Native population augments it; the

[1] *The South African Institute of Race Relations, 1931,* p. 39 ff.

White family's difficulty of adjustment to a Rhodesian habitat aggravates it; the investment of fixed capital adds an intriguing element to it, while the growing threat of gradual mergence of White and Native into a miscegenate race similar to that of Porto Rico and Jamaica gives it plausibility.

Again, the longer experience of the Union is ever before the Rhodesian. While the colour bar in Northern Rhodesia has not as yet entrenched itself in legislation, it is none the less real. The Poor White group which is the Native's actual economic competitor has already found its way into the Northern Rhodesian towns.[1] The competition is keen and the spoils are not always to the White. There are sections of the North-Western Transvaal in which Dutch Whites are wage labourers for Native employers—a fact which affronts the dignity and race pride of the more fortunate White and sharpens his sense of fear. From this it will be seen that the fear complex has an obvious explanation. It rests, however, on a fallacy as fundamental as it is pernicious and results from superficial economic thinking. As Professor Henry Clay has pointed out,[2] the Native population, far from being a menace, properly understood, is the country's greatest asset. It is indeed a misconception to assume that if the Native becomes better educated and better skilled he will supplant the White worker. This implies that the White worker holds his place in industry not because of his skill and versatility, but because he can artificially keep others from competing with him for it. If the European has ability and a willingness to exercise it he would be pushed upward in the industrial scale as the Native rises in industrial importance. Far from trying to

[1] At Ndola during November 1932, 193 "poor Whites" were being fed under the auspices of the local District Commissioner, and at Lusaka 400. As yet the ratio of "poor Whites" to the total White population is not as great as in the Union, where 17·5 per cent of all White families are described as "very poor" (*The Poor White Problem in South Africa*, Joint Findings and Recommendations, vol. i. p. 7), but the direction of the trend in the North is similar to that in the South.

[2] Prof. H. Clay, *Report on the Industrial Relations in Southern Rhodesia*, p. 42.

keep the Black man down, the European should encourage his advancement, for he is a potential asset. To be sure, the poor Whites would temporarily suffer by the removal of the artificial barriers behind which their inefficiency now precariously masquerades, but in the long run they too would share the stimulation of honest competition on the basis of merit rather than of colour. Furthermore, as the Native becomes a more proficient worker and secures higher wages he will be financially able to purchase the goods produced by the still more highly skilled White man. While there is a definite limit to the consumption of food, there is no known limit to the power of a group with increasing wages to consume manufactured products. So the opportunity for White employment is without any upper limit save that of human enterprise. This fear complex also gratuitously assumes that there is a definite limit to White ingenuity, and that if the Black comes into industry the White must go out. Surely this is absurd. The rise of Native skill, the improvement in Native standards of living and the stimulation of Native wants means rather that there will be added opportunities for all, both White and Black, and the facilitation of the welfare of the group as a whole.

F. *Race Co-operation and Psychology*

The last problem has to do with the changes necessary in the psychological attitudes of both races before there can be any adequate working basis for racial co-operation between Whites and Blacks. This necessity underlies all other needs. Europeans in Africa evidence a growing interest in this need for a rational and defensible attitude toward the Native. What, it is inquired, creates the apparently unbridgeable gap between the two races? Is the difference physical and instinctive, or is it social and due to differing race histories and traditions? Should we try to make over the Bantu Society into an imitation of our own? What changes would be necessary in the attitudes of both White and Bantu to ensure a better co-operation between them?

To answer these questions fully lies outside the limits of this report—on the other hand, to refuse on that account to analyse and estimate the significance of the mental attitudes underlying them would be like describing the functions of the human body with no mention of the ductless glands because as yet their functions are imperfectly understood.

Attitudes determine human behaviour and relationships. They furnish the drive for human action. When, as sometimes happens, they are built on prejudices uncorrelated with facts they may swing from one extreme to the other. Especially is this the case with attitudes regarding race.

In the early days of Dutch settlement in Africa the Native was regarded frankly as belonging to a different "class of beings" from Europeans. He was thought incapable of development. He could never be other than a servant of the European. The Creator had made him so. That notion has undergone a gradual modification but it has not entirely disappeared. One encounters it still in the remoter White settlements of Africa. By the early part of the present century, however, the pendulum of White opinion had swung from this absurd and untenable attitude to the opposite extreme and the Bantu was referred to as "just a black Scotchman".[1] Below both uncritical attitudes lay the confusion of racial difference with racial inferiority.

Racial difference is demonstrable even between the sub-groups of the Caucasian, Mongolian and Negro stocks, but inferiority has never yet been proved. The Bantu is a variety of the human species. He differs from other human varieties. Perhaps the difference between White and Bantu might be compared with the difference between a pointer dog and a setter. Racial differences are measurable in terms of head shape, hair, throat, lungs, pelvic and other structural peculiarities. The biochemist has traced the differences down into the blood stream and shown their permanency.[2]

---

[1] Sir George Cory, *The Rise of South Africa* (London, 1910), vol. i. p. 8.

[2] Dr. Ludwik Hirchfeld and Dr. Hanka Hirchfeld, "Serological

The primary causes of individual variation (which underlies group differences) and the complex laws under which it occurs are as yet so little known that no individual variation in animals or humans can be predicted. However, it happens. If the variant is adapted it persists, if not it disappears in a few generations at most. The important thing is that a series of such adaptive variations may quite differentiate a race from its parental stock. Whites and Blacks seem to be variants in opposite directions from a common ancestor. Each best fits its respective environment, which is another way of saying that each has become adapted to the conditions under which it lives. Comparative isolation and deliberately supervised selective breeding, as the killing of twins, weaklings, aberrant types and the like, has further specialised each human variety or race.

Race on the physical side is not, then, a matter of superiority or inferiority, potential or actual, but rather of difference due to a long process of adjustment to environment; thus the Bantu is suited to a certain set of environmental conditions, the White to another. These differences are in the germ plasm and are unchangeable other than by generations of interbreeding with other races or by a long subjection to the environmental influences already mentioned, but they are sometimes over-emphasised in working out a basis for racial respect and co-operation. More significant differences lie in the social customs which are demonstrably subject to change. Fundamentally these approved group ways tend to be transmitted without modification from one generation to the next: individuals are coerced to conform to them so early in childhood and so continuously that in adulthood it is difficult to distinguish them from instincts with which they are sometimes mistakenly confused. They are not in the germ plasm, however, but are entirely social in character.

It has long been a popular fallacy to list the psycho-

Differences between the Blood of Different Races", *The Lancet*, October 18, 1919, pp. 676-7.

logical differences between the two races as indisputable
evidence of innate difference, forgetful of the fact that one
is but contrasting traditional usages of which individuals
are the carriers. When an observer says the Black is an
extrovert, a materialist, highly impressionistic, imitative,
superstitious, without business acumen, ambition or the
power of self-direction, he is characterising not the individual but the standards and customs of the group to
which he belongs. Such characteristics are invested in him
by his society. They are not innate. Many of them are
readily explicable in the light of the history and vicissi-
tudes of the Bantu race. The Natives' social characteristics, though they are more stubborn than is usually
supposed, are capable of being modified. Indeed, on careful
examination the vast majority of them, particularly those
of a communal sort, are found to be rooted in his tribal
organisation; on the other hand, the Westerner, in his
mental attitudes and social relationships, has for many
centuries been activated by an increasingly exalted individualism. His commerce, property concepts, industry
and even his religion force him to be individualistic. His
mental attitudes thus necessarily differ from those of the
Bantu.

Thus while there are physiological differences which
will prevent the Native from becoming a "Black Scotchman" the gradual modification of his culture will more and
more permit the expression of latent powers long repressed
by tribal custom. Only as the Bantu's culture is changed
can his "natural" limitations be known. Individuals here
and there in Africa have demonstrated their intellectual
equality with Europeans and found a place in White
society. A Native institution at Fort Hare[1] has for eighteen
years successfuly carried on educational work of college
grade for African boys. So that although no African group
has yet reached a stage on which co-operation with the
White approximates perfection, the process is already
under way.

[1] Fort Hare College, Alice, Cape Province.

The second question as to the wisdom of trying to make over Bantu society after the pattern of our own cannot be so easily answered. Western civilisation has discovered that too great standardisation of individuals and functions makes for stagnation rather than progress, so individual and group specialisation is welcomed. There are distinct values to a group, nation or race made up of individuals differing widely in physique, abilities and functions providing there continues to be mutual respect and co-operation between the specialists; so also race differences may be a real advantage to human society. To make over the African Native and his society, then, into a replica of the White and his society, even if it could be accomplished, is neither desirable nor wise, but to create a better psychological basis for co-operation is necessary if both races are to be advantaged.

The answer to the third question as to the exact basis of such co-operation, for the time at least, must be a compromise between present policy and the ultimate ethical ideal. No plan which can be carried through in a year or even in a generation can possibly suffice. The method of adjustment may be laid down and the direction of the next few steps indicated, but any long-time plan, however essential as a guide for the immediate future, must be cogent enough to ensure conformity and at the same time tentative enough to permit of adaptation as the adjustment proceeds.

Race adjustment is primarily the outgrowth of individual adjustment, for, while the modification of personal attitudes is limited by the attitude of the group, the aberrant thinking and feeling of the individual gradually changes the sentiment and mental slant of the group. Effective modifications of group attitudes begin with far-sighted and courageous individuals. For example, it requires no little courage under present conditions for Europeans in Africa to insist on the recognition of the individual Bantu on his merits rather than as a race type. But until the Native is so recognised he will tend to be classified as a "raw Kaffir" whatever his attainments may be. On the other hand, few Europeans are willing to encourage the Native to recognise the White man on the basis of his merit rather than as a representative of the White race. Yet without such mutual recognition no permanent relationship can be established which will ensure the conformity of each to the best standards in his own society and to the highest common standards of both. The absence of it means the absence of ordinary civility of which the Native now complains and the "cheekiness" of the emancipated Bantu which so exasperates the White. The need is not for a sentimental Bantuphilia on the one hand or a Bantuphobia on the other, but for a relationship built on mutual confidence and respect.

It has been observed that it will not be possible much longer for the White man's skin alone to see him through. Natives are already beginning to discriminate between White men. A Rhodesian trader phrased it thus: "We cannot keep up the bluff that all White men are just a little lower than God". Nor on the other hand can the White man continue to refer to all Bantu as "low Kaffirs", "spoiled niggers", or by other similar humiliating epithets.

A changed personal attitude on the part of White men will necessarily manifest itself in an increase of economic opportunities to the Native and the gradual removal of trade and labour disabilities, especially if accompanied by a frank declaration that the upper limit of economic advancement will depend on the Native himself. It would mean in Northern Rhodesia an even more equable manner of handling the assignment of land, Native administration and the adjustment of wages on the basis of individual efficiency rather than on the basis of race and colour, but it can come about only as White attitudes are modified.

It should not be forgotten, however, that the need of changed attitude is reciprocal. The psychology of the Native during the present transitional period must also be modified. He must know that until he produces or creates that which is desirable and acceptable to the White man, the White attitudinal changes will be spurious and thin. Until the Bantu has come to value the satisfaction of a task well done, the approximation of a standard of perfection yet undreamed of, and the necessity of carrying out his tasks, however menial, with intelligence and initiative, regardless of the wages paid, the irritation of his fumbling and slipshod methods will ever annoy his White employer or associate. In the field of politics the adoption of the new attitude need not occasion concern as it does not necessarily mean immediate political equality. European governmental institutions are the outgrowth of European culture. The White race has had to struggle determinedly through the centuries for political rights and functioning and in the process it has acquired peculiar abilities in self-government. Any sound basis for the right to political participation must be rooted in Native economic and cultural attainments. But the new attitude does require that no disability should be placed in the way of his reaching this ultimate goal. A recognition of this principle has resulted in the limited enfranchisement of the Native in the Cape Province of the Union of South Africa.

Socially also the attitude permits of the present separation of the races. White social recognition can come to the Native only as he develops a pride in the achievements of his own race, as he builds up his own agencies, organisations and institutions and does it with diminishing help from the White group. In welfare work there is insidious danger of social pauperisation. Giving to him gratis educational facilities, medical service, recreational and social welfare agencies, beyond those provided for by taxes collected from him, is a questionable expedient unless it be regarded as a responsibility which he may and should take over as rapidly as circumstances will permit. As has been indicated, the beginnings of the process are already evident in Africa. The more intensive experience with the Black in America has demonstrated that the growth in race pride, self-direction and self-sufficiency of the Negro tenth of the population has done more to stimulate and encourage individual and group achievement than any other thing, and, what is more significant still, it has been effective in winning for the Black social recognition by the White group.

One of the forces effectively discouraging the building up of this race integrity on the new plane is the sporadic occurrence of intermarriage and miscegenation. The White group has been the offender in this particular to the increasing resentment of the Native. A growing public opinion condemns it in Northern Rhodesia, but the imposition of heavy penalties on Europeans having immoral relations with Native women, including immediate dismissal from public service, would help to keep this dangerous practice within bounds.

The changed attitude would perhaps mean a slighter modification for the religious workers and missionaries, as, by reason of their altruistic purpose, they lead in this field. This is not to say that the situation even in this quarter cannot be improved. It unquestionably can. The attitude counsels the better adaptation by the missionary of educational objectives to Native needs, a better understanding and recognition of the finest qualities in the Bantu culture, a building upon and improvement of Native beliefs and religious practices, a greater emphasis on anthropological studies, and above all a consistency in following the plan of keeping the religious life and moral sanctions of the Bantu group on a par with or in advance of the changes taking place in the industrial, educational, political and other spheres of Native life.

Many methods have been suggested for effecting the needed change in attitudes. Obviously frankness in statement of Native policy is desirable. In Europe and America it has been discovered that the most effective method of correcting false propaganda is by promulgating sound theories and facts. Little has been done in Africa toward this end. The Natives' misunderstanding of White motives, purposes and policies might well be corrected in this way.

A sheet published in his own language under joint governmental and missionary auspices would pay high dividends in better understanding, loyalty and co-operation. And, incidentally, it would lay the foundation for the not-distant system of giving radio talks to the Native villages on health, agriculture, markets, local improvement possibilities, current events and world topics.

But even this is not enough. The strategy of the situation would require a beneficent and consistent propaganda of the White minority of the population, through the already established press; and by addresses at such occasions as the Kafue Agricultural Show, farmers' meetings, gatherings at the mines, Rotary clubs, etc., appealing if need be to the self-interest of the White population, emphasising the place and value of the Native in Rhodesian society and the possibilities of capitalising his development for the benefit of both White and Black. Press facilities are already at hand which could well be turned to account under a responsible publicity committee representing the administrational, educational, religious and other interests involved.

The problems dealt with in this chapter are necessary of solution before any reintegration of Native society on a level which will permit of better co-operation with White society can possibly take place. We shall now turn to a consideration of the reconstructive forces at work in the Native territories.

CHAPTER VII

THE impact of the returning mine-worker generally on the life of his kraal in theory should be obvious and measurable. In accordance with this *a priori* theory an imposing list of influences was compiled from various sources. No doubt was anywhere expressed about their being universal, tangible and available for observation and measurement. For the investigator it should be but a matter of correlating and estimating the significance of the factors in the rapidly changing order.

It was, therefore, with some surprise that we found so few and widely scattered tangible evidences of the influences. A longer period of investigation of the Native kraals might perhaps have revealed more—a careful selection of villages near mission stations unquestionably does. But over the Territory, so far as it was visited, and in spite of many contacts, the results were found to be intangible and difficult of definite measurement.

Subsequent questioning of Government officials, missionaries, business men and settlers to obtain specific data revealed a paucity of concrete results of civilisation's impact. This is not to say that vital changes are not taking place, but that they are subtle, chaotic, unconscious and transitional.

In the health, hygiene and personal habits of the Native villagers there seemed to be little deliberate improvement outside those who had been directly influenced by a local Christian mission. It is true that life on the copper belt had slightly changed food, accommodations and conveniences. Occasionally a sun-dried brick house, with simple furniture, kitchen utensils and European hoes, more occasionally still a few fruit-trees, domestic fowl and

European clothes, attested the Native's contact with the White man at the mines or on the missions. In a Native village near Chitambo we stood in the broiling tropical sun as we talked to the Native headman and his council. The former wore a heavy cast-off overcoat buttoned to the chin. It was his official regalia and, with the exception of a youth in shorts and sweater, the only visible European clothing in the group. When we examined the huts, in spite of the fact that every able-bodied man had been working at the mines, the paraphernalia, utensils and trinkets had been spread so thinly through the village that there was little evidence of them left. It was difficult to exercise personal property rights against communal claims. Indeed, the only property of European manufacture recognised as personal seemed to be the sewing-machine, gramophone, gun and bicycle. The early tribal usages still set the limits of personal property. The machines for war, the chase and agriculture had long been *approprius*, and the new machines, because they were machines, were the inalienable property of the individual. Clothes were generally stowed away as a bank account, and the bank for their meagre savings was a pit dug in the kraal.

It would seem that the Native when he returned home, however skilled in handicrafts he had been under White supervision, feared to show that skill by improving his living quarters, his kraal or garden. Tradition reigned. The White man's ways, ideals and material equipment were measurably sublimated. They belonged to another world and might render him suspect of witchcraft—with only one end: death. Not infrequently the worker easily and fatalistically slumped back into, or became vigorously the exponent of, his former tribal life. Even students, however emancipated, on their return home find it expedient to conform to the usage of the tribe. The following case is typical: "I had bad feeling against the Chief and Headman. Many a time . . . I felt like knocking them down with a big kerry, but I have to regard the authority of the Chief and

Headman. When I meet them I clap hands and kneel down."[1]

It is generally supposed that there is an improvement in the physique of the Native on his return from the mines, due to regular work, cleanliness, hygiene, attention when sick, and better-balanced food rations. "The physique of the men is undoubtedly improving", says Moffat Thompson, Secretary for Native Affairs for Northern Rhodesia. "This statement is based on the evidence of medical officers of wide experience and knowledge of the people. These medical officers examine the Natives recruited for work and see them on their return, and they are constantly in touch with Natives in the villages and at various Government stations."[2]

It was rather in the intangible field of psychic attitudes and social organisation that the new civilisation had taken root. Mental attitudes, whatever the behaviour, had unquestionably changed. The worker was more discriminating, more favourable in his attitude toward Native reform, more impatient with the inefficiency of his Chief, more interested in education, more critical of old codes and social taboos, more emancipated from tribal superstitions, more ambitious to attain the standards of the civilisation of which he had temporarily been a part. That these attitudes were inhibited of expression need not prevent their bearing fruit in succeeding generations. The new and subversive ideas of their children, exposed to similar contacts, will find a readier reception and sympathy because of the earlier experience of the parents, just as the children of former Native Christians find it immeasurably easier to think and live their Christian lives.

In organisation also the reintegrative process is already

[1] From the life-history of a Shangaan student after a visit to his Native kraal.

[2] Answer to a question on the accuracy of statements in the *Northern Rhodesia Government Report for 1931*, submitted to the Acting Governor and referred for written reply to the Secretary for Native Affairs, November 7, 1932.

under way. Under the recently adopted system of indirect rule the authority of the Chief has been defined and
strengthened by the Government. His rights and duties
have been regularised and brought into conformity with
local administration in surrounding areas. It is the beginning of a standardisation which will permit the Native
to meet Bantu from other areas on the common basis of
citizenship instead of the old basis of sublimated tribal
hostility. Labour in industry, on the mines and more
especially on the farms of local White settlers, together
with the White man's system of medicine and hygiene, has
taught the Native something of the consistency and regularity of the laws of Nature, and thus indirectly, but
effectively, is undermining the former magical and superstitious practices of village life. This industrial labour has
familiarised him with a wage economy and trade in terms
of money rather than barter in kind. On the other hand,
missions, through a long period of secular education and
religious instruction, have disseminated through the territories substitutes (as yet not altogether understood) for
the modes, ideas and ideals of the past.

By reason of the play of these new forces on Native life
there has crept into Bantu consciousness a specious individualism and way of thinking which is at variance with
the tradition of his group and something in defiance of it.
During the present transitional period the expression of
this individualism is somewhat random and uncorrelated
with any well-balanced philosophy of life. He has not yet
discovered the true inwardness of the White man's moral
system. Thus his newly-born independence is rather negative. It manifests itself in resentments of discipline, in the
eschewing of tribal and family responsibilities, in chafings
under traditional modes of expressing respect to the Chief,
the elders, and the Europeans, in divorce, in his refusal to
extend customary hospitality, and even in his unwillingness
to conform to the discipline of his church or mission and
the building up of a separatist cult of his own. Again, this
must be recognised as a transitional phase in his develop-

ment. It shows that the reintegrating process of effective reconstruction in Native society is incipient only.

So this transitional generation calls as no other for unremitting thought and service on the part of the European; for an intelligent long-time plan; for emphasis on the note of confidence in the future; for sympathetic and patient understanding; and, above all, for courage, perseverance and the ability to face failures.

PART THREE

THE ECONOMIC PROBLEM

E. A. G. ROBINSON

CHAPTER VIII

THE ECONOMIC PROBLEM

THE economic organisation of Northern Rhodesia as it existed in the recent past has in its broad outlines been described in the preceding section. The centre of the system was the self-sufficient family group,[1] organised to satisfy its own needs in almost every respect. By its own efforts the family fed itself, clothed itself within the primitive bark-cloth of the country, equipped itself with its simple tools, housed itself and manufactured for itself the few articles of furniture and of pottery that it required. Within the family unit there was some division of labour. As was described in the previous section, to the women fell the tasks of cooking and of hoeing; to the men the lopping of trees, the building of houses; to the men also in some cases the care of the cattle. Outside the family unit specialisation and exchange of products was practically unknown. A few men possessed the skill of working metals, and in their leisure from agriculture would, with the assistance of their friends, make the weapons, the hoes or the axes for the community. A few individuals traded the salt or the tobacco of one district with their neighbours. The fishermen of the rivers and the lakes exchanged their catches for the grain or roots of the nearer tribes.

The elementary agricultural methods produced barely sufficient for the family group itself. Outside the area of the tsetse-fly the main task was the care of the cattle, and the diet was derived in large measure from the herds. Within the fly-belt area they cultivated each year an acre, or a little more, of garden, cutting some ten acres of forest annually to burn the brushwood on the selected spot. The

---

[1] As has been explained in the previous section, this group is considerably wider than the family as understood in Europe.

garden yielded a barely sufficient crop to keep the family until the next harvest. In many years there would be shortage in the last months. They grew no crops that could be sold for cash. Apart from the mission stations and the Government offices there were no purchasers for the products of these undifferentiated producers. Each produced himself what his neighbour produced, and had therefore no interest in exchanging products with his neighbour. Like the social system with which it was intertwined, the economic system formed a simple, consistent, intelligible framework for a simple order of technique and of wants. The interdependence of the different family economic units was slight. The customs of marriage defined clearly the adherence of the next generation to the one unit or to the other. If for technical reasons the standard of living of the people was deplorably low, if the gains of division of labour and of specialisation had been inadequately secured, yet at least the poverty, hunger and suffering which can come from the periodical breakdown of a system of commercial interchange was unknown. The risks of the seasons were constant. The vagaries of world markets were a matter neither of their knowledge nor of their concern.

Adequate as was this simple organisation so long as the country was isolated, so soon as contacts with the outside world increased its weaknesses began to be manifested. In the wake of explorers and missionaries came traders with new goods to offer. Cotton cloth, blankets, factory-made hoes, kerosene oil, candles, sugar, tea, all presented themselves almost as necessities to the unaccustomed consumer. Moreover, an established government began to need and to demand the payment of taxes for its support. But the primitive economic system in which he lived afforded the Native no ready means of payment. He grew no cash crops; unlike many of the Oriental countries in similar circumstances, he had no valuable indigenous handicrafts to offer; there were, in the early days at least, no rich natural products which could command a sale in the world's markets. Thus a problem of disequilibrium, previously unknown,

was introduced into the economic system. The economic
problem of Northern Rhodesia to-day is the re-establish-
ment of equilibrium in the face of cumulatively increasing
forces making for disequilibrium. The earlier problem of
adjustment created by the establishment of peace and the
opening up of trade has grown gradually more difficult
with the steady improvement of means of transport, with
the increase of trading companies, with the steadily developing taste for foreign products, and with the growing
need of Government to raise revenue in cash to finance
administration, education, road-building and a multitude
of other services.

The equilibrium of an economic system depends upon a
multitude of factors, comparatively few of which need concern us here. The essential conditions are two: first, that
no one shall receive so much more for his services, either
as owner of capital or supplier of labour, in one place than
in another, that he is induced to move; second, that the
inward and outward payments of any group shall balance.
The first is sufficiently obvious, and though it will greatly
concern us later, it need not delay us now. The second deserves a moment's consideration. It is true of any group
that expenditure in the widest sense must equal receipts,
again in the widest sense. In expenditure we must include
not only what is ordinarily so called, but also the acquisition of investments or of currency, and any gifts or loans
or interest payments made to persons outside the group.
In receipts we must include not only payments for products or for services, but also gifts or loans received from
persons outside the group, and any interest payments received. Clearly, defined thus, a balance of payments is inevitable. Any funds received must be devoted to some
purpose or other among those which we have included in
expenditure. On the other hand, any incoming goods must
be balanced either by a payment or by an addition to the
loans or gifts received. The problem is not the establishment of some balance of payments (some such there will
always be), but the establishment of a balance that con-

forms to the desires for trade on the part of the two parties
to the trade, and throws undue strain upon neither.

This conception of balance can be applied to any group
that we may imagine. It is equally true of the individual
family, the individual village, the individual district or the
individual country in their relations with the world outside
themselves. We are accustomed in the countries living
under a Western economic system to think of it as it concerns the payments of one country to other countries. We
are accustomed to ignore it in Western countries so far as
it applies to the smaller groups inside a country. We can
afford as a rule to ignore it because, in a Western country
with a highly developed system of specialisation and exchange, and with a highly developed system of banking
and credit, adjustments are as a rule sufficiently automatic
and immediate to cause us no concern. It is because the
processes of adjustment are difficult in international trading that our attention is called to it. In more primitive
countries, among which Northern Rhodesia is for this purpose to be counted, the satisfactory adjustment of balances
between individuals and between places is not facilitated
by any credit organisation, and in the conditions of production which prevail these other problems of the balance
of payments are often more difficult than the adjustment
of the international balance.

The groups for which payments must balance need not
be purely geographical groups. They may equally be social
groups or groups based on any common bond. Thus in
order that Government expenditure on education may be
increased there must be, directly or indirectly, a counter-
vailing increase in the payments of taxpayers to those per-
forming the tasks of education. The problem of adjustment
here will depend upon how far the teachers are prepared to
take directly those things which the taxpayers can most
easily put at their disposal. A Native teacher, living in the
village and spending his salary on local produce, may cause
little or no problem of adjustment. A European teacher
who wishes to spend his income on the maintenance of his

own family in England may cause very considerable problems of adjustment.

Beside the problems of adjustment between Northern Rhodesia and the world outside, the most important balances that we shall have to consider are those just mentioned, between the taxpayer and the tax receiver, and those between the remoter agricultural areas and the towns which sell the imported products. If Natives in a country village wish to buy cotton cloth, two questions arise. First: Is Northern Rhodesia exporting sufficient to pay for this import into the country? Second: Is the village exporting sufficient to the town to pay for its further importation into the village? There may be a breakdown at either of these points, and at a later stage these problems must be examined more closely. For the moment it is important to emphasise the part which has been played by the movement of labour in the achievement of the necessary balance. Having nothing else to sell, the Native has sold himself. The need to find the money to pay his taxes, his mission or education dues, and to buy the products of the store, has led him to seek work in the towns, on the farms, at the mines, both in Northern Rhodesia and the surrounding countries. For the time being, this method of payment may suffice. But the drift to the towns and to the neighbouring territories has already thrown strains both upon the organisation of the Native agriculture, and upon the social and political structure, which these are at present ill-equipped to bear. There is almost certainly some upper limit, and it may well prove to be a comparatively low one, to the number of workers who can without harm be absent at any time from the village. If then the increasing demands for payment by the country to the town can no longer be safely met by the temporary migration of labour, it will become urgently necessary to devise some alternative means of payment to take its place and make it so far as possible unnecessary.

. If we are to understand fully the problems of disequilibrium and of readjustment that are involved in the recent growth of the copper-mining industry, we shall need to study its effects largely in terms of two balances, that of the external balance of payments of Northern Rhodesia with the outside world, and that of the balance of payments within the Territory, between the labour-supplying areas and the labour-using areas. The first of these must involve us in some examination of the prospective exports of the copper industry, and therefore of the markets for copper and the power of the Northern Rhodesian producers to compete in those markets. The second of these must involve us in a consideration of the demands for labour not only of the copper industry itself but also of other industries in Northern Rhodesia. The emergence of the copper industry and its considerable demand for labour would in itself, in isolation, cause no considerable problem. As will be seen later, it has served in many ways to simplify the problems of the country. It is because it is added to the existing sources of demand for labour that its effects have been in some cases serious. Northern Rhodesian labour has found its way to mines and to other work for many years past, and at great distances from home. Until the imposition in May 1913 of the restriction on recruitment north of latitude 22° South, a certain number of workers found their way to the gold-mines of Johannesburg. So long ago as 1907 there were 7590 Northern Rhodesian Natives recruited by the Rhodesian Native Labour Bureau to work in the mines of Southern Rhodesia. They moved also, as will be seen later, to the Belgian Congo and to the plantations of German East Africa. By 1930 the number of Natives working for wages within the Territory or outside it [1] had increased to about 100,000 at any one time.

Some of this labour force is permanently urbanised. It would be difficult to make any accurate estimate of the proportion, but it is almost certainly less than 10 per cent of the whole, and quite probably far less. The vast majority

---

[1] In 1932 this number had fallen to about 60,000. Deduction has been made in each case for foreign Natives working in Northern Rhodesia, and included in the published statistics.

of these workers keep their roots in the country. They regard a distant village as their home. In many cases their
wives and families remain there. They work for short
periods of time, often as little as a few months, seldom more
than a couple of years. Thus there has been evolved in the
past thirty years an urban economic system superimposed
upon a rural social and political system. This paradoxical
organisation has met successfully both the needs of industry and those of political life so long as individuals have
been content to move freely and frequently back from the
new system to the old. It has its analogies farther south in
the Union, where the industrial life of Johannesburg is
built on the labour supply afforded by the rural societies of
Basutoland, the Transkei and Ciskei, of Portuguese East
Africa and other Native areas. But the situation in Northern Rhodesia differs fundamentally from that in the south.
The continuance of the latter is assured for the time being
by the impossibility of housing the vast numbers involved
on the limited areas of the Rand mines, and by the absence
therefore of any family life in the industrial area, so that
recruitment from outside is continuous. In the north, survival of the dual economic system is conditional upon the
willingness of the individual to live alternately in the two
places. Already the older mines are beginning to build up
a nucleus of permanently urbanised workers who have not
returned for long periods to their homes. At the Wankie
coal-mines in Southern Rhodesia, for example, out of a
sample of 692 workers, largely recruited in Northern Rhodesia, 173, or exactly 25 per cent, had in 1932 been with
the firm ten years or more without any break of service.
Other mines, as will be seen later, are consciously building up stable labour forces living a normal family life in the
mine locations. Thus conscious urbanisation is becoming
added to the inertia of those already in the towns.

Meanwhile the pull of the town upon those remaining
in the country grows year by year greater. Wants increase, and taxation does not lessen. If present processes
continue through a generation as they have begun, the

drift to the towns must inevitably grow greater, and the
social and political systems built upon the framework of a
rural economic organisation must gradually die of inani-
tion. Economic change of this sort is seldom catastrophic.
The old order imperceptibly declines, the new order as
imperceptibly advances until it ultimately supersedes
the old, and the change is complete and radical. If by
some such process the whole economic system of Northern
Rhodesia is not in one, two or more generations to be transformed, active steps must be taken in this generation to
control and make unnecessary the drift to the towns, and
to build a permanent and stable economic life in the rural
areas. Already political changes have been instituted which
for their full fruition must require two or more generations.
If nothing is done, or can be done, to make the economic
foundation of this political structure secure, the whole
policy may ultimately prove vain. For the time being, however, it would be a mistake to exaggerate the difficulties of
the problem. Individuals still move freely and willingly
backwards and forwards from town to country. It is only
small numbers who have become definitely urbanised. The
policy of stabilisation in the mines has scarcely yet been
formulated, and affects only a comparatively small proportion of the whole wage-earning group. But the process of
urbanisation has started, and unless controlled it can
scarcely fail to increase.

CHAPTER IX

THE COPPER-MINES

THE copper belt of Northern Rhodesia is limited for the main part to a narrow strip which extends from the railway at Ndola westward some two hundred miles along the frontier of the Belgian Congo. Across the frontier in the province of Haut-Katanga is a similar area exploited by the Union Minière du Haut-Katanga. The whole extent of the reserves of copper in these two contiguous fields has not yet been fully discovered. But the proved reserves form over one-third of the world's known resources of the metal. Northern Rhodesia alone possesses about 28 per cent of the total.[1] The reserves already calculated are sufficient to enable the territory to produce a quarter of a million tons annually for a hundred years.

The existence of copper in this district has long been known. Copper has been mined for tools and for monetary purposes by the Natives beyond memory, and the presence of the metal was known by the earliest explorers. The discovery of the mines by White prospectors was in the majority of cases made easy by the existence of earlier Native workings. The expedition organised by Mr. Robert Williams,[2] which traversed in 1899 the border-lands of Northern Rhodesia and the Congo Free State under the leadership of George Grey,[3] owed their finding of the Kansanshi mine to the ancient workings shown to them by the old Chief Kapiji Mpanga. Ancient workings were found also at Bwana Mkubwa and at Nkana in Northern Rhodesia, and at Kambove and other places in Katanga. By 1903 many

[1] See *Mining and Metallurgy* (New York), December 1931, article by Mr. Chester Beatty.

[2] Now Sir Robert Williams, Chairman of Tanganyika Concessions Ltd.

[3] A brother of the late Viscount Grey of Fallodon.

of the deposits at present being exploited had already been located. The Bwana Mkubwa and Roan Antelope deposits were discovered by Collier about that time. Grey had explored the Katanga field and proved the existence of several of the deposits which are now being worked by the Union Minière. The existence of valuable deposits of copper in this area has thus been known for some thirty years, though their full extent and their richness have only recently been recognised.

Attempts were made to work these ores almost immediately. First the Rhodesian Copper Company, and later the Northern Copper Company, started to exploit the minerals at Bwana Mkubwa. But the railway at that time did not reach beyond the Victoria Falls. Transport over some five hundred miles depended largely on carriers, assisted sometime later by traction engines. In these conditions no great progress was possible and development was inevitably difficult and slow, not only in Northern Rhodesia but also on the Katanga side of the border. The railway reached the zinc and lead mine at Broken Hill in 1906, and by the end of 1909 had reached the Congo border. The Belgians completed the extension to the mines of the neighbourhood of Elisabethville in 1910. The copper-mines were now provided both with an outlet for their products to the port of Beira, and with facilities for bringing to the copper deposits coal from the large mine at Wankie in Southern Rhodesia, some seventy miles south of the Victoria Falls, and stores from the port and from the Union of South Africa.

As soon as transport was available more serious development was begun. A small concentrator was erected at Bwana Mkubwa in 1912 and was worked intermittently until the end of the War. The Kansanshi mine was also developed on a small scale and produced some copper, but work was suspended when war broke out. In Katanga more considerable progress was made. This was largely due to the fact that the earliest discoveries of ore in Katanga were richer than the corresponding discoveries in Northern

Rhodesia. On both sides of the border the earlier finds were of oxidised ores. But whereas in the Congo much of the ore averaged 15 per cent copper, and some was as high as 25 per cent, in Northern Rhodesia the oxidised ores averaged only some 3 to 5 per cent copper, and ores as rich as these were going on the dumps as waste on the Katanga side of the border. It is the later discovery of sulphide ore bodies averaging 3 to 6 per cent or more of copper which has made the Northern Rhodesian area commercially profitable.

The Northern Rhodesian field lay dormant from 1913 until 1923. At that time the satisfactory price of copper and the success of the Katanga mines led to an increased interest in the deposits south of the border. Moreover, in that year the British South Africa Company introduced a new policy of granting over considerable areas the sole prospecting right to substantial prospecting companies on the condition that they made in any year a certain minimum expenditure on their work. The most important of these companies were those which were later combined into Loangwa Concessions, and the Rhodesian Congo Border Concession. The former covers an area of almost one-half of Northern Rhodesia, extending from Mporokoso in the north to the River Luangwa at a point south of Serenje, thence to Kasempa in the west and Livingstone in the south. The latter concession follows the Congo border from its eastern limit to beyond Mwinilunga, and reaches as far south as Kasempa. Enclosed within this latter concession is the smaller concession known as the Nkana concession, which after changing hands several times came in 1924 into the possession of the Bwana Mkubwa Company. These various concession-holders began at once the scientific exploration of their areas. The deposits of Northern Rhodesia are not so readily discoverable as had been most of those of the Congo. Whereas in the latter country the copper is found usually in large hills standing above the level of the country, in Rhodesia the copper is more often at considerable depth with few surface indications.

It could only be proved by expensive and repeated drilling operations, and yielded itself only to the investigations of trained geologists assisted by modern equipment.

As a result of their work the discovery was made at the end of 1925 that, unlike the deposits in the Katanga which remained oxidised to the lowest depth mined, the deposits in Northern Rhodesia entered a sulphide zone at a depth of about one hundred feet.[1] This discovery completely changed the outlook for Northern Rhodesia. Sulphide ores of 3 to 5 per cent of copper were enormously profitable, whereas oxidised ores of similar grade were almost valueless. The richest discoveries of ore were made in the Nkana Concession and in the Rhodesia Congo Border Concession. The Bwana Mkubwa Company had granted to the Selection Trust certain options and rights to explore the Nkana Concession, apart from the Nkana mine itself, and the latter company succeeded in proving the existence of profitable deposits of ore at the Roan Antelope, at Mufulira and at Chambishi. In the Rhodesian Congo Border Concession a valuable new deposit was found at Nchanga. The various companies concerned gradually explored their areas by means of drilling, and the great extent and value of the deposits was by degrees realised. In 1927 a separate firm, the Roan Antelope Copper Mines Ltd., was formed with a majority of American capital. Development of the mine and construction of the surface plant began immediately.

Meanwhile in 1922 the Bwana Mkubwa mine had been re-equipped with new plant and reopened, and began to produce copper, gradually increasing its output until it reached over 5400 tons in 1929. Considerable difficulties and disappointments were met with in its operation. The oxidised ores nearest to the surface, when worked by the open-cast method, yielded a lower percentage of copper than the average of the mine, and the technical

[1] For an account of these discoveries see *Mining and Metallurgy* (New York), July 1931, article by A. M. Bateman, and December 1931, article by A. Chester Beatty.

problems of recovery proved somewhat difficult to master
and expensive to work. The Bwana Mkubwa Company
pushed on, therefore, with the exploration of the Nkana
mine and ultimately discovered in 1927 valuable deposits
of sulphide ore. The Company continued to investigate
the resources of the area by means of drill-holes, until by
1929 it was clear that sufficient reserves existed to justify
their commercial working, and the development of the
mine and the construction of a surface plant were put in
hand. In order to finance the great expenditure at Nkana
and to provide for a closer working between that mine and
the mine at Nchanga which was also under development,
the Bwana Mkubwa Company, the Rhodesian Congo
Border Concession and the Nchanga Copper Mines amalgamated in 1931 under the title of the Rhokana Corporation.

By 1930, then, the copper belt of Northern Rhodesia
was in the midst of a construction boom. Apart from the
zinc, lead and vanadium mine at Broken Hill, there were
copper-mines at Bwana Mkubwa, at the Roan, at Nkana,
Mufulira, Nchanga, Chambishi and Kansanshi, all either
producing or under development. Other smaller properties
were being explored. The town of Ndola, the centre for
the copper belt, was growing daily. Labour, whether European or Native, was scarce, unemployment unknown,
wages high. Trade flourished both in Ndola and at the
mines themselves. Credit was freely asked and freely given.
This state of prosperity continued into 1931, but early in
that year it became plain that it was not to last indefinitely.

Since 1926 most of the large producers of copper, both in
the United States and in the rest of the world, had been
united in an organisation known as Copper Exporters Incorporated, whose aim was to eliminate speculation and to
stabilise the price of copper. The price per long ton of
standard copper, which varied from 1921 to 1928 between
a maximum of £77 and a minimum of £56, in 1929 reached
almost £100, and even in the disastrous later months of
that year never fell below £66. But in 1930 stocks increased
rapidly and further price maintenance proved to be im-

possible. The price of standard copper fell from about £72 in February to £44 in November. The fall continued through 1931, and the maximum for that year was £47 and the mimimum £27. The first consequence of this collapse was the sudden shutting down in February 1931 of the Bwana Mkubwa mine. It was known that this mine was producing only at a high cost, and it had been foreseen that it would be closed as soon as the Nkana mine of the same Company began to produce; but its immediate closing was wholly unexpected. At the Nchanga mine development work was curtailed, and when the mine was accidentally flooded in September it was decided to suspend work there for the time being rather than incur the cost of pumping it out, and to concentrate all activities at Nkana. Just before Christmas Mufulira had actually reached the point of production when the order was given to close down. Development work at Chambishi and Kansanshi was also abandoned or reduced to a mimimum. Thus by the end of 1931 only two mines in the copper belt were active, the Roan Antelope and Nkana. At the former copper production had begun in October, at the latter construction was nearly finished and regular production began in March 1932.

Between the beginning and end of 1931 an exaggerated confidence in the future of the Northern Rhodesian copper belt gave way to an almost equally exaggerated despair. The time has now come for a more sober analysis of the prospects of this area. Northern Rhodesia possesses certain very great advantages over other copper-producing areas. In the first place the ores are in general unusually rich, and while the grade of the ore is not the only factor affecting mining costs, it is an important one. For the period 1927 to 1930 the average grade of all copper ore mined in the United States of America was approximately 1·41 per cent.[1] The Roan Antelope mine has proved reserves of 108,000,000 short tons of ore, averaging 3·44 per cent of copper. The Rhokana Corporation has reserves of some

[1] *Copper in 1930*. United States Bureau of Mines, Washington, 1932.

271,000,000 short tons, averaging 4·3 per cent copper. The deposits at Mufulira, Chambishi and Baluba are estimated at 162,000,000 short tons of 4·14 per cent ore. With the exception of the Nchanga properties of the Rhokana Corporation, where very rich mixed ores are found, about 95 per cent of the ore in each case is in the form of sulphide. Most of the mines possess certain areas of even higher grade which can be worked profitably in bad times. The high grade of ore means that smaller amounts of ore require to be mined, crushed and concentrated for a given tonnage of copper. Moreover, the ore is comparatively cheap to mine. Little timbering is necessary, and in the Roan mine none at all is at present employed. In the majority of the undertakings in Northern Rhodesia the ore is mined below ground, but at no great depth. In the Congo the oxidised ores are found mainly in exposed hills and are extracted with electric shovels after the overlying strata have been removed.. This method was employed in Northern Rhodesia at Bwana Mkubwa and is likely to be used at the Kansanshi mine. Underground mining is found in the Congo only in the Kipushi mine. The second great advantage of Northern Rhodesia lies in the comparative regularity of the sulphide ores, which can be crushed, concentrated and smelted by simpler and cheaper methods than can usually be applied to the oxidised ores of other areas. The third great advantage lies in the cheap and increasingly efficient labour supply available. This point will be considered later and need not be examined in detail at this moment.

These three advantages conspire to make Northern Rhodesia one of the lowest-cost copper-producing areas in the world. The total cost of copper at the mines in July 1932, including all local costs but excluding any financial charges or expenses incurred abroad, was less than £16 per long ton of blister copper. The cost of rail transport, ocean transport and handling increased this to about £23 at a European port.[1] At that time neither mine was working at

---

[1] This cost has been reduced in 1933 below £20.

as much as half the capacity of its surface plant, and there is no doubt that costs could be even further reduced if the mines could work at full capacity. Information regarding costs in other areas is meagre, but it has been said that "only seven of the United States owned mines produce copper under £40 a ton, eight at from £40 to £45 and thirty at over £45".[1] Another recent investigation into American copper costs in 1931[2] gives the average operating cost, which excludes interest, taxes and depreciation, and is therefore as nearly comparable as is possible to the Northern Rhodesian figures quoted above.[3] For all American mines, including those in Mexico, in South America and in Canada, the average operating cost in 1931 was 8·21 cents[4] per pound.

With these considerable advantages we might expect the Northern Rhodesian copper belt to be able to undersell its rivals and to expand its sales even in a time of depression. It is important, therefore, to consider the relation of this area to the market for copper. Effective routine production of copper only began at the Roan Antelope mine in October 1931, and at Nkana in March 1932. At that time the world demand for copper had already declined catastrophically. The world consumption of copper reached a peak in 1929 of about 1,860,000 long tons.[5] It had increased steadily since 1880 at the rate of about 6 per cent per year. In 1930 consumption declined to 1,531,000 long tons, and in 1931

[1] Sir Edmund Davis, at a meeting of the Rhodesian Anglo-American, Ltd., in May 1932.

[2] *Mining and Metallurgy* (New York), July 1932, article by G. W. Tower.

[3] It is, however, important to note that for American mines miscellaneous receipts and the receipts from the sale of metals other than copper exceed the allowance necessary for the items omitted, so that total cost is only 8·06 cents.

[4] This is equivalent to about £38 a ton at an exchange rate of $4.86 to £1, or at an exchange rate of $4 to £1 to about £46 a ton.

[5] Three units of measurement are ordinarily employed in copper statistics, the long (or English) ton of 2240 lb., the short (or American) ton of 2000 lb. and the metric ton of 2204 lb., which is equal to 1000 kg. Statistics in Northern Rhodesia are usually in short tons on the production side, but in long tons as regards sales. In the Belgian Congo they are usually in metric tons.

to 1,256,000 long tons. In 1932 a further considerable reduction has occurred.[1] The decline in consumption was
inevitably accompanied both by the fall of price which has
already been described, and by an increase of stocks. At
the beginning of 1929 the total stocks of copper in North
and South America, in Great Britain, in France and Japan[2]
had been at the artificially low level of about 296,000 long
tons, or a little less than two months' consumption at the
current rate. By the end of 1931 stocks had risen to some
682,000 long tons, or rather more than six months' consumption at the current rate. Other more recent estimates
put the stocks at the end of 1932 at about 750,000 long
tons, or about ten months' consumption at the very reduced
rate of the time. Of these stocks by far the greater part
(85-95 per cent) were in the United States.

In July 1932 the price fell below £25 per ton, and no mine
could cover its costs and meet its financial obligations. In
such circumstances survival depended upon the husband-
ing of financial resources. Price-cutting by low-cost producers without the necessary reserves was more likely to
destroy than to assist them. Moreover, it must be remembered that the present low costs of the Northern Rhodesian
mines have only been achieved in the last few months of
1932, and had not been fully anticipated before routine
production began. It was consequently to the interest of
the Northern Rhodesian companies as such, and quite apart
from their connections with other copper-producing interests in other parts of the world, to join in an agreement to
limit the output of copper. A conference of most of the
copper producers agreed in November 1930 to a considerable curtailment of production. Nevertheless, stocks increased and prices fell. This earlier agreement did not immediately affect the mines in Northern Rhodesia, for they
were not yet in production, but it played an important
part in slowing down the rate of development. When a

[1] A recently published figure puts the consumption for 1932 at
901,000 long tons.
[2] *Year Book of the American Bureau of Metal Statistics for 1931*,
p. 13 (converted into long tons).

second conference was called in August 1931, the Northern Rhodesian mines were represented. Before the end of the year agreement was reached, and from January 1, 1932, interests representing 90 per cent of the production of the world agreed to limit output for the first quarter of 1932 to about 26½ per cent of capacity.[1] From April the output was reduced to 20 per cent. The two mining companies concerned decided to concentrate all output at their two chief plants. Mufulira was closed and its quota distributed by agreement with the Rhodesian Selection Trust, approximately two-thirds to the Roan and one-third to Nkana. The latter mine also received the quota of Nchanga. Even so, both mines have been working far below capacity. The Roan has been working at the rate of some 25,000 tons a year with a capacity for some 80,000 tons, and Nkana at about 36,000 tons a year with a mill capacity for perhaps 120,000 tons. The Union Minière, which in 1930 actually produced nearly 145,000 tons and has now a considerably greater capacity, agreed to limit its output to 82,000 tons a year, of which a certain part was to be stocked in Africa.

In June 1932 the United States of America imposed a duty of four cents a pound on copper with the intention of helping the American high-cost producers, who had complained that they were being ruined by copper from areas which enjoyed the·advantage of low wages. The Union Minière, as well as three of the other largest producers of copper outside the United States, the International Nickel Company of Canada, the Chile Copper Company and the Cerro di Pasco Corporation, withdrew from Copper Exporters Incorporated. The result was the

[1] According to a statement by the Chief Secretary (*Northern Rhodesian Legislative Council Debates*, 7th Session, p. 111), the quotas originally assigned to the Northern Rhodesian mines were as follows: Rhokana, 69,000,000 lb. copper per annum; Roan Antelope, 40,000,000 lb. copper; Mufulira, 25,000,000 lb. copper. He further said that the companies operating in Northern Rhodesia and Belgian Congo were at that time estimated to be capable of producing at least 350,000 tons of copper per annum. The Union Minière was equipped to produce 225,000 tons per annum, and could quickly augment that.

immediate collapse of Copper Exporters Incorporated. But the underlying association survived, and the limitation to 20 per cent of capacity was effectively continued down to the end of the year. Meanwhile the Ottawa Conference had met. The general limitation of output had been made conditional on the absence of any measure of protection in Great Britain, and the agreement at Ottawa to impose a preferential tariff of twopence per pound on all copper from extra-imperial sources once more created an element of confusion.

In December 1932 a further conference of copper producers was held in New York. At this conference the Roan Antelope copper-mine claimed an increase of quota. It had become clear that the productive capacity of the Northern Rhodesian mines was considerably greater than had originally been calculated. Moreover, as low-cost producers they had least to gain and most to lose by restriction of production. In these circumstances it was inevitable that protest should be made against the more irksome clauses of the agreement, and in particular against the power of American producers to transfer their quotas to foreign subsidiaries. The refusal of other producers to give way led to a breakdown of the conference. Thus for the moment unrestricted competition has returned. With such a wide divergence between the high-cost and low-cost producers in the market, it is now to the interest both of the consumer and of the low-cost producer to eliminate rather than subsidise the inefficient. The newly revealed strength of the Northern Rhodesian mines would appear to be such that they can afford to enter into an agreement on their own terms or not at all.

With its very rich deposits, its cheap but comparatively efficient labour supply, and its now much improved transport facilities, there can be no doubt that in time the Northern Rhodesian copper belt must become one of the great producers of the world. It is far more difficult to judge how soon such developments will come about. The high-cost producers both in the United States and in other countries have great financial resources. They are integrated with the refineries and with the consuming industries. In the United States they have the world's largest users of copper within their own political boundaries, and enjoy for the time at least the advantages of a protective tariff. In these circumstances the competition for the remaining markets by the expanding low-cost producers can hardly fail to keep the price unremuneratively low for some years to come. In present conditions supplies far greater than can be needed would be forthcoming at £40 a ton and, apart from definite control of output, prices are not likely to rise much higher than this. At £40 a ton it is almost certainly not profitable to invest large sums of money in developing new properties. Until there is a fairly certain prospect of copper remaining above £40 a ton it is unlikely that those various projects will be carried to completion which were first planned with hopes of a consumption of 3,000,000 tons a year in a free market for copper at about £55 a ton.

As regards immediate prospects, then, it is likely that when trade recovers to a more normal condition the existing mines will find a fair market. There is reason to hope that Mufulira may be enabled to produce. It may be that at Nchanga some solution of the technical problems of recovering the rich mixed oxidised and sulphide ores will be found which will justify their exploitation. Rapid progress beyond that point must be regarded as unlikely in the present conditions of the market. Of the ultimate development of the area there can be little doubt; it is only the profit and likelihood of early expansion in this area which are in question.

If we assume that the probable output of the Northern Rhodesian mines during the next six or seven years is not likely to exceed 240,000 tons a year, what is likely to be the form and size of the industry? In particular, how many Native workers will be required to produce this? In the past large numbers have been employed in the mines. The following table shows the actual number of Native workers in employment at the end of each month in different years.[1]

	Natives employed on all Mines and Concessions. Actual Number at the End of each Month (approximate only).					
	1927.	1928.	1929.	1930.	1931.	1932.
January .	8,592	10,517	16,673	23,226	28,974	11,339
February .	8,395	10,234	15,500	24,224	25,643	10,093
March .	8,666	9,862	14,406	23,307	23,319	9,663
April .	8,421	9,100	15,697	22,981	22,074	8,623
May .	8,488	11,001	16,032	26,297	21,193	8,305
June .	8,698	11,229	16,568	25,473	19,966	8,095
July .	9,056	11,625	17,928	28,714	19,514	7,523
August .	10,131	11,807	19,050	31,023	19,771	..
September .	10,904	12,637	20,214	31,941	19,313	..
October .	11,849	13,637	20,743	31,283	16,645	..
November .	11,257	13,476	22,186	29,758	15,273	..
December .	10,946	16,073	22,341	29,689	13,261	..

Not all of these were employed in copper-mines. A figure varying from about 2500 in 1929 and 1930 to 750 in 1932 requires to be deducted for mines working other minerals. In the main, however, this table shows the variations in activity in the copper industry. It will be seen that employment increased steadily, with occasional set-backs due rather to the difficulties of recruitment than to a decline in demand, up to a maximum in September 1930. From the beginning of 1931 there has been a steady decline until less than one-quarter of the maximum were employed in July 1932. The explanation of this enormous change is to be found in the changed conditions at the mines themselves. In 1930 simultaneous development and constructional work was being undertaken by a number of mines. Labour was employed mostly upon tasks which once completed did not require repetition. Buildings were erected, machinery and head-gear installed. European townships and Native locations were cleared and laid out, roads

[1] These figures include all employees of the mining companies, but exclude servants, store-boys and others who are employed in the mining townships by private employers.

and water services created. In September 1930 only 13 per
cent of all Native labour was employed underground; by
July 1932 as much as 34 per cent of the Native labour was
underground.

The actual number of men required to operate even a
large copper-mine is comparatively small once construction is completed. No accurate estimate of the Native
labour supply required can be made unless it is known
exactly what tasks can be entrusted to Native workers.
This point must be considered later. For the moment it
will be assumed that present conditions will continue. In
August 1932 about 4600 men were employed in mines
actually producing copper. At that time their output was
equal to about a hundred tons of copper per month for
every eighty-two men employed. If we apply this ratio to
an assumed future output of 240,000 tons per annum, the
necessary Native labour force would be about 16,400 men.
But in fact it would not be necessary to increase all employees proportionately to a given increase of output.
One estimate would place the numbers required for full-
capacity working at only about fifty men per hundred tons
of copper per month. In that case the necessary number of
Native workers would not exceed 12,000. Perhaps a more
conservative estimate would put the labour strength of
producing copper-mines at about 14,000. To this must be
added some 2500 for mines other than copper, and the
number who may be employed at any time on construction
and development work. This latter number obviously
cannot be estimated with any accuracy. It will depend on
the growth of the market and on many other factors. But
it is unlikely that there will again be any such volume of
simultaneous construction as took place in 1930. Apart
from Kansanshi, the area is now controlled by two large
groups which will only expand their activities as circumstances permit and demand. Of the mines which are most
likely to be brought next into production a considerable
amount of the preliminary construction work is already
completed. If we assume that at any moment 3500 men

are so employed, our estimate is probably sufficiently
generous. This would give a total of between 18,000 and
20,000 employed at the mines when trade is flourishing.
With moderately good trade 12,000 would be a fair
estimate. These estimates fall very far below the figure of
employment in 1930. They fall still farther below the very
high figures which have been quoted in earlier discussions
of this problem. A Native labour strength as high as
60,000 to 65,000 had been suggested as being necessary
for such outputs as have been discussed, and even more
reasonable estimates have put the numbers necessary in
the near future at about 25,000 and in times of expansion
at 50,000. In the light of more recent events, even these
figures must be regarded as exaggerated.

Since any decisions of policy in the copper belt must
depend in considerable measure upon the numbers that will
be employed there, it will be useful to verify our conclusions so far as it is possible from the figures of the Union
Minière. In 1927 the Union Minière employed about 209
men per hundred tons of copper per month. By 1931 this
had been reduced to 109 men.[1] In 1932 with a very reduced
output the figure rose to 111 men. It is now said that, with
improved organisation and the increased output per man-
shift which has lately been achieved, no more than 6000
men would now be required for an output of about 120,000
tons per year, or about 60 men per hundred tons of copper
per month. This figure agrees very closely with the estimates which have been made for the Northern Rhodesian
area.

In conclusion it must be repeated that any long-period
forecast of developments in Northern Rhodesia must in the
very nature of things be uncertain. If we look beyond the
next few years, with which we have here been mainly concerned, the activity of the copper belt will be determined
largely by tariff policies and by political decisions which

[1] It must, however, be remembered that the copper yield of the ores
worked in 1927 was about 5 per cent and that in 1931 was over 9 per
cent.

are beyond our present powers to predict. If the consumption of copper expands in the way that the history of the past fifty years has led us to expect, and as the probable development of the copper-using industries gives us reason to hope, then Northern Rhodesia may well become the greatest copper producer in the world. Such changes have occurred before in the copper industry. For the first fifty years of the last century England was the world's largest copper producer, and turned out almost 40 per cent of the total production. By 1930 her share was negligible. For the years 1911 to 1914 the United States produced 56 per cent of the world's output. By 1930 her share had fallen to 40 per cent, and South America, Katanga and other producers were advancing. It is well within the bounds of possibility that Northern Rhodesia should take her turn as the leader of the world's copper industry, and offer employment to considerably greater numbers of Native workers than are at all likely to be required during the next few years.

CHAPTER X

THE ORGANISATION OF NATIVE MINE-WORKERS

IT has already been shown that the profitable commercial working of the Northern Rhodesian mines depends in large measure on the available supply of cheap and relatively efficient Native labour. We must next proceed to consider how this labour is recruited and organised. The responsibility in this matter rests in the main with the local officials of the companies. While certain broad lines of policy are established by the boards of directors, their interpretation is left to the men on the spot.

The possible sources of labour supply open to the Northern Rhodesian mines lie not only in the Territory itself but in the surrounding countries also. The Native when in search of work has never recognised political boundaries. Their recognition is sometimes forced upon him by Governments, but is not a matter of his own immediate thought, apart from the variations of treatment which political frontiers enclose. Unlike the European worker, he will travel distances which may be more than a thousand miles, and are frequently more than five hundred miles, to secure work of a type that he desires. But though Natives from other territories are often to be found at the mines of Northern Rhodesia, the great majority are, as has been shown in the previous section, derived from the Protectorate itself. Northern Rhodesia has for many years past afforded a recruiting ground for labour not only for work at the mines and in other employments within the country itself but also in the surrounding territories. The Congo mines were developed and worked in the early days largely by the labour of Natives derived from the Mweru-Luapula and Awemba provinces of Northern Rhodesia. In 1920 some 5500 Northern Rhodesian Natives were employed in the Katanga mines and they represented about 48 per cent of all Native workers employed. In 1921 they accounted for over 56 per cent. In Southern Rhodesia in 1920 some 24,000 Northern Rhodesian Natives were employed on mines, farms, railways and other work. In more recent years the numbers employed outside the Territory have declined somewhat, partly because motives of policy have led to a greater employment of local Natives, partly because the total volume of such employment has declined. But as late as 1930, when construction work at the mines in Northern Rhodesia was at its peak, it was estimated that as many as 38,056 Northern Rhodesian Natives were employed outside the Territory. The reason is not far to seek. Until motor-lorry transport became generally available it was necessary for Natives to travel on foot in search of work. To the Native of the East Luangwa province the mines of Southern Rhodesia were not only more familiar, but also more easily reached than those of their own territory. The Natives of the extreme north-east of the Territory have become accustomed to seek work in the sisal and cotton plantations in the neighbouring Tanganyika Territory.[1] The Natives of the west have preferred to travel south into South-West Africa rather than east to the railway belt. Though mine work in the Congo no longer required such large numbers of foreign labour as in earlier years, some 10,000 Northern Rhodesian Natives were still believed to be in employment in that country. And though recruiting for the Rand mines was not permitted north of the 22nd parallel of latitude, small numbers of Northern Rhodesian Natives found their way into employment, mostly as house-boys and store-boys, in Johannesburg.

Moreover, the volume of other employment in Northern Rhodesia itself is considerable. In 1930 the number of Natives employed at work other than mining was estimated at 48,639, of whom 10,883 were employed as agricultural wage-earners away from their own lands, 6808 on the railways and 12,470 in domestic service. Thus in

[1] *Annual Report upon Native Affairs, 1930*, p. 19.

that year, a boom year it is true, some 114,702 Natives were in wage-earning employment inside the Territory or outside of it. This, however, includes about 12,000 alien Natives working in Northern Rhodesia. If we exclude those, about 102,700 Natives of the Territory out of an estimated number of 276,386 able-bodied males, or some 37 per cent of the whole, were on average at any time during that year employed in wage-earning work, and the actual number of individuals who found employment at some time during the year was certainly considerably greater than this. The aggregate amount of work spread over all the able-bodied males was equal to an average of 3·6 months' work per man.

It will be evident from what has been said that Northern Rhodesia cannot for purposes of the supply of labour be regarded as a single separate economic unit divorced from its neighbours by rigid and seldom-passed frontiers. In this it differs wholly from the conditions of Europe. Labour so infrequently migrates, for example, from France to England that they can both be regarded for all working purposes as self-contained units. Northern Rhodesia, though a separate political unit, forms a single economic unit, so far as the supply of labour is concerned, with Southern Rhodesia, the Belgian Congo and Nyasaland. If wages or conditions are widely different in the different territories labour will be rapidly attracted or repelled. In this matter conditions rather than wages, and in particular feeding and health conditions, appear to play a predominant part. But though this unity is in many respects important it must not be exaggerated. The wages to be earned in any work so far exceed the possible earnings in the village that untrained labour can now usually be obtained in any quantity that is desired at any reasonable wage that may be offered. Shortages are the result rather of ignorance of possible opportunities than of a limited supply of willing workers. Wages can and do vary considerably within the group of adjacent territories without completely depriving low wage payers of all labour. But the more skilled, the better trained, the more enterprising workers will within the area move toward the places of highest opportunity.

For the present the group of adjacent countries that we have considered is divorced almost completely from the more southern areas. The Rand and Kimberley, the towns, farms, railways and workshops of the Union derive their labour almost exclusively from south of the 22nd parallel of latitude. The mines of the Witwatersrand draw mainly upon the territories of Basutoland, Bechuanaland, Swaziland, Zululand, the Transkei and Ciskei territories of the Cape Province and upon the parts of Portuguese East Africa south of the 22nd parallel. There is at present no important group which unifies the two systems by exercising a choice as to whether it shall work to the north or to the south. It has, however, been recently recommended that the restrictions imposed in 1913 on recruitment for the gold-mines north of the 22nd parallel be withdrawn.[1] The Mozambique Convention has resulted in the progressive diminution of the number of workers who may be recruited for the Rand mines in Portuguese East Africa, and thus seriously curtailed the possible area of recruitment.[2] As the efficient operation of the mines requires the certainty of an adequate labour supply, and as the numbers available in the Union and the Protectorates south of the 22nd parallel are not usually sufficient in years of good crops and satisfactory wool prices, Johannesburg is being forced to look to the North. Since Southern Rhodesia cannot supply her own needs, the demand for labour, if it comes, will fall mostly upon Nyasaland and Northern Rhodesia, and may have quite considerable effects upon the rates of wages paid for mine labour in Southern and Northern Rhodesia.

It has been said above that the Rhodesias, Nyasaland

[1] *Interim Report of the Low Grade Ore Commission, Union of South Africa.* U.G. 16, 1932.

[2] The Convention reduces the number who may be recruited from 100,000 in 1929 to a maximum of 80,000 in 1933. In 1931 only 54,076 Portuguese Natives were actually recruited locally on the Rand and in Portuguese territory.

and the Congo form naturally a single source of labour supply. The various political authorities have attempted artificially to break up this unity and to reserve for their own territories their own local workers. In the Congo, a labour-using area, the authorities of the Government and the Union Minière have created a policy of employment which has replaced the immigrant labour of Nyasaland and Northern Rhodesia by Natives recruited in the Kasai district of Katanga and from the distant mandated territory of Ruanda-Urundi. In 1921, as has already been seen, Northern Rhodesia supplied some 56 per cent of the labour force of the Union Minière. In 1931 the Northern Rhodesian share was only 0·7 per cent of the total, while the Congo supplied 66 per cent as compared with 38 per cent in the earlier year; Ruanda-Urundi supplied some 24 per cent, though none had been recruited there ten years before.[1] Nyasaland, a labour-supplying area, has made various attempts to limit the movement of Natives out of the Territory. Recruitment within the country itself was prohibited by the Employment of Natives Ordinance (1909). In debate on the Second Reading of that ordinance the Deputy Governor said that the labour needs of the Protectorate were the first consideration. The view that predominated in the council would appear to have been that, while they ought not to prevent men who themselves wished to go in search of work from leaving the Territory, they should not allow recruiters to denude the villages. The ordinance may have been successful in fulfilling this latter object, but it never succeeded in diminishing considerably the number of Nyasaland Natives working abroad. They have either found their own way to work, without the often valuable assistance of recruiters, or have allowed themselves to be recruited in the contiguous districts of Northern Rhodesia. In 1931 some 30,000 Nyasaland Natives, out of an estimated male population between the ages of seventeen and forty-five of 300,000, were working

[1] The remainder (approximately 9 per cent) came from Nyasaland and from Angola.

outside the Protectorate, chiefly in the Rhodesias and the Union of South Africa.

In the same way Northern Rhodesia, when the demand for labour at the mines increased, attempted to restrict the flow of labour out of the country. The agent who recruited labour for the Congo mines was informed that the number of men that he might recruit would be gradually reduced. The Rhodesian Native Labour Bureau, which recruited for Southern Rhodesian employers, was limited progressively to a much lower figure than the average of previous years. But these devices came too late to be of value to Northern Rhodesian mine-owners. In 1930 at the peak of construction they were not yet effective. By 1932 the depression had come and the supply of labour everywhere vastly exceeded the demand.

In these conditions of the labour market the mines were faced with the problem of securing adequate supplies of Native workers. From the beginning two methods of employment were used. In the first place Natives were engaged for work on a monthly basis at the mine itself. Secondly, recruiters were sent into the districts to persuade workers and to assist them to reach the mines. Since the costs of recruiting are considerable a more lengthy contract of service is necessary to yield an adequate return for the expenditure involved. In the early stages the mines recruited individually, and, as was inevitable, in competition to some extent with each other. Recruiters on occasion trespassed across that indefinite boundary which separates the crying up of one's own goods from the crying down of others. This state of affairs was unsatisfactory not only to the mines but also to the Government, and yielded no compensating advantage to the Native worker, and at the instigation of the Government the mines joined together in March 1930 to form the Native Labour Association. This takes the form of a private company whose shares are held by the various mining companies in proportion to their normal labour complement. With a single exception all the mining undertakings in

Northern Rhodesia, whether occupied in working copper or other minerals, are shareholders. The capital of the Association has been employed for the equipment of the offices and buildings necessary for the conduct of the work of the Association. It makes a charge to the mining company concerned of £5 for each recruit obtained. This covers the full expense of bringing the worker to the mine and providing him with the necessary food, blankets and clothing, including where necessary provision for his wife and family. The repatriation of the worker and his family at the end of his contract, which costs from thirty to forty shillings, according to the distance involved, is done at the expense of the mine concerned. If on any year's working the Association makes a profit, this is distributed to mines which have taken recruits during the year in proportion to the number taken. If a loss is incurred a call is made upon them in the same proportion to meet it.

In the early days of recruiting the period of service was ordinarily six tickets. From the middle of 1930 it has been for twelve tickets, each representing thirty days' labour. These normally take about thirteen months to complete. The recruited worker must sign a contract of service at the place of recruitment in the presence of the District Officer, declaring his willingness to enter the service of the Native Labour Association for work at whatever mine he may be sent to, under certain specified conditions of employment. These latter provide that his employment shall be subject to the conditions laid down by the Employment of Natives Ordinance (1929), that he shall be supplied with food while travelling and with rations while at work on a scale not less than that laid down in the Mining Regulations; that he shall be paid a certain rate of pay, which varies according to whether he volunteers for underground work or for surface work; that he may, if he wishes, be re-engaged for a period or periods of a month at the end of his service; finally, that he shall be repatriated to his district of origin at the end of his contract. It is required that he shall be examined by a Government medical officer. It has been

regarded as impossible to provide that Natives in the recruiting areas may be contracted definitely to individual
mines.[1] Popular mines, it is said, would be surfeited, the less
popular starved, and the Association would find its limited
accommodation packed to overflowing with recruits awaiting vacancies at some particular mine. The Association
does, nevertheless, do all that is in its power to send men to
the mines which they themselves would choose, well knowing that its own best recruiter is the satisfied repatriate.

In the initial stages the mines were more dependent upon
recruited than upon voluntary labour. As late as the last
quarter of 1930 the number of men recruited in the districts exceeded those who presented themselves unassisted
at the mine. But from the beginning of 1931 the supply of
voluntary labour began considerably to exceed that of
recruits. For the whole year 13,838 voluntary workers
were engaged as against 6086 recruits. As the total
number employed declined the need for recruiting diminished, until in October 1931 it ceased completely. For the
time being the Native Labour Association is concerned
solely with the repatriation of men who finish their
periods of contract or re-engagement. At the Roan Antelope
the average proportion of voluntary workers during 1931
was 68·8 per cent of the whole. Since October 1931 they
have represented, of course, a steadily increasing proportion, until by the end of 1932 all the remaining contracts
were finished[2] and all the workers were on a monthly
basis.

It would appear that the main function of the Native
Labour Association is now completed. It has been the
experience of other territories, and of individual mines in
Northern Rhodesia itself, of the Broken Hill mine in particular, that, once a firm connection has been established
with the labour supply areas by a system of recruitment,

[1] Such choice is, however, allowed farther south to Natives who are
recruited for the Rand gold-mines, and no insuperable difficulties have
been encountered in its operation.

[2] A considerable number of workers still, of course, retain their right
to repatriation under the original terms of their contract.

further supplies may be left to provide themselves. The Native Labour Committee of Enquiry in Southern Rhodesia found that workers preferred to come down independently. "It is evident to your Committee that it is the intense desire of these labourers to choose their own master and arrange their own terms of service, and as the northern Natives gather knowledge of the country and its conditions, and by work become more efficient, they determine to act for themselves."[1] Neither the Broken Hill mine nor the Globe and Phoenix gold-mine in Southern Rhodesia, a large proportion of whose employees are from Northern Rhodesia, found it necessary to recruit workers even during the boom of 1930. It is the opinion of the majority of location managers that in any likely expansion of activity an adequate labour supply will quickly be obtained without recourse to recruiting. In some cases the mine is working short time, and full-time working will increase output without addition to the labour supply. In other cases there is maintained in the location itself a small reserve of Natives who are seeking work. In the copper belt there are said to be a number of unemployed workers living with their relations and friends who were estimated by one location manager to amount in October 1932 to almost a thousand.

The Native worker, when he has been recruited or selected, requires training for the work to be performed. In both the mines at present working in the copper belt provision is made for some elementary training on the surface before the man undertakes regular underground work. He is trained to use the various implements. At Nkana, for example, a complete dummy working-place of concrete exists in which he is taught to use a drill. He is taught also the English names of all the tools ordinarily in use, and is given some elementary instruction in safety regulations and precautions and first aid. After some days in this school he is drafted to his normal work.

[1] *Report of Native Labour Committee of Enquiry, Southern Rhodesia, 1921.*

The mines ordinarily work two shifts each day underground and three on the surface. The main tasks of the Native workers lie in the mining of the ore, and in a mine working in normal conditions considerably more than half of the Native labour force would be employed underground. If we take an individual day in September 1932, there were 2594 men actually working on that day at the Nkana mine. Of these 1445 were employed underground. Of the remainder 502 were employed on certain administrative duties, including 230 in the location and 118 on sanitation. On engineering duties 261 were engaged, of whom 183 were in the workshops. Only some 389 Natives were employed in the routine production of copper on the surface, made up of 151 working at the concentrator, 34 at the power plant and 204 at the smelter. No one who sees the actual production of copper from the ore can fail to be impressed by the automatism of the process. The mined ore is raised at the shaft and the tubs are tilted into bins. The ore falls automatically into crushers. It is carried by endless belts to further crushers and mills. The fine material is carried in a stream of water and still further reduced in size. When it has reached the necessary fineness it is pumped to the flotation tanks. The mineral, now some 50 per cent pure, is entrapped in an oily froth; the waste is carried off. The concentrates are pumped to a dryer and carried thence on a belt to the reserve bins or to the smelter. From first to last there is no labour involved other than that necessary to secure that accidental interruptions shall not arrest the continuity. There is no task here for Native labour except the oiling of machinery and the poling out of temporary blockages; some fifty men on each shift suffice with the European supervisors to keep the whole process in operation. For the smelter and convertor, and for the casting of the final blister copper, somewhat greater numbers are required, but they are small as compared with the numbers engaged in mining operations.

Underground two shifts are worked. At the Roan Antelope mine the day shift is from 7.30 A.M. to 3.30 P.M., the

night shift from 7 P.M. until the work is finished, usually
between 3 and 4 A.M. The day shift does all the drilling,
charging up and blasting. The night shift extracts the ore
from the stopes and clears away all the waste rock in
development work. Of the two the day shift is considerably
the larger. On one given day, for example, the day shift
consisted of 45 Europeans and 550 Natives, the night
shift of 13 Europeans and 144 Natives. The work of
mining is carried on in stopes. These are large rock-
chambers, inclined according to the dip of the ore-bearing
stratum, which reach a final width of some seventy feet
and run downwards from one haulage level to the next.
Each stope is separated from its neighbour by a pillar of
unmined ore some fifteen feet thick. In the stopes there is
a European miner in charge who may be responsible for
two or three faces. The European miner will have under
him one or more Native boss boys and some sixteen
Native workers. These will be organised on the day shift
into drill crews, each of four boys, who work a pneumatic
drill. One boy in each drill crew is the senior and is responsible for his crew. The Native boss boy exercises general
control under the miner, helps to see that the work is
properly done and the regulations are enforced, and occasionally acts for new workers as interpreter of the miner's
orders. Both on the day shift and on the night shift there
is a certain task to be performed. On the day shift so many
holes must be drilled. When the task is satisfactorily performed the crew is free to leave the mine. Similarly, on the
night shift when the task of removing the necessary quantity of rock is completed the worker may go. A keen
worker will often finish his task in six hours or less.

The hours of work in mines in Northern Rhodesia are
limited by the Employment of Natives Regulations (1931),
made under the powers conferred by the Employment of
Natives Ordinance (1929). The regulations require that
"Wherever it is reasonably possible all Natives employed
on mines and works shall be given at least 24 consecutive
hours' rest in one week; where Natives are employed on

shift work they shall not work for a longer shift than 8 hours, provided that in any prosecution for a contravention of this regulation the onus shall be on the employer to prove that it was not reasonably possible to provide the minimum prescribed by this regulation." In practice the mines are closed regularly on Sundays, and during the depression have on occasion worked only eleven days or less in the fortnight.

The Government, through the Department of Mines, is responsible also for the issue and enforcement of the necessary regulations governing the safety of mine-workers and the conditions of mining. In the last few years a most complete series of regulations have been drawn up and put into force, and in this respect the Territory has gone considerably farther than has Southern Rhodesia. In the latter country the Government has been satisfied to leave the mining companies to secure the safety of their employees by whatever regulations they might individually consider most satisfactory, inquiring carefully, nevertheless, into the causes of any accident and holding officials responsible rather for the results of their policies than for adherence to Government-made rules.

In 1931 there were in the Northern Rhodesian mines 42 fatal accidents and 205 serious accidents, and the death-rate from accidents and the accident rate per 1000 employed both on the surface and below ground were 1·80 and 8·80 respectively. These rates compare favourably at first sight with those for the Union of South Africa. The death-rate per 1000 from accidents in the Witwatersrand gold-mines in 1931 was 2·35. But, quite apart from the added risks in the latter area from the great depths at which mining is carried on, if comparison is made only of the rates below ground it is far less favourable to Northern Rhodesia. In the gold-mines the rate below ground in 1931 was 2·97 per 1000; in Northern Rhodesia it was as high as 6·05 per 1000 below ground. This figure was quite considerably greater than those for 1929 and 1930, which were 4·3 and 3·6 per 1000 respectively. Where the absolute numbers involved are comparatively small, some such yearly variation is only to be expected, but the authorities concerned have given increased attention to the problem of accident prevention. The causes of accidents have been analysed as follows:

CAUSES OF ACCIDENTS, 1931

	Fatal.	Serious.	Total.
	Per Cent.	Per Cent.	
Falling material . . .	4·76	14·66	12·96
Falls in shafts and raises . .	21·43	8·76	10·94
Fall of rock	19·07	14·16	15·00
Machinery	7·14	14·66	13·36
Electrical	4·76	0·49	1·22
Trucks	7·14	13·16	12·15
Other causes	8·53	25·82	23·05
Explosives	26·17	8·29	11·32

It will be noticed that accidents due to explosives account for more than a quarter of all the fatal accidents. The regulations governing the use of explosives have recently been revised and the new regulations came into force in October 1931. The majority of the accidents attributed to explosives are in fact due to the fumes caused by the explosion. Workers who have returned too soon, or have delayed in leaving a stope after lighting up, have been overtaken by the fumes and gassed. Every attempt is being made to reduce the possibility of further accidents of this sort. The Secretary for Mines possesses the power of insisting where necessary on improved ventilation and the abandonment of dangerous and defective practices. The Inspector of Mines attends any inquest on the victim of an accident and the causes are most carefully considered. But apart from Government regulations the mines themselves are concerned to do everything in their power to reduce accidents to the minimum. Their own safety regulations are in several respects more strict than those imposed upon them by Government. The training in first aid has reached an astonishingly high standard of efficiency. At the Roan Antelope mine all boss boys are trained in first-aid work.

They learn to diagnose the more likely fractures and to handle men who are suffering from such accidents, from gassing, or from electrocution. A very similar training is given to all candidates for blasting certificates at Nkana.

The use of explosives is limited to men who are in the possession of blasting certificates. These certificates are in no way confined to European workers. At no point in the regulations is any distinction other than that of competence introduced. On September 26, 1932, there were 328 blasting certificates in all outstanding, of which 89 had been issued to Natives. The majority of these have been issued to Natives employed at the Nkana mine, which has encouraged its workers to secure certificates. A school is provided at that mine in which candidates for the certificate receive a training. While the management and supervision of the school is in the hands of a European expert, a considerable part of the actual teaching is carried on by a remarkably competent Nyasaland Native instructor. It is necessary for the candidates to be familiar with the practical handling of explosives, the regulations governing their use, as well as the elementary principles of first aid. The examination of candidates is conducted by one of the inspectors of mines, and exactly the same standards are required of Natives as of Europeans. It is by no means a simple and straightforward test. The examiner makes deliberate attempts to trap his candidate, and to be successful a candidate must possess a very thorough knowledge of his work and of the regulations, and the power to see that the latter are being enforced in every detail.

Though the regulations permit Natives to use explosives, the larger mines in practice insist on all charging and shot-firing being done under the direction and supervision of European miners, and the comparatively high death-rate from explosive accidents is not a consequence of the careless and ill-controlled handling of explosives by Native workers.

The payment of Native workers in the copper belt is for

the moment almost entirely on a fixed daily basis. Until
recently underground workers were paid 30s. for a ticket
of thirty days and surface workers 17s. 6d. for a ticket.
These rates were increased at intervals when the worker
proved himself efficient. Owing to the depression in the
industry, and the competition for the work, the rate has
lately been reduced for all new workers taken on by 5s. a
ticket. This reduction does not apply to workers already
employed at the higher rate. A recruited worker who continues beyond the end of his contract period goes on at his
finishing rate of pay. Natives doing special work receive,
of course, special rates of pay. Locomotive drivers underground get from 1s. 4d. to 1s. 10d. a day. For sharpening
drills Natives receive from 1s. 4d. up to, in one or two cases,
2s. 4d. a day. A few Native carpenters are earning as much
as 4s. a day, individual transport drivers 2s. 8d. a day.

Some attempt is now being made at Nkana to devise a
system of payment by the piece, which will probably take
the form of a standard daily rate for a given task with a
bonus for excess over the task. In some other cases in surface excavation work a task has been set which must be
completed in order to earn the day's pay. On completion of
the task the worker has been allowed to undertake a second
task and has been paid proportionately more for the extra
work, which is in most respects the equivalent of piece-
work. It must be remembered that most tasks have only
recently, since the end of construction and development, become sufficiently standardised to be made easily amenable
to piece-work. It is said, moreover, that in the majority
of cases the Native worker prefers the additional freedom
and leisure that he is now given on the completion of his
task to the additional income which he might earn under a
piece-work system. For overtime a Native worker is paid
in addition to his ordinary day's wage an extra amount
proportionate to the extra time. For an extra four hours,
that is, he gets an additional half-shift's pay at the standard rate.

It is difficult to make any satisfactory comparison of

earnings with those of other areas for two reasons. Firstly, money wages form only a part of the total remuneration of the worker; secondly, the monetary units in which wage comparisons must be made are extremely fluctuating, and no accurate measurement of local purchasing power exists. In Northern Rhodesia expenditure on feeding, housing, medical attendance and other forms of welfare considerably exceeds direct wages. At the Roan Antelope mine the average wage per shift was, in August 1932, 1·01s., whereas the cost of compound maintenance, food, welfare and repatriation added a further 1·32s. for each effective shift worked, making the average labour cost 2·33s. per shift. In the Union Minière, where the average wage is 11 francs, the cost of social services amounts to about a further 15 francs. The proportion between wage and social services is in each case about the same. In the Witwatersrand gold-mines the average earnings in 1931 were 2·25s. per shift, and the additional cost of quarters and food was estimated at 0·85s. per shift worked.   That is, in the gold-mines wages were considerably higher, and social services somewhat less, even when allowance is made for currency differences, than in the North.

It is of more interest to compare the labour costs of the Northern Rhodesian copper-mines with those of other copper-producing areas. Mining costs vary, of course, enormously with local conditions. Some ores can be exposed by stripping and then mined at very low cost. Others must be worked by cutting the ore underground and then filling into trucks. Thus the Utah Copper Company had in 1929 a mining cost of $0·504 per ton of ore stripped to the mills, of which about half was the cost of the preliminary stripping.[1] In mines which are operated by methods more closely similar to those of Northern Rhodesia mining costs vary from about $2·50 per ton of ore to $4·50 per ton. Thus the Champion mine had a mining cost of $2·528 and the Magna mine one of $4·416.[2] The mining cost of the Roan Antelope

[1] *Mineral Industry in 1929*, p. 120.
[2] See *Information Circulars* of the United States Bureau of Mines,

mine for the ten months of the accounting year 1931–32 was on average 4·58s.[1] For more recent months the cost has been further reduced,[2] and in April 1932 was 3·24s. per ton.[3] These results are considerably better than the original estimate of the cost of mining, which had provided for a cost of 7·25s. per ton. It is thus evident that the Northern Rhodesian mines have the double advantage of low mining costs per ton of ore mined, and of a high grade of ore which diminishes the tonnage of ore which requires to be mined for a given output of finished copper.

The Northern Rhodesian mines have been operating on a production basis for such a short time that any attempt to measure the ultimate level of efficiency of the Native worker is bound to be premature. The workers in the mines had few of them the advantage of any experience before they came to work in Northern Rhodesia. A certain number had worked in the mines of Southern Rhodesia, and when in the early days there was a shortage of underground workers, special efforts were made for a time to recruit in Southern Rhodesia the necessary number of Northern Rhodesian Natives. Others had experience in the Katanga mines, but whereas the recruiting for the Congo was mainly in the Fort Rosebery area, the recruiting for the Northern Rhodesian mines was in the areas farther east. The vast majority of workers were thus completely untrained. During the construction period living conditions, for European and Native alike, were difficult. It must not be forgotten that the copper-mines under construction were forty miles or more from the main railway line at Ndola, that in the early stages the present railway branches were not in existence, that unmetalled roads, with the heavy traffic of construction to carry, rapidly

Nos. 6515 and 6168, also *Engineering and Mining Journal* (New York), October 1932, article by M. J. Elsing.

[1] *Annual Report, No. 5, Roan Antelope Copper Mines, 1932.*

[2] *Engineering and Mining Journal* (New York), November 1932, article by R. M. Peterson (of the Roan Antelope Company).

[3] At $4·86 = £1; 4·58s. = $1·10; 3·24s. = $0·788.

At $3·42 = £1; 4·58s. = $0·73; 3·24s. = $0·53.

deteriorated. Food supplies were difficult to organise; fresh milk, fresh vegetables, fresh fruit and all the minor amenities of life were usually unobtainable. The work itself was severe and constantly changing. Unaccustomed tasks had to be performed with the utmost possible expedition, frequently under trying conditions of heat or of rain. Heavy pieces of metal had to be handled in a sun which made them scorching to the touch. Inevitably in such conditions the weaker men found themselves exhausted and dispirited. As inevitably the explanation of constantly changing requirements in an imperfectly known language, and in conditions which might fray the mildest temper, led to difficulties between the European in charge and his team.

During the period of construction desertions were numerous, and the causes not far to seek. The atmosphere of construction was one of hard men living hard. To apply to this heroic phase the sober canons of judgment of a workaday existence is to misunderstand it completely. In Northern Rhodesia this phase was completed, so far as the two operating mines were concerned, in March of 1932. Routine production is of a very different type. As has already been explained, individual workers are specialised on individual tasks, which they perform regularly day after day. The mechanical processes involved are familiar to all concerned. The names of the tools in regular use are known. The worker can understand immediately what is required of him, and even if his boss's attempts to speak a Native language do not conform to the strictest standards of grammatical constructions, he has learned to interpret for himself the meaning that lies behind familiar idioms.

It is the opinion of mine officials, whose experience in the South enables them to judge, that the Northern Rhodesian Native is now almost, if not wholly, equal in efficiency to the average worker in Rand mines. His efficiency is steadily increasing. At the Roan Antelope mine, for example, output per man-shift has increased very considerably since stoping began in June 1931. The following figures show the improvement:

OUTPUT PER NATIVE MAN-SHIFT BELOW GROUND

		Short Tons.	Per Cent.
July	1931 . . .	1·5	100
November	1931 . . .	3·3	220
May	1932 . . .	5·1	340
July	1932 . . .	4·7	313

The lower figure in July than in May 1932 is accounted for by a reduction in the output of the mine, which necessarily diminished efficiency. While part of this increase must be ascribed to improved organisation and underground management, to the stabilisation of working conditions, and an increase in the proportion of productive work, a large part is certainly due to the increased efficiency of work on the part of the Natives engaged in underground work. It is interesting to find that a very similar improvement has occurred in the Katanga mines. There the policy of stabilisation which was put into effect in December 1927 has led to progressively increasing output. For the Kipushi mine the following figures show the percentage change in output calculated on the basis of the cubic metres of ore extracted per man-shift.[1]

OUTPUT PER MAN-SHIFT—KIPUSHI MINE

Year .	1927	1928	1929	1930	1931	1932 (1st qtr.)	1932 (3rd qtr.)
Per Cent	100	132	104	149	160	198	260

These figures show clearly the advantage which is to be

[1] Dr. Mottoulle of the Union Minière has commented on these figures as follows:

(a) *On est prié de remarquer cette chute du rendement de la main-d'œuvre indigène en 1929 qui ne fait que confirmer les bons résultats de la stabilisation, car cette chute est due à la suppression dans les chantiers en question des anciens travailleurs Rhodésiens et à leur remplacement par une main-d'œuvre nouvelle non encore entraînée.*

(b) *Si une petite partie du meilleur rendement signalé ci-dessus peut être attribué au perfectionnement des procédés industriels d'exploitation, la grosse part en revient néanmoins à l'amélioration de la valeur professionnelle de la main-d'œuvre indigène.*

The very considerable increase during 1932 he attributes partly to the regular process of improvement, partly to a careful selection of the most competent workers for retention during a period of retrenchment.

secured by the stabilisation of a labour force and by special-isation of workers on particular jobs. In the Katanga mines this policy has been in operation for five years, and so far as concerns the efficiency of work it has been completely justified. Under the old system of short contracts (the con-tract in Katanga for Northern Rhodesian Natives was of six months only) the Native worker had barely begun to reach a stage of physical and technical efficiency before he left on the expiration of his period of service. While the constant change of staff was to the advantage of the Native, in that it secured for large numbers a certain measure of training, it was costly and unsatisfactory to the Union Minière.

The Union Minière has sought to secure the stabilisation of its labour force and the increased period of service by insisting upon a three-years contract. This method is in the particular circumstances of the country probably the most satisfactory. Stabilisation in the Belgian Congo has gone hand in hand with the development of indigenous sources of labour supply. Whereas in 1921 only 38·1 per cent of the workers came from Belgian territory, in 1931 89·7 per cent were derived either from the Congo or the Mandated Territory of Ruanda-Urundi. The extra expenses involved in recruitment, the transport of whole families, their acclimatisation and training could only be faced if a suffi-cient security for long service were obtained.[1] The Northern Rhodesian mines are aiming at stabilisation by a different method. They are content that contracts with "voluntary" workers shall be for one month only. They seek to retain

[1] The Union Minière has calculated that the cost of recruiting a man varies from 2700 francs to 3000 francs according to the distance from which he is brought. By the time that he is acclimatised, trained and stabilised his capital cost amounts to about 12,000 francs, since for each stabilised worker some three men require to be recruited. The Company has a most interesting accounting arrangement whereby a department is charged 1000 francs for each Native worker who may die from any cause whatsoever, up to a death-rate for the department of twenty per thousand, and 5000 francs for each Native worker who may die in excess of that death-rate. Thus departmental heads who wish to show the best results are given an added incentive to safeguard the health and working conditions of all their labour.

their workers not by a long-binding contract, which may
well prove irksome before it is completed, but by providing
conditions and attractions which will induce workers to
remain for the longest possible time. It has already been
shown that workers at Broken Hill and at Wankie have
remained for very long periods on a similar monthly basis,
and the copper-mines have every reason to expect equally
long periods of service from their workers. There is no
industrial disease, comparable to the phthisis of the gold-
mines, which makes an occasional holiday from mining
desirable, and the gradually increasing average period of
service shows that workers, since the beginning of routine
production, have preferred to remain for long periods. At
the Roan Antelope mine the average period of service [1] of
all Natives who were actually in employment at August 1,
1931, was 6·6 months. By February 17, 1932, the average
period of service had already increased to 11·9 months.[2]
Thus the Northern Rhodesian mines, while adhering to the
short period contract, are aiming at stabilisation of their
workers by the same methods by which in other countries
manufacturers have sought to reduce their labour turnover, and in particular by creating conditions which will
make the worker remain of his own volition and apart from
any contract.

While from the point of view of efficiency and from that
of the social and living conditions of the workers the arguments in favour of the stabilisation of the industrial working force are overwhelmingly strong, there is a danger
which must be considered and faced. The copper-mines,
unlike the gold-mines in the South, are liable to extreme

---

[1] The average period of service of all workers in employment at any
moment must be distinguished from the average length of service of
workers who may leave employment during some period. The latter
figure is likely to be very considerably larger than the former, which
includes many individuals whose service has only recently begun.

[2] These figures are obtained by taking the actual periods that all
workers have been in employment at some given date and averaging
them. If workers were arriving and leaving at a steady rate, the period
of completed service at leaving would be twice the average period that
all men had been in employment at any one moment.

fluctuations of activity. The world output of 1921 was barely 38 per cent of that of 1917; the output of 1932 has been only some 47 per cent of that of 1929. There cannot fail to be similar variations in the future. The world is far from having achieved such control over industrial fluctuations that we should be justified in building upon their future disappearance. The variation here is bigger than that which most industries in Europe, even in the depression of the last few years, have been forced to undergo.

The average working force of the Union Minière has declined from 17,257 in 1929 to 3758 at July 1, 1932. The numbers employed in mines in Northern Rhodesia have declined from a peak of 31,941 in September 1930 to 7523 in July 1932. Despite a reduction of 78 per cent in the former and 76 per cent in the latter case, the suffering of displaced workers cannot be described as severe. There have been cases of real hardship, cases where individuals have found readjustment to the old conditions difficult. But the great majority have returned quietly to their villages and have fallen back into the old habits of their agricultural life. They have cut their gardens and grown their crops as if the interruption of the mining adventure had never occurred.

That is possible in this generation, because almost without exception the mine-workers have been brought up in a village and have learned the everyday tasks of agriculture from their childhood. Will it be possible in the next generation? Already in a Union Minière location has been born the first child of a father and mother brought up themselves under the supervision of the company. There are many children in Katanga, and a few already in Rhodesia, who have known no other life than that of the mine. They are the forerunners of an industrial population with the strength of those who have been brought up to the activities of an industrial life, but with the weakness of those who have no alternative open to them. At the mines, with good food, good sanitary conditions and expert medical attention, infant mortality has been reduced to a small fraction of its former level. The rate of increase is almost certainly greater than elsewhere, but even in the rest of the Territory population increased by some 36 per cent between 1921 and 1931. Unless the expansion of the mines and of other urban industry, is to be very rapid, the absorption of the town-born children must prove increasingly difficult. Northern Rhodesia is less well equipped than almost any other country to carry a load of unemployment.

We must recognise that we are here brought face to face with a conflict between two incompatible objectives. Stabilisation will give us the opportunity on the industrial side of securing far greater efficiency, on the human side of making possible the growth of a stable society with all the advantages of family life, of a permanently raised standard of living, of education and outlook. But these gains must be bought by exposing the stabilised population to very great risks of unemployment which it will become progressively less fitted to face. Northern Rhodesia has few other industries which could absorb men who are unemployed in the copper-mines. Those which it has are so dependent upon the copper industry and upon the earnings in the copper industry that they are likely to be depressed when it is depressed. Unless the unemployed are fitted to return to agricultural work they must be maintained either by their friends or by the Government and the industry. Stabilisation in its completest form is a grave risk unless the Territory is prepared at each succeeding depression to carry more of the responsibility for those who have become urbanised. If, nevertheless, we are prepared for its obvious advantages to advocate stabilisation and the complete severance of the urban worker from the land, we must also be prepared to propound plans to deal with unemployment when it next returns. But until it is possible to make such provision it is important that every bond of unity between town and country shall be maintained.

CHAPTER XI

THE development of the Northern Rhodesian mines has affected the economic situation of the country in various ways. In the first place, by greatly increasing the demand for labour it has accelerated the process of transition to a wage-earning economy. It has speeded up the growth of the urban, capitalistic, economic organisation and has brought it into stronger contrast with the self-sufficient, communistic, rural existence. In the second place, life in the mine location has for many men and their families developed new tastes and habits of life which even upon return to their homes they have not wholly abandoned. In particular they have grown to demand imported products, clothes, cottons and many other things. In the previous section of this report some light has been thrown on the various ways in which wages have been spent. Wages on the mine represent, as was there pointed out, a surplus above living expenses, pocket money which may be spent as the individual sees fit. It is impossible to estimate with accuracy the total volume of wages paid in the Territory, but from such information as is available it may be said that somewhere about £900,000 was earned in 1931 by Natives working inside and outside the Territory, of which about £250,000 was earned on the mines. From the point of view of the balance of the trade of Northern Rhodesia it is important to know more about the expenditure of these earnings. An estimate has been made of the expenditure of Natives working at the Roan Antelope mine by one who is well situated to obtain the most accurate results which in the circumstances are possible. He has estimated that a total of wages which amounted in 1931 to approximately £100,000 was spent in the following way:

Spent on Native trade-goods	£56,000
Beer-hall	12,820
Eating-house	3,650
Bakers, shoemakers, fish, tobacco, etc. . .	3,730
Taxes, licences, fines, etc., at Luanshya[1] . .	2,800
Remitted through post	4,000
Silver hoarded or taken out of area . . .	15,000
Unaccounted for	2,000
	£100,000

The first figure is exclusively composed of imported goods. All locally produced goods are included in the fourth figure. It will be seen that, so far as may be judged from these figures, about 56 per cent was spent on imports, 44 per cent on local produce, on taxation and saving. About 13 per cent was spent on drink,[2] and approximately 20 per cent in all on immediately consumable goods. The amount by which the recruiting areas might be said to benefit is measured by remittances and money taken out of the mining area (about 19 per cent) by taxes paid (about 3 per cent) and by the proportion of the Native trade-goods which are ultimately brought back. If this were no more than half of the purchases they will have benefited to the extent of 50 per cent of the total sum paid in wages.

It was suggested in an earlier chapter[3] that with the development of industry and of international trade on a considerable scale a new problem of the balance of payments had arisen. The time has now come to examine this question more closely and to consider how Northern Rhodesia is able to pay for the volume of imports which both Natives and Europeans demand. Unfortunately, there are many obstacles to such an inquiry. None of the statistics of the Territory have been collected with this object in view, and few of them are in such form as to facilitate it.

---

[1] The tax office was open only for two months in that year.

[2] This is, of course, 13 per cent of the cash wage. It is equal to about 5½ per cent of the total wage, including food, housing, and other services provided. A later calculation for the same township puts expenditure on drink at 18 per cent of the total of cash wages, or about 7½ per cent of the inclusive wage.

[3] See pp. 132-6.

As at present organised, the statistics of imports into Northern Rhodesia divide all imports into four groups: goods from countries outside British South Africa imported via the Union; goods from countries outside British South Africa imported via Beira; goods removed under customs agreement from the Union; goods removed under customs agreement from Southern Rhodesia. Since customs are collected on the value free-on-board at the port of shipment the first two groups, the direct imports, are valued in that way. Under the customs agreements, on the other hand, Northern Rhodesia is credited with the tax on goods which have broken bulk in the Union and in Southern Rhodesia and have been forwarded to Northern Rhodesia. The adjustment is made by applying certain factors to the cost, free-on-rail at the station of shipment, calculating thus the original cost free-on-board, which is the basis of the tax calculation. For the second two groups, therefore, the values are those free-on-rail at the station of shipment. Thus none of the values published indicate the sum which is paid by an importer in Northern Rhodesia for the goods delivered in Northern Rhodesia. Some include, others exclude, tax paid ultimately to the Northern Rhodesian Government. All exclude a certain quantity of transport service, some the whole cost of transport from Europe, America or Japan. The total reached by the addition of these dissimilar calculations is meaningless from the point of view of any comparison of imports and exports. An attempt has been made to adjust these figures with the assistance of information from the Customs Department, the African Lakes Corporation and the rate-book of the Rhodesian and Mashonaland Railway Company. The calculation itself is too complicated and not of sufficient interest to reproduce here. The final figure is included in the subsequent table. A further difficulty is concerned with the valuation of exports. The capital of the copper companies is owned only to an insignificant extent in Northern Rhodesia itself. If the exports are valued at the selling price in Europe, allowance must be made for transport costs and for dividend payments abroad. It is more convenient to value exports at cost, which represents the amount remitted by the copper companies to Northern Rhodesia. In the second calculation that follows copper has been valued at £17·5 per ton, which is approximately cost on rail at the copper-mine and half the transport cost to Beira. This may be taken to be the value of exported copper at the Northern Rhodesian frontier.

The following table is an attempt to construct a balance of the payments to and from Northern Rhodesia in 1931:

BALANCE OF PAYMENTS, 1931

£ (thousands)

Imports . . .	5988	Exports . . .		989
Imports of specie . .	12	Re-exports . . .		191
Pensions, leave pay, etc..	150	Exports of specie . .		22
Home remittances . .	180	Re-exports of specie .		8
Payments abroad for services and interest .	950	Remittances of missions, tourists and interest .		80
Interest on Government debt and other payments . . .	45	Government borrowing .		565
		Private investment .		5470
	7325			7325

It must be emphasised that few of the figures here included are much more than intelligent guesses. They indicate the order of magnitude of the figures involved, but no undue reliance must be placed upon them. It will be seen that of the payments made in that year some 82 per cent were the result of borrowings. But obviously these borrowings were directly accountable for a considerable proportion of the actual imports. During 1931, in addition to heavy investment by the mining companies, there was also a considerable investment by the railways, and by other undertakings such as shops, stores, cinemas and hotels, as well as in the building of houses.

The imports for 1931 may be divided roughly as follows:

	£ (thousands)
Consumption goods, European .	2600
„ „ Native . .	400
Industrial stores and constructional goods	3000
	———
	6000

The exports for 1931 may be divided as follows:

	£ (thousands)
Copper	505
Zinc	201
Vanadium	92
Gold	35
	———
Total of all minerals . .	833
Total of all other exports .	156
	———
	989

In many ways the year 1931 was abnormal.[1] The investment in the copper-mines was at its height, and the Government was also borrowing for the building of the new
capital and for other purposes. A very large proportion of
the £3,000,000 of industrial stores and constructional goods
was material directly imported for the construction of the
plants and townships of the mines. While the situation in
1931 is of interest in showing the approximate balance as it
has been in the immediate past, it gives little indication of
what may be expected under more normal conditions. In
order to attempt to do this a second calculation has been
made. It has been assumed that imports of constructional
goods have ceased. It has been assumed that European
consumption has been diminished in the proportion in
which the European population has declined and that
Native consumption has declined proportionately to the
decline in wages. The resulting total of imports is about
equal to the figure for 1928 if the latter is corrected to give
the values of goods at the Northern Rhodesian frontier. On
the exports side the value of copper has been increased to

[1] In 1932, with investment much reduced, the situation was far less
satisfactory.

that which would result from the sale of 200,000 tons.
Other figures have been adjusted in accordance with the
estimates of the Finance Commission of 1932. The result
is a balance for a hypothetical post-depression normal year.

BALANCE OF PAYMENTS: NORMAL YEAR
£ (thousands)

Imports . . .	2800	Exports . . .	4200
Pension and leave pay .	150	Re-exports . . .	100
Payments abroad for ser-		Remittances of missions,	
vices and interest .	900	tourists, interest, etc.	80
Home remittances . .	160		
Interest on Public Debt .	80		
Total .	4090		
Credit available for added			
imports . . .	290		
	4380		4380

The total balance available to finance imports in such a
year would be about £3,100,000. This should suffice in present conditions to meet the expenditure of the European
population, the necessary recurrent expenditure on industrial stores, and a Native expenditure on imported goods
at a rate equivalent to that of 1931. Thus if we can assume
that copper exports will be at least 200,000 tons in a normal year, the problem of paying for the imports of European products should not create any very urgent difficulty.
But Northern Rhodesia will be acutely susceptible to those
risks and fluctuations from which single-product or few-
product countries are liable to suffer. In the recent depression Brazil, Australia and other countries which depend
largely upon a single export have been among the first to
encounter difficulties. In the assumed normal year minerals
account for 94 per cent of all exports. For this reason,
therefore, it is desirable to do everything possible to foster
alternative exports. On the other hand, there is valid
reason to doubt the frequently expressed argument that it
is necessary, if Northern Rhodesia is to import European
goods, that crops and other products shall be found which

can be sold on the world market. In normal conditions of the copper market the copper exports should suffice.

The foregoing calculation would appear to suggest that the problem of the payment for the imports of the country will not in normal times prove unduly difficult. If, as may be reasonably hoped, the copper industry steadily expands, the means of purchase abroad will develop, in all probability, sufficiently fast to satisfy the demands of the population. But a second and more obstinate problem remains. It is not only necessary for the Territory as a whole to pay for its total imports, it is necessary also for the rural areas to pay the urban areas for the goods which they receive from them. For this a balance of payments between the country and the town is necessary. If, as is at present the case, the people in the country areas are under-employed and wish to purchase more imported goods, they can offer in exchange either their products or their labour. At present for lack of suitable products they are forced to offer labour, and this fact is having unsatisfactory reactions upon their social and political life and organisation. Moreover, the absence of the men is possible for a year or two without the complete collapse of the present agricultural system, but more protracted absence becomes progressively more dangerous.

In the case of the foreign trade of the Territory, while accurate statistics were not to be had, sufficient information was at hand to give us some idea of the order of magnitude of the figures involved. In the case of the internal trade even that degree of accuracy is impossible. But a few figures are available which may give us some idea of the size of the quantities involved. In 1931 the number of Natives at work inside and outside the Territory was estimated at 110,108.[1] Their total earnings will have been approximately £900,000. The most reasonable estimate that we can make is that about one-fifth of this,[2] or £180,000, was taken back in the form of cash, about £250,000 in

[1] This includes some 10,000 Natives from outside Northern Rhodesia who were working in the Territory.   [2] Compare p. 179.

the form of goods, and about £50,000 in the form of tax receipts, making about £480,000 in all. We may regard this last figure as an approximation to the value of the export of labour to the towns and mines and to the European farms and plantations. Quite obviously this export could not be completely discontinued without destroying the whole basis of industry in the Territory, and no one would be so foolish as to propose that. But to enable those who cannot at present find employment and are forced either to go outside the Territory or to go short of necessary purchases, to sell suitable products as an alternative to offering their labour cannot fail to be an advantage. Moreover, the problem is in some ways becoming aggravated with the passage of time. Hitherto the rapid turnover of labour has made it possible for many families to benefit from the available work. It has not been difficult for money to be earned to pay taxes and buy imports, but with the process of stabilisation the industrialised groups will, it is almost certain, gradually lose contacts with the country. The proportion of total earnings which will find their way back ultimately to the rural areas will diminish, and, with the best jobs permanently filled, those who remain in the country will find it increasingly difficult to sell their labour. The Government of the Union of South Africa has dealt with this same problem during the present depression by requiring the gold-mines to discharge a certain proportion of their total labour force each month and thus spread a given volume of earnings over a larger number of families. It is not suggested that a similar policy should be adopted in the North. Conditions are wholly different, and the pressure on the land, which has prompted the policy in the South, has no parallel in Northern Rhodesia. But the probable emergence of the problem must be foreseen and considered. Stabilisation on the mines and in the towns can only be achieved without causing a progressive drift to the towns of Natives from the country areas in search of work if it is accompanied by a parallel stabilisation of the rural areas.

If the nature of the problem be admitted, there follows the practical question of how it can best be remedied. The adverse balance of the country can be improved either by selling more produce to the towns or by buying less from the towns. Since the gap to be bridged is considerable, both these methods must be employed so far as is possible. The discovery of suitable exports from the country to the town is not a simple task. Both missionaries and officials have been thinking and experimenting for many years past, and they have not found a solution of the problem. In order to appreciate the difficulties it must be seen in a typical setting.

Kasama is the centre of the province from which the largest proportion have been absent at work. It is some 458 miles from the railway at Kapiri Mposhi and about 1830 miles from the sea at Beira. Any heavy produce must be carried by motor-lorry to the railway, since ox-cart transport is made impossible by the existence of numerous fly-belts. The present rates for carrying goods amount to about 1d. per lb. per 100 miles, or about 4½d per lb. from Kasama to the railway. The difficulties of Kasama are greater, but not vastly greater, than those of many other districts in the Territory. There are certain areas more favourably placed. A strip of some fifty miles' depth on either side of the railway and the areas round Fort Jameson and Abercorn have sufficient access to markets and a considerable development of trade has already taken place. In the remainder of the Territory the difficulties of transport have hitherto proved an almost insurmountable barrier.

For an agricultural population it is natural to seek first to discover suitable agricultural products. For the cattle-raising tribes of the west it is to be hoped that, once the difficulties of disease have been mastered, a trade will develop within the Territory itself and with neighbouring districts of the Congo. It has been suggested that in this trade the European farmer may come to play an increasingly important part by buying Native cattle, bringing

them into condition for slaughter and organising the
marketing. But in North-East Rhodesia, from which the
main stream of labour has come, and which constitutes,
therefore, the core of the problem, no similar self-trans-
porting produce is available. Grain can find a market only
in the immediate neighbourhood of where it is grown.
Many instances are quoted of great variations of price
over comparatively short distances, which owing to the
high cost of transport have not resulted in the movement
of produce. Coffee, cotton and tobacco have all been suggested as possible crops. In present conditions they are
none of them very suitable for Native production. Success
depends on most careful and intelligent handling, and on
the control of the various pests which attack them. Fear
has been expressed in some quarters that careless and irre-
sponsible growers may infect the crops of their European
neighbours. Whatever may be the truth of this, these crops
require both more capital and greater knowledge than is at
present at the disposal of most Native agriculturalists. Moreover, in the present state of the market the possible margin
of profit is too small to make active development advisable.
A successful crop which cannot be sold at any remunerative price will only dishearten the experimenter. For this
reason, among others, the experiments with cotton in the
Lufu Valley have now been abandoned. It is, however, too
early to say that none of these will afford outlets in the
long run for Native agriculture. Crops which are as difficult to handle are being grown by Natives in West Africa.
Coffee and cotton are being produced by Natives in the
Belgian Congo, cotton in Uganda. The present time is a
difficult one in which to judge of economic possibilities over
longer periods. There is hardly an agricultural product in
the world which could be found to be remunerative to-day
to the ordinary producer.

If primary agricultural products hold little promise,
semi-manufactured products must be considered. It has
been suggested that pea-nut oil and other essential oils
may be produced in the Territory and exported. Paper

pulp in the half-manufactured state might, it has been suggested, prove profitable. Other small-scale outlets could perhaps be devised. Apart from these possibilities the uncomfortable truth must be faced that the remoter districts in and behind the fly-belts possess no agricultural product which can support the expense of four hundred miles of road transport. Improvement, if it is to come in these districts, must come principally from a raising of the standards of self-sufficient agriculture and from the reduction to the lowest possible levels of taxation and other cash payments which make exports a necessity.

Within the area adjacent to the railway and to the mines the growth of economic crops has considerably developed. Natives can often grow maize more cheaply than European farmers because they rarely employ any labour outside the family circle. Wherever an assured market at a reasonable price has been open, Native output has considerably increased. The main source of demand is from the mines and the towns. The mines buy on a large scale and require a good quality. For these reasons they have hitherto obtained their supplies in the main from the European growers and from outside the Territory. There has thus emerged the present paradoxical system whereby European farmers grow Native crops for Native consumption. So long as their grain is dirty and of unequal quality it is unlikely that Native growers will make any considerable inroads into this market. But quality is being gradually improved with better methods and better seed, and the existence of numerous European grain-buyers and storekeepers is making it possible for Native-grown crops to fill comparatively large contracts. In the railway strip the primitive methods of Native agriculture have in many districts been abandoned. Ploughs and ox-carts are now common. Harrows, cultivators and drills are coming into general use. It is stated[1] that this revision of time-honoured methods has occurred "because of the pressure brought to bear upon the men by the women who no longer

[1] *Annual Report upon Native Affairs, 1931.*

agree to work in the fields with the hoe. But that the men are not expected to undertake all agricultural work in addition to training oxen and supplying the yokes and reins is shown by the fact that women are following and directing the plough whilst the men carry the whip and look after the oxen."

The efforts of the Department of Agriculture, so far as concerns the Native side of their work, have rightly been concentrated on the improvement of the existing methods of the self-sufficient agriculture. The problem which they have to face is very much more difficult than that which confronts the officials of the territories farther south. In Southern Rhodesia, in Basutoland or the Transkeian territories, for example, Native agriculture is different in scale and organisation rather than in type from the agriculture practised by their European neighbours. In Northern Rhodesia no European farmer grows crops, other than coffee or tobacco, in a fly zone. The methods which Natives have evolved to deal with their own peculiar problems have to be examined and analysed before improvements can be suggested. This is being done now in the Nsokolo Reserve near Abercorn and at one or two other points. There is no doubt that the *chitemene* system of agriculture is wasteful of area and of resources. An area of trees which may be so great as twelve acres, and is probably nowhere less than two and a half acres, is cut to provide branches to be burnt on each acre of land. An inquiry made during a recent locust campaign showed that the average area of a man's millet garden was about one and one-eighth acres. As a rule a new garden is cut each year. It takes some twenty years for the trees to recover. Thus a man requires some two to three hundred acres of woodland to keep himself and his family alive. A village works out all the land within a radius of some three miles in about five years and it must then move. Consequently permanent improvements, satisfactory buildings, the planting of fruit-trees, are all impossible. Where villages are permanently established, as in the neighbourhood of mission stations,

it may be necessary to go very great distances to find satisfactory sites. Cases are quoted where gardens are as much
as eleven or twelve miles from the village, and in exceptional cases very much greater distances have been found.
They are worked during the annual seasons of agricultural
activity from temporary garden huts built in the gardens
themselves.

A system that depends upon an area of two hundred
acres or more of woodland for each family cannot endure
indefinitely with a growing population and declining wood-
lands. Since 1911 the numbers have increased, according
to the population estimates, by about 62 per cent. Already
in some areas, where until recently only the branches
were lopped, whole trunks are beginning to be cut. Gardens
are being made on the slopes of hills, where the work is
harder. The cutting of trees in stream-beds,[1] and their
destruction by the increasingly prevalent grass fires, have
aggravated the problem of erosion. Streams in some districts are beginning to dry out as evaporation increases.
The time must soon come when the pressure of circumstances will dictate a change of the methods which produce
such consequences.

Experiments are now being made to discover the
peculiar advantages of this system in the local conditions
and to devise alternative methods of securing equal
results. Its main virtue, it has been found, lies not in the
value of the ash as manure, but in the excellent seed-bed
which this method produces. Once the trees have been
cut and burned and the seed planted the main work of the
year is complete. No weeding or cultivation is necessary.
Germination is more certain than with other methods and
the crop rarely fails. It is almost impossible to discover
another method equally safe and equally efficient. The
work is carried on in a series of spurts; a burst of energy at
the time of tree-lopping, another when fencing must be

---

[1] This has for some time been forbidden by certain Native authorities,
and a number of cases have come before the Native courts. See below,
p. 258.

done, a third at harvest time. Between these are long periods of pleasant inactivity, when a man can travel, or go away to work, or follow his own inclinations. Any alternative method means harder and more continuous activity. If manure is employed, weeds immediately appear. If it is suggested that the garden be used for longer periods, or that a rotation of crops be introduced, the problem of weeding and cultivation immediately arises. There is little doubt, however, that these changes will soon be forced upon the Native, and when the time comes he will probably adapt himself without difficulty. "Instances of Natives being compelled by force of circumstances over which they have no control to change their methods of agriculture have not been unknown in the past. Owing to a scarcity of timber some villages that had practised the tree-lopping method of agriculture for generations were compelled to cease the growing of finger millet and change their staple food to cassava. In other areas the people who cultivated finger millet by the tree-lopping methods were forced by exhaustion of the timber to cultivate millet in open country. In neither case did the population experience any hardship; they adapted themselves to the new conditions quickly and they have as good crops as before with much less expenditure of labour."[1]

Once the necessary knowledge of improved methods has been secured, the problem of spreading it arises. It is here that at the moment organisation is weakest. Following the example of other territories, a system of agricultural demonstrators was devised and a training course for prospective demonstrators was organised at Mazabuka. Unfortunately, it has proved necessary, partly for financial, partly for other reasons, to close down this experiment. It was found that the programme of research work had not yet reached a stage at which it was desirable to press on with the popularisation of new methods. But the main difficulty lay in the quality of the pupils who were under training for the work of demonstration. It was found that their general

[1] *Annual Report upon Native Affairs, 1931.*

education had not reached a stage at which they could readily comprehend or pass on the new ideas which were being taught them, and it has been decided to offer to those of the first batch of students who are willing and qualified to accept, posts on the existing experimental stations. It would be very regrettable if the whole plan were allowed to be abandoned for lack of immediate success. Very similar difficulties were encountered at the outset in the organisation of a similar scheme in Southern Rhodesia. In that instance initial failure was retrieved largely through the goodwill of one mission station, that of the American Board of Foreign Missions at Mount Selinda, which persuaded some of its best pupils to enter for this work and supplied the greater number of recruits for several years. In Southern Rhodesia, in the Native territories of the Union, and in the British protectorates in South Africa, a system of Native agricultural demonstrators has been built up which has done much already to introduce improvements. It has been found that once the methods to be employed have been determined, Native demonstrators can impart them and persuade their fellows to adopt them more successfully than a far better qualified instructor of another race. It is very much to be hoped that as soon as a programme of agricultural improvement is established another trial may be given to the scheme of educating demonstrators.

In addition to the experiments being carried on by the Government agricultural officers, certain mission stations are doing useful work in the way of agricultural experiment and demonstration. They are helping to discover the types of seed and methods of cultivation most suitable to the areas in which they are working, and by demonstrating the better yield which arises from suitable methods of cultivation to procure the spread of better agricultural practices. It is most important that all missions which are engaged in agricultural work shall share the lessons of their own experiences with the Government agricultural department and be well acquainted themselves with the results of the work of the department. At present the interchange of ideas depends largely upon the personal relations between the agricultural officers and the missionary. In some cases they are perfectly familiar with each other's work, in other cases almost completely ignorant. Where so much requires to be done, any unnecessary duplication of work is to be regretted.

It must be regarded, nevertheless, as improbable that in the present conditions of transport the more remote parts of Northern Rhodesia can find economic crops which can be sold to the towns or in the export market. This is not in itself surprising. Trade between country and town developed in other parts of the world only by slow degrees and at first over comparatively short distances. Other countries in Northern Rhodesia's stage of economic development have exchanged only the more valuable products of manufacture or mining whose intrinsic worth enabled them to support the higher costs of inefficient carriage. It is only within the last hundred years that the widespread exchange of primary products of low value has become general, and it has been made possible only by the existence of the cheap transport facilities offered by railways and ocean shipping. If suitable crops cannot be found we must turn our attention to manufactures. It has already been suggested that if these are to redress the balance of trade they should be either such things as may be exported to the towns or as may be substituted for imports from the towns.

Various suggestions have been made at different times for the development of different industries. At the 1927 General Missionary Conference of Northern Rhodesia papers on Native industries were read both by the Rev. J. A. Ross and the Rev. J. R. Shaw which were concerned with this problem. The proposals which were then made included in one case cotton- and flax-growing and their spinning and weaving, and the making of ropes and soap; in the other case tailoring, bootmaking, carpentry, building, iron-working, basket-working and weaving. It would take too much space and serve little purpose to examine all these and other proposals in detail. While practical experiments with some of these products have not been very successful in the initial stages, they were made at an unusually diffi- cult time and in not wholly favourable circumstances. Success with any particular product must depend largely upon local conditions, and what may be best for one part of the country may be wholly unsuitable for another. The problem will be solved, if it can be at all, not by discovering one single panacea, but by finding a multitude of local treatments for local difficulties. It will be of more general service to examine the conditions in which any such solu- tion is likely to be found. In the first place, if it is to bear transport to the railway area the product must be light and not easily damaged by carriage. When it reaches its destination it must be able to command a sale against local or imported products. To do this producers in the remoter districts must make full use of any peculiar advantages which they possess. The chief advantage of Northern Rho- desia lies obviously in large supplies of cheap, fairly ener- getic, but not yet highly skilled labour. Against goods which can equally well be made by machinery competition will be difficult. So far as it is possible, therefore, we must find products which cannot be made in satisfactory quali- ties by machinery—Native handicrafts which can command a ready sale. This type of product is still made and exported to the more advanced countries by the countries which are in a state of economic backwardness. The carpets of Persia or of Turkestan, the fine cloths of Benares or of Chan- deri, the silks and embroideries of China and Japan, the shawls of Spain, the fine metal-work of Damascus, afford examples of such exports. Unfortunately, these are almost all the products of trades which have developed for cen- turies under the influences of monarchs and courts, and with the local demand which has been afforded by great inequalities of wealth. The equality of the African tribe, almost unparalleled in other societies, has in the develop- ment of craftsmanship proved a handicap. But great as may be the initial disadvantage, it is in this type of product alone that ultimate success can be found.

The alternative of increasing the local manufacture of many of the things which are at present imported has been left till the last. It is along this line that the best hope of immediate success would appear to lie. At present the largest imports of goods for Native consumption are those of cottons and blankets. It is not possible to distinguish Native from European goods with accuracy in the customs returns, but of £139,000 worth of cotton piece goods and £45,000 worth of cotton blankets, the greater part is probably sold for Native use. Since Native-made bark cloth disappeared before the cotton cloth of the store it is usually said that any attempts at local manufacture are doomed to failure. This cannot be regarded as wholly convincing. It is almost certainly true that hand-spinning cannot compete against machine-spun yarn. But it is by no means so clear that handloom weaving must fail. In many parts of India, where wages are the equivalent of about ten shillings a month, cloth continues to be woven by hand from imported yarn. It is dyed and printed locally and is sold at prices which enable it to compete successfully even with the products of the Indian mills. It was estimated [1] in 1921 that hand-woven cloth accounted for about 29 per cent of the total consumption of India.

Among other imports into the country districts picks and hoes (which are valued at £3204) and pots and pans play an important part. These are all things in which the village till recently was self-sufficient, and which might well be made again. Because in the early days of the British occupation blacksmiths who were also gun repairers were almost inevitably harried by officials responsible for the maintenance of peace, there would appear to be a widespread but completely erroneous view that the Government discourages blacksmith's work. If this error can be removed, and smiths actively encouraged, a useful trade will almost certainly develop. As regards pots and

---

[1] See Wadia and Joshi, *The Wealth of India*, p. 412.

pans, the village also until lately provided for itself. But the
iron or enamel-ware pot is rapidly driving out of use the
old and very dangerous earthenware pot. It is not necessary, however, that progress should replace a Native with
a foreign product. The Indian village is in this respect
usually self-sufficient. The brass pots of everyday use are
made by a local brass-worker, who turns or spins them on
his primitive lathe. It is paradoxical that Northern Rhodesia, which is now one of the world's greatest producers
of copper and zinc, should possess no indigenous brass
industry of any kind. As regards china and earthenware,
several mission stations have already begun to teach the
elements of the work to some of their pupils. The potter's
wheel has been introduced into the country for the first
time by mission agency, and it may be hoped that its use
will gradually spread.

The industrial schools of missions have hitherto been
concerned chiefly with a different problem from that
which has been considered here. They have been concerned
firstly to train the craftsmen who are needed to create the
mission station itself, and secondly, to provide craftsmen
who can fit into the needs of a Europeanised society. In
this they have done excellent work. The first needs of the
mission itself have been for buildings and for furniture, and
so the trades which have been chiefly developed have been
those of builders, carpenters and joiners. What is more
important than the trade itself, they have built up a pride
in honest craftsmanship which is almost wholly new to the
Bantu mind. The work done by some of the teachers in
industrial schools has given a moral training which is
hardly second to the technical training itself. Once a feeling
for craftsmanship has been built up the application of it to
other trades may proceed.

It has been hoped that the craftsmen trained in these
schools will help to raise the standard of living in the
villages. To some extent this has happened. Square huts
of Kimberley brick with windows and doors are steadily
increasing in number under the influence of mission and

Government example. But the craftsman who seeks to ply his trade in a village finds himself confronted by great difficulties. In the first place, the communal habits of tribal life have not accustomed the Native to pay another Native for work. Money is used at the mines to buy Native produce, but elsewhere the trade is largely a matter of barter, and such exchange as takes place is concerned mainly with goods, such as salt or tobacco, which are brought from a distance. Within the village there is, generally speaking, no specialisation and no exchange. In the second place, the Native has little or no money with which to buy. The insistent demands of the tax collector, of the storekeeper for necessary purchases, sometimes of the mission for educational fees, exhaust his available resources. He has no means and little inclination to purchase something that he can if necessary make for himself. This is a weakness of the present system of industrial training. Craftsmen are being educated to provide neither products which the village is accustomed to buy outside nor things which it can sell outside, but things in which the individual has long been accustomed to be self-sufficient. They are, therefore, the very things which it must be most difficult to persuade purchasers to buy. In practice many of the craftsmen who have been trained have been absorbed by the missions themselves either in their own building work or in teaching. Others have found their way to Government stations or to the big towns and have in many cases earned a good living there. Comparatively few have contributed to raise the standard of living of the village, and those who have succeeded have done so because during the period of intense demand for labour at the mines men have been willing and able to find the money to pay others to build for them in their absence. If one of our main objects is to diminish the necessity of travelling to find work, a system of craftsmanship must not be built on the assumption that earnings from such work are the source of payment.

This difficulty of the establishment of craftsmen in the

middle of a self-sufficient population is not confined to Northern Rhodesia. It affords an almost equally intractable problem for countries as different as Southern Rhodesia, Basutoland and the Ciskei. The difficulty is a really fundamental one. Craftsmanship, as understood by those who are in charge of the training work in the industrial schools, is a feature of a comparatively advanced society in which specialisation and the exchange of products is a normal event. At the present moment boys after being trained are launched into a society which is not fitted to absorb them. The inevitable consequence is that they have to adapt themselves to the society. They cannot in most cases make a whole-time living by their trade, so they become once more self-sufficient agriculturalists, growing their own produce and exercising their craft in their spare time.

If Northern Rhodesia is to make progress along the same lines of internal development that have been followed by other countries, the next stage must be a gradual evolution of specialisation and exchange. This when it comes will bring a very considerable increase of productivity and wealth. There is no doubt that even with existing methods a family can, if it wishes to do so, produce a fairly considerable excess of foodstuffs over its own immediate needs. An estimate puts the present surplus at about 25 per cent, which is largely absorbed in beer. Where markets have been available in the railway belt the Native output of economic crops has been considerable. The means exist of setting free a quite considerable number of men to make things other than the food, drink and housing at present produced. The immediate problem then is how such a transition can be assisted and facilitated. In theory the change is not difficult. If in a village in no contact with the outside world a man had the faith to buy his food from his neighbours, he would put into their pockets the money with which they could buy his wares in exchange. But in practice many difficulties arise. The village has many contacts with the outside world, and his money will disappear probably in taxation or the purchase of foreign goods, and will find its way back into his pocket only by circuitous routes and in trifling amounts. In self-protection every individual is precluded from doing that which would be safe if all did it equally.

In Northern Rhodesia there is an added difficulty. In Europe even at a similar stage of development the population was sufficiently dense for a craftsman to be accessible to a sufficient number of persons to give him a fairly regular market. But Northern Rhodesia, with an area equal to that of France, Belgium, England and Wales together, has a population less than that of Northumberland and Durham. Moreover, in Europe the demand for a craftsman's products was at first more localised. The inequalities of wealth, which were earlier mentioned, provided centres where a market was assured. In Northern Rhodesia much the same part which was played by the Church and by feudal courts in Europe is played by missions and Government stations. They provide the nucleus of a town and a market round which growth can take place. In such a thinly populated territory specialisation can grow up only if everything possible is done to facilitate exchange. The latter is obviously the condition of the former, and it is the difficulty of exchange that has made specialisation almost impossible. The greatest present need is an increase of facilities for trade, and trade means not only selling but also buying. At present the chief opportunities which exist are for the buying of imported produce for money. The African Lakes Corporation and other trading firms have done a great deal to bring goods to the Native. They have done far less in recent years to help him to sell his own products. Some traders accept grain in payment, but seldom do so with any intention of selling it at a distance. In many cases it is sold back to those from whom it was originally bought, at a later date and at an enhanced price. It has in effect served as a security until someone shall go to the mines to earn the money to make the final payment. In the railway strip, grain merchants buy crops for sale, offering sometimes cash, sometimes goods in exchange. In Basutoland and in the Transkei the trader has become a really valuable feature in the economic development of the people. He has found a market for their produce outside the territory and has himself created a market for his own goods by doing so. A similar expansion of this side of the activities of the trading companies in Northern Rhodesia would be a great benefit to Native economic development.

At present the Indian trader, who has done so much to increase the petty trade of the East Coast of Africa, is rarely to be found in Northern Rhodesia. While this has contributed to the slow expansion of Native trade, it is probably for the ultimate good of the Territory. It is far better that the local Native trade should be, so far as it is at all possible, in Native hands.

Native traders are slowly increasing in number in Northern Rhodesia; in 1931 there were seventy-two Native-owned trading stores, of which more than half were in the East Luangwa province, around Fort Jameson. There were in addition 617 Native hawkers in possession of a licence. They are handicapped to some extent by the Credit Sales to Natives Ordinance, which by making it impossible for them to secure goods on credit limits the quantity of stock which they can carry and makes competition with European storekeepers difficult. At the present stage, however, it is probably necessary to prevent individuals who have little idea of the value of money, or of commercial methods, and who usually keep no books, from involving themselves and others in disaster. The Native storekeeper and the hawker are both engaged mainly in the sale of imported goods. For the trading of Native goods no licence is required. This trade is almost confined to the marketing of fish, tobacco and salt. It is said that Natives of the Luwingu district sold over a hundred and fifty tons of dried fish during 1931 at a price of 1½d. a pound. The fish is either transported on bicycles to the copper-mines or sold to European buyers on the spot. Since the depression the buyers have disappeared and only the more laborious means of outlet remains. Moreover, competition has begun from fish caught at Lobito Bay and carried by railway to the copper belt.

The development of a Native trade in Northern Rhodesia has long suffered under one very severe handicap. There is no unit of currency in ordinary circulation less than the silver threepenny piece. This extraordinary limitation has been imposed not by the Government but by the banks and stores concerned in the local trade. This may be of little disadvantage to Europeans living in a country in which they must expect a high level of prices. It effectively precludes any dealing in the units in which a Native trade might arise. The threepenny piece represents in many parts of the country a day's wage. Little trade could exist in England if the smallest unit were the ten-shilling note. In Southern Rhodesia, where the same condition of affairs had long existed, the penny was recently introduced and immediately found favour. But the penny itself is too large a unit. A suggestion that the farthing be employed is usually met in Northern Rhodesia with derision. But that is the value of the unit in which a very large part of the business of India is transacted to-day. If specialisation and exchange are to develop, it must be possible for everyone to buy and sell in those quantities which suit them, and prices must become adapted to their needs. A pot of beer costs a day's wage at the mine, or four days' agricultural work. There is no unit in which the amounts of grain or of relishes consumed in a day can be bought or sold. There can for the present be no equivalent to the marketing of the European housewife.

Government officials are alive to many of these difficulties and it is to be hoped that something will gradually be done to remove them. Attempts have already been made by individual District Officers to institute markets for Native produce. Hitherto, with one or two exceptions, these have not been very successful. At the mines, however, markets for fish, tobacco and Native foodstuffs have grown up even despite a quite considerable charge for stands, and the custom will doubtless in time spread to other places. In the Belgian Congo there has been a greater development than in Northern Rhodesia, but even there the market is still in a primitive stage and far less popular and successful than on the west coast of Africa.

In addition to the daily or weekly market, dealing chiefly in foodstuffs, there is room also for the annual fair. The fair played an important part in the exchange of products between different parts of the country in mediaeval England; it still plays a large part in the economic life of India. Mission stations, and particularly those which are engaged in agricultural work, might well give consideration to the possibility of an annual show at which facilities for trading could be added to agricultural and industrial exhibits and demonstrations. By such means as these something may be done gradually to develop increased openings and opportunities for Native craftsmen and to help them to fit into the society in which they have to live.

CHAPTER XII

THE DIFFICULTIES OF ECONOMIC TRANSITION

WE have seen in the last four chapters that an economic transition is in progress in Northern Rhodesia which in its scale and its violence is comparable with the industrial revolution of the eighteenth and nineteenth centuries in Europe. Forms of economic organisation and of the technique of production which have existed for centuries are being modified and transformed within a single generation. The revolution is in some respects more ruthless than that of the industrial revolution as it was known in Europe, for there the changes involved were the spontaneous changes of an indigenous economic system, the next stages in a process of change which had been proceeding less rapidly, but none the less certainly, during the previous centuries. Here the changes are the consequence of the importation of an entirely new and exotic technique, in circumstances which for the first time have favoured radical change. In the past such contacts as had occurred with other tribes and with other races had not induced great changes, because the tribe itself selected certain features of their neighbours' technique for adoption and the full weight of conservatism resisted change. It has even been claimed that apart from intermarriage widespread technical change was unknown. But with the coming of the Europeans new seed-beds of change were for the first time cultivated. Not only did the adults come into the new environment, but the children also were exposed to the influences of an educational system which helped to break down the resistance to innovation and to prepare them to accept new ways and ideas.

There are two wholly different types of economic change at present in progress in Northern Rhodesia. In the first place, economic organisations and institutions after the European model are growing up and in part taking the place of earlier and cruder alternatives. In the second place, the indigenous forms are being modified to make them better adapted to the new conditions. The central problem of economic change is to secure that this process of modification shall keep in step with the process of innovation, so that the adaptation of Native institutions shall play a part complementary to the development of European industry on the railway line and in the copper belt, and shall not be stifled or destroyed by the developments in the latter. The danger of the moment is that modification will proceed too slowly and that, for lack of the necessary change in Native methods, industry after the European model may grow faster and more generally than is in the ultimate interest of the country.

To anyone who is watching this transition two questions cannot fail to present themselves. Do we wish to control and direct this transition? Have we the power to do so if we wish to? The answer to the first of these questions must depend in large measure on the end that we have in view in the development of Northern Rhodesia. If our sole criterion of policy is the most rapid possible economic exploitation of the Territory and the greatest possible immediate creation of wealth, then the grounds for intervention and control are few. In Europe in recent years immediate economic results have been the first test of any policy, and politicians have hesitated to recommend anything that might interfere with the greatest possible addition to productivity. With the person who would apply this same criterion to the condition of Northern Rhodesia, convinced that there is no more urgent problem than that of poverty and that what has been held to be of paramount importance in Europe cannot fail to be *a fortiori* paramount in a far poorer territory, we cannot argue by any appeal to logic. It is a matter of judgment whether other problems do not require equal consideration. In particular we must have in mind the effects of economic

changes upon the political, social and moral life of the
country, and upon the future political problems of the
country. The wisest economic policy for the moment may
reasonably be regarded as that which grapples effectively
with the problem of poverty without creating insoluble
problems of political and social adjustment in the present
or of racial relations in the future. But it must always be
remembered that most of these adjustments have to be
made either sooner or later. Our power to postpone them is
only limited, and it is only an advantage to use it if the
adjustments can be made more painlessly in the future
than in the present. The future will inevitably bring its
own problems, and if we delay adjustment too far we may
increase rather than diminish the total of difficulties. An
attempt to use such powers as we may have of resisting the
forces of economic change in order to maintain unchanged
outworn forms and institutions and to prevent their
modification or replacement by new types better adapted
to the needs of the present, is doomed sooner or later to
failure. It may be most desirable to proceed slowly in the
political sphere or in the educational sphere. That is the
more reason for attempting to delay economic change.
But economic change is going to take place in any case. It
may be slowed down like a cyclist attempting to keep pace
with a man on foot, but if the man stands still he cannot
fail to be left behind.

The actual form that the economic transition will take
must depend in large measure upon the political background against which it takes place, and in particular
upon the part that it is proposed that Europeans shall
play in the future economic system. There have been a
number of different types of economic policy in Africa
which may be distinguished into three broad categories.
First, there is the policy of the parallel independent development of White and Native, the policy, that is, of
economic as well as political segregation. This policy is
never carried to its logical conclusion of making the White
community independent of Native labour as well as

segregating all Natives not actually in White employment. Second, there is the policy of unified development of the two races, fitting them both into a single homogeneous economic structure in which each race makes the contribution that it is best fitted to make. Third, there is the policy of the development of the Native economic system, using the European not as a permanent part of the structure but as a temporary provider of technical, financial and organising knowledge. The third policy differs fundamentally from the first two in regard to the assumption which it makes as to the permanency of the European element in the country.

To the south of Northern Rhodesia are the Union and Southern Rhodesia. In these countries economic policy, never clearly defined, would appear to be an attempt to compromise between the first policy and the second. But it is clear beyond all doubt that both these countries, as well as Kenya to the north-east, contemplate a permanent place for the European settler in the economic and political structure of the country. To the north and north-west are the Belgian Congo and West Africa. In these it may be said that economic policy is of our third type. The Belgians are not at present colonising on any considerable scale. Officials are, as in the British colonies and protectorates, temporary *émigrés* from Belgium. The technical experts who run the railways and the industries are almost all on short contracts and look forward to a return to their own countries. If the time comes when they cease to be required they can cease to be recruited. Northern Rhodesia politically as well as geographically lies between these two types. There is along the railway belt a small body of settlers whose intention is to remain permanently in the country. They were encouraged by the Government to settle there, and any policy must be built upon the assumption that they can and will remain. There are other similar groups of settlers in the Fort Jameson district and in the Abercorn district. Native reserves have been created in these three districts, leaving considerable areas open for European development. The policy of West Africa, therefore, in its purest form cannot in any case be applied to the Territory. On the other hand, the area of European settlement is so small and so localised that an economic policy designed for the rest of the country, provided that it adequately safeguards the interests of the settlers, must be determined in the main by a consideration of other factors. More important in many ways are the communities in the towns and the mining areas. The European staffs of the mines have been recruited almost entirely from outside Northern Rhodesia. The higher officials would not regard Northern Rhodesia as their permanent home, apart from their work. They are accustomed to follow copper, or mining of some other kind, to any country which may offer suitable opportunity. The more permanent element in the country is to be found among the lower grades of the mining staffs, in the building industry and in commerce. The numbers even in these groups are at present small and have diminished very considerably during the recent depression.

The problem of racial readjustment is not likely to prove as difficult as it must be in countries where the numbers of the two races are more nearly equal. The steady development of the Native's abilities, and the encouragement of the growth of Native industries and crafts, need not, and indeed will not, be at the expense of the White community in the towns. As the Native grows in wealth his demand for European products cannot fail to expand, even if in some respects these alter in type. The first need of the European trader or craftsman is for wider markets in which to sell their goods or services. What Professor Clay has written of Southern Rhodesia is equally true farther north. "Such a development of native capacity is sometimes regarded with fear, and in the neighbouring territory of the Union has inspired colour-bar legislation. It is thought that the native, as he acquires skill, must necessarily displace the white worker. Such fears do less than justice to the economic quality and adaptability of the white worker, and imply that his present wage is not based on his skill and capacity as a worker, but on an artificial scarcity of skilled labour, maintained by excluding natives and the under-payment of the mass of natives employed. They are, moreover, unfounded. The relation of advanced and backward labour is much more complementary than competitive. The increased employment of natives increases the number—and possibly the remuneration—of supervisory, responsible and specially skilled posts which white men must always fill. Even if in some occupations the native does displace the white man, now that he is able to earn more he can demand more, and so offers a market for an increased output of goods in general, in which additional white labour will find employment. Already the railway receipts from native passenger traffic exceed those from first-class passenger traffic. These fears are indeed based on the fallacy that there is a limited amount of work to be done, and that if the native does it the white man cannot do it. This fallacy, if it were true, would constitute an equal objection to the admission of any more white men to the country for fear that they should take away the work of those already in the country. It would constitute an objection to the influx of capital in the form of labour-saving machinery. In fact there is no rigid limit to the work awaiting additional resources in labour and capital. There is no more social danger in cheap labour than in cheap capital, cheap power or cheap land. All alike, by increasing the output of the community, increase the opportunities of economic welfare; all alike, by increasing the power to purchase of those that supply them, increase the demand for labour in the community fortunate enough to possess them."

In Northern Rhodesia European settlers and traders have in the past played a large part in improving the economic status of the Native. One missionary of great experience in the country regards the civilising and educating influence of suitable settlers as so valuable that he would wish to see a great increase in their numbers. Many who would hesitate to agree with him in wishing to see European substituted for Native institutions on a considerable scale would pay their own tributes to the influence of many individual settlers and traders. It is not a condemnation of individuals that leads to doubt whether a wholesale and immediate substitution of a foreign for a Native system of economic organisation would be unmitigated gain. This doubt applies more particularly to the growth of industries and workshops. There are some industries in which the benefit which they confer on the country far exceeds any possible losses. There are others in which the gain is far less clear. The advantages which have resulted from the opening of the copper-mines almost certainly outweigh any possible disadvantages. They have raised the general standard of living and given the country the export which it needed. They have widened the available basis of taxation and have made possible expenditure on Native education and Native agricultural development that was previously impossible. But there are economic consequences of the growth of the mines which are likely to need thought and control. The higher standard of living which they offer makes the mines the greatest consuming centres in the country. They are likely to attract toward them the subsidiary industries which may provide the goods to be consumed there and offer employment to further Native workers. There are likely in time to grow up round them small industries providing goods for the consumption of the Native workers employed, probably also for the European community.

So far as the mines themselves are concerned, it is both inevitable and desirable that they should be employing the most efficient technical methods of production that are known in America or Europe. These methods require, it is true, great aggregations of people, but the efficient and wealthy mining companies can provide conditions of life, and of health and housing, which are better than those of the districts from which their employees come, and vastly better than those of the town locations. It is far more doubtful, however, whether it is desirable that industry after the European method should grow up around the richer mining areas. The employees will almost inevitably be housed in the town locations, under conditions very different from those that prevail on the mines. Small firms and industries will probably have neither the resources nor the far-sightedness to treat their men as the mines have done. If the gains of employing a European technique of manufacture are overwhelming, it may perhaps be desirable that by degrees such industries shall grow up in the towns. But if they are to grow there only because knowledge and initiative are lacking in the country areas, or because transport in the initial stages is difficult, then all the other considerations of the political and social changes involved, and of the harmful effects of migratory labour, can properly be given their due weight. At the present moment, unless the technical advantages of production on the railway belt employing the latest European methods are enormous, the arguments which count in favour of the encouragement of industry in the present rural areas must preponderate.

The copper-mines have created a nucleus round which industrial development is taking place. What is needed most in the rural areas is to find similar nuclei, comparable to the market towns of European countries, which can provide trading centres for craftsmen and places where grain or other produce may be exchanged for simple manufactures. If such nuclei already existed the pull of the European town would be far less strong. The *Boma* stations are usually about a hundred miles apart and far too scattered to provide the full equivalent of the market town, though they do, of course, to some extent serve their own neighbourhoods in that way. Mission stations, though in some parts more frequent than this, are still too far apart to satisfy this need in full. It may be hoped that the Chief's villages will gradually come to fill this place in the economic organisation of the Territory.

If the answer to our first question is that for various

reasons we should wish to control and direct the transition which is in progress, we are brought to our second question: What powers do we possess to do this? The weapons, such as they are, are possessed partly by the Government, partly by the missions. Apart from the general influence which a Government can exert on economic policy through the opportunities and privileges which it is able to give to certain individuals or groups or industries, there are three main weapons of control: fiscal policy, Government enterprise where private enterprise cannot undertake some task, and education in the widest sense of that word. Let us consider these in turn. Protection may be a useful weapon later, but it is only valuable in isolation if there is reason to think that the necessary knowledge and initiative to start new industries exist but cannot profitably be employed. This is not at present the case in Northern Rhodesia. A tax on cotton or blankets would probably increase the aggregate sum which people in the rural areas are obliged to pay for these things without stimulating their local production. Moreover, a protection which can operate only at the borders of a territory can do little to foster industry in the country in competition with industry in the town, and, as has happened in some other countries, may produce the very opposite effect to that intended by increasing the rate of growth of urban industries.

Government enterprise or assistance in economic development is not impossible. In India, where the problems have in the past been in some ways similar to those in Northern Rhodesia, the Government has taken a far more active part in economic life than do most European Governments. In Northern Rhodesia, partly perhaps because the Government itself was until comparatively recently in the hands of a company, more has been left to commercial initiative. More important, probably, was the fact that the Chartered Company was running the country at a considerable annual loss, which has only in a few recent years been converted into a surplus. Thus the resources available for economic development have been meagre, and for some years to come may again prove hard to find. The Government of Northern Rhodesia is responsible for the administration of a large territory in which distances are great and travelling difficult. The number of officials must necessarily be higher than in most countries in proportion to the number of persons governed. Apart from the copper industry and other mines, the country has few taxable sources of income, and even so far as concerns the mines the White tax-paying population is not a large one. The main sources of revenue in 1931–32 were the following:

REVENUE, 1931–32

Customs	£342,017
Income tax	126,567
Native tax	148,263
Licences, etc. . . .	54,016
Fees and payments . .	55,585
Post Office	50,229
Colonial Development Fund . .	37,457
Miscellaneous, etc. . . .	42,242
	£856,376

Of this total it is calculated that about £180,000 was contributed directly and indirectly by Natives. On the other hand, about £62,000 was spent directly on Native welfare, including Native education, provincial Native agricultural and veterinary services and provincial expenditure on medical services. There remains, therefore, a contribution of about £118,000 from Native sources to the cost of the Provincial Administration (which alone amounted in that year to £128,854 apart from pensions) and to the expenditure on police, justice, roads, central agricultural and veterinary administration and research, and all the other activities of government which the Native shares with the European population.

During the past year the depression which has overtaken the copper industry has seriously affected the financial position of the Government. A Finance Commission was appointed in April 1932 to survey the position. It found a great falling-off in the receipts which were to be expected from import duties, and a smaller but nevertheless serious decline in the probable yield of Native taxation and of Posts and Telegraphs. The estimate of the amounts by which receipts were likely to fall short of revenue was £172,000, or about 22 per cent of the revenue. The decline of revenue from customs during the first four months was as much as 43·8 per cent.

The Finance Commission has recommended additional taxation to produce in a full year £69,000 and economies for immediate adoption which in a full year would produce £82,000, and has prepared a schedule for further and more drastic retrenchment which, if it proved necessary to have resort to it, would yield another £20,000. In these circumstances no considerable addition to the expenditure on Native development and on education can be expected. Native education was estimated to cost, in 1932–33, £24,740, of which £13,410 is for grants to missions for educational work. The economies recommended by the Finance Commission have been confined to administrative costs and to the costs of operation of schools maintained by the Government itself. An economy of £500 on the grant to missions is anticipated by the non-appointment of mission staff for which estimate had already been made, and from stricter conditions for the earning of boarding grants. The Commission in making these recommendations has stated:

We are of opinion that Government may reasonably require Missionary Societies to render an account of the manner in which they have expended grants received from public funds for any specific purpose. In expressing this opinion we are influenced by information that, in certain cases, such grants have not been fully expended in the year to which they were applicable.

We feel that closer control should be exercised over expenditure of this kind and where it appears from enquiries made by Government that any Missionary Society did not fully expend its 1931–32 grant before 1st April 1932, the unspent balance should be recovered by deduction from the amount of any

assistance promised to that Society by Government in respect
of the year 1932–33.

We further recommend that the principle involved in the
above suggestion should, in future, guide Government in paying annual grants of every description.

Unless the financial situation rapidly improves it may be
impossible next year to continue annual grants to missionary
bodies on the same scale as in past years, and we suggest that
all Missionary Societies at present in receipt of Government
assistance should be warned forthwith that it may be necessary
seriously to reduce, or even to cancel, their grants in 1933–34.
As missions may have committed themselves to expenditure
and may have engaged staff on the basis of assistance promised
for the current year, we refrain from recommending any reduction in 1932–33 other than the adjustments suggested above.

One of the greatest handicaps to any scheme of advanced
native education to benefit the natives of this Territory appears
to be lack of knowledge of the three R's. It is considered that
the necessary instruction can best be achieved by encouraging
more intensive elementary education in village day schools
rather than by undertaking the expense of boarding institutions for sub-standard pupils at Missions: and this should, in
our opinion, dictate Government's policy in making educational grants.

In these circumstances it is clear that no great expansion
of Native education or development can be financed for
the present out of the internal revenues of the country.
It is incumbent, moreover, upon the missionary societies
to co-operate with the Government in securing the
greatest possible return from the expenditure on Native
education and to make all economies that are reasonably
possible. But while they will sympathise heartily with
the difficulties that confront the Government at the
present moment, they cannot be expected to acquiesce
in a proposal that the Government shall divest itself
of all financial responsibility for Native education in
the Territory before a further attempt has been made
to balance the budget by taxation. A married man with
a wife and two children has hitherto paid no income
tax if his earned income was below £1150. Even under

the Finance Commission's proposals he will pay only some £17, and the man with £920 will escape completely. The Government, as well as the missionary societies, has now a responsibility for the education of the Native and the partnership cannot be dissolved at a moment's notice.

One of the chief contributions which a Government can make is the improvement of the means of transport. "The material development of Africa", wrote Lord Lugard, "may be summed up in one word: 'Transport'."[1] Roads and railways are often regarded with suspicion as a means of opening up and so destroying primitive groups. In the initial stages this is often true, but when a country has reached the stage to which Northern Rhodesia has now come the effects are likely to be the very opposite. The absence of facilities to export goods has forced the people themselves to come out. Anything that now facilitates the sale of their products will be a stabilising rather than a disintegrating influence. Over a great part of the country the only methods of transport are the heads of carriers or bicycles. There are only 2160 miles of trunk roads and 4959 miles of district roads, or about one mile of road to forty square miles of territory. With the present resources of Government this is probably unavoidable, but the only alternatives in the fly districts to these elementary forms of transport are the motor-lorry and the railway. The existing roads are simply tracts of sufficient width cleared in the bush. Bridges are flimsy structures of unworked trees which are seldom properly fastened and may collapse under the passage of a car or be burnt in a grass fire. The surface of the road is smooth where there is little traffic; where the traffic is dense it deteriorates until an enterprising driver makes another track. After rain the roads are practically impassable. Over these roads lorries attempt to carry passengers, mails and goods. The state of the roads results in rapid wear and tear and heavy depreciation. Even at the comparatively high rates that are paid many haulage companies have found it unprofitable. The roads

[1] *The Dual Mandate in Tropical Africa*, p. 5.

are being gradually improved in some parts; more permanent bridges are being substituted, but it must be years before the general standard is considerably raised. At present it does not appear profitable to improve roads unless a traffic is forthcoming. On the other hand, until transport facilities are cheaper the traffic can hardly offer itself. The only permanent solution for many of the difficulties of the remoter districts must be railway construction; but unless minerals are discovered the immediate probability of any considerable extension would appear to be small.

The main weapon, then, for the control of the present economic transition must be education, if we may include in this word every attempt to increase the knowledge and to guide the actions of individuals in the direction in which we should wish them to go. At present, education in the ordinary sense of the word is almost entirely in the hands of the missionary societies. The missionaries, moreover, are, by virtue of their independence and their disinterested position, better placed than any, except perhaps Government officials, to influence the thoughts, tastes and ideas of those who have passed the ordinary age of schooling. A grave responsibility for the future therefore rests upon them.

There are two main tasks which education must undertake: first, the creation of the knowledge and initiative required to bring about the necessary change; second, the creation of an atmosphere in which the change can take place. It is partly through the industrial schools of the mission stations, partly through working for European employers, that Natives come in contact with new technical methods. The missions possess the opportunity of selecting suitable crafts for their students. Much has been said regarding this in the last chapter and it need not be repeated here. But it is important to emphasise that a suitable craft is one adapted both to the technical capacities and to the financial resources of the Native. More thought might in some cases be given to this second consideration.

However well suited copper-mining may be to the technical capacities of Natives, it is utterly remote from their financial resources. The same is true in less degree of other less obviously improbable industries. The financial suitability of any industry will depend largely upon how far the craftsman can be taught to· make his own tools and equipment. Some schools are already teaching this. Others have hitherto made little attempt, with the result that their pupils are more dependent on employers and on their environment, and are less well equipped to fit into a society in which their leisure is likely to be considerable and their earning power in money only meagre.

The problem that remains for our consideration is that of creating an atmosphere in which the necessary changes and modifications of the present Native economic organisation can take place. The most important task is obviously to change the attitude to change. No one would propose that every old custom must be abandoned. The main object of almost all who are interested in the welfare of the Native in Northern Rhodesia is to retain everything in his economic life, as in every other branch of his life, which can be profitably retained. But the most effective way of retaining the essentials may be to jettison the unessentials. If some custom stands in the way of development it is better to sacrifice it than to divert development into less desirable channels.

What conditions will prove necessary to improvement it is impossible to forecast with certainty. Very much will depend on the attitude of the individual to the institutions under which he is living, and until the time comes his attitude cannot be foreseen. But if a system of division of labour and the exchange of products is to work effectively, certain prerequisites can be stated. Obviously if a craftsman is to buy his tools and the materials with which he is to work he must be paid sufficient to cover the wear and tear of the former and the cost of the latter. There have been cases in other territories where craftsmen after training have been summoned by a Chief and expected to work for him without payment. It may be possible in some cases for craftsmen to give their services to the group in which they live, or to the Chief as representing the group, but they cannot also pay for things which they themselves must buy. The craftsmen may perhaps come to be in a sense the servants of the group, receiving in exchange for their services sufficient to keep themselves and to cover their outgoings. Such until comparatively recently was the place of the craftsman in the Indian village. In exchange for his services as smith or carpenter, a man received his fixed share of the crop on the threshing-floor. By some such system of barter the incorporation of the craftsman may perhaps, in the first stages, be facilitated. So far as concerns a man's tools, it seems almost inevitable that, as these increase in complexity and value, an increasing measure of individual responsibility and ownership must emerge, as well as individual ownership of the materials which have been purchased for some particular task. This can all happen, probably, without any grave strain to the existing scheme of things. The severest test must come with the problem of savings and of working capital. If a craftsman is to work continuously, he must at intervals sell products and convert part of the proceeds into the raw materials which he will again require. This is no part of his profits, and if other members of the group are to take this from him he must remain idle. It seems necessary, then, that a craftsman should have some measure of individual ownership in money, unless the group can achieve such sense of responsibility that he is assured of the necessary funds without himself owning them. But an increase in individual ownership on the side of production need not necessarily imply an equal growth of individualism in expenditure. In many parts of India the joint family still persists because it has succeeded in uniting the individual earning of an income with the communal spending of the individual contributions.

The other important prerequisite of a system of exchange is an effective law of contract enforceable without undue expense in a local court. Goods must be made to order, and materials bought to serve some particular purpose. The craftsman must be in a position to hold a customer to his promise or recover payment for his work. There would appear to be no fundamental difficulty in the entrusting to the existing Native Courts of the responsibilities of enforcing contracts. In the Employment of Natives Ordinance they have already been made responsible for the enforcement of a complicated code of European-made regulations.

A more difficult problem is that concerned with land tenure. At present land is assigned by Chiefs, and can be recovered by them. This power is occasionally used to the detriment of progressive Natives. If better methods are to be used, sufficient security is necessary to make it worth while to make improvements. If agriculture is stabilised and the present movement of villages ceases, the opportunity to make permanent improvements, both of buildings and of cultivation, will become more than ever desirable. Southern Rhodesia has met a very similar need in two ways. In the reserves, by demarcating arable areas and separating them from the commonage, the lands of individuals have been practically fixed. By working rotations of crops they are being taught how to keep them in such condition that movement will be unnecessary. In the Native purchase areas Natives are to be permitted to buy farms and work them with all the advantages which are given by ownership and security. At first sight the advantages of security and efficiency appear to weigh heavily on the side of wider opportunity for private ownership. But there are very real disadvantages. In the Glen Grey area of the Ciskei, where Native tenure has existed for some forty years, a large landless class has already emerged. This is a much more serious matter in an almost exclusively agricultural community than in a more modern society. In Northern Rhodesia the area per head is so large [1] that with any method of farming other than the present there can scarcely be any serious shortage of land for many generations. In

[1] About 130 acres per head.

these circumstances there would appear to be no strong
objections to a modification of the system of land tenure if
a strong feeling arises that it is necessary. But it would in
many ways be regrettable if the more progressive individuals were encouraged to move out of their tribal environment so that they might improve their methods elsewhere.
The obvious remedy for an abuse of authority by the chief
is an increase in his sense of responsibility and duty toward
his people.

By far the biggest problem is that of creating a public
opinion in which trade can develop. The bringing of the
great mass of the ordinary people to some understanding
of the various parts which are played by individuals in a
more advanced system can only be slow and elementary,
but is nevertheless a task worth undertaking. Northern
Rhodesia cannot be touched by the great forces of the
press or the broadcast, which can change ideas like the
shift of the wind. But public opinion, for that reason
the more stable, exercises a real power and is open to be
moulded by those who have the opportunity. In a modern
society the adaptation of our tastes to the manufacturing
capacities of the economic system in which we live is
achieved by the ceaseless and most insinuating persuasion
of advertisement and propaganda. In some more appro-
priate fashion it is surely legitimate to attempt to encourage the Native consumer to want what the Native
craftsman is equipped to give him.

In many parts of the world, in India in particular, the
stimulus and encouragement to the individual that are
so necessary at the moment in Africa have come from
the growth of co-operation and the opportunities that
have thus been opened for thrift and self-development.
In Africa the co-operative movement has hitherto made
little advance. So long as Natives are engaged in self-
subsistence agriculture the sphere of co-operation is
limited. But so soon as transitions such as we are here
considering are in progress, co-operation has a valuable
part to play. Lord Lugard has described it as the counter-

part in the economic sphere of "Indirect Rule".[1] The
latter, he says, might better be named "Co-operative
Rule". Co-operation, like Indirect Rule, may not always
be the quickest way of achieving results, but in the end
it is the surest, for it builds on the foundation of the
wishes, the ideals, even the prejudices of the Native
himself. The part which Co-operation may play in building a new healthy Native society in Africa deserves the
closest study, for the spirit of co-operation is peculiarly
sympathetic to the communal outlook of an African
tribe. By fostering co-operative enterprises missions may
effectively assist in enabling the Native to develop the
elements of a local trade.

In these various ways the missions, working in conjunction with the Government, can help to create the
environment in which the Native craftsman can gradually
develop his own industries, and make it easier for the men
that they are themselves training. But they cannot do
more than this. Success or failure must depend ultimately
on the Native himself and his power to develop his own
capacities. As to what are the limits of his capacities the
most careful observers differ profoundly. Almost everyone
would set some particular limit, but few agree in defining
it. Native workers differ between themselves as widely as
do Europeans, and almost anything that may be said of
one group can be shown to be false of another. If general-
isation is at all legitimate, it may be said that the Northern
Rhodesian Native has already shown himself quickly adaptable to the learning of routine repetition tasks. In the
mines they are driving electric haulage locomotives and
motor-lorries, sharpening drills and doing repair work in
the workshops, the last usually under close European
supervision. In the Belgian Congo they drive the trains on
the railways and operate the lathes and other machine
tools in the railway workshops. Natives, almost without
supervision, dismantle, repair and re-erect the bogies and

[1] See *Co-operation for Africa*, by C. F. Strickland, I.C.S., introduction
by Lord Lugard.

brake-gear of the railway coaches. This has been achieved by concentrating certain men on certain work until they have completely mastered it. They have at present none of the versatility of the European craftsman, and little of the self-confidence that arises from the knowledge of a power to deal with any problem or emergency.

At present it is in most cases the task of the European supervisor to supply the knowledge of how some strange task shall be tackled, the initiative to set to work and organise the job, the conscience to see that the job is properly done. But he is gradually imparting these qualities to the Native worker. The Native's best schoolmaster is the lazy European who leaves to his Native helpers as much as he can of the work to be done. It may nevertheless be said that the technical qualifications of Native craftsmen have in some respects run ahead of the moral qualities which are as necessary to the creation of confidence in honest work, and that the task of those who are concerned with the education of the next generation of workers must be to impart not only technical knowledge but also the will to use it thoroughly.

In these five chapters some attempt has been made to describe and analyse the more important features of the economic transition which is now in progress in Northern Rhodesia. Some of the changes which have been discussed have been proceeding for a generation or more. Others show at present only the faintest indications of beginning. That is not sufficient ground for neglecting them or underestimating their probable importance. A long view is being taken of the political problems of the country. It is equally important that a long view shall be taken of its economic problems. Before the direction of change has become set, it is far easier to influence and control it. During the last generation superficially the change has been small. Natives still live in the same villages, building the same huts, employing the same methods of agriculture. A few non-essentials have changed. Cotton is worn; candles are used;

other small European luxuries have crept in, but out-
wardly things are much as they were. But in reality
change has been profound in the Native's economic life,
as in all other departments of his existence. He has become
already a part of the world's economic system. Whether
we like it or not, his income, his power to pay taxes, to
educate his children in the mission school five hundred
miles from the nearest European town, are all dependent
on the whims of the copper market, on the number of
wireless sets or motor-cars sold in Europe and America.
This dependence on world conditions can hardly fail to
grow with each decade, and the country must become
increasingly more exposed to the danger and difficulties of
economic fluctuations and the unemployment which they
bring in their train. Wealth must lie along the road of
specialisation and concentration upon copper- or zinc-
mining, or upon whatever other tasks individuals or
groups or districts are best fitted to perform. But security
lies in the self-sufficiency of subsistence agriculture.
Copper, unfortunately, is likely to remain one of the most
fluctuating of industries. Some compromise, then, will
require to be found between the conflicting interests of a
solution to the problem of poverty and a solution to the
problem of unemployment. We may perhaps be forced to
modify our views as to the desirability of a complete
stabilisation of the labour force in the towns and on the
mines. Dependence on world conditions brings other difficulties also. The general level of prices, and the relation of
individual prices of different goods, will be decided less
and less by local conditions, more and more by conditions
outside the Territory. Where hitherto tradition and fixity
have played an important part, flexibility will become
increasingly necessary.

In this process of economic adjustment the missions have
a very important part to play. One of their most valuable
services may often be to interpret to those who have been
brought into conflict with the forces of economic change
the meaning of what is happening and to help them to meet

their difficulties intelligently. Progressive adaptation of old methods of production, old ways of doing things, to the new conditions of life to-day, cannot fail to throw strains upon the social and political frameworks within which the people live and produce. Some of these strains may become so irresistible that to attempt to withstand them must lead to disaster. Our objective in such cases must be to discover the most easy and painless way of yielding before them. Other strains may be less insistent, and we can profitably study the methods whereby we can assist to diminish or to delay the impact. Few countries have attempted to weather the storm of industrial revolution without such control as may be afforded by social legislation, by the protection of industries in a process of re-adaptation, by the use of an educational system to foster or to protect the technical knowledge of valuable groups, by influencing tastes to harmonise with the capacities of the economic organisation.

As we attempt, however, to estimate our power to influence the trend of the transition in such a country as Northern Rhodesia, it is impossible not to be impressed by the feebleness of the weapons with which we are seeking to oppose the great but slow-moving force of economic change. We must always remember that economic forces are only the manifestation of the ever-changing wants and desires of ourselves and of our fellow-men. When we are in conflict with economic forces we are in conflict with ourselves. By changing ourselves and others we can radically modify the forces that encompass us. In some cases the power of the people of one country to influence these forces is small, in other cases it may be considerable. In the circumstances of Northern Rhodesia to-day much can be done within the Territory itself to control the change that is taking place. A great opportunity to guide the whole process of economic development, and to establish a firm basis for political development, rests with those, missionaries, Government officers, mine officials, and others, who are shaping the character of the Native and moulding his tastes for good or for bad.

PART FOUR

THE PROBLEM OF GOVERNMENT

LEO MARQUARD

CHAPTER XIII

THE GOVERNMENT OF NORTHERN RHODESIA

(a) INTRODUCTORY

WHILE it is true that people cannot be made good by act of parliament, it is at least equally true that good laws are a condition of the harmonious and progressive evolution of society. Rousseau's remark that "man is born free and is everywhere in chains" has as much validity to-day as ever before in human history and everything depends on how the chains are forged. They may chafe the wearers and hamper development; or they may preserve them from falling and promote orderly progress. In an African dependency no less than in a modern State the general proposition remains true that the law is a conditioning factor circumscribing the action of society; but while, broadly speaking, it is true to say that in a modern State society itself is responsible for the extent to which its action is circumscribed, in an African dependency the law is imposed from above by an alien government. This fact greatly increases the responsibilities of those who govern in Africa, for there is no easy and automatic check on laws which may be good in themselves but which are nevertheless unsuited to the needs of society.

Mission societies operating in such a country as Northern Rhodesia have to work within the proscribed limits of the law; either that or they must change the law. From both points of view a knowledge of the administration of the country, of the motives actuating Government and of the goal at which legislation aims, is an essential equipment for missionaries. Without an intelligent and sympathetic understanding of the methods of government, the work of the missionary will lack contact with reality and any criticism of administrative action will be valueless and

227

irritating. With such an understanding missionaries can co-operate with Government to the greater benefit of the Native, whose interests they wish to serve. In view of the importance of such co-operation, some aspects of government in Northern Rhodesia are discussed in this and the two following chapters.

(b) EXECUTIVE AND LEGISLATIVE

In 1924 the Charter in terms of which Northern Rhodesia had been administered for a quarter of a century expired and the Territory became a protectorate of the British Crown. In that year the framework of the new administration was created by three instruments—the Northern Rhodesia Order - in - Council, the Northern Rhodesia (Legislative Council) Order-in-Council and the Instructions to the Governor.[1]

The Governor and Commander-in-Chief of the Territory is appointed by the Crown to exercise all the powers and jurisdiction of the Crown, and for the purpose of advising him there is an Executive Council which consists of the Chief Secretary, the Attorney-General, the Treasurer, the Secretary for Native Affairs and the Director of Medical and Sanitary Services; these are styled *ex officio* members. On instructions from the Secretary of State for the Colonies, the Governor may appoint more official and some unofficial members, and he may, without instructions, summon anyone whose advice he desires as an extraordinary member of the Executive Council for a special occasion. The Governor presides over the Executive Council and is bound to communicate to it all instructions from the Secretary of State and to consult it on all actions unless, in his discretion, the matter is too trivial or too urgent to brook of delay, or when he considers that the interests of good government would not be served by such consultation. Minutes of meetings must be kept and copies transmitted

---

[1] *Vide*, for all three, *Northern Rhodesia Government Gazette*, No. 211 of 1/4/1924.

to England twice a year. The Governor alone submits
questions to the Executive Council, but should a member
make a written request that some particular matter should
be placed on the agenda, and should such a request be refused, the member has the right to have it recorded in the
minutes. The Governor may act in opposition to the advice
of the Executive Council, but must report his reasons for
doing so to the Secretary of State, and any member whose
advice has been rejected has the right to have his opinion
recorded in the minutes.

The Governor has powers to make appointments, suspend officials, grant pardons, subdivide the Territory into
provinces and districts and make grants of land; his
assent is necessary to legislation. Among the duties of the
Governor which are specifically mentioned is that of promoting to the utmost of his power ·'religion and education
among the Native inhabitants of the Territory, and he is
especially to take care to protect them in their persons and
in the free enjoyment of their possessions and by all lawful
means to prevent and restrain all violence and injustice
which may in any manner be practised or attempted
against them".[1]

The Governor is responsible to the Crown through the
Secretary of State for the Colonies and thus to the British
Parliament, where his actions may be called in question or
criticised during the debate on the Colonial Office Vote
or by other parliamentary procedure. The powers of the
Crown as exercised by the Governor are far wider than
those in the neighbouring colony of Southern Rhodesia,
which has responsible government and is in consequence
not subject to the same control by the British Parliament.

There are several ways in which laws may be made for
Northern Rhodesia, but, ultimately, there is only one
source from which laws derive their authority, and that is
the British Parliament. Thus when, in 1924, Section 21 of
the Northern Rhodesia Order-in-Council declared that all

[1] *Vide* Instructions to the Governor, paragraph 23, *Northern
Rhodesia Government Gazette*, No. 211 of 1/4/1924.

existing laws, regulations, proclamations and rules should remain in force until repealed, it is from an instrument of the British Government that these laws derive their force. Again, such Native law and custom as is enforced in the courts derives its authority not from the fact that it is Native law and custom but from the fact that the British Government has declared that it shall be enforced. Up till 1911 any act of the British Parliament applied equally to Northern Rhodesia, but while Parliament may still legislate for the Territory, no act is applicable to-day unless it is specifically intended to be so. The King may make Orders-in-Council, and the constitution of the Territory is, in fact, based on such orders. One of these provides for the establishment of a Legislative Council.

The Legislative Council consists of the Governor as President, five *ex officio* members, not more than four nominated official members and seven elected unofficial members. The five *ex officio* members are the same as for the Executive Council; the nominated official members are appointed by the Governor subject to the approval of the Secretary of State, and the election of the unofficial members is regulated by two ordinances,[1] one of 1925, the other of 1929. The voting qualifications provide that the applicant for the franchise must be twenty-one years of age, or if a woman twenty-five years, must be a British subject,[2] must not live a communal or tribal life, and must be able to fill in the application form. Further, the applicant must have resided either for six months within the electoral area in occupation of a house of the value of £250, or for thirty months anywhere in the Territory during the four years preceding the date of application if he or she is the owner of real or personal property, anywhere in the Territory, of a clear value, free of encumbrance, of £2000.

[1] Vide *Laws of Northern Rhodesia*, 1930, vol. i. pp. 154-78.

[2] It is interesting to note that since Northern Rhodesia is a protectorate Natives are, presumably, not British subjects, and would, as the law stands, not be eligible for the franchise. This was manifestly not the intention of the ordinances.

The Legislative Council meets at least once a year and is elected for three years, but the Governor may dissolve it sooner; an election must take place within three months of dissolution.

Subject to certain restrictions, the Legislative Council may make ordinances for "the administration of justice, the raising of revenue and generally for the peace, order and good government of Northern Rhodesia".[1] Ordinances must respect Native laws and customs provided that these are not incompatible with public safety nor conflict with natural justice and morality. In practice, this means that such matters as tribal ownership of land, tribal authority, customary marriage and divorce, inheritance customs and polygamy are recognised by law, while the practice of witchcraft and ceremonial murder are prohibited. Any member of the Legislative Council may initiate a bill provided it is not a money bill for raising or disposing of revenue; such a money bill may be initiated only by direction of, or with the express sanction of, the Governor. When a bill has been passed, the Governor may either assent to it, refuse his assent, or reserve the bill for the signification of the King's pleasure. Certain kinds of bill must be so reserved. These are bills which discriminate against non-Europeans, except in the matter of arms, ammunition and liquor; bills which affect mining revenues, railways or the construction of new railways; bills which provide for divorce; bills which affect currency and banking, impose differential duties or affect foreign policy and existing treaties. When urgency demands it the Governor may give his consent to such a bill, but the matter must be reported immediately to the Secretary of State. Apart from these bills which are specifically reserved for the allowance or disallowance by the Secretary of State, he may disallow any ordinance passed by the Legislative Council.

In action the Legislative Council resembles a parliament in certain superficial matters such as procedure and debate, but there the resemblance ends. The Governor has a

[1] *Vide* Northern Rhodesia Order-in-Council, 1924, paragraph 20.

deliberative and a casting vote, and the presence of the
official majority which is bound to vote with the Government ensures the passage of any resolution that Government may desire or the defeat of any adverse proposal.
The Governor, though acting as President of the Council,
by no means occupies the position of the Speaker in Parliament, and he intervenes in debate whenever he thinks it
necessary or desirable. For various reasons the debates in
the Legislative Council wear an air of unreality. The unofficial members, representing the European community,
can never carry a resolution against the Government. The
Governor's veto is not exercised according to the advice
of a responsible ministry, and the British Government
exercises a very effective control over legislation. Finally,
the European population is so scattered that the creation
of a representative public opinion is a matter of great difficulty. But it would be a mistake to underestimate the influence of the unofficial members; their power of public
criticism and the authority with which they are clothed as
duly elected representatives give them a position from
which they can bring pressure to bear on administration
and on legislation. The Government's policy of requiring
that 50 per cent of the skilled labour used by building
contractors on Government buildings shall be European
is probably a result of such pressure.[1]

Historically, the logical conclusion to the existing type
of government in Northern Rhodesia is full responsible
government, and the European inhabitants tend to speak
of the advent of such a government as a mere matter
of time. Needless to say, the position as regards Native
administration would be greatly complicated by such a
development, for once responsible government has been
granted it is well-nigh impossible for the Imperial Government to exercise any control. Experience in southern
Africa and elsewhere has shown that, where a small group

---

[1] It should, however, be noted that this policy does not apply to road
or bridge work nor to work carried out departmentally. Further, the
necessity for good workmanship is an important factor which merits
full consideration.

of Europeans gains control over the government of a territory in which it is seriously outnumbered by Africans, it
cannot resist the temptation to entrench its position by
restrictive legislation and by discriminating against the
Africans. There is no reason why Northern Rhodesia
should be an exception to this rule. The existence of a parliament in the ordinary sense of the word would inevitably
raise the question of the representation of Natives; moreover, the orderly development of Indirect Rule, a subject
which is discussed in a subsequent chapter, would be seriously hampered by any premature attempts to represent
Native and European interests in the same parliament.
Well-informed European opinion in Northern Rhodesia—
though it is probably a minority opinion—is quite confi-
dent that responsible government as it is known in the
South will not be granted for a very long time. The present
European population is small and scattered and the rate
of immigration is almost insignificant. Even a superficial
view of the agricultural possibilities of the country makes
it seem unlikely that this rate of immigration will increase
or that the country is sufficiently suited to Europeans to
encourage settlement. In these circumstances the British
Government, with the present state of British public
opinion, would scarcely contemplate handing over the
government of more than a million Africans to a parliament dominated by a handful of Europeans.

In a discussion on the political future of Northern Rhodesia the question of responsible government is closely
connected with that of affiliation with the South, since
union with her two southern neighbours presupposes
responsible government in Northern Rhodesia. Will the
Territory unite with Southern Rhodesia and, further, will
the two Rhodesias join the Union of South Africa? These
are, naturally, questions for the future, and all that can be
done here is to note some of the determining factors.
Northern Rhodesia differs from her two southern neighbours in having a comparatively small European population which is mainly concentrated in the railway strip

from Livingstone to Ndola. This fact alone is likely to make union with the South uncomfortable, and it has led to the suggestion that North-Western Rhodesia, including Barotseland as a Reserve, should be joined to Southern Rhodesia.[1] At the moment, economic interests link the North-West strongly with the South, but it may be expected that the existing outlet to Lobito Bay on the west coast and a prospective railway to the East will lessen this influence. They will lessen, too, the flow of political ideas on Native administration which now run strongly from their sources in the South. That such a diminution of influence will be of advantage to Northern Rhodesia, whose administrative problems are essentially different from those of the South, can hardly be doubted. The apparent similarity of interest with the South is largely due to historical accident and to the direction of railway development, but from the administrative point of view the destiny of Northern Rhodesia is linked with the East rather than with the South.

(c) NATIVE LEGISLATION

A description of some of the laws in force affecting Natives will give a clearer view of the general principle underlying administration in Northern Rhodesia.[2] Since the Territory is a protectorate, the legal status of the Native inhabitants is not easy to define. The African is not a British subject but a protected person whose rights have been defined by legislative and executive action on the part of the British Government. The Northern Rhodesia Order-in-Council lays down that no discriminating legislation may be made without the consent of the Secretary of State, except in the matter of arms, ammunition and

---

[1] *Vide* Cmd. 3234 of 1929 (Hilton Young Report), p. 264. The majority of the Commission rejected this proposal, which was made by the chairman, the Right Honourable Sir E. Hilton Young.

[2] The description given here of the administration of Northern Rhodesia does not include Barotseland, where conditions differ greatly from those in the rest of the Territory. A note on Barotseland will be found on p. 247.

liquor. A Native may "acquire, hold, encumber, and dispose of land on the same terms as a person who is not a
Native" provided that if he encumbers or alienates land
the contract is not valid unless made in the presence of
and attested by a magistrate.[1] This is not the case in most
parts of the Union of South Africa, and both in the Union
and in Southern Rhodesia the policy is to have separate
areas for Native and for European ownership. Though
there are signs in Northern Rhodesia that a few Natives
are beginning to desire individual ownership, the overwhelming majority live on tribally owned land, and the
question is not likely to arise to any great extent in the
immediate future. Tribal lands are sufficiently safeguarded
in that no Native may be removed from a village or from
any land assigned to him for occupation except after full
inquiry by and by order of the Governor.

The policy of Native reserves has been embarked upon.
Apart from Barotseland, which is virtually a protectorate within a protectorate, reserves have been demarcated in three areas, the railway area, the East Luangwa
Province and the Tanganyika Province. In these three
areas, chosen because European settlement had already
taken place there, reserves were set aside for the use of
Natives "in perpetuity" and the delimitation followed
investigations by a Reserves Commission. Various factors
were considered by the Commission; water, suitability of
soil, probable future occupation by Europeans and railway expansion, existing Native occupation and probable
future needs of an increasing Native population, these
were all taken into account. It should be noted that non-
reserve areas are not European reserves but are Crown
lands and may be sold or leased to anyone. After the
boundaries of the reserves had been drawn, villages falling immediately outside had gradually to be moved in,
and while there is little evidence of actual hardship being
entailed, there was some dissatisfaction on the part of the

---

[1] *Vide* the Northern Rhodesia Order-in-Council, 1924, paragraphs
40 and 42.

Natives, particularly since the areas vacated have not been occupied by Europeans. In some cases the removal of villages along main roads caused inconvenience and hardship to Native travellers, who found themselves without their customary ports of call on a journey.

There is no doubt that in the policy of reserves the Government is actuated by the soundest motives. Taking warning from the difficulties of expropriating land for Native use in the Union of South Africa, it desires to secure reserves for Native occupation before it is too late. Any friction that may have been caused by over-anxiety to have the movement into the reserves completed soon is fully realised by the Government, and there has been a very considerable slowing-up of the policy. Opinions differ as to the wisdom of reserves in Northern Rhodesia. The principle is open to attack on the grounds that it is doubtful whether the land reserved for future European development will ever be required, and, secondly, whether "in perpetuity" is likely to be interpreted literally if any rich discovery of minerals be made in areas which are now called reserves.[1] In the Union and in Southern Rhodesia, where European occupation is not only far more extensive but is increasing more rapidly, there is much to be said for the policy of reserves as a protection of Native interests; but in Northern Rhodesia it would hardly seem to be necessary and might result in land being locked up.[2]

The basis of taxation in Northern Rhodesia is different for Natives and for Europeans. For the latter there is an income tax [3] and for the former a poll tax, while both alike contribute toward the large revenue derived from customs duties. The poll tax is assessed at three different rates, 7s. 6d. per annum in the extreme North-West, 10s. in

[1] In this connection should be noted the recent controversy in Great Britain and in Kenya regarding the discovery of gold in the latter country.

[2] An alternative policy is to create reserves not for Native but for European occupation. Granting the necessity for reserves, there is much to be said for such a policy.

[3] As an emergency measure a personal tax has been imposed on every non-Native for the year 1933.

the North-East and 12s. 6d. in the railway area where earning capacity is higher. Every male Native over eighteen years of age is liable for the tax, which is collected in the province in which he happens to be working but at the rate of the province from which he comes. This system of varying rates is in vogue in the Belgian Congo too, unlike the Union of South Africa where a flat rate applies irrespective of earning capacity. In the existing economic circumstances the payment of the tax is not always an easy matter, and when a man cannot find the money Government is prepared to give him work, if such is available, or to assist him to find work, at standard rates of pay. Generally speaking, a month's work enables the tax-payer to discharge his obligations. In both the Belgian Congo and in Tanganyika Territory work may be done in lieu of the tax, but in Northern Rhodesia the cash transaction must actually take place, though there seems to be no difference in principle involved. Legally there is nothing to prevent the tax being paid in kind, but this is not the practice; nor may the tax be paid in instalments. European officials collect the taxes, which are all paid into general revenue, and there is no system of local taxation from which purely local needs might be served. If a district requires a road or a bridge, funds must come from the central Government. The obvious difficulties of such a lack of local revenue may be met by the institution of tribal treasuries, which will be discussed more fully in the next chapter.

There is not, as in the Union of South Africa, an arrangement by which a definite proportion of the tax is earmarked for Native development, and the experience of the Union is not sufficiently happy to warrant the introduction of such a system. It tends to stabilise the amount of money spent on Native development without any consideration of the expanding needs of society. There is, however, a Native Reserves Fund which is being built up from rents, grazing fees, timber royalties and other funds collected from the reserves. This fund is to be spent for the advancement of Natives occupying the reserves. More than seven thousand pounds has been collected so far, and the money has been invested pending schemes for expenditure. Native authorities are to be consulted in the allocation of funds.[1]

Apart from the ordinances regulating the sale of arms, ammunition and liquor, there is very little legislation which discriminates against the Native. There is, legally, no colour bar.[2] The railways are privately owned, and there European trade union pressure has been sufficiently strong to prevent the employment of Natives on skilled labour; but on the mines and in Government employ Native skilled labour is used more extensively than in either the Union of South Africa or Southern Rhodesia and to about the same extent as in the Belgian Congo. There is, of course, social segregation, and signs are not wanting of pressure being brought to bear on Government for colour-bar legislation as it is known in the South. It is not in the least likely that Government or the Colonial Office will give way to these demands, but the growth of towns, with the influx of a European artisan class, is bound to increase the pressure, especially in times of unemployment such as the present.

An example of legislation which discriminates against Natives is the Native Registration Ordinance, which requires all Natives in prescribed districts,[3] and those who wish to enter such districts, to carry an identification certificate. This is not a pass and is not a form of taxation. The system was instituted partly to be able to control movement in a mixed European-Bantu area and partly to protect Natives by enforcing the payment of wages due; it differs radically from the pass system in vogue in the Union. The ordinance is apparently not working well at the moment, since Natives from other districts can easily destroy a certifi-

---

[1] Vide *Annual Report upon Native Affairs, 1931*, p. 10.

[2] It might be noted here that the jury system, that fruitful source of racial clash, is fortunately absent from Northern Rhodesia.

[3] The only districts prescribed at present are in what is commonly known as the railway strip; but the desirability of prescribing the Fort Jameson district has been under discussion.

cate and get another, and because European employers do
not trouble to comply with the law by filling in the period
of the engagement and the last wage paid. The last wage is
normally the highest, and Natives are dissatisfied because
the certificate does not protect them sufficiently in this
respect. It is probable, therefore, that the ordinance will
soon be amended.

The only other restriction on movement is in force in the
town locations, where curfew regulations prevail. While
no Native may be outside the location without a pass
after nine o'clock at night, it is equally true that no European may enter the location at night without permission.
Natives in the rural areas who wish to change their domicile must obtain the permission of the Chief, but this may
not be refused, though Chiefs will sometimes try to prevent
women from moving. There is also evidence that Chiefs try
to extort a small payment for permission to leave, but this
is illegal and not of sufficient frequency to constitute a
restriction on movement.

The use of penal sanctions for the enforcement of tax
payment and of the terms of the Employment of Natives
Ordinance may be considered as discriminating legislation,
and it is excused on the grounds that it would be useless to
impose fines on people who have no cash, and that therefore
the only method of enforcing the law is by the application
of penal sanctions. It is a method used in practically all
African dependencies, and provided that it is wisely used
it need not, in the circumstances, be objectionable. At the
same time it is a system which is very easily abused, and it
should never bo considered as more than a temporary
measure.

The recognition of Native law and custom in Northern
Rhodesia, as in other parts of Africa, produces some
features of administration that merit discussion. Not only are
principles which would not be recognised in English law
applied under Native custom, but even where English law
is applied, as in most criminal cases, Native custom tends
to modify the application and even the law itself. The inter-

action of English law and Bantu custom is of the utmost
importance in the development of Bantu society and provides some of the sharp distinctions that exist between the
code of Government and that of missions. Some examples
will illustrate what is meant. Polygamy is recognised by
law, and a husband or wife may give evidence in a trial
where the wife or husband respectively is involved, provided they belong to a polygamous tribe.[1] Government
feels the impossibility of forbidding polygamy without running the risk of seriously disorganising the whole of Bantu
life. As African society is constituted there are really no
such persons as widows, orphans and paupers, and the
creation by legislation, in certain polygamous tribes at
least, of such a class entails a responsibility which Government is not prepared to assume. On the other hand, mission
societies feel that they will be upholding polygamy as an
institution if they admit polygamists into the Church. This
policy is based, in the last analysis, on the conception of
Christian society as an individualist society and on the
assumption that Christianity can flourish only where the
family, in the European sense of the word, is the basis.

Another difference in code arises from the fact that
Government recognises as legal only marriages contracted
according to Native custom. In Southern Rhodesia, and
elsewhere, the law provides for Native Christian marriages,
but though the matter has been frequently discussed in
Northern Rhodesia the Government is not prepared to
legislate. To do so would entail parallel legislation prohibiting bigamy, since cases frequently occur where a
Christian Native who has been living with one wife for
many years, suddenly decides to take a second wife.
Tribal influence has been too strong for him or kinship
obligations must be acknowledged, and to prosecute such
a man for bigamy would be manifestly unjust.

Two examples of the modification of English legal
practice will suffice to show the tendency. The practice of

[1] Vide *The Statute Law of North Eastern Rhodesia, 1900–1907*, pp.
122, 123.

witchcraft is prohibited by law and is severely punished as a criminal offence. But if a Native is found guilty of murder, for example, and it is proved that he acted under the fear of witchcraft, the death sentence is frequently commuted by the Governor. Again, adultery is not a crime in English law, but, in some tribes at any rate, adultery with a Chief's wife used to be punishable by death; in other tribes it was simply a tort. These facts are recognised in law, and in the former tribes adultery is now treated by the courts as a crime[1] while in the latter it is not.

An interesting piece of legislation, reminiscent of the early English law of group responsibility, is to be found in the Collective Punishment Proclamation.[2] Under this proclamation the Governor may impose fines on all or any of the inhabitants of a village or the members of a tribe or community if, after due inquiry, he is satisfied that they have failed to prevent a criminal escape, failed to restore stolen property, combined to suppress evidence in a criminal case, wilfully disobeyed a lawful order of a Native authority, or if their conduct has been such as to necessitate the use of force to suppress riot or to collect taxes. If someone is found dangerously wounded or unlawfully killed, the community may be held responsible unless it can prove that it is innocent either of complicity or of negligence. This law was used in connection with the Watch Tower movement, and again when an epidemic of petty theft broke out in the Abercorn district. Though seldom invoked, it is an instrument that can be used when other methods fail and it is not unsuited to the existing state of Native society.

It remains to be said in conclusion that a great deal of legislation directly affecting Natives is made by executive and administrative action rather than by enactment. An enabling ordinance is passed by the legislature, and the Governor then makes regulations which are, of course,

---

[1] This is not invariably true, and adultery is treated criminally only when occasion demands. It still remains true, however, that English legal practice has been modified to this extent.

[2] Vide *The Statute Law of Northern Rhodesia, 1911–1916*, pp. 191-3.

subject to the control of the Secretary of State. Though this tendency to legislation by regulation is much deplored in other countries because of the power it places in the hands of a bureaucracy, it works well in Northern Rhodesia and ensures that the final form of the regulations is the responsibility of the Government officials, who know how to consult Native opinion and to study varying local conditions.

(d) The Courts

The Northern Rhodesia Order-in-Council of 1924 provides for the establishment of a High Court, Magistrates' Courts and Native Commissioners' Courts. Such courts were, of course, in existence before 1924, but slight modifications have been made from time to time. The High Court has the same criminal and civil jurisdiction that is vested in the High Court of Justice in England, and an appeal in a civil suit in which the amount involved exceeds £500 lies to the Privy Council. The Court itself acts as a court of appeal from Magistrates' Courts and has full powers to reverse and vary judgments, order a new trial or alter a sentence. Native law and custom, when not contrary to "natural justice", equity and good government, are largely applied if both parties are Native, and even in mixed cases when the judge is of opinion that a strict adherence to the rules of English law may result in an injustice. When Native law and custom are in question, the Court may appoint Native Chiefs or other persons as assessors, but the decision on the case rests with the Court. In cases where Europeans only are concerned, English law and the ordinances of the Territory are applied, and the rules of procedure are so framed that civil suits shall be "decided on their merits according to substantial justice and without excessive regard to technicalities of pleading or procedure and without unnecessary delay".[1]

Magistrates' Courts[2] have criminal jurisdiction in all

---

[1] *Vide* Northern Rhodesia Order-in-Council, 1924, paragraph 30.

[2] *Vide* Magistrates' Courts Ordinance, Chapter 4 of *The Laws of Northern Rhodesia, 1930.*

cases arising in their districts, but their powers of punishment are limited to a maximum fine of £25, or imprisonment with or without hard labour, and with or without spare diet and solitary confinement, not exceeding twelve months, or a whipping or caning not exceeding twenty-four lashes or strokes, or to any two of these punishments. If the Magistrate is satisfied that the accused is guilty and that the heaviest punishment that he may by law inflict is inadequate, he may convict the prisoner and report the matter to the High Court with a recommendation as to a fit sentence. On instructions from the High Court he may then pronounce sentence; this provision included murder cases. The civil jurisdiction of the Magistrate is limited to debt or damages not exceeding £100, to issues of writs of habeas corpus, and to making orders for the custody of infants.[1] He may not deal with suits involving title to land, title to office, wills, the legitimacy of a marriage, or divorce other than under Native custom. The same rules regarding Native law and custom that apply in the High Court apply in the Magistrates' Courts.

Subject to certain limitations, Native Commissioners' Courts [2] have, as to Natives in their districts, the jurisdiction and powers of Magistrates. They may try civil suits in which both parties are Natives and criminal cases in which the accused is a Native, and they may try mixed cases if both parties give their consent. The powers of punishment of a Native Commissioner are limited to imprisonment not exceeding six months, with or without hard labour, to a fine not exceeding £5, to a whipping or caning not exceeding ten strokes, or to any two of these punishments. If a Native Commissioner is satisfied as to the guilt of a prisoner but cannot give an adequate sentence, he may report to the Provincial Commissioner, who may, in turn, adopt the same procedure and report to

---

[1] The civil jurisdiction of Magistrates includes also ejectment orders, affiliation, maintenance, and any order which may be made under the Summary Jurisdiction (Married Women) Act of 1895.

[2] *Vide* Native Commissioners' Courts Ordinance, Chapter 5 of *The Laws of Northern Rhodesia, 1930.*

the High Court. Appeals lie to the Provincial Commissioner sitting in the Magistrates' Court and all cases must be sent to him for review. He has full powers to vary or reverse a judgment, order a new trial or pass a new sentence, and must forward a copy of the return from the Native Commissioners' Court to the High Court, which, in turn, has full powers of review. As before, provision is made for the use of Native law and custom and for the appointment of Native or other assessors.

In practice the offices of Magistrate and District Officer are at the present time filled by the same official. Thus Provincial Commissioners, Acting Provincial Commissioners and District Officers of the first or second grade are given magisterial powers, and a Native Commissioner may be a District Officer of the first, second or third grade. Such a District Officer is, in most cases, District Commissioner, Magistrate and Native Commissioner all in one. As the first he administers the district; as the second he tries European or mixed cases; and as the third he tries Native cases. At the present time there is no real need to separate the judicial and administrative functions, and it can be done at any time under existing legislation. At Ndola and at Broken Hill it has been done by seconding a District Officer for purely magisterial work; such an officer is called a Police Magistrate.

Finally there are the first and second class Native Courts, but these can more conveniently be discussed in Chapter XIV. under the heading of Indirect Rule, as they form an integral part of that policy.

(e) ADMINISTRATION

The secretariat at Livingstone, which remains the capital until Lusaka is ready to house the different departments, is the central control of all administration. The Department of Mines is more conveniently situated at Ndola, but it nevertheless forms part of the secretariat. The whole field of administration is divided into departments such as Native Affairs, Education, Justice, Agriculture, and while Government is naturally responsible for policy, the departmental officials exert a great influence through their intimate knowledge and through their control of the routine work of the departments. It is bureaucracy in the better sense of the word, and conditions in Northern Rhodesia are well suited to this form of administration. The Secretary for Native Affairs, for example, has an *ex officio* seat on both the Executive and the Legislative Council, and all the weight of his experience can be fully utilised whenever legislation affecting Natives is proposed.[1]

The Territory is divided into nine provinces, Awemba, Tanganyika, Mweru-Luapula, East Luangwa, Barotse, Batoka, Kafue, Luangwa and Kasempa, though the recently published report of the Finance Commission recommends a reduction to seven. At the head of each province is a Provincial Commissioner, and the provinces are divided into 33 districts in all, each in charge of a District Commissioner who is the senior District Officer in that district. There are three grades of District Officer, first, second and third, and there are Cadets who serve a probationary period of two years. Usually there are at least two officers, or an officer and a cadet, on each station. The provincial staff in 1931 consisted of 9 Provincial Commissioners, 91 District Officers, 15 European clerks, 95 Native clerks and 553 Native messengers.[2] The District Officers are responsible to the Provincial Commissioners and report to them; in their turn the Provincial Commissioners report to the secretariat, and their reports form the basis of the annual government reports on the state of the Territory.

Though the great bulk of the work of District Officers and Provincial Commissioners is concerned with Native administration, they are in charge of all matters whether distinctively Native or not. They have magisterial powers

---

[1] It has latterly been the custom to have a Provincial Commissioner as one of the nominated members of the Legislative Council.

[2] Vide *Annual Report upon Native Affairs, 1931*, pp. 43 and 48.

and in townships and municipalities they perform important functions in connection with the administration of the European inhabitants. The District Officer spends a great deal of his time touring his district, inspecting villages, giving advice to and listening to complaints from Chiefs and headmen, attending to roads and bridges, collecting taxes, and, generally, keeping in close touch with the Native population in his area. Recent legislation (described in Chapter XIV.) has set the District Officer free from having to judge numerous petty civil and criminal cases; and while his responsibilities have been increased rather than diminished, he has more time for the real work of administration. The system by which District Officers are moved from district to district, coupled with the terms of their contract, which provide for six months' leave every three years, makes it difficult for an officer to become fully acquainted with the language and customs of any one district before he is moved to another. There is much to be said for and against this policy, but, on balance, the present system would appear to have a slight advantage over any other that has been suggested. It tends to make administration rather more impersonal and it gives an opportunity for judicious changes without prejudicing an officer's position. The recent Finance Commission stated that transfers of officers had been too frequent of late and militated against efficiency as well as involving expense.[1] Government is considering a scheme for reducing the number of transfers, but whether this is purely an economy measure is hard to say.

Provincial Commissioners hold conferences of District Officers in their province and are themselves called to periodic conferences with the Secretary for Native Affairs. This valuable piece of machinery, which is being threatened under present economic conditions, provides for the pooling of ideas and experience, and militates against the dangers of isolated action based on individual interpretations of policy. It gives cohesion and force to what might

[1] Vide *Report of the Finance Commission, 1932*, p. 47.

be termed the extra-secretariat opinion, and thus acts as a brake on any tendency to overcentralise.

The work of the administration will depend for a long time to come on the Provincial Commissioners and District Officers. They carry a heavy responsibility, for they more than most people come into very close contact with the Native population and exert a powerful influence on their surroundings. Under trying climatic conditions they have to play the most difficult of all games, that of being content to go slowly and to allow for and guide a natural evolution rather than to force a spurious progress. Being in comparatively lonely positions, they are subject to the strain of severe criticism, often of an ignorant and unsympathetic nature, from European settlers and missionaries. They have to administer both European and Bantu, religious and non-religious, while the missionary deals primarily with the Bantu. This difference of function is bound to produce a difference of emphasis which, if incompletely comprehended, will result in friction. Northern Rhodesia is fortunate in its administrative officers and, provided there is mutual understanding of aims and methods, a full and fruitful co-operation between missionary and administrator may confidently be expected. It cannot be sufficiently stressed that such co-operation is essential to what is, after all, the common object of mission societies and Government, namely, the welfare of the African.

Note on Barotseland

The administration of Barotseland differs in so many respects from that of the rest of Northern Rhodesia that it is necessary to indicate where the distinctions lie. In 1890, Lewanika, Chief of the Barotse nation, who had dominion in varying degrees over many tribes, granted a mineral concession to the British South Africa Company. In 1900, Coryndon, on behalf of the Company, concluded an agreement with Lewanika and his Council by which the Company gained the right to administer justice between

Bantu and European, but not in purely Native cases. The
Company was to protect the Chief and his nation and
assist in education and in the work of civilisation. The
Chief retained all his customary rights and was to be paid
£850 per annum by the Company. European immigration
was not allowed except with the consent of the Chief and
his Council. In 1905, by another agreement, the Barotse
Trust Fund was created and 10 per cent of the tax from
North-Western Rhodesia was paid into it. The money was
to be used for educational, medical, veterinary and other
services for Barotseland. This was felt to be unfair to those
Natives who did not live in Barotseland, and in 1924 the
agreement was altered to provide that 30 per cent of the
tax from Barotseland itself was to be credited to the fund.
In 1924, too, a number of the Chief's customary rights
were, by agreement, commuted for cash payments by
Government.

By the earlier agreements the Chief and his Council
retained extensive political and judicial rights. Thus the
proclamation of 1916 providing for the appointment by
Government of Chiefs and headmen did not, in large
measure, apply to Barotseland. Again, in the administration of justice between Natives, Government has no jurisdiction except in serious cases, and there is no appeal from
the Native Courts to the European Courts. Finally, the
very important provisions of Indirect Rule have not been
applied in Barotseland, though the present Chief has agreed
that this should be done and the matter awaits the consent
of the Colonial Office.

At present, then, Barotseland is a protectorate within a
protectorate and the Chief and his Council or *Khotla* have
far wider powers than a Native Chief has in the rest of
the Territory.

CHAPTER XIV

TILL the advent of European governments Bantu tribes were ruled by their Chiefs and Councils. Broadly speaking, the tribes were independent of one another, and within the tribe a body of customary law grew up which suited the needs of primitive hunting and agricultural communities. The Chief was seldom despotic, and the amount of power allowed him depended on his own personality and on public opinion as expressed by the Council. These Councils differed so widely in constitution that a full description would require much space; but it may be said, generally, that they were semi-hereditary bodies on which the wise men of the tribe served. These elders were either appointed by the Chief or took their places by hereditary right, and they, with the Chief, guided the tribe in peace and war. No important decision could be taken without the consent of the Council; laws were administered by the Chief in his Council, and the appointment of a new Chief was the responsibility of the Council. In return for leadership in war and peace the Chief was maintained by his people, who paid tribute in labour and in kind, while the religious nature of the Chieftainship added enormously to the prestige of the office. Even when one tribe ruled over others, as in Barotseland, there was usually no violent interference with the customs of the subject tribes, and the ruling race contented itself with the exaction of tribute. Between these independent and semi-independent tribes there was no common law except the simple rule that one tribe was either at war or at peace with another. When the British South Africa Company established its administration in Northern Rhodesia it brought the tribes under a common rule and naturally abolished what had now become private war. It was then faced with the task of maintaining law and order between the tribes and within the tribes, and was bound to superimpose a body of statute law over the customary law of the African.

In Northern Rhodesia, as elsewhere in South and Central Africa, the simplest and least expensive policy was to "use the Chiefs" in the administration of the tribes, and it was carried out in a way that constituted a radical break with the past. On the one hand, the European administrations, here as elsewhere in Africa, greatly exaggerated the powers of the Chief when it came to treaty-making for cession of land. Throughout Africa, literally thousands of treaties [1] were made between Native Chiefs and European Government or Company officials, and for the most part these treaties, while useful in pushing claims against a rival Government, were not worth the paper they were written on. On the other hand, when it came to administration, the Chiefs were greatly reduced in status by being turned into salaried officials of the administration. The abolition of intertribal wars had deprived the Chief of his traditional method of maintaining authority at home by resorting to a foreign war, and his power was further reduced when he was forbidden to exact tribute from his subjects. Shorn of political powers and forbidden to exercise some of his most important traditionally religious functions, he was paid a small salary in return for doing police work. In many cases appointments to Chieftainships were made for purely political reasons without much reference to tribal traditions, and it is small wonder that the annual reports from all parts of Central and Southern Africa repeated with monotonous regularity that the power of the Chiefs was declining.[2] Gradually and surely the District Officer was

[1] For what must surely constitute an international record in treaty-making, as regards numbers at any rate, *vide* Johnston, *British Central Africa* (1897 edition), p. 85 *et seq.*

[2] The references are too numerous to be quoted, but the following may serve as an example. It is taken from the *Report of the Chief Native Commissioner, Mashonaland, 31/12/1910*, p. 2. "The Native Commissioner is now the person who supplies the blank left through the taking away of the Chief's power, consequent on the removal of the tribal system."

taking the place of the Chief in administration, though the latter's unofficial influence and power remained.

While destroying the authority of the Chiefs, European administrations retained the greater part of Bantu law and custom, particularly where it was of a tribal or domestic nature and provided that it did not conflict with natural justice or European conceptions of morality. Thus the marriage laws were retained, including polygamy, and the greater part of what may be called Bantu civil law. But knowledge of Bantu custom was scant and traditional law was too often interpreted in the light of European legal conceptions. It is perhaps fortunate that difficulties of transport and considerations of economy prevented a more thorough interference with Native customs than did, in actual practice, take place.

Though this system of government did maintain order, it was largely a negative or disruptive policy which took little or no account of the political requirements of Bantu society and in many cases applied nineteenth- and twentieth-century theories in the administration of a primitive people. Since the Great War, and particularly in the last ten years, there is evidence that a new attitude toward the needs of Native races is beginning to obtain. Politically this change is expressed in the phrase Indirect Rule. The theory and practice of Indirect Rule were understood and applied many years ago on the West Coast, in Nigeria and in Uganda, but it has only recently come to be more generally accepted by those European nations that are responsible for the government of African dependencies. It may almost be described as the theory of self-determination applied to Native tribes, and the new attitude is more particularly noticeable in such territories as the Belgian Congo, Northern Rhodesia and the mandated territory of Tanganyika, in none of which has there been any considerable European settlement.[1] It is much less noticeable in those areas, such as the Union of South Africa, Southern

---

[1] Indirect Rule is, of course, of long standing in Nigeria, where it was introduced in 1903. *Vide* Lugard, *The Dual Mandate in Africa* (1920).

Rhodesia and Kenya, where the European population is sufficiently numerous to have gained complete or partial control of the government of the country.

Properly understood, Indirect Rule is a positive theory of government based on the assumption that sound administration rests on the traditions of the people and should continuously evolve a new technique to meet changing social and economic conditions. Granted that Chiefs can no longer be allowed to exercise independent sovereign powers and must submit to a law that is above tribal law, the institution of the Chieftainship and of the tribal Council may be effectively used for local government. The practical method of giving effect to this theory is to invest the Chieftainship and the Council with political, administrative and judicial powers and to establish tribal treasuries. While maintaining authority, as much responsibility as possible must be thrown on to the Chief and his Council, and the task of the administrative officials must become the much more subtle one of guiding rather than of directly controlling.

This policy differs radically from the older one, which still obtains in most of the protectorates,[1] of "using the Chiefs". Chieftainship ceases to be purely an instrument for maintaining order and becomes an integral part of the administration. Indirect Rule does not seek merely to rehabilitate the Chief, but it endeavours to take the African institutions of Chieftainship and the tribal Council and to revitalise them for the service of the tribes. Native law is no longer something to be tolerated because it is impossible to enforce European law. Under Indirect Rule it becomes an instrument to meet the developing needs of Native society.

In Northern Rhodesia the first steps toward Indirect Rule were taken in 1929, and it is merely a matter of time before the policy is applied to its fullest extent. In that

[1] Although, for example, Chiefs are recognised and used in Bechuanaland and Basutoland, it is incorrect to say that these protectorates apply Indirect Rule.

year the Native Authorities Ordinance[1] and the Native
Courts Ordinance[2] inaugurated the new régime. By the
first of these the Governor is empowered to appoint
Chiefs and to notify such appointments in the *Gazette*; in
the case of a dispute as to the rightful successor to a Chieftainship an inquiry may be ordered. The Governor may
declare that there shall be a Native Authority for any
given area and may direct that any Native Authority may
be subordinate to another. In practice this means that a
Chief and his Council of sub-Chiefs constitute the Superior
Native Authority, while each sub-Chief will constitute a
Subordinate Native Authority; in cases where, from various circumstances, there is no Chief of sufficient standing,
no Superior Authority is appointed, or else a Council of
Chiefs is constituted a Superior Authority. It is the duty of
Native Authorities to maintain order and good government in their respective areas, and to enable them to do
this they are given certain powers. In the first place, they
retain those customary powers which have not been
directly forbidden by Government, and, in the second
place, they may issue orders, subject to the provisions of
any existing law and to the directions of a Superior Authority, for all or any of the following purposes: controlling
the sale of liquor and firearms; controlling gambling;
prohibiting acts likely to cause a breach of the peace;
preventing the pollution of water and controlling the
cutting of trees; preventing the spread of disease; suppression of crime; engaging, under adequate safeguards, of
paid labour for essential public works; controlling the
migration of Natives; registration of births and deaths;
controlling the movements of live-stock; providing food
for travellers; suppressing prostitution; making inter-
village roads; assisting in tax collection; controlling the
burning of grass or bush; **exter**minating tsetse-fly and other
pests; requiring Natives **to cultiv**ate sufficient land; and for
any other purpose specially sanctioned by the Governor by

---

[1] Vide *Laws of Northern Rhodesia, 1930,* Chapter 57.
[2] *Ibid.* Chapter 6.

notice in the *Gazette*. All orders made in this way are subject to the control of the administrative officer, who may,
if necessary, compel an Authority to make an order.
Native Authorities may, further, make rules for the peace,
good order and welfare of the Natives within their areas;
such rules are subject to the concurrence of the Superior
Native Authority, if there is one, and to the approval of
the Governor, who may at any time revoke a rule. A distinction must be drawn between the orders made for the
specific purposes mentioned above and the more general
rules. Broadly speaking, the orders are in the nature of
executive regulations made under an ordinance, while the
rules are legislative in character; the orders enable the
Native Authorities to cope with the day-to-day business
of administration, and the rules provide the machinery by
which they can adapt that administration to new needs.

The Native Courts Ordinance provides for the creation
of Native Courts and empowers the Governor to make
regulations concerning jurisdiction, rules of court, fees
and fines, etc. By Government Notices No. 24 of 1930 and
124 of 1932 these regulations were promulgated and provide that there are to be two grades of Native Courts,
those of the first and those of the second class. The
courts administer Native law and custom provided these
are not repugnant to "natural justice" and morality. They
have criminal jurisdiction in respect of acts which are
offences against Native law and custom, in respect of acts
which are an offence against a scheduled list of ordinances
such as the Cattle Diseases Proclamation (1913), the Game
Ordinance (1925) and the Employment of Natives Ordinance (1929), and in respect of acts which are offences
against the Native Authorities Ordinance or any rules or
orders made thereunder. The Native Courts have no
criminal jurisdiction in cases where the accused is charged
with an offence punishable by death or imprisonment for
life, or with an offence in consequence of which death is
alleged to have resulted; in cases relating to witchcraft; in
cases where the accused is a Government servant, unless

the authority of the District Commissioner has been obtained; and in cases in which a non-Native is involved,
or is an essential witness. A Native Court of the first
class may punish by imprisonment not exceeding three
months with or without hard labour, or a fine not exceeding
ten pounds, or a caning not exceeding ten strokes, or any
two of these punishments; the corresponding punishments
in a second class court are one month, five pounds and
six strokes.

The Native Courts have civil jurisdiction in all matters
relating to marriage, divorce and return of dowry under
Native custom; inheritance and succession under Native
custom; the custody and maintenance of children. A
court of the first class has jurisdiction in cases involving
recovery of debt or damages where these do not exceed
fifty pounds, and, in the second class courts, twenty-five
pounds. They have no jurisdiction where one party is a
non-Native or is in Government service unless, in the
latter case, the authority of the District Commissioner
has been obtained.

All fees and fines are to be paid in cash and go into
general revenue; receipt-books and case records must be
kept and all sentences must be served in a Government
prison. Native Courts are under the control and supervision of the District Officers, who may direct that a new
trial be held, may remove a case to their own or to any
other court, and may quash convictions and alter sentences.
Appeal lies from a second to a first class court, and while
there is technically no appeal from the decision of a first
class court, the power vested in the District Officers
achieves the same result; further, a Native may petition
to have his case tried by the Native Commissioner's Court,
and such a request, if well grounded, is not likely to be
refused.

The two ordinances by which Indirect Rule was instituted in Northern Rhodesia are complementary and constitute the declared policy of the Government. They
establish Native Courts and provide the machinery for

local government, and it is necessary to discuss in some detail the practical application of the ordinances.

In the appointment of the Chiefs,[1] who may become the Native Authorities, Government is now at great pains to see that the rightful heir succeeds, and in practice it is the elders of the tribe who select the successor for the Governor's approval, which is seldom withheld. The elders do not necessarily select the man who would succeed according to European notions of Bantu succession laws; they will not go outside the royal family, but have been known to reject one claimant in favour of the man they want, and the "rightful heir" is the member of the royal family whom the tribe desires as Chief. In the appointment of the present Chitimukulu at Kasama, for example, there seems to have been a reasonable doubt as to whether he was, strictly speaking, the legitimate heir, and Government went to extraordinary lengths in investigating the dispute. Evidence was taken on both sides, villages were consulted and historical records were carefully read. Actual fitness to govern was not a large factor in the mind of the administration. Tribal custom as interpreted by the wishes of the tribe was the final criterion.

On the other hand, in deciding which Chiefs should be declared Superior or Subordinate Native Authorities, Government took into account fitness for the position, personal status of the Chief in the eyes of the Natives, and territorial divisions. This latter consideration has led to the appointment of too many Superior Authorities merely from the desire to have such an Authority in a particular district and not because the Chief was sufficiently important for, or sufficiently worthy of, the position. With the wide difference between the powers of a Superior and a Subordinate Native Authority it would seem necessary to exercise great care in the appointment of the former.

---

[1] Excluding Barotseland, there were, in 1930, 201 Chiefs, 240 sub-Chiefs, 43 Superior Native Authorities, 365 Subordinate Native Authorities, 30 first class Native Courts and 346 second class Native Courts. It will be noted that all Chiefs are not declared Native Authorities or recognised as Native Courts.

Further, some of the tribes have more political cohesion than others, and Government has the power, though it has not used it to any extent, of granting more authority in some cases than in others. If judiciously used this could have the effect of giving more power to those Native Authorities most fit to exercise it and of encouraging the others to strive after an increase of powers by amalgamating with other smaller units.

Chiefs generally appoint their own headmen for the villages and Government will seldom interfere. The position is not hereditary, but it often remains in the same family, and, in any case, the village is very much of a family unit or an extension of such unit. The headman is unpaid and his work consists chiefly of settling petty village disputes, maintaining order and cleanliness in the village and doing minor police work. Some steps might well be taken to strengthen his position somewhat so that he and the village elders may become the nucleus of village government just as the Chief and his Council are the nucleus of local government.

The orders and rules made thus far by Native Authorities show little initiative or originality. In practically all cases they are either suggested by the District Officer or else copied from previous regulations. This is partly due to ignorance and partly to the desire not to worry their people with new rules. It should be remembered that Chiefs are unaccustomed to legislative power. It is doubtful whether, in Bantu society, the Chief ever had legislative authority apart from his influence on custom; and while the old machinery of tribal government can be adapted to modern needs, it cannot be expected that it will immediately respond to the new stimulus. For more than a generation society in Northern Rhodesia has been accustomed to look upon the European as the source of all law, and the change from this attitude will probably be slow.

At the same time there is evidence that Native Authorities are beginning to be worried by new conditions and are taking the first halting steps toward rules that will suit the altered circumstances. Near the mines, for example, we find a Native Authority proposing rules to deal with the very difficult subject of intertribal marriages and the subsequent questions of divorce and custody of children. There are also attempts, to control the movement of women to the mines and towns and to compel men going to the mines to make ample food provision for their dependents. Other orders include prohibitions against insolence to Chiefs and headmen, against tree-cutting near streams and against the building of permanent grain bins in the forest. In some districts meetings of Chiefs are being held for the discussion of common difficulties and this is bound to have a stimulating effect on law-making. On the whole there is sufficient evidence to conclude that Native Authorities will soon begin to make a more extended use of their powers under the ordinance.

Though there are cases where Chiefs abuse their authority in their own interests, the evidence is not sufficiently strong, nor are the abuses sufficiently common, to warrant any accusation of oppression. Government has ample powers to depose or punish Chiefs for neglect of duty or for other causes, but in general the policy is not to interfere too much. The question when, and when not, to interfere with apparently arbitrary action on the part of the Chiefs is a most difficult one and it is impossible to lay down hard and fast rules. It is quite natural that some Chiefs will look upon the recently inaugurated policy as a restoration of purely personal power. This phase will pass, and in the meantime it should be borne in mind that to refrain from interfering action does not necessarily indicate an absence of policy on the part of the Government.

Chiefs deplore the loss of their customary rights, which have been abolished by law, to tribal labour and to taxation in kind. In practice labour for Chiefs is still given and is winked at provided that it is reasonable and moderate in amount. In this connection it must be remembered that the custom is deep-rooted and very natural. The Basutos, for example, who are more advanced than the Natives of

Northern Rhodesia, do work for their Chiefs, and as far as can be gathered from conversations with the more sophisticated Basutos, among whom opposition to the system might be expected, the work is done willingly. In Northern Rhodesia a Chief may not compel a man to work for him, but moral pressure is probably all that is required.

Chiefs are paid small subsidies by Government varying from one pound to sixty pounds per annum, the average being probably not more than ten pounds if Barotseland, which is treated separately, is excluded. This subsidy bears no fixed relation to the amount of the tax. In some cases payments have been increased as a slight compensation for the abolition of customary tribute, and both payment and increases are usually dependent on good behaviour. In these low salaries is to be found one of the causes for the petty abuses to which Chiefs resort in order to augment their income. In any case this method of payment is out of keeping with the principles of Indirect Rule and may be expected to disappear when the Government moves in the direction of tribal treasuries. Such a step lies in the logic of Indirect Rule, and until it has been taken it cannot be said that the policy is really being applied.

As the system of tribal treasuries works in the mandated territory of Tanganyika a percentage of the tax, which is collected by the Native Authorities themselves, is paid over to the tribal treasury; in addition, all fees and fines of court and other small revenues are paid in and from this revenue, the Chief and Native officials are paid and local works are undertaken. There is strict control over tax collection and over expenditure, and such control will probably be necessary for some time to come; but the principle of giving the Native Authorities financial responsibility and control in local matters is sound, and it does away with the conception of the Chief as a private individual in Government pay. He becomes what he was in Bantu society, a public servant responsible for the welfare of his people. Further, the introduction of tribal treasuries in Northern Rhodesia will provide the much-needed facility to finance purely local works from local revenue instead of having to depend on central funds. There have been, and probably will be, cases of corruption and of malversation of funds, but these happen in the best-regulated countries and are no argument against tribal treasuries.

There is a consensus of opinion among Government officials that the Native Courts Ordinance is working well and that the Native Authorities understand their judicial functions better than their legislative. The Native Court may, by the ordinance, consist of a Chief, a headman, an elder, or a council of elders, as the Governor may direct, but in practice it consists of the Chief alone. Provision is, however, made in the Native Court Rules for elders to sit as advisers, and when this happens, as it usually does, it is the Chief who pronounces judgment but the elders who deliberate. Case records are kept either by the Chief himself or by a salaried clerk, and in most cases they are well kept. Returns of cases and of money received are made at regular intervals, usually monthly, to the District Officer. A few cases of wrongful or exorbitant fines have been reported and corrected, but as a general rule the Chiefs appreciate their duties and are anxious to avoid charges of corruption or unfairness. (One Chief fined himself for wife-beating.) Sentences tend to be less severe than a European magistrate would impose, and fines are sometimes estimated according to ability to pay, even being altered after judgment has been pronounced. The Courts do not understand clearly the difference between criminal and civil cases and sometimes exceed their jurisdiction by trying cases of homicide as if they were civil suits. There are very few appeals from Native Courts, and though this may be due in small measure to fear of the Chief or to the fact that Government tends to uphold the decision of the Native Court, it is largely due to the general satisfaction with the judgments, which, though the procedure may seem strange to Europeans, are substantially just and in accord with public opinion. The public nature of the Courts is a great

check on any possible corruption, and the part played by
the elders makes a despotic use of the Court by an individual Chief very difficult.

Most of the civil cases are matrimonial and the figures
from one district may be taken as typical. From April to
June of 1932 there were 68 civil cases, of which 51 were
matrimonial. In the same period there were 73 criminal
cases, of which 26 were for common assault, 15 for illegal
tree-cutting, and the remainder for such offences as failure
to remove a village and building outside a village.

The evidence is strong that the introduction of Indirect
Rule into Northern Rhodesia has greatly strengthened the
authority of the Chiefs, whose influence is sufficient to advance or to retard progress among the Natives. Chieftainship has been strongly reinforced as a tribal institution,
and Government's policy of supporting the Native Authorities and of being patient with them as they take their first
steps is bound further to enhance the influence of the Chiefs.
They are the leaders of the people, but the present generation of Chiefs is old and conservative and unaccustomed to
the work of leadership and it is doubtful whether much
progress can be expected from them.

There are, however, two ways in which the institution of
Chieftainship may be made to be of greater service. In the
first place, some measure of education for future Chiefs is
of paramount importance. There are, admittedly, difficulties in the way, and not the least of these is the uncertainty
as to the final successor to the Chieftainship, particularly
under matrilineal succession.[1] Other difficulties are connected with the relation between a school for Chiefs and
other schools which are run by mission societies; with the
scope and content of education for Chiefs; and with the
prime necessity of avoiding the creation of a class of Europeanised rulers out of touch with the realities of tribal life.
But these and other difficulties have been overcome else-

[1] The fact that a certain tribe appealed to the Secretary for Native
Affairs to have its rule of descent changed from matrilineal to patrilineal suggests one possible method of overcoming this difficulty.

where in Africa, and the need for trained leaders who are able to cope with the changing economic and social circumstances of the tribesmen is of paramount importance. Missionaries sometimes have a deep knowledge of Bantu custom, and if they take the trouble to understand clearly the principles of Indirect Rule they will be able to render invaluable service to the Government in this connection.

In the second place, the Chief's Council provides a splendid instrument for government, and much more emphasis can with advantage be placed on this aspect of tribal politics. In Bantu society the Council played a very important rôle, and by careful study on the part of Government officials and missionaries its true functions may be revived and the old Council may be moulded to suit modern needs. It is a more flexible instrument than the Chieftainship and it could easily be used for the purpose of associating the more progressive elements in the tribes with the business of administration. There is a strong tendency now for semi-educated Natives to decry the power of the Chief, and it is largely because they fail to find a part in tribal government. This is particularly true in those parts where Natives have come into closer contact with European communities and with mission stations, and Indirect Rule will have to adjust itself to this factor. Societies advance by the play of progressive ideas on the conservatism of the mass of the people, and the Chief's Council is the most useful machinery for providing that such a play of ideas shall continue.[1]

The political machinery for tribal government will have to face other difficulties. At the moment society in Northern Rhodesia is based on a larger group than the family as that word is understood in Europe. Kinship ties are strong and individualism is comparatively unknown. The business of making a living is largely communal, and Bantu law and custom, which are administered by the Native Courts, are

---

[1] *Vide* for this subject and for much other information on Indirect Rule in Tanganyika Territory: *Reports on Tanganyika Territory, 1919–1930*; *Tanganyika Territory Native Administration, 1927* (East Africa Pamphlets, No. 91); and *Report on Native Administration in Tanganyika Territory*, H. D. Aplin (published by Nyasaland Protectorate), 1931.

based on that communalism. But individual taxation and individual work on the mines and in the towns may be sufficiently strong in their influence to change this state of affairs. Further, it seems probable that economic advance in the villages may tend toward individualistic production, and that will mean a gradual change in the basis of society and of law. The political machinery will have to adapt itself to these changes; but there is nothing inherent in Indirect Rule to make progressive adaptation impossible, and the fact of generations of administration based on a non-individualistic society may facilitate the avoidance of the worst evils of an acquisitive society.

In discussing the implications for the missions of Indirect Rule it is necessary to think of it as it will be rather than as it is at the moment. We must take it for granted that Government will move in the direction of tribal treasuries, of a fuller use of the Chief's Council and of educating the Chiefs; and such an assumption is well justified by the attitude of the Northern Rhodesian Government. Looking even farther ahead, we may find the local units of tribal administration being compelled by the exigencies of economic and social development to co-operate in ever-widening circles until some sort of National Council, with its roots firmly planted in the tribal life, will evolve. There is no need to be perturbed as to the form which this Council will take, whether it will be democratically elected or not; the form will take care of itself provided the local units are soundly administered. When this complete form of Indirect Rule comes about the effect on local government, and by implication on central government, will be profound and mission societies will have to define their attitude toward the new process and assist in shaping its course. In one mission school at least, in Northern Rhodesia, there exists a very intelligent appreciation of the situation that is arising and Native teachers are being encouraged to discuss the questions involved and to make it their business, when they take up positions as village teachers, to assist the Chief. Along such lines mission-trained Natives, instead of constituting a discontented so-called educated minority, will be able to exert a powerful influence on the course of local politics and on the growth of a healthy public opinion.

But this presupposes a sound knowledge and understanding on the part of missionaries of the whole theory of Indirect Rule; it means active co-operation with Government officials and a real appreciation of the many difficulties involved, a co-operation which Government might well assist by the issue of explanatory pamphlets somewhat along the lines of those issued in Tanganyika Territory.[1] Intelligent criticism is always welcome to the administrative officer who knows his job, but it must be based on thorough knowledge and must take cognisance of the fact that to apply Indirect Rule requires the kind of patience and restraint that is able to refrain from precipitate action. It is necessary to realise that Indirect Rule is dynamic and not static; that, ideally, it respects the past for its achievement and welcomes the future for its possibilities; that it is not only a political theory, but involves ethical and moral problems which require to be viewed from a new angle. It would be a fatal mistake on the part of missionaries to oppose the development of Indirect Rule either directly or by failing to take it into account. The temptation to do this will be strong, especially while the present generation of Chiefs lasts; but it should be remembered that the Chieftainship as an institution is above the Chief as an individual. By intelligent co-operation with Government, mission societies will be able to render the country an invaluable service.

[1] *Vide* also the Nigerian Political Memos. as revised in 1918.

CHAPTER XV

EXPERIENCE throughout Africa, but particularly in the Union of South Africa, has shown that the problems of administration in urban areas are far more serious than in rural areas. Where European towns and villages spring up they are invariably accompanied by Native settlements, and the conflicts of social cultures and economic conceptions are intensified, setting administration a task compared to which the government of rural areas is simple. In their tribal life Africans are under the powerful and conservative influence of a well-established public opinion which, together with their allegiance to the Chief and their kinship obligations, constitutes a set of rules of conduct which are probably stronger than most European conventions because they are reinforced by superstitious fears. From this well-regulated existence they go out, driven by various forces, to seek cash wages from Europeans on mines and in the towns, and are immediately brought into an atmosphere which differs radically from the one to which they are accustomed. Tribal sanctions are severed, and the African finds that what were considered good conduct and good manners are of little account in his new environment. Instead of a community he finds a heterogeneous collection of people living under laws which are not sanctioned by tradition and which are made to suit the requirements of the employer rather than the needs of the employee. Living has ceased to be a communal effort; it has become a stern individualistic process involving his relations with an employer of a different race and necessitating a mental and moral adjustment to totally new conditions. And all these changes make demands on his adaptability in circumstances where, deprived of the customary moral support of his social group, he has no reserve strength upon which to draw; his lines of communication have been cut and he has almost ceased to be a "political animal" in Aristotle's sense of the word.

Looked at from a strictly administrative point of view and leaving social economics out of account, the disruptive influence of the mines is far less serious than that of the towns. On the mines in Northern Rhodesia and in the Belgian Congo the African lives in a "compound", though it would be far more correct to call it a Native village so as to avoid confusion with the term "compound" as used on the mines in South Africa, where conditions are entirely different.[1] These Native villages are on mine property and are controlled by the mines, though Government lays down certain minimum conditions regarding such matters as food and sanitation. The workers are encouraged to bring their families and to settle down, and large numbers of the same tribe come together. From a purely business point of view the mines try to make the Native villages as attractive as possible and with as little destruction of tribal tradition as is compatible with the main object of mining. The men on the mines are engaged in a common task; they labour for one employer; they are subject to the same discipline and to the same regular hours; their treatment is practically uniform. All this tends to produce a corporate feeling which is not unlike that existing in the villages, and while it would be manifestly absurd to push the analogy too far, there is a real sense in which the change from the villages to the mines means a substitution of authority rather than a destruction of authority. On some mines appointed elders are consulted in the settlement of minor disputes and Chiefs are encouraged to visit the mines and, while they are there, to try civil cases, thus

---

[1] In South Africa "compound" is used to describe the men's barracks on the mines. The word commonly used there for the Native Area next to a European town is "location". In Northern Rhodesia "compound" is frequently used to describe the Native quarters both in the towns and on the mines, and a change might well be made to some such terms as Native Village or, better still, to its Bantu equivalent.

further bridging the gap between the village and the mine. So long as the mine-workers remain under the control of the mine authorities no serious administrative problem arises for the Government except that of general supervision by inspection and of carrying out the excellent regulations which exist concerning recruitment and employment of labour.

There is another aspect of the matter to be considered, and that is the effect on rural administration of the absence of numbers of villagers and of the return to the villages of men who have worked on the mines. There is not much evidence that the absence of men complicates Government's task unduly, but as local government becomes more the affair of the Chief and his Council this absence may have a detrimental effect in withdrawing the younger and more progressive men from taking their part in local politics. As time goes on, however, a state of political equilibrium will be reached, particularly if the mines continue the policy of stabilising the industrial population.[1] The returning mine-workers appear to fit back into village life with remarkable facility, and there is little evidence that they complicate the task of the Native Authorities. In most cases a man takes back a present to his Chief, and it is hardly likely that this custom would be as general as it is if the men resented the authority of the Chiefs.

In the towns which have sprung up along the railway strip of Northern Rhodesia the position is far more serious and constitutes one of Government's major problems. The disciplinary forces tending to lessen the strain of a sudden political change are as notable by their absence in the towns as they are by their presence on the mines. The individuals who go to the towns are exposed to all the stresses mentioned above, but they have no common employer whose

[1] A greater complication is the absence of men who find work outside of the Territory and particularly in the mines in Southern Rhodesia. In 1930 there were 38,000 Northern Rhodesian Natives employed outside the Territory. These men, while absent, fall under an administration which differs not only from their own tribal custom but also from that of their own European government.

business it is to make their stay attractive; the uniform
treatment and the corporate feeling involved in perform-
ing a common task, which their fellows on the mines get, is
not present in the towns to assist them to a more gradual
adjustment to the new political conditions.

The government of the European townships with their
adjacent Native settlements is provided for by two ordinances, the Townships Ordinance of 1929,[1] and the Municipal Corporations Ordinance of 1927 as amended in 1929.[2]
Two towns, Livingstone and Ndola, are municipal corporations, while the remainder are townships. Under the
Townships Ordinance the Governor may appoint a board
of management as the local authority for a township. In
practice two Government officials have seats on the board
and exercise a powerful influence on its decisions. If a
board is not appointed, the senior District Officer is the
local authority. The duties of the board are, subject to the
control of the Governor, to attend to such local matters as
lighting, sanitation and streets, and its revenue consists of
rents, half the fines for contraventions of local regulations,
and a grant-in-aid from general revenue. Estimates of
revenue and expenditure must be approved by the Governor, and the Governor-in-Council makes those local regulations which are usually regarded as part of the duties of a
municipal council. Thus Government, through its control
of the local authorities, has control over Native affairs
in the townships.

Under the Municipal Corporations Ordinance a corporation has far wider powers than a board of management
and is not merely an administrative body carrying out
the instructions of the central government. A council is
elected by the European rate-payers, and though the
Governor may appoint three Government officers as
additional councillors, the elected members form a
majority. The council has powers to make bye-laws concerning the whole range of subjects usually considered as

[1] Vide *Laws of Northern Rhodesia, 1930*, Chapter 26.
[2] *Ibid.* Chapter 25.

falling within the province of local government, and such
bye-laws are subject to the approval of the Governor-
in-Council. These powers include the control of Native
locations within the municipal area.

Some account of the administration of Native affairs
in one of the two municipal corporations will serve to show
the difficulties of the problem. The control of the location
falls under the general purposes committee of the council
and the location manager and his assistant are servants of
the council. There is no provision, as there is in the Union
of South Africa, for a separate budget for the location,
though the accounts are kept distinct; any deficit would
have to be met from municipal rates. There is nothing in
the nature of the advisory boards which, in South Africa,
represent the opinions of the Native inhabitants, and the
location manager has no statutory means of consulting
public opinion in the location.

There are about 4000 Natives in the location, which lies
some little distance away from the European area, and
of these probably 40 per cent are employed in domestic
service, another 40 per cent as clerks, shop-boys, and in
skilled and unskilled labour; and the remainder, which includes a small number of independent craftsmen, are in
miscellaneous employment.[1] The Natives do not own land
but rent stands and pay a water rate. The cost per stand
is 2s. 6d. per month and the water rate 6d. per hut, while
a four-hut stand costs an additional 6d. per month per
hut. In many cases the European rents a stand in the
location for his employees, but he has no guarantee that
the stand houses his own employees only. At present the
Native erects his own hut, but in the new location which
is being laid out the municipality is building houses and
rents will have to be increased to meet the additional expenditure, particularly since half the labour employed in
building is European.

No regulations exist governing trade in the location.

---

[1] Excluded from these figures are those domestic servants who live
on their employers' premises in the European quarter.

At the present moment the council rents a trading site to a European and there is a small open-air market where Natives pay 2s. 6d. per month for a stand. Provision has been made for trading sites in the plans of the new location and there is division of European opinion, on the council and off, as to whether trading rights should be granted to Natives. Those who have vested interests in the Native trade are opposed to granting such rights, and unless Government intervenes a repetition may be expected of the struggle which has been going on for some time in the municipal areas in the Orange Free State Province of South Africa. There the municipal councils are unanimously opposed to granting trading rights to Natives.

The location manager spends about half his time running and controlling the beer-hall, which is municipally owned, and the profits from which have to be devoted to Native amenities, though these are not clearly specified. These profits are large, and the takings in one beer-hall for 1932 are estimated at £3400. After deducting expenses, which include interest and redemption on capital outlay, wages and material and the salary of the location manager, there will probably be a surplus of £950.

The natural tendency will be for townships to grow into municipal corporations, and thus for the control of the Native population in the towns to pass from the Government to councils elected by the European population. The results would be similar to those which would occur, on a national scale, were responsible government to be granted to Northern Rhodesia. The principle is the same in both cases. Municipal councils are, like all elected bodies, primarily interested in their constituents; and since these are Europeans, Native affairs are made to subserve the interests of the European employers. Locations are looked upon merely as places where those Natives employed by the European population must live, and there is seldom any realisation of the common interests of employer and employee. Individually the councillors may, and very often do, have good intentions toward the Native inhabitants of their towns, but economic and social forces are too strong for them.

Further, from what was said above of the differences between the surroundings from which the African comes in his village and those upon which he enters in the towns, it will be realised that the administration of Natives in urban areas is the most arduous of all tasks set to European governments in Africa. It is a task that would tax the abilities of a first-class officer, who would have to foster the growth of a new public opinion among the Natives before he could build an administrative system. By constitution municipal councils are not suited to this kind of administration, and to ask them to undertake it is to place too heavy a load on their shoulders.

Another very important point to be borne in mind is that the gap between Indirect Rule in the tribal areas and municipal administration in the urban areas is so large as seriously to imperil the steady progress of rural local government. Natives returning home from the towns are more difficult to reabsorb into the village life than Natives returning from the mines, and the evidence is strong that the closer a tribal area is to the towns the more difficult does the enforcement of tribal discipline become. Even if, as will probably happen, the town population tends to become stabilised, there will always be a movement to and fro between town and country. It is thus essential that the differences between rural and urban administration should be minimised and not emphasised. In the nature of things a great deal of Bantu law and custom will have to be superseded by European law in the towns, but there is no reason for the almost complete break that now occurs. Stated in general terms, what is required is the introduction of a modified form of Indirect Rule in the urban areas, and this is a task for Government rather than for municipal councils.

The policy adopted by the Belgian Government in the Congo is very well worth studying in this connection. By a decree of 23/11/1931 the Governor-General may create

what are called *centres extra-coutumiers*, and such a *centre*
has been proclaimed at Elisabethville among other places.
The Governor of the Katanga, of which Elisabethville
is the capital, is called the Tutelary Power, and he has
delimited the area of the Native city and may divide it into
quarters according to personal status, ethnic origin, or
civil state or profession. The *centre* has civil personality
and may raise rates, and the *commissaire du district* of
Elisabethville may appoint a *chef du centre* and a council
of from five to twelve members from among the inhabitants,
whose wishes must be consulted in this matter. The *chef*
and council exercise power under the supervision and
direction of the Tutelary Power, and the Governor may
appoint a European temporarily as *chef*. In Elisabethville
this has been done and a Government Officer of high standing fills the position of *chef* until such time as an African
can be found to take his place. The *chef* legally represents
the *centre*. He convokes meetings of the council, proposes
rules and introduces the budget. He and his council are
responsible for law and order and for transmitting the
wishes of the inhabitants to the Tutelary Power. The duties
and powers of a *chef du centre* are practically those of
a customary Chief, so that the judicial, legislative and
administrative functions of a Native Authority under
Indirect Rule have been imported, with slight modifications, into an urban area.

The budget for the Native city at Elisabethville is to be
made up from the following sources: (1) a subsidy on the
pound-for-pound system from the Government (this corre-
sponds to the grant-in-aid given to townships in Northern
Rhodesia); (2) local taxes such as a tax on beer; (3) fines
and fees of court; (4) dance licences; (5) a small addition
to the Government tax.

There is a European committee of protection for each
centre on which there are three officials and three non-
officials nominated by Government; their powers are supervisory. While Natives do not yet own land, full ownership
will be introduced as soon as Government can itself obtain

ownership from the Katanga Company. It is hoped that the
centres will become communities with a corporate existence of their own, and not places controlled by European
councils whose main interests do not lie in the *centres*. In
this way the gulf between Indirect Rule in the country
and urban administration is bridged and the Native city
becomes in reality an advanced tribal area.

In Southern Rhodesia, too, the Government has felt the
need for Native villages not controlled by municipalities,
and plans exist for building such villages near to towns
and allowing Natives to elect councils to administer the
villages under the guidance of a Government official. The
plans are excellently conceived and should, when put into
operation, provide model villages where Natives may own
land and houses. Something similar is happening outside
Ndola and Broken Hill in Northern Rhodesia, where a
small number of Natives rent plots, quite separate from
the location, and do market gardening. Here councils
have been formed and, in one case, Government has extended certain minor powers under the Native Authority
Ordinance. These settlements are under Government and
not municipal control.

In the Union of South Africa urban locations have in
the past been allowed to develop with little or no conscious
direction, and municipal councils are now struggling in
vain with the problems created by the very existence of
the locations. As a rule they are bleak, wind-swept, tree-
less places where Natives live in semi-slum conditions,
and where discontent and crime are bred. Such conditions
will be reproduced in Northern Rhodesia if similar methods
of local administration are adopted.

While the towns remain the severest administrative
test for the government of Northern Rhodesia, they are
also one of the greatest potential assets. In the task of
realising this asset mission societies can play a very important part, particularly along the lines of assisting
Government to recreate in the urban areas a sound public
opinion upon which to build. For no government that

does not ultimately rest on public opinion can achieve lasting effects; it may be able to keep order but it will be a purely negative policy. Whatever steps are taken, a new society is developing in the towns in Northern Rhodesia as it has done in towns throughout Africa, and it will depend on the co-operative efforts of Government and missions what kind of society it is. If Native clubs, Native welfare associations, possibly joint councils of Natives and Europeans, schools and churches, and the beer-hall, can all be pressed into service to build up this public opinion; if Native Courts and Native Councils with their own treasuries can be established on the foundation of this public opinion; if, eventually, the African who leaves his tribal village to go to town finds himself, not in a collection of untidy huts, but in an African village where the best of Bantu life has been preserved; if these things can happen, then the new Native towns will become sources of great strength to the community. There need then be no fear of the results of town life for the rural Native. There need then be no fear of the influences which flow from the towns to the tribal areas, for such influences will be progressive and founded on Native life. Instead of being a source of weakness the Native towns will be examples in administration to the Native Authorities.

In the description, contained in these three chapters, of the administration of Northern Rhodesia it will be noted that the Government has embarked on a policy that is based on sound principles. It takes its stand on administrative conceptions that are not national but universal; for such principles as local government and a system of justice rooted in the traditions of the people are not peculiar to one nation or to one climate but form the essential basis of all sound administration. Government officials are becoming fully aware of the implications of the present policy, and in putting Indirect Rule into effect in town and country, in guiding Native society in a natural and orderly progress, in avoiding the evils of a population deprived of its customary incentives to good order, these officials will need every ally that is available. Mission societies and Government in co-operation have before them an opportunity which the traditions of their respective services should prompt them to seize with avidity.

PART FIVE

THE PROBLEM FOR MISSIONS

J. MERLE DAVIS

CHAPTER XVI

THE IMPACT OF THE MINES UPON MISSIONS

LONG before the modern discoveries of gold, diamonds and copper in Central Africa, in fact before the earliest appearance of the White man, there existed a type of Native labour which was a forerunner of the service at the mines. This was the employment of porters for carrying impedimenta that attended every move of the European, whether missionary, administrator, hunter, explorer or trader.

In a wilderness, thousands of miles from bases of supplies, with no roads and few waterways, and where the presence of the tsetse-fly made animal transport impossible, a self-contained European expedition required large numbers of Natives for transport. It was a slow and costly method of travel, since the load for a single Native was between 40 and 50 lb.; food for the entire entourage was carried, and the porters had to be returned to their homes. These journeys frequently entailed absences from home of six months or a year.

The "Safari" accustomed the people to the periodic journeying and absence of their men. It trained the Native to work under the direction of White men and introduced him to wage labour and a supplementary source of income. With the building of highways and railroads and the coming of the motor-car the "Safari" has gone into the background. To-day, except in remote districts and for hunting parties, it has nearly disappeared.

We have already seen that the demand for large numbers of Northern Rhodesian men in the mines of Katanga and Southern Rhodesia existed for some years prior to the opening of the copper belt. The extension of the railway from the Victoria Falls to the Belgian Congo frontier gave work to further large numbers of Natives, in building the

line and constructing the towns and farming settlements
that followed. Thus during a long period the Territory had
been accustomed to a degree of social and economic dislocation and to the entrance of alien ideas and commodities.
This had prepared the people in a measure for the heavy
demand for labour on the new copper belt.

It is necessary that these preparatory developments in
the people's life should be kept in mind in attempting an
appraisal of the effect of the copper belt upon the Natives
and upon the missions of the Territory. The significance of
the most recent labour movement in Northern Rhodesia
lends itself to exaggeration both because of the speed of its
development and the numbers of the men employed. Fore-
casts were made during the period of mine construction
that a labour situation could eventually be expected ap-
proaching the Rand mines in numbers of men employed.
We have seen that a maximum of 31,941 men were employed on all the mines during the peak of the construction
period in 1930, and that these large numbers were partly
due to the demands for building the mines and the towns
which served them, and by no means represented the
normal labour force for operating the mines themselves.[1]

It has been pointed out in the Economic section that a
maximum of 12,000 Natives will be the probable force
required for operating the mines under moderately favourable trade conditions.[2] To this number should be added
the large group of house servants of the European population, the shop-boys and the general workers of the townships adjoining the mines, aggregating some 8000 additional men. If compared with the total of 102,700 Northern
Rhodesia wage-earning Natives of 1930, or the 10,883
working on farms and the 38,056 employed outside the
Territory, this total of 20,000 workers of the copper belt
would appear to have no unusual significance. Why, then,
should special concern attach to a labour group which will
probably constitute less than 10 per cent of the able-
bodied men of the Territory?

[1] Part III. Chapter IX.   [2] *Ibid.*

Other than numerical considerations, however, furnish ground for this concern and the importance of this labour movement to the Protectorate and its missions. Among these should be mentioned:

A. The accessibility of the Rhodesia copper belt to several of the chief centres of Native population and missionary activity.

B. The great financial strength of the mining corporations and the responsibility with which they have undertaken the organisation of their labour provides for missions a factor of stability in dealing with an industrialised population.

C. The stabilisation of increasing numbers of families on the mines.

D. The highly repetitive nature of the employment, through which men return again and again to the mines.

E. The discipline under which the men work, with the comparative ease of handling and influencing them.

F. The repercussions of the mines upon a wide rural territory.

G. The growth of urban communities of detribalised Natives on the copper belt and in the railway zone.

The opening of the copper-mines in the Territory brought the problem of absentee labour closer home and into a clearer focus to the missions than had the labour demands of the previous decades. These had drawn men from a wide territory with a distribution of the strain upon the population. The new mines, however, were within walking distance of several districts such as the Luapula and Luanga Valleys, and the Fort Rosebery, Kawambwa, Kasama and Fort Jameson districts, which were long-established mission areas. These soon became popular recruitment fields for the mine agents. The miners were able to return to their homes from the new copper belt after a short period of work, and a certain number also began to take their wives and children with them back to the mines.

When the Native Labour Recruiting Association was opened, access was still further facilitated by the use of lorries for labour transport. Workers from centres of population 500 and 600 miles distant now found themselves only a three or four days' journey from their new work.

A large movement of population now set in toward the copper belt, a movement which in some areas amounted to a temporary depopulation of males. In certain districts of the Awemba country as high as 60 per cent of the able-bodied men were away from home during the peak of construction on the copper belt.[1] In some villages the proportion of absent men was even higher. The effect upon the missions in these areas was alarming. The bread-winners were drawn out of the Native communities. In cassava planting, where a cycle of two and three years of crops are tended simultaneously, the absence of the cultivator for a single season results in the cutting off of the supply of food for two years. The women, old men and children could not satisfactorily take the place of the able-bodied men in this cultivation, and a very serious food shortage arose throughout a wide area. This condition in its most acute form was temporary, but the forces giving rise to it remain as a permanent threat to the development of agriculture in the Territory.

This situation not only reduced the Natives of certain districts to the verge of famine, but it also affected various missions. The usual supply of local produce in grain and cassava was not forthcoming. Foodstuffs had to be purchased farther afield with added cost. One large mission boarding-school found the sources of its food so curtailed that the classes were dismissed and the majority of the students returned to their homes for a period of several weeks until new supplies could be found.

The high wages paid to Natives on the copper belt soon affected wage standards in the Territory. Missions began to lose helpers, carpenters, bricklayers, cooks, house-boys, teachers and even catechists. Mission-trained boys who

[1] See Part II. Chapter IV. p. 57.

could speak English and were accustomed to work with
Europeans were in high demand. The sixpence per day
paid to trained workers at the mission could not compete
with the shilling wage at the mines. Missions found themselves drained of the helpers whom they had developed
and who were carrying many of the mission activities. It
was a disheartening situation. The director of a technical
school told us that for a period of years he had trained
a group of skilled artisans with whom the building programme of the mission was being carried on with increasing success. Within a year of the opening of the mines
every one of his skilled men had disappeared—the result of
the training of years vanished and the mission construction brought to a standstill. A missionary of a different
region, speaking of this loss of trained helpers, said: "It is
hard to see our best boys leave us, but we have to remember that the demand for them is a tribute to our work and
to Christianity. The going out of these Christians from our
missions is a casting of bread upon the waters. If it is a
loss to us it is gain to the whole Christian movement of the
Territory."

To hold their workers under these conditions wages
should have been raised immediately, but this could not
be done under the limitations of annual budgets. Mission
loyalty competed with the high wages at the mines. In
Northern Rhodesia the inevitable result of industrialisation
has been that wage-levels have been raised throughout the
Territory. Missions in the end had to meet the higher
standards with higher salaries.

Price-levels of most commodities have also risen during
the last seven years, in some cases as much as 200 and
300 per cent. This is notably the case in areas contiguous
to the markets of the railway zone and the copper belt.

The rise in wages and in prices has brought a definite
upward trend in living standards among Natives. Mission schools have to pay higher salaries to their teachers,
higher prices for food, uniforms, housing, labour, building
materials, equipment and transportation. The result has

been that missions have had to charge higher tuition fees. Certain schools in Northern Rhodesia charge an annual inclusive fee of as much as £4 for their upper standard pupils. As compared with the average annual Government poll tax of 10s. this is a heavy burden in a country where the average yearly cash income of men in employment is in the neighbourhood of £8 or £9, and the average cash earnings of tax-paying men is about £33. It is a result of introducing the people to a more abundant and costly way of life. A stable administration, better homes, clothing, a wider dietary, education, and many conveniences in commodities, tools and accessories of life, accompany the new culture.

The experience at the mines stimulates the worker to a new independence of thought. The horizon has widened beyond the mission station. He comes back an experienced man, questioning mission ways of doing things. He often becomes a disturbing element by stirring up his fellows to question and criticise the missionary. He has begun to think for himself and has new criteria of judgment with which to measure the mission. On the other hand, the training in the mine has disciplined the Native in the handling of heavy and technical tasks and has increased his value as a worker. A missionary who was building a large church said: "Some of my boys have come back from the mines greatly improved. Instead of standing about and criticising me and doubting whether it is possible to do things they have never before seen, they take hold with an entirely new confidence. They have learned how to use their hands and to trust the leadership of the White man to carry through what he attempts."

The immediate effect of the mines upon the Church of the recruitment areas is disappointing. Spiritual interest tends to be overwhelmed by the material. A few of the men return to the mission stronger Christians, with tested and deepened faith, and become more valuable as Church workers than before. Many find their main interest in their new clothes, bicycles and knick-knacks, and in planning for earning more money and increasing their possessions. From the poverty of bush life they have suddenly broken into a world of fascinating things which can be had for the money that they have found they can earn. It is only natural that the spiritual values should be less attractive to these children of Nature than the new toys of civilisation. However, the experience of the American Congregational Mission on the Gold Rand between 1915 and 1925 indicates that this may be a passing aspect of the sudden introduction of the African to civilisation. The evangelistic work carried on by this Mission through a long period of years for the Rand miners recruited from Portuguese East Africa, resulted in the Christian boys who returned to Inhambane opening bush churches and schools in seventy different places without missionary help. Many of these primitive churches have continued to live and are to-day centres of Christian influence.

A shrinkage of giving to the Church has been a concomitant to the new earning power of the people at the mines. Native contributions are less than in the years before the mines opened. The African has learned that not only his labour, but his foodstuffs, can be turned into money. Money has suddenly become imbued with a new power. He no longer gives it away. His gracious hospitality and giving to strangers are disappearing. Compared with the resources of the White man his money seems so little that he does not feel called upon to give to the Church.

The copper belt has opened new opportunities of Christian leadership to Native Christians. Energetic, ambitious men have found on the mine opportunity to break away from mission tutelage and to launch out as organisers of independent Native denominations. As in the Union of South Africa, so here, the Native finds that about the only sphere of organisational leadership and self-expression which is open to him is that of religion, and he readily tries his hand at a new variety.

As previous chapters have described, the life at the mines is responsible for a certain amount of social and moral disintegration in the areas from which the men are recruited. The mines offer to the Rhodesian youth an escape from the difficulties, obligations and ennui of his village. At the mines he is out of reach of tribal law and family discipline. If he has quarrelled or broken faith with his relatives or Chief, the eventuality of becoming an outcast from the tribe no longer frightens him. The road to the copper belt is open, a place where he can lose his identity, make a living and enjoy a certain status. In fact he need never return to his village, and may join the growing army of detached and detribalised Natives who drift from one centre of European employment to another along the railway line or copper belt. A Government official in the Ciskei Native Territory[1] stressed as a menace to the morale of the Bantu people the ease with which their youth could shirk disagreeable situations or responsibilities at home by signing a contract for work on the Rand. The unfitting of young men for citizenship is imminent under the system of absentee employment.

The long absences from home are a strain upon the fidelity of both husband and wife. Temporary unions at the mines are a frequent source of unhappiness on the return of the worker. Prostitution on the copper belt takes its toll of disease and wages from the men. On the other hand, the young wife left at home under these conditions is peculiarly susceptible to the advances of older men and strangers. Missionaries state that marriage difficulties and the breaking up of homes among their people have increased since the opening of the mines. The increase of divorce cases in the courts of the Territory, and of personal family problems dealt with by the missionary, are witnesses to this trend.

Missionary work in the immediate vicinity of the mines has severely suffered from the opportunities for immoral earnings offered to young Native women. The work of a mission established among the Lamba people, situated ten miles from the newly opened Roan Antelope mine, was

[1] Cape Province, Union of South Africa.

brought to a standstill and the girls' boarding-school destroyed through these influences. Within a year of the opening of the construction work at the mine not one of the twenty-five girls of the school remained. One by one they had slipped away and succumbed to the allurements of the new world of machinery and high wages.

There are, however, not a few positive assets gained by the Native in his life at the copper belt. The regular exercise, good sleeping conditions, ample and balanced diet and general physical care tend to increase the weight and vitality of a large proportion of the men. The average weight of a group of 250 new recruits at Panda, Katanga, increased by 3·8 lb. during 1930–1931.[1] In spite of a certain amount of pulmonary trouble and other sickness, it is probable that a majority of the men return to their homes physically improved and more fit from the experience. The mines stimulate the desire for a larger and more varied diet. On returning the men are dissatisfied with the monotony and meagreness of village fare. They crave a change. This encourages the people to keep more fowl and goats and to grow vegetables and plant fruit-trees. This influence upon their dietary habits is of the first importance for the health and stamina of the people of Northern Rhodesia, and the vigour of the new society the Church is seeking to build up.

The mines introduce the Native to new standards of sanitation and personal hygiene. He has discovered the advantage of cleanliness in person, in his hut and surroundings. He will not happily return to dirt and slovenliness. He has learned the function of soap, and in some cases begins a regular use of it. He has also found the practical and aesthetic advantages to be had from clothing for himself and his family. To satisfy this new taste the worker is compelled to return again and again to the copper belt.

Life at the copper belt is also a mental stimulus. The experience of travel, contact with men of other tribes, introduction to the world of European industry, contact with

---

[1] Statement of Superintendent, Panda Location, based on annual physical measurements.

White men and their laws, ways of living, amusements, commodities and ideas, amount to a liberal education.

The discipline of the mines is another constructive experience. The tribal discipline has been exchanged for an industrial discipline with its own régime of law, order, authority and obedience; a daily round of regularity, responsibility, rewards and penalties. These are values of the highest order, and in a measure compensate for what the Native has temporarily lost under tribal authority.

New ideas of building, village-planning and sanitation are now and then brought back by the men from the copper belt. In some districts villages are being rebuilt with a view to proper drainage. Men are beginning to select the site of their homes with reference to the appearance and welfare of the village. "In all the villages of the Luapula Valley[1] sun-dried brick houses with several rooms are springing up. This is directly due to the mines. A man employed on the copper belt sent up £10 the other day to a local builder with a good plan of a house and asked him to go ahead with it and have it ready for his return. The incident shows that the men of this district have no intention of making a home on the copper belt."[2] A similar effect upon the building tastes and methods of returning miners from Katanga was cited by members of the Methodist Episcopal Mission of Kabongo, Belgian Congo.

The equipment of the Native house is also changing. Enamel pots, dishes and saucepans have become a necessity in many Native homes. Soap, needles, thread, scissors, safety-pins, mirrors and matches are increasingly used, while women and children's clothing, umbrellas, European blankets, writing materials, and medicines are finding their way to the bush. In rarer cases the home is equipped with a sewing-machine, a gramophone and a bicycle. Cot beds are found in the homes of many returned miners, and tables and chairs are occasionally seen. Although missions have supplied a part of the impetus

[1] Luapula, the Upper Congo river.
[2] Quoted from Miss Mabel Shaw, Mbereshi.

toward these European commodities and the results are more apparent in the vicinity of mission stations than elsewhere, the greater comfort of life at the mines is responsible for their being widespread in many parts of the Territory. While these conditions are true of many villages and areas, other areas still remain practically untouched by the influence of the mines and reveal few outward signs of contact with Western civilisation.

On the other hand, the mines must share with the trader and missionary the responsibility for the marked decline in village Native industries. The enamel and iron utensil has driven out the handicraft of the potter; the machine-made hoe of Birmingham replaces the Native tool; Bantu cloth has entirely disappeared before the cheap prints of Lancashire and Bombay. The money earned at the mines makes possible these conveniences and creates a taste in both husband and wife that can only be satisfied by repeated employment at the copper belt or European settlement.

The mines have given to thousands of Natives their first experience of rapid transportation. Districts situated two, three and four weeks' walk apart can now be reached by auto-lorry in as many days. A careful Native is able to save enough from a year's wages to ride home on his own bicycle, in one-fourth the time it took him to walk to the mine. The bicycle is a social factor. It has put isolated villages into communication with each other, has stimulated visiting and the spread of news and ideas, and is breaking down provincialism and tribal lines. The bicycle is a heavily worked vehicle in Rhodesia, the wife or children frequently clinging fore and aft of the rider.

Trade is being stimulated by the bicycle. It is placing the fish of inland rivers and vegetables, ground-nuts and other light produce within reach of the markets on the railway zone and copper belt. Within a radius of two hundred miles of the mines we repeatedly met lines of bicycles bringing in produce in large wicker baskets carried in front of and behind the saddle.

At the mines the Native experiences the possibilities of making money through buying and selling. He carries the habit back to the more progressive villages and begins to trade with the other Natives in foodstuffs, clothing and furniture.

The copper belt is also enhancing the social life and recreation of the people in the country areas. Concerts and wedding feasts are a new feature of village life. The gramophone has stimulated dancing and brings a new type of hilarity and amusement to the village.

The Native is being introduced to modern sport during his stay at the mine. Here and there villages are beginning to have their football club, organised by returned workers. As at the mines, Sunday is the day for matches. The whole village turns out for these football contests, and the players are treated as heroes. Singing, dancing and beer-drinking usually accompany these athletic meets.

The interplay of influences at the mines upon the Native worker is similar to the experience of the European adolescent youth who goes from limited home surroundings into the freedom of the outer world. There is a spiritual cutting adrift from his old foundations. He finds himself free to break tribal laws. Family sanctions are left behind, nor has his spirit world followed him to the mines. His spirits and the taboos connected with them no longer dominate him. The mine is a place where he can defy all taboos—of food, ceremonials, purifications, sex relations, ancestral sacrifices—and nothing happens to overwhelm him in disaster. He is no longer dependent upon his tribe for support or protection. He finds he can take care of himself. On his return to his village there is an obvious lessening of respect toward his elders. He has been out in the great world, seen many wonders, lived an independent, individualistic life and broken the bonds of communalism and family discipline. Not only is disrespect shown to his elders; it is evident in his relationships with Europeans. On the copper belt he dropped the salaam and handclapping with which the Rhodesian Native salutes superiors.

Why should he resume it again for the missionary and administrator of his district? A new criticism born of disillusionment of the White man now shows in his dealings with Europeans. He has begun to discern, discriminate and question, and these uncomfortable faculties are turned upon all White men, including the missionary. Fortunate is the missionary who sees in this mental and spiritual awakening the birth of a new man, and who can successfully readjust his attitude of mind, assumptions and his message to the needs of this prodigy that has been created on the copper belt.

CHAPTER XVII

NORTHERN RHODESIA and Katanga were among the last of the unopened areas of Africa. The vast watershed between the Zambesi and Congo rivers, by reason of its remoteness, the immense physical difficulties of travel, the peril to man and beast from the tsetse-fly, and the hazards of malaria, sleeping-sickness and other tropical diseases, had withheld its secrets from the outer world until the last three decades of the nineteenth century.

David Livingstone was the pathfinder and inspirer of Christian missions in this immense area. From Victoria Falls on the South to Tanganyika in the North-East, and from Lake Nyasa to the Congo watershed and across to Portuguese West Africa, the territory was traversed step by step by the great missionary explorer and for all time will be connected with his memory.

Livingstone's death on the marshes of Lake Bangweulu, facing the unopened Congo and praying for Africa, deeply moved Christians in Europe and America and inspired the founding of several of the principal missions in Central Africa.

Christian missions were the spear-point of the modern occupation of these areas. In 1885, five years before the British South Africa Company secured a concession for mining rights in Barotseland and twenty-six years before an established government was set up in Northern Rhodesia, François Coillard opened a station of the Paris Evangelical Society in the upper Zambesi Valley. In like manner the British missionary, F. S. Arnot, had been at work in Katanga for fifteen years prior to the first mineral development of the Tanganyika Concessions Ltd., in 1901, and five more years had passed before Belgian administration followed.

The main streams of mission as well as governmental activity flowed into Northern Rhodesia from the South and East. Following in the trail of Livingstone across Bechuanaland and the Zambesi came the Paris Evangelical, Primitive Methodist and Dutch Reformed Societies. From Tanganyika and Nyasaland entered in succession the London Missionary Society, the Livingstonia Mission, the White Fathers and the Universities Mission. At first settling near the frontiers, the missions have spread northward, eastward and westward to occupy the areas which are largely affected by the copper belt.

Of the nineteen mission societies at work in Northern Rhodesia, seven were established between 1885 and 1900, seven opened work between 1905 and 1912, and five have come into the Territory between 1923 and 1932. In a total of 282 missionaries, 153 belong to four Roman Catholic orders established on 33 stations, and the 129 Protestant workers represent fifteen societies with work centred at 57 stations. About three-fifths of the mission work in the Territory is in areas that are directly influenced by the activities of the copper belt.[1]

The Christian missions of Central Africa have felt a deep concern over the opening of the copper-mines, their influence upon the Territories and the obligations that these new centres of population have placed on them. We will now sketch briefly the steps which missions have taken to cope with this situation.

The copper belts of Northern Rhodesia and Katanga offer valuable examples of the pooling of missionary activity and the growth of a united Native Church. The outstanding feature of the Christian work on the Rhodesia copper-field has been the spontaneous coming together of Native Christians of various denominations to form a

[1] For a list of the missionary societies of Northern Rhodesia with their stations the reader is referred to Appendix A and to the missions map at the back of the volume.

united, self-supporting Church. The Katanga field is notable
for harmonious mission co-operation and the uniting of
various mission interests under the leadership of a single
society.

The first mission work on the future Rhodesia copper
belt was an extension of the Nyasa Industrial Mission, a
Baptist Society, which opened a station at Kafulafuta in
1905, near the future site of the Roan Antelope mine. In
1914 the South African Baptist Mission took over this
work and the permanent occupation of the field began. Ten
years later, with the opening of the Bwana Mkubwa mine,
the mission extended its work to Ndola, the new railway
and administrative centre of the copper-field, built a missionary residence and began a school in the Native location.

During this period a spontaneous Church movement
emerged among the Christian Natives from different districts who were working at Ndola and Bwana Mkubwa.
These people appealed for help to the mission. Since there
was no missionary immediately available, the responsibility was thrown upon Native leadership. In this way a self-
governing, self-supporting church unit soon evolved with
the encouragement of the mission. The members of this
church represented many Protestant denominations, but
they worked harmoniously together, organised a vigorous
evangelistic work in surrounding Lamba villages and developed their own Church life. Except for the support of
its missionary, the Society has never been asked to pay a
penny toward the upkeep of this Ndola Native church.
Buildings have been erected, evangelists supported and the
running expenses of the work met entirely by the Native
Christians.

This development at Ndola led the Mission to take hold
of the religious problem of the locations in the larger mines.
At Nchanga mine a church building was put up by the
Christian Natives before the missionary's first visit, and
the work was marked by the same fine spontaneity and
unity as had been shown at Ndola. Later the Company
built a commodious Native church and a guest-house for

the visiting missionary. At Mufulira mine a number of the Native employees had come under the influence of the Methodist Episcopal Mission in the Katanga copper-field. Here also a good building was provided by the management, and a flourishing church continued until the mine closed at the end of 1931. At the Roan Antelope mine the Natives also erected their own church building. The Company soon replaced this by a permanent structure, and a self-supporting work has continued there from the beginning. A work begun by the mission at Nkana mine passed over to the care of Rev. H. C. Nutter, the Welfare Officer of the mine, in 1930.

"The Mission's policy in dealing with the mine location and township work has been governed by the principles of making the fullest use of the available Native leadership, establishing self-governing, self-supporting Church units, and encouraging evangelistic effort, preaching and other Church activities by unpaid voluntary Native helpers."[1]

There are at present four Church groups that are caring for the spiritual needs of the Native employees of the Rhodesia copper belt, viz. the Roman Catholic, the Anglican (Universities Mission in Central Africa), the Dutch Reformed Church of South Africa and the South African Baptist Church. The Rev. A. J. Cross, the missionary of the South African Baptist Society, however, is considered by several other missionary societies as the spiritual shepherd of their church members on the copper belt. He has successfully cared for a wide group of believers of different denominations and has co-operated effectively in the growth of a union Native Church. This is a unique and vital movement and, though now curtailed by the closing of many of the mines, reveals the possibility of united Christian effort in Central Africa. It also shows the initiative, leadership and sacrifice of which the Native Christian is capable.

---

[1] Rev. A. J. Cross, "Statement on the Work of the South African Baptist Missionary Society in the Copper Belt of Northern Rhodesia", December 1932.

Mr. Cross's time is divided between the union Native churches on the copper belt and the European Baptist Church in Ndola of which he is pastor. He also supervises the Native rural evangelistic field near Ndola.

There are three European clergymen resident on the copper belt. In addition to the Baptist pastor at Ndola, a priest of the Universities Mission is in charge of the local Anglican church. His ministry extends to the Europeans of all the mining communities and to a less extent to the Native communicants employed in the mines. This work is under the missionary Bishop of Northern Rhodesia, who visits the copper belt at least once a year. At Luanshya, the government township which adjoins the Roan Antelope mine, a Congregational minister is resident. His work is jointly responsible to the Congregational Colonial Society of London and the Congregational Church Society of South Africa, and is limited to the Europeans of the community. At Nkana mine the Welfare Officer of the Company, a former missionary of the London Missionary Society, holds a weekly religious service and Sunday School for the European community and ministers to their needs in addition to his religious work for the employed Natives. Until the closing of Nchanga mine a minister of the Wesleyan Church was in residence there.

The large Dutch (Afrikander) element of the population on the mines presents a language problem. The majority of these people do not understand English sufficiently to feel at home in an English-speaking service. The Dutch Reformed Missionary Society of the Free State, which is in charge of the Northern Rhodesia field, arranges for the periodic visitation of the copper-field by its missionary stationed at Broken Hill, 130 miles south of Ndola. He not only holds services for the Europeans but for Native Christians as well.

Until 1931 the interests of the Roman Catholic Church on the copper belt were looked after in a somewhat similar way. Priests of the White Fathers' Mission at Chirubula and of the Jesuit Mission at Broken Hill paid occasional visits to their members on the copper belt. In 1931 an Italian Order established stations close to the Roan Antelope and Bwana Mkubwa, and in 1932 opened work near Nkana mine.

Thus at the present time there are one Anglican and two (Free) Protestant European churches with ministers established in the copper belt, but only one Protestant Missionary Society with a resident missionary for Natives operating in the area.

A spirit of church co-operation exists on the copper belt. Until the closing of Nchanga and Mufulira mines a monthly exchange of pulpits was arranged whereby the Protestant ministers visited one another's parishes and co-operated in meeting their common problems.

The policy of the mining companies in relation to religious work for Natives has been liberal. Suitable buildings have been provided at Nchanga, Mufulira, Roan Antelope and Nkana mines, for church services and Sunday and day schools. Separate buildings are usually given to Protestant and Catholic groups, though at Nkana the commodious hall erected last year in the mine location is used in turn by the Roman Catholic, Anglican and Protestant Free Churches.

The policy of the mines management toward the building of European churches has been conservative and has differed between the mines. Various reasons are given for reluctance to comply with requests for church sites on mine property. The chief alleged obstacle is sectarianism; with the possible compulsion of giving to each of a half-dozen denominations the land for building a church for the handful of its European communicants. The presence of Government townships adjoining mine property has also postponed the granting of permission by the mines for church construction. These townships are equipped with railway station, hotel, police station and school. They are laid out with streets and building stands and are supplied with most of the necessities of a town, but have few people. These prefer to live on the mine property adjacent to their work. It is stated that until the community has further developed and more light is gained on community needs and centres it would be premature to fix permanent church sites. The present depression with the retrenchment of many employees engenders further caution, and the presence of commodious social halls for the use of Church services gives an added cause for delay.

There is reason to believe that these powerful corporations, which have spared no expense in providing for the physical welfare of their European employees, will in due time make suitable provision for the spiritual needs of the people whom they have brought together under such isolated conditions.

In the older copper-field of Katanga on the Belgian Congo side of the frontier the interests of all the Protestant Churches, with the exception of the Seventh Day Adventists, are served by the American Methodist Episcopal Mission. From Elisabethville, the metropolis and capital of the Province, to Kambove, a distance of one hundred miles, the Methodists have for twenty years vigorously cultivated the field of the copper belt, with a recognition of its importance for the spread of Christianity in the Belgian Congo and adjoining territories. One of the most striking buildings of Central Africa is the church erected by this mission in Elisabethville. It is an imposing building, seating 1800 people, finely situated between the European and Native towns. This costly church for people who in their own villages use pole and grass structures, has been freely criticised. The criticisms, however, do not take into account the influence of such a centre of civilisation in Africa as Elisabethville. If the White man invests millions of pounds in great material enterprises, it is fitting that the spiritual enterprise he brings should not suffer through lack of dignity and equipment. This building is well suited to the responsibility which the Methodist Mission has undertaken, i.e. of serving the interests of all the Protestant missions of Central Africa on the copper belt of Katanga.

The influence of the Katanga mineral field is shown by

the immense area from which its workers are drawn. Christians come from the schools and churches of more than fifteen different mission societies situated in the Belgian Congo, Northern Rhodesia, Southern Rhodesia, Nyasaland, Tanganyika, Kenya, Uganda and Portuguese East Africa. Angola, Sierra Leone and other West African territories are also represented. The principal societies represented are London Missionary Society, Anglican, American Methodist Episcopal (North and South), Plymouth Brethren, South African General, Congo Evangelical, Westcott, Free Church of Scotland, Paris Evangelical, Baptist, American Presbyterian and American Congregational. These missions do not feel able to establish their own stations on the copper belt. Moreover, a responsible mission has been for many years working in this field, and it has been felt that it should be able to minister satisfactorily to all the Protestant Christians gathered in the area. The need that Protestant missions should present a united front in a Roman Catholic country is a further consideration supporting this policy. In this way one of the finest examples of the pooling of mission interests in Africa has come about. It is a situation that deserves careful study as the principles it embodies are capable of being usefully applied upon other mission fields.

The American Methodist Mission in the Katanga copper belt is in charge of Dr. J. M. Springer, with Jadotville as headquarters. Here two Native churches and two day schools are in operation, and a Sunday school and evening church service are held in the missionaries' home for the Europeans of the community. Dr. Springer visits many out-stations up and down the copper reef as well as the five mission stations of his society in Katanga Province.

The mission at Elisabethville, the capital of the Province, is under the direction of Rev. E. Irving Everett. The work includes church services, two day schools, work for women, catechist training and out-station visitation. A most interesting aspect of the Elisabethville work is the ministry to Christians coming to the copper belt from different churches and districts. The communion service in the Elisabethville church is most impressive. Newly arrived members of various churches are called by name to the altar, and as they join in communion with Christians from many different tribes and districts, a glimpse is had of the future African Church united in allegiance to one Lord.

The new member brings a certificate from his home church as an introduction. This is exchanged for a membership certificate in the Elisabethville church and a record of attendance and giving is kept upon it. On leaving the copper belt a card of dismissal is given to the member to the church of origin. A few of the missions write in advance of the departure of their members to the copper belt, but by far the greater number of Christian men arrive unheralded, since their final location is not usually known until they reach the copper-field. The missionary and his assistants discover these Christians, receive them, and attend to their proper dismissal on departure. The work also requires a large amount of correspondence and personal visitation of the mines and labour camps. It is a tribute to the breadth of Christian fellowship of this mission that it has been able to make a church home for so many Natives baptized in other churches. The result is a solidarity and a sense of strength among the Christian Natives on the copper belt that could scarcely exist upon the basis of many denominational centres.

The Protestant mission work in Katanga is under severe restrictions in respect to the mining locations. Subsequent to the liberal policy of its pioneer period, the Union Minière has for many years refused to Protestants the right of entering mining property to hold preaching services or do evangelistic work.[1] Neither is social service or secular teaching permitted. The whole field of religious training and social welfare has been assigned to the Roman

[1] During the first ten years of the Methodist Mission work great freedom was granted its missionaries by the Union Minière in preaching, teaching, colporteur work and in social and recreational activities among its camps. From 1925 onward these activities have been greatly curtailed.

Catholic orders. The splendid hospitals are staffed by well-trained Sisters; the day schools in these locations are taught by them, the industrial training for girls is in their care, as are the kindergartens, the day clinics, the pre-natal and post-natal care of mothers and the welfare of the babies. As far as one can judge from repeated study of these activities, they are being carried on with thoroughness and fine devotion.

The Union Minière has declined to share responsibility for its welfare programme with mission groups which represent an alien language, culture and confession. Centralisation is required in the management of such a highly organised programme, and the officials consider that this can best be secured with the leadership of nationals and of Catholics.

A similar case, however, cannot be made for the policy of excluding Protestant religious work from the mine locations. A careful estimate of the religious affiliation of the Native Christian employees of the Union Minière shows that approximately one-half are Protestants. It would therefore seem obligatory upon the Union Minière, in the interests of fair play and of the religious freedom to which the Belgian Government is pledged,[1] to permit ministration to this large group of workers on their pay-roll. Petitions from the Mission for land for chapels adjacent to mine property were entertained by Government without action for several years at both Elisabethville and Jadotville. The Mission was finally notified in the summer of 1932 that sites for church and school buildings adjacent to mine property in both centres had been granted. The reason given for excluding Protestant services from mine property is the strained relations of Roman Catholic and Protestant Native employees, and the alleged difficulty of keeping order on the location and of protecting Protestants. The multitude of Protestant sects in the Congo and the possible necessity of giving equal privileges to all is a second alleged reason for withholding privileges from the Methodist Mission.

[1] For text of Revised Treaty of Berlin, Art. XI., see Appendix D.

The Methodist Mission has under these circumstances directed its energies to the town locations in the mining centres—increasingly large and important groups. It has also served the mines' Protestant employees who attend the church services in town, and in this way keep in touch with their fellow-Christians.

The town Native locations, too, have presented barriers to the free conduct of religious meetings. The Elisabethville location superintendent has ruled it a civil misdemeanour for Natives to hold religious meetings without the presence of a European, save in a house with windows barred and blinds drawn.

In the town locations, the bulk of the educational work is done by the Roman Catholic Church. Schools with classes up to the Third Standard are carried on by the teaching orders, and the education of the European children is also in their hands. The Salicien Fathers' Mission near Elisabethville conducts a most efficient technical and farm school which enrols 175 boys and 50 girls. Boys are trained as tailors, dressmakers, cobblers, printers, leather-workers, carpenters, blacksmiths and bricklayers. An experimental farm gives training in agriculture, the raising of fruits, grain, vegetables, poultry and hogs. The school employs eighteen European teachers and is heavily subsidised by the Government, which depends upon it for official printing and other contract work.

The Seventh Day Adventist Society has been established for about twelve years on the outskirts of Elisabethville. Its representatives conduct a training-school for evangelists and a day school for children. The Mission has a small plot in Elisabethville and has purchased a site for a chapel near the Native location at the Lubumbashi smelter. Its work, however, has been related more to its general field than to the copper-mines.

Save for day schools, the Protestant movement since its early years of activity has attempted little social welfare work on the copper belt. It has stressed evangelism and the care of the Christian Natives gathered from many parts of Africa. In view of the highly centralised system of the Union Minière and the imposing social efforts of the Roman Catholics, this has been a natural development and has resulted in focussing the energy of the Mission upon building a dynamic church.

CHAPTER XVIII

SOCIAL WELFARE AND MISSIONS

THE opening of the copper belt in Northern Rhodesia is a challenge to Christian missions to both widen their activities and unite their efforts. A study of the mining communities and the conditions under which they live reveals the overwhelming opportunity and responsibility of those who have brought these people together.

The manager of an African copper-mine holds the destiny of a small army of Natives like clay in the potter's hands. Through these employees he is forming the pattern on which Native society in the whole territory is being refashioned. He is also laying the foundations of the future industrial cities of the Protectorate. Seldom has such far-reaching control over human destiny been vested in an industrial enterprise.

The answer to the riddle of the old Greek philosopher is being found in the Rhodesia and Katanga Bush. What happens when the irresistible force of Western capital meets the immovable object of African society? Though Western capital is far from irresistible and Native society is dynamic with progress, the result of the collision is a titanic struggle. Out of its heat and pressure is emerging a new African—an African with peculiar physical, social, educational and religious needs. Of these human needs, in all of which the Church is inevitably interested, which are those upon which it should focus its efforts and what is the priority of their urgency?

Before we attempt to analyse the central spiritual task which the mines have created for the Church, we will consider the secular needs of the workers. The selection, conditioning and physical care of the men is well looked after by the mines and leaves little to be desired. It is clear that missions need not attempt to supplement this programme. The social welfare field of responsibility in the copper belt, however, is a marginal area, not so clearly defined as the physical. It includes the use of the spare time of the workers, their recreation, opportunities for self-expression, outlets for emotion and social relationships. The social factor conditions in a measure the contentment, self-respect and happiness of the men and the zest with which they take up their daily task. Since it is closely related to the morale of the working force, social welfare is the responsibility of the mines and is generally accepted by them.

Important initial steps in Native welfare have already been taken in the Rhodesian mines. Well-equipped hospitals are provided under skilled supervision, officers are employed who give their whole time to recreation and social welfare, and halls have been built for recreational and educational purposes. Roan Antelope mine has installed a modern playground and arranges a weekly cinema entertainment, and both here and at Nkana school-classes have been provided. Mufulira mine employed a trained woman welfare worker for its women and children. Notwithstanding this good beginning, there is a possibility that the field may suffer from experimenting with inadequately trained welfare workers, and that on the basis of their success or failure decisions of policy of great importance to the future of the copper industry and the Rhodesia Native may be reached. It is reasonable to expect, however, that corporations commanding such financial strength and able direction as the Rhokana and the Rhodesia Selection Trusts will in due time put their welfare work on as adequate a basis in organisation, equipment and leadership as any of the other departments of the industry.

Social welfare is a recent activity in Africa and one in which technique and tested programmes adapted to Native needs are limited and experienced leadership is rare. An effective welfare officer calls for a person of excep-

306 MODERN INDUSTRY AND THE AFRICAN CH.

tional ability and unusual preparation. He should have
facility in handling Natives, skill in the use of at least one
Native language, should be genuinely interested in Native
people, with a desire to help them, and should have had
training in the science of social welfare. Such a combina-
tion of qualifications is rare and difficult to secure in people
who are willing to work in the African Bush.

The question of welfare activities for the Bantu miners
presents a group of new factors to the European social
worker. These inhere in the social structure of Bantu life,
without a knowledge of which the alien worker will accomplish little. Strenuous organised play is foreign to the
African and not entirely to his liking. Football attracts
many, but the average Bantu prefers to take his recreation
in his own way. The provision of social halls and games,
without reference to the Bantu's recreational instincts and
without trained leadership, is useless.

The work of the welfare officer is that of directing the
leisure time of the people toward wholesome ends. The
leaders among the men should be found and used in leading, organising and inspiring their fellows. The constructive aspects of Native recreation may well be studied and
utilised. Adaptations of Bantu games and contests of skill,
strength and dancing could advantageously be given a
large place in the programme. The welfare officer will
organise sports and games for different ages and groups,
manage the recreation-hall, arrange for lecture and discussion groups for the more advanced Natives, and supervise the library, reading-room and night school. Music
may be a useful welfare feature, as has been shown by the
popular fife and drum corps of the Roan Antelope location.
The Native's musical ear lends itself to the use of band or
orchestral instruments, and to training in glee and mass
singing with adaptations of his own tribal songs.

The welfare officer should not be responsible for religious work in the location. However, he should secure the
co-operation of all the religious bodies and be able to work
with any Church. He may well look upon the various

churches in his location as allies, while the Churches, on the other hand, will see in the welfare programme a vital means of strengthening the morale of the mines community.

The importance of the cinema as a means of Native education as well as recreation is dealt with in a later chapter.[1] There are, however, social and cultural possibilities for the Bantu in the cinema which await development. Not alone the realm of European culture, but Bantu culture, lore and history, with the wealth of geographic, animal, insect and other wonders of his continent, might be used as subject and background material to stimulate the African's interest and pride in his own country and people.

The relative merits of the system of employing men unaccompanied by their wives and housing them in compound barracks contrasted with that of stabilising the family in villages at the mine has been widely discussed in South Africa. It is a question that has many conditioning factors which make it impossible to give an unqualified approval of either system. The special conditions on the Rand do not exist in the copper belt of Northern Rhodesia.[2] Chief among these are the physical proportions of the problem and the close presence of a great city like Johannesburg, with the necessity of safeguarding men away from home under these conditions. To provide quarters for the families of the 215,000 men employed on the Rand mines would be impossible. The proximity of a centre of 375,000 people with its ready market for prostitution and illicit beer is a factor so demoralising as to have created wide opposition among the rural Bantu of the Union to the going of their women-folk to the Rand.

There is a marked contrast between the conditions existing on the Rhodesian copper belt and the gold Rand of the Union. The copper-mines are still small settlements which have just emerged from the primeval bush; the mine location is close to the forest, and the rural hinter-

[1] Chapter XIX. pp. 324-6.
[2] *Vide* Ray E. Phillips, *The Bantu are Coming* (Student Christian Movement Press, London).

land and the location huts bear a resemblance to those of
the Native villages. Thus, although there are moral and
social dangers to which the wife is exposed, her experience
in coming with her husband to the Rhodesia mine is quite
different from that of the Bantu woman who goes up to
the metropolis of South Africa.

On the other hand, the policy of the Union Minière in
Katanga in the compulsory stabilisation of families on
its mines through its three-year contract and intensive
welfare methods is not favoured upon the Rhodesian
copper belt. The Union Minière has followed this policy to
overcome the expense of recruiting workers from a vast
area and to build up an industrialised population. A large
proportion of its people are transported from great distances, such as Kasai and Ruanda-Urundi, and the moving
of the women and children with the men is an essential
part of the stabilisation plan.

The Northern Rhodesian mines are not under the same
need of holding their people. Their sources of labour are
nearer and a larger number of experienced workers are
available. Though favouring the presence at the mines of
wives with their husbands, neither Roan Antelope nor
Nkana are following a deliberate plan of compulsory stabilisation of their workers. Stabilisation of an industrial
population on the mines during a period of prosperity may
become a source of acute distress in case of such an economic depression as now exists, and involve a company in
the necessity of repatriating or assisting many of its people
who have broken their tribal connections. However, stabilisation on the Rhodesia mines is a trend which is automatically developing because of its advantages to the
workers themselves rather than from deliberate stimulation.[1]

Under these circumstances, to evaluate the moral and
social dangers of stabilisation over against the dangers in-

---

[1] This is illustrated by the very large proportion of stabilised workers
employed at the Wankie coal-mines in Southern Rhodesia. These mines
have been continuously operating since 1903.

cident to the men working alone on the mines is extremely difficult, if not impossible. The opinion of the Commission, supported by the judgment of officials, missionaries, traders and mine officers, is that in spite of certain grave dangers with which it is attended, the presence of the wife at the mines under prevailing conditions in Northern Rhodesia creates a sounder physical, social and moral environment for the worker and is productive of lesser evils for Native society than the Rand compound system of employment of men unaccompanied by their families.

The coming of the families of the workers to the mines opens a new group of social problems and widely extends the field of the welfare officer. Well-trained women welfare workers are needed who are equipped to deal both with the health and hygienic needs of the women and children and their problems of social and educational adjustment. The sudden transition from the busy life of the village to the unaccustomed leisure of the mine location calls for the training of the women in home industries and handicrafts suited to helping them to a productive use of their time. The provision of garden plots for the women to tend has already been successfully undertaken by some of the mines. Demonstration groups in child welfare, dressmaking and other branches of domestic science, exhibitions of handwork, the giving of prizes for best-kept homes and gardens and the raising of poultry could all be undertaken. The children could be happily organised out of school hours into boy-scout and girl-guide groups, and competitive drills and exhibitions of all such activities could be arranged between the mines.

The Mufulira mine made a good beginning in 1930 in meeting the health needs of the women and children of its location by the appointment of a trained visiting nurse. With a staff of Native assistants the following programme was followed. Daily visitation of each family for the discovery of sickness, eye-sores and tropical ulcers. The attendance of all such cases at the department clinic. The weekly weighing and examination of all young children on the location. A daily shower-bath for all children, followed by physical drill and games. A daily inspection of all family huts on the location, with the cutting down of food rations for those who failed to meet a reasonable standard of cleanliness. The attendance of a nurse at confinement cases, with a daily report of births and the condition of the mothers and babies. Every confinement case was visited by the director for four days after birth, and soap as well as milk and sugar were given to the mother. Serious cases were referred to the location hospital. Vaccination of the 750 women and 500 children of the location and of all new babies was carried out. The suspicion of the women and their reluctance to co-operate was rapidly overcome, but reveal the need of a personality and technique suited to such work. During the fifteen months of its operation this Mufulira mine programme demonstrated the possibilities of welfare work under competent direction.

Shrewd observers have commented upon the peril to the Native family that may come from too much direction of its life by welfare work. A programme that takes all responsibility for enforcing and supervising the care of the children may defeat its purpose, i.e. the training of parents to new standards of health and hygiene and raising their interest to a point where they will intelligently care for their families.

It is significant that missions have been largely drawn upon to supply the personnel for the welfare work of African mines. The Rand Chamber of Mines has placed a large part of its welfare activities for the last fifteen years under the direction of a missionary of the American Congregational Board. The welfare system of the Union Minière of the Belgian Congo is largely carried on by Roman Catholic missionaries. Of the three Northern Rhodesia mines which have conducted welfare activities, Nkana and Mufulira have both put their work in charge of directors with mission experience. Location managers from the Belgian Congo to the Rand pointed out that mission circles

provide many of the qualifications of the successful welfare worker for Natives. Missionary preparation, however,
does not usually include training in social work or courses
in sociology or anthropology. However important devotion to the interests of the Native may be for the welfare
worker, this cannot take the place of a knowledge of those
modern sciences which have given a new approach to the
problems of society and the understanding of primitive
peoples.

Missions cannot but be profoundly interested in the
social welfare opportunity that the copper belt opens.
However, we do not look upon such welfare programmes as
described as the task primarily of missions. Activities so
directly related to the efficiency, morale and health of the
worker are clearly the responsibility of the mines. Moreover, welfare programmes necessitate such intimate adjustments to the schedule of the labour organisation as to
make it difficult for them to be directed by anyone outside
of the managing staff.

What part then should the mission have in this work?
Several types of co-operation come to mind. First, because
of its knowledge of the factors in the problem and its contacts in the home land, a mission could bring to the attention of the mines well-prepared men and women of Christian character and with the spirit of service who are available for welfare positions. Secondly, missionaries are well
placed for studying the effects of the mines upon the people
of their districts, calling the attention of mines and Government to such effects and suggesting measures for coun-
teracting them. Thirdly, a highly trained mission welfare
worker would be of great value in co-operating with mines
and Government in welfare experiments related both to
the copper belt and recruitment areas. Finally, with the
growth of churches at the mines the mission will develop a
sensitiveness to the social needs of its people, and could
offer its services in intensive activities such as educational
classes and mother training groups directed toward meeting
such needs. In these various ways it would be possible for

the missions to keep close to the problem of welfare on the mines, sensitive to specific needs, and alert to possible ways of meeting them, without tying their hands with ambitious programmes or accepting primary responsibility for them.

The Native location of the town of the railway zone and copper belt is a distinct community from the mine location and presents different characteristics and problems. We describe elsewhere the administrative and social organisation of these groups, and are here concerned with the peculiar difficulties which missions face in meeting the needs of this type of community and its significance for the Christian movement in the Territory.[1] The town location is ever present in the new Africa. Wherever a European settlement appears, at its door springs up a motley of huts of the Natives who follow the fortunes of the White man and depend on him for work. In contrast to the mine location there is an absence of discipline in the life of the town Native community. Few general rules exist. Uniformity in hours, work and pay is absent. Each worker is on his own with responsibility to his individual employer. The residents of these locations offer wide contrasts. The sophisticated and the raw Native, the seasoned worker and the novice, the well paid and the unemployed, live side by side and present a variety of types with which the welfare worker must deal. It is, moreover, a fluctuating population; families may be here to-day and gone to-morrow.

The Native of the town location is often in closer contact with Europeans than the mine worker. As house-boy, gardener, store clerk or worker on municipal jobs about town, he frequently meets White people. He also enjoys a larger freedom of movement than the mine worker. Under these conditions a sophistication born of familiarity with the European and his ways develops. The town location is a definite detribalising influence. Here the worker, in contrast with the recruited Native at the mine, has few links with his home village. His identity is easily lost.

[1] See Part II. Chapter V., also Part IV. Chapter XV.

Opportunities for keeping up tribal friendships and solidarity are few. No one is responsible for notifying family or
Chief in case of accident or death, nor for repatriating the
worker should he desire to return to his village.

In these loose agglomerations of families and single men,
kinship obligations, the restraints of public opinion and
the gossip of the home village are absent. People may live
as they please and with whom they please. The town
location tends to become a reservoir for unemployed mine
workers who do not wish to return home. Its population is
elastic and receives casual visitors and gives indefinite
shelter. It lends itself in these ways to sexual promiscuity,
the growth of vice and the harbouring of a useless and
dangerous type of Native. The location undermines the
Native home, shatters tribal solidarity and makes it easy
for the African to remain permanently severed from those
obligations and relationships that render him a useful
member of his tribe. Such a community broken from its
moorings is in need of all the stabilising and regenerative
influences that can be brought to bear upon it.

These communities of detached Natives are the advance
guard of the future urbanised population of Northern
Rhodesia. The managing director of one of the great mining
syndicates predicts the steady growth of Native communities at or near the mines. This growth will probably attend
the appearance of various subsidiary industries related to
the production of copper, such as small blast furnaces,
milling, machine shops and possibly brass foundries. It
may also be expected that shops and small factories for the
manufacture of many of the commodities used by the
miners and their families, such as clothing, shoes, etc.,
will appear.

The experience of the South African Union and Southern
Rhodesia with Native populations which have followed in
the wake of the mines points to the importance of dealing
thoroughly and promptly with the Native locations of
Northern Rhodesia while they are yet in their infancy and
the whole position is still plastic.

In contrast to the mines, the Native town location offers a definite social responsibility to the Christian Church. The door of the location is wide open to the mission. It is impossible for the employer of two or three Natives to provide fully for their social needs. On the other hand, the sense of corporate responsibility is sluggish in a pioneer community. The White population is small, its resources slender, its social needs many, and after providing for them there is little either of enthusiasm or funds left over to spend upon the Native. Where Government directly administers Native locations there is a more paternal interest in meeting Native needs, but the best-intentioned administration is hampered in fully putting its policies into effect by lack of funds for Native amenities.

The Church has a challenging opportunity in the town location. It not only can serve the multiple needs of the Native residents, but may serve as a bridge between the Black and White communities. Missionaries of various societies in the South African Union have secured notable co-operation from the European community in Christian social-welfare projects for Natives.[1] Hospitals, day clinics, domestic science schools, social settlements, day and night schools, playgrounds and Sunday schools are being served by laymen and women as teachers, visitors, nurses, physicians, counsellors and members of boards and committees. A second group of citizens have become regular contributors to the upkeep of these activities. The Municipality and Provincial Government, too, have generously supported several of these mission philanthropies. By pioneering in such forms of Christian social service the Church may demonstrate to a sceptical White public the possibility of upbuilding the Native, awaken the social conscience and stimulate community action in the solving of its own race problems. The two races by these means may also gain an acquaintance with one

[1] Bantu Men's Social Centre, Sophiatown Social Settlement, Bridgman Memorial Hospital, The Helping Hand Club, etc., etc. (all of Johannesburg).

another and secure an understanding of their peculiar and
mutual difficulties.

The mission in the town location, as at the mine, has the
opportunity of studying the whole need of the new Native
community in relation to the development of the Territory. In carrying on a welfare programme for these detached Natives it will be sensitive to specific needs of
the people, such as housing, sanitation, trading rights,
beer-halls, recreation facilities and schools. To some
of these needs the mission will directly minister; others,
which may be beyond its capacity or responsibility to
handle, it may serve by interpreting them to the Municipality and the White community and co-operating in
drawing up remedial plans and programmes. On still
other social problems of the location the mission will be
able to stir the Natives themselves into action through
creating public opinion, and will help them in planning
measures for their own betterment. In these ways the
mission will actively supplement its spiritual activities
and help in building foundations of morale, self-respect
and self-help, on which a safe structure of urban Native
society and a Christian community may develop in
Northern Rhodesia.

CHAPTER XIX

EDUCATION AND THE COPPER BELT

It is not within the scope of this report to attempt an analysis of the educational task of missions in Africa. This has already been done by others.[1] Education will be treated only in its relation to the new industrial trend of the territory, and the implications that may be drawn for the work of missions and the development of the Bantu people.

The copper belt is a pioneer field for educational experiment. A vivid impression gained from a study of the mines is their effectiveness as a means of education. A process has been set up in the heart of Africa, quite apart from a purpose of Native uplift, which is drawing large numbers of picked men from their rural homes and putting them into contact with one of the most highly organised activities of European civilisation. The stay in these surroundings is prolonged and is repeated again and again. The men work under conditions that improve the health, awaken the mind, widen horizons and bring them new ideas, liberties and desires. When they return home their horizons narrow and the blanket of tribal and heathen custom envelops them. They acquire little experience or skill at the mines that is useful in their rural homes, and, due to the pressure of custom and superstition, the new ideas, skills and tastes gained are apt to be short-lived and make small headway in the village.

Here is a deplorable waste of opportunity. Quite independent of Government's Native policies or Mission programmes the mines are moulding the economic habits of

[1] *Education in Africa. Education in East Africa* (Reports of 1st and 2nd African Education Commissions, Phelps Stokes Fund, New York). Oldham and Gibson, *Remaking Man in Africa* (Milford, 1931). J. W. C. Dougall, *Religious Education in Africa* (International Missionary Council).

the Native, his social customs, political ideas and moral and religious life. We question, however, whether the stay of the Native at the copper belt cannot be utilised far more than at present for the benefit of the workers themselves and the Territory.

A limited number of men are trained at the mines in handicrafts, such as carpentry, iron-work, cement and brickwork, and tin-smithing. Some of this knowledge may be used with advantage on their return home. These trades are of more definite value where the worker seeks employment in a European settlement. However, a real dilemma for a majority of the men is how to use what they have learned on the copper belt in their tribal surroundings. The Roan Antelope mine has taken a valuable step in giving garden plots for all who wish to work them. In this activity the Native is at home. Such plots could be given on condition that modern methods should be used in seed, fertilisers, preparation of the soil, etc. It would then be possible for a family to acquire some practical knowledge at the mines which could be usefully related to the activities in the village and so advance the agriculture of the Territory.

Group instruction for the women of the location could be best related to the care of the family and the home. Training in child nurture, preparation of food, bathing, clothing and the treatment of the common children's diseases are of first importance. The cleanly care of the hut, protection of food from flies, the making of simple garments, and lessons in weaving and other handicrafts suggest themselves.

The attendance of all the children at the day school would keep them out of mischief, assist in the discipline of the location and add to the contentment of parents, who by this means would have less reason for sending their children home to the village. The location school offers the Department of Education a rare chance for experimenting with the training of children detached from tribal surroundings. Such education to have permanent worth would have to be put upon a compulsory basis as it is in many civilised countries, with penalties for parents who refuse to co-operate. The question of school attendance is on a wholly different basis from that of the town locations from the fact that the mines ration their children, which carries with it a right to enforce attendance at school. The Union Minière of Katanga asserts this right with the children of its locations for this same reason.

The mines present a commanding educational opportunity to the Administration of the Territory. The men are living under well-controlled conditions in which a part of their idle time could be used in educational classes. After making due allowance for the exhaustive nature of the work, much could be accomplished. English lessons, already available in the Rhodesia mines, though useful, are not what is most needed. We refer rather to the use of the Native language in giving simple instruction that will help the men to adjust themselves to the whole of the new life, political, economic, social, ethical and religious, which they are entering. To this end there might be given simple talks on Government; its nature and functions; the reasons for levying taxes and how they are used; the nature of the principal laws affecting the people; the policy of Indirect Rule, and the sphere of authority of Chiefs. Talks illustrated with maps could be given on the position of Rhodesia and Africa in the world; the special contributions of Africa to other peoples; and the uses and properties of copper and its place in world trade. Most valuable would be talks with lantern slides or charts, on health, hygiene, physiology, sanitation, diet; disease germs, the fly and mosquito as disease carriers; cleanliness in preparation of food, care of huts, etc.; remedies for common illnesses and accidents; first-aid treatment for snake-bite, wounds inflicted by animals, drowning, burns, etc. Simple talks on thrift, savings, and the use of money and its earning power could be given. The dangers of indebtedness, the theory of private ownership, the value of diversified vocations and the principles of trade could be explained.

The potential value for the whole Territory of education
on the copper belt is apparent. Each year a small army of
picked men passes through the mines; they return in most
cases to their homes in all parts of the Territory. The
opinions and prejudices, no less than the objects which the
men have acquired, are passed about and discussed from
hut to hut and from village to village. There could hardly
be devised a more effective way for Government to communicate its purposes to the people and to spread knowledge of a practical kind to the whole Territory than
through this ready-made instrument.

Missions can no more dissociate themselves from concern for the education of the people on the copper belt
than for those in the rural areas, and must stand ready to
support Government in whatever measures it undertakes
to provide schools for the mines and town locations. It is
true that the mines management has direct control and
responsibility for all activities upon its property, but it
admits its inability to provide complete schooling for all
its people and recognises the ultimate responsibility of
Government for this education. In discharging this responsibility there is every reason to believe that here, as
elsewhere, Government will welcome the aid of voluntary
agencies and thoroughly prepared mission teachers. But
whether conducted by Missions, Government or Mines, or
jointly by all these agencies, so important an educational
programme must be put on a high plane in point of personnel of staff and adaptation of studies to the unusual
needs of these communities. The problem of education on
the copper belt could well be made a subject of conference
and study by representatives of the three major interests
concerned, Mines, Government and Missions. In this way a
practical plan suited to the needs of Native society and one
which would secure the co-operation of all could be devised.

Modern industrialism has placed a new necessity upon
those who are educating the people of Northern Rhodesia
to define the goal toward which education is directed. This

will require an understanding of the economic forces that
are at work in the Territory, the strength and extent of
their influence, a forecast of their future growth and the
new groups of Native society that are forming under them.
It will also require a clear grasp of Indirect Rule, the trend
of its influence and the nature of the society that it fosters.
Education must be conscious of the conflict that exists
between the economic and political principles that are operating in Rhodesia. The mines are tending to weaken tribal
life and are developing a type of Native and a social group
that are independent of it. Government is strengthening
the Chieftainship and tribe and striving to stabilise Native
society in its traditional forms.

Where do missions stand in relation to these conflicting
policies? They are both detached and involved in the situation that has arisen. While they must accept the entrance
of economic forces no less than the Native policies of the
Administration, missions are far from helpless in relation
to both of these factors. They hold a key position toward
Native development, for through the schools of the Territory which are in their hands and through the religious
training of the people they can throw a determining weight
into the scale.

In considering the bearing of the industrial movement
upon the progress of Northern Rhodesia there are three
types of education that should be noted. First, is the
schooling suited to the bulk of the population living in
isolated rural villages within the framework of tribal
organisation and with agriculture as their occupation?
With the economic implication of the copper belt calling
for rural stabilisation in mind, education will continue to
be carried on in these village schools by mission-trained
teachers, with an increased emphasis upon schooling for
rural life. A second type of education is that which is
adapted to the needs of the detached Native communities
on the copper belt and railway zone: the location Native.
With a recognition of the rural and tribal background of
these groups a schooling must be devised which will inter-

pret for the pupil the influences and demands of the industrial and urban surroundings and help him to make the best possible adjustments to them and a satisfactory preparation for life in these surroundings. A third educational need is for a school suited to those Native communities that are in a transitional stage between the rural and urban types. These are villages that are in close contact with mission stations, Government posts, and European settlements along the railway line. They include also villages from which men and women are constantly passing back and forth from the copper belt or other centres of European employment, and which have kept up a contact with the outer world. This type of community presents the most difficult educational problem of all. It is here that the question "For what kind of life are we preparing our young people?" is most perplexing to answer. It is in this transitional type of community in which the weight of mission influence will be most felt in the direction of rural or urban stabilisation, in guiding population trends and in the forming of social and economic patterns.

There is for the present no clean-cut division between the educational needs of the three communities outlined above. The margin of each tends to merge with that of its neighbour. A guiding principle for all will be an adaptation of courses to prepare the pupil for the life of the group to which he belongs. Moreover, all of these groups are changing so rapidly that educational policies and syllabi must be susceptible of frequent revision. This necessitates a grasp of population, cultural and economic trends in the Territory on the part of both missions and Government if progress and not confusion in education is to be attained.

It then becomes clear that the rôle of the mission school in this conflict of forces is not to support either the rural or urban stabilisation trend at the expense of the other. The issue is far from being so clear-cut as this. The mission is compelled to face in two directions, addressing itself to serving the different social and economic groupings that are forming, as it were, both in front and in rear.

The fundamental question that faces the missionary educator must be how he can train his pupils to best serve Native society. The needs of the mission, the mines, Government offices, European farms and households, all fade into the background before this prior demand. Until the basic needs of Native society are determined and types of schooling adapted to them are evolved, there is danger of hastening the present trend of preparing Natives primarily to serve European society and to render them more and more dependent on alien cultural and economic activities for their livelihood and their ideals.

Adult education, simply and cheaply offered, is needed for the Bantu groups that are in process of transition between the rural and urban community. The possibilities of such education have been demonstrated on a large scale by the Mass Education Movement of China. This popular movement has in the last ten or twelve years taught five million people to read and write, on the basis of 1300 of the most commonly used Chinese characters. It has given the people elementary arithmetic, simple courses in history and civics, and has created a simplified literature which places the news of the day and a wide field of practical information at the disposal of the common man and woman. This course of education has been organised at a total cost of text-books of twenty cents (Mex.) per student. The teaching is done entirely by volunteers, and public rooms and temples have been furnished as class-rooms, rent free, by the municipal officials in hundreds of Chinese cities.[1]

If the growing Native communities in urban and mining districts are to be helped toward intelligent adjustments to the new order, it must come through the enlightenment of the adults rather than by waiting for the generation of children now in school to come to maturity.

Ability to read rules and laws, railway time-tables, shop signs, advertisements and official directions would go far toward helping the Native to find his place in the new

---

[1] *The Reorganisation of Education in China*, pp. 188-95. League of Nations Institute of Intellectual Co-operation.   Paris, 1932.

scheme of things he has entered. Access to newspapers and other literature would gradually be possible, and the Government would have a medium through which these communities would make progress toward citizenship.

A training in numbers, in the simplest processes of addition, subtraction, multiplication and division, would be of immense benefit to the Native in his dealings with the trader and in his growing commercial relationships with his own people.

One of the most effective ways of educating an illiterate peasantry *en masse* has been used by the Soviet Government. The Soviets have taught with startling and realistic posters the contrast between old and new methods of hygiene, sanitation, agriculture, stock raising, housebuilding, political principles and communistic ideals. By this and other methods millions of illiterate people have been given something of an understanding of the advocated advantages of the modern and Soviet way of life over the old. In this way a desire for change and a willingness to cooperate with Government and with one another on the new basis has grown.

This method is well adapted to conditions in Central Africa. It is inexpensive and resourceful, can be varied through a wide range of subjects, compels the attention and is vivid in the lessons it teaches. The poster also is well suited to the fine powers of observation of the African. It could be used on mission station, mine location, European railway zone, Government post and village. Bulletin boards could be installed where series of the educational posters could be fastened and changed at regular intervals. The principle is used by the Union Minière in Katanga. In the power plants of the Company, wherever the Native worker is in close proximity to high-tension wires, vivid posters depict the various ways in which he may be menaced by the death-giving current. The posters show the electricity as a red demon leaping at the careless worker, and the danger is traced by a red line back to the dynamo so as to make clear to him its source. These realistic pictures fascinate the Native and startle him into an attention which spoken or printed warning could not arouse.

The moving picture widely expands the educational possibilities of the picture poster. There are many striking advantages of this means of educating the Native African. First, the cinema goes far toward meeting the problem of the illiteracy of the adult. In any grouping of Natives only a minute number is capable of reading. If the mass of present-day Africans are to understand the wider world which they are entering, it will be by means of what they see and hear rather than by reading. His intimate dealing with Nature has sharpened the African's capacity for noting details, and for remembering and describing them. The cinema is also suited for teaching peoples in the mass and with all ages and types of audience. Several thousand Natives can get the benefit of its instruction together, as contrasted with the limitations of the class-room. Through a large part of the tropical year the cinema can be used in the open air without the need of a specially designed hall. It is suited to the African by teaching through life and action. It deals with the concrete, illustrates through the experiences of people and gathers up its message in a story which moves rapidly and holds the attention. The cinema uses the flank rather than the frontal attack. Fundamental principles may be woven into the picture story. It maintains a freshness and vigour and rivets the interest as no other form of instruction. The cinema can be used in the teaching of every variety of subject: hygiene, sanitation, Government administration, religious and moral instruction, economics, agriculture, art, child nurture, land utilisation, trade and commerce, geography, travel, natural science, physics, biology, physiology, astronomy, etc. etc., may all be depicted with success.

A moving-picture outfit with suitable films could profitably form a part of the equipment of every African mission, and would have special value for those missions whose people are being influenced by the copper belt. The great expense of producing films and the difficulty of planning subjects thoroughly suited to the African, and the further difficulty of organising an adequate supply, point to the necessity of joint action and financing. An impossible programme for a single mission might be carried out through the pooling of the resources of a dozen mission societies in co-operation with Government or large industries.

The cinema as an aid to mission work is well known in South Africa. The long experience of the American Congregational Board with the moving picture as a means of social welfare for the Natives of the Rand mines is deserving of careful study. For a number of years, under the direction of Rev. Ray E. Phillips and with the generous support of the Transvaal Chamber of Mines, a semi-weekly film service has been provided for the workers of more than fifty of the mines. More recently this service has been very widely extended to include many industries, schools, societies and missions in various parts of the Union of South Africa, and even reaching points in Southern and Northern Rhodesia. Two hundred centres or more are regularly served by this cinema circuit. This imposing Christian social work is an example of what can be accomplished through energetic mission co-operation with a large industry.[1] The possibilities of the constructive use of the cinema in relation to the indigenous peoples of British colonies are being studied by the Colonial Office.[2] This is obviously a field in which extensive experiment and testing must be carried out under expert leadership. Missions should follow closely these developments and be prepared to co-operate with Government and industries in giving practical effect to any serious efforts in this direction. Unless prompt measures are taken to enter the Central African field with wholesome films, the commercial exploitation of the Native will proceed with a type of picture that caters to his worst instincts and

[1] For an account of this social-welfare programme on the Rand mines *vide* Ray E. Phillips, *The Bantu are Coming.*

[2] A. C. Cameron (Governor-elect of the British Film Institute), "The Constitution of a British Film Institute". Paper read before the British Social Hygiene Congress, July 1933, Craven Street, London.

depicts an unreal and corrupt European civilisation. Missions should be among the first to throw the weight of their influence against such a development and study the problem of providing the African with sound and constructive pictures.

An outstanding implication of the copper belt for Christian missions is the necessity of a stronger emphasis upon the education of girls and women. The development of the Territory has for thirty years through one means or another provided for the practical education of large numbers of its men. Safari, highway, railroad, town and mine have given a glimpse of the outside world to probably at least one-half of the able-bodied men. During 1931, 110,108 Northern Rhodesian men were engaged in some form of service away from their homes.[1] There is nothing corresponding to these liberalising influences in the experience of the women. It is true that small numbers of wives are beginning to accompany their husbands to the copper belt, but the vast majority of the women of the Territory stay at home in their isolated villages. The women of the Bantu are the keepers of the traditions and the defenders of conservatism. They hold the key position in the problem of the advancement of the people. Broadly speaking, the men of the tribes can go no faster nor farther forward than their women will go with them. If the new impulses and ideas of the men who have been in contact with European influences are to take root in the home villages, it is the women who will make it possible by creating a congenial soil for the germinating of these ideas.

Members of the Commission were told repeatedly by Native men that the foremost need of the Territory was an education for girls which would prepare them to become suitable mates for the educated men. The prospect of marrying an ignorant Native woman is disheartening to the ambitious man who wishes a home and a life on a higher level than the old style affords.

A factor of great importance in Bantu society is the

[1] See Part III. Chapter X.

rôle of the old woman as the teacher of youth. The young
children are put in charge of the grandmother for discipline.
The long period of preparation of girls for womanhood,
known as the initiation school, is in the hands of the old
women of the tribe. The old woman in this way dominates
Bantu life. Thus in dealing with the tribal village the
mission has to reckon with the strategic position of the
elders and their control of the public opinion of the group.
Such a situation requires time for the emergence of a
generation of Christian grandfathers and grandmothers,
who as children and young people have had their minds
opened to the Christian way of life.

One of the foremost training-schools in Africa is the
Livingstone Memorial Girls' School situated at Mbereshi,
Northern Rhodesia, near Lake Mweru, in a district widely
recruited by the copper-mines. This school, which has been
in operation for eighteen years, seemed remarkable to the
Commission for embodying principles of the first importance for women's education in Africa. The school introduces the girls to the Christian way of life and opens their
minds to a wealth of universal knowledge but does not
unfit them for re-entering their villages and living as loyal
members of the tribal group. A striking principle is the use
of tribal customs, phrases and concepts in the religious and
corporate school practice. The school is the tribe of Christ.
Christ is the Chief to whom all owe loyal obedience and
for Whose service and commendation all aspire. Familiar
Native religious ideas and practices are utilised and placed
in the Christian setting—such as All Souls' Night, Harvest
and Planting festivals. The question of the preparation of
the girls for womanhood has been so ably handled that
parents bring their daughters to the principal to be trained
with this in view. The Livingstone Memorial School is also
notable for the long period of training which its girls receive. Many of the pupils enter at the age of six and seven
years and remain until sixteen or eighteen. Often the
whole girlhood is spent in the school, with a consequent
maximum of influence and Christian development.

The school reproduces so far as possible the essential elements of village life.

"The school is a tribe in miniature, living a life centred around an invisible Chief, trying to obey His law—it is a community of loyalty, of interest, of work and play. The government of the school village is in the hands of the house mothers (the older girls), assisted by the teachers and all the other grown girls. The house mothers are responsible for the cleanliness of the school village and its environs; they are responsible for the well-being and behaviour of their own houses. Every child, even the smallest, contributes her share to the life of the whole community. They seek guidance and direction from the Chief, who came not to destroy but to fulfil—His commandments are the Law and they rarely conflict with the old tribal laws of the people. Respect for the elders is cherished—respect and obedience based on love and loyalty—not on fear." [1] Here is a centre of new life where the Bantu girl is not dislocated and uptorn from that which has made her a Bantu, but where wisdom, insight and sympathy have used the Bantu framework and clothed it with the spirit of the living and universal Christ—the Bantu Christ. This conception of Christianising the Bantu tribe needs to be widely spread in Northern Rhodesia through many schools patterned on this Mbereshi principle, and led with something of the depth of insight, artistry and courage that marks its leadership.

Missions must see that an educational policy directed at the training of boys alone is not only inadequate as a means of bringing forward Native society, but may even be a waste of effort. The Native man who marries an uneducated and backward woman often finds both a negative lack of sympathy with his higher aspirations and a positive drag which at length pulls him back to the level from which he had risen. The steady increase of monogamous marriage also brings a need of adjustment to the single wife, who finds an increase of duties in the home for

[1] Mabel Shaw, O.B.E., *God's Candlelights*, pp. 53-57. Edinburgh House Press. London, 1933.

which she needs training if she is to succeed. Since a large proportion of Church members are women, an ignorant womanhood means an ignorant Christian Church—one in which a majority of its members are not intellectually freed from superstition, but in whose beliefs a thin Christian veneer is spread over the mass of inherited heathen tradition. No Church can go far in changing Native life if it is compelled to carry this double load of ignorance and superstition upon its back.

Missions cannot afford to carry education for boys a step farther or faster than education for girls, for they are the two wings of the bird which must be equal if Native society is to lift itself and make substantial progress.

CHAPTER XX

THE position of modern missions in Central Africa resembles that of the missions of the monastic orders of the Church in Central Europe from the seventh to the tenth centuries. The monks found backward, illiterate peoples, living in squalor, with agriculture, industries and craftsmanship of the crudest kind. It did not suffice for these monastic missionaries to bring a knowledge of Christ to pagans living on so low a scale. The whole life of the people needed to be changed—reorganised, instructed and inspired—if a stable Church were to be established. The Benedictines, Cistercians and Franciscans established monastic foundations among the Germanic peoples where a practical Christianity was demonstrated by many generations of missionary monks. Such monasteries as Fulda, St. Gall and Reichenau were centres of abounding life, little islands of civilisation in a period when the religion and culture of Christendom were nearly extinguished. Large numbers of lay brothers joined the priests in a practical ministry of love. The monks taught a wide variety of subjects, from the Gregorian chant and the catechism to fish culture and wheat-raising, and from the illuminating of manuscripts and staining of glass to stone masonry, carving and metal work. During four or five hundred years this practical ministry went hand in hand with the preaching of the Gospel, until leaders among the people themselves emerged as patrons of the arts and sciences.[1]

It is impossible for the Christian mission in Africa to free itself from social and economic responsibility for the Bantu. Such responsibility accompanies the giving of a dynamic philosophy of life to a backward society. It is the result of

[1] Vide *Acta Sanctorum* and *Historica Ecclesiastica Germanica*.

the life of the mission station in the African Bush. Long
before the coming of the mines there had been created in
Northern Rhodesia many centres which were representing
a new social and economic order. The dress of the missionary, his home, food, garden, furniture, equipment and
tools were silent teachers of a different economic order.
His hygiene, baths, sanitation, water supply, medicines,
care and preparation of food pointed to a new way of life.
His cultivation of flowers, vegetables, fruits, cereals, poultry and live stock, with the regular and varied supply of
food which these provided, reinforced the trend of mission
influence. The organisation of his household, its variety of
activities, regular work, study, books, play and worship,
his family and personal relationships in respect of wife,
children and fellow missionary pointed clearly to a new
social order. Imperceptibly the ways and ideas of the mission began to penetrate the countryside. New interests were
aroused, new needs were born and new values and standards began to emerge.

Christianity in Europe and America is an expression of
the social and economic order with which it has grown.
Thus the missionary finds difficulty in disentangling his
message from the civilisation which has produced him.
There is a great gap between the economic levels of the mission and those of its converts. The new way of life is expensive. It assumes a standard of equipment and a supply of
things that require money. Mission work and wages can only
meet the needs of the few. The enlarging economic wants of
the countryside must look beyond the mission for satisfaction. At this point the European industrial enterprise provides a means of paying the cost of the new way of life.

As we have seen, the mining of copper in Northern Rhodesia has accelerated processes that were already operating
through various media for some decades. The situation
points to the urgency of defining the Native policies of the
Territory—administrative, economic and missionary—and
securing a clear understanding of the position of the Native
in the light of this complex of influences to which he is

exposed, and the co-ordinating of programmes suited to achieving accepted policies.

It has been pointed out that the present system of the development of the mining areas in Central Africa is tending to stabilise the Native population at the mines and in the town locations; that the effect of these detached Native communities upon the rural areas is disruptive; and that the economic trend of the Territory suggests the importance of a concurrent stabilisation of rural Native life as the soundest answer to the problem.[1] An effective rural stabilisation implies a degree of stabilisation of social and political forces, but for the moment let us address ourselves to the economic question.

Although missions have themselves initiated certain economic changes and have contributed to the economic unrest of the Territory, they have been superseded by other factors for which they are not responsible and which are forcing the pace of change. The mine, the farm, the European settlement, the railway, the motor-lorry and the trader are all contributing to the process.

As outlined more fully below, missions under these circumstances may do three things: try to understand the economic forces and changes taking place in the Territory; help their people to meet these changes wisely and make adjustments to them, and, finally, endeavour to control the direction and, so far as may be possible, the speed of these changes.

With rural stabilisation in mind as a means of control, how can missions co-operate effectively? The central position of agriculture in Native African life should be deep graven on the consciousness of the Christian mission. However insistently industry and domestic service may call upon certain sections of the population, the climatic and physical conditions of Central Africa point to agricultural and pastoral pursuits as the basic and permanent occupations of the bulk of the people. The missions could profitably study this fact and its implications for their pro-

[1] See Economics section, Chapter XI.

gramme, message and personnel, for it conditions every step they take. If the people are to stay at home the inducements of the home occupations must be strong enough to hold them. Agriculture must be made profitable: crops must not only be sufficient to supply food, but also a surplus convertible into the cash required to provide the enlarged needs of the family. Markets for produce, roads for transport and the organisation of credit arrangements for financing such enterprises are also problems for the rural community which adjusts itself to the new economic order.

The modern mission in Africa, as elsewhere, is not agriculturally minded. Its missionaries usually have an urban background, point of view and interests; they are trained in the arts, theology and many of the sciences, but rarely in agriculture. They come prepared to give many of the finest elements of Western culture to a people whose main interest and destiny in life is farming. Moreover, it is a farming so crude and inadequate that it requires a reorganisation and adjustment to modern community and market conditions before it may serve as a basis for building the Christian community. This the graduate of the university, theological or Bible school is not prepared to attempt. Here is a task in the main for the specialist. But more than the leadership of a specialist is required to meet such a basic need. The whole mission personnel must grasp the significance of the agricultural process in the life of their people. The co-operation of the farmer with the Creator of all life, through preparing the soil for the germination of the seed, and in care of the plant and nurture of the ripening crop, together with the beauty and dignity of the whole creative process, might well have a central place in the services of the Church, the teaching of the schools and in the attitude of the missionary. With this in view, the task of the mission would be, not only the creating of catechists, pastors and teachers, but the building up and inspiring of a community of Christian farmers.

The work of the Galangue Mission in Angola (Portuguese

West Africa) illustrates the possibilities of the agricultural approach in dealing with a backward community. Here a group of American Negro missionaries, under the auspices of the American Congregational Board, have been carrying on evangelistic, educational and agricultural work for some ten years. The Natives were depressed, superstitious and helpless in the face of Government taxation. By the study of local conditions and by first-hand demonstration of methods suited to meet them, the life of the district has been markedly improved. The Natives were cultivating only the thin soil of the ridges, believing the rich bottom-lands to be haunted by the spirits of their dead. The Negro missionary cultivated the bottom-lands, ploughing deep, with oxen. After four years the heavy yields of wheat and the absence of disaster following the breaking of taboos interested the Natives. The missionary helped in the selection of seed and loaned his oxen around the district. By the tenth year Native farmers were raising wheat in the bottom-lands of several neighbouring valleys. The missionary turned his attention to the improvement of Native live-stock. With imported animals he cross-bred a sturdy type of hog suited to withstand local climate and diseases. He then organised a village circuit for demonstration of his specially bred stock. Several pairs of animals were circuited through the countryside, each pair remaining long enough in a village to prove their breeding capacity. One half of the litter remained as the property of the village and the other half reverted to the mission, while the parent hogs continued their educational tour to the next village.

By these and other methods many people have been helped to a position of comparative independence. We saw these Native farmers selling to the local trader enough of their own wheat to enable them to pay their poll taxes. The effects of these improved economic conditions upon the Native community, in increased support of the Church, in a desire for education for the children and for better homes and standards of living, were apparent. The removal of the dread of enforced absentee labour for pay-

ment of taxes and the increased solidarity of community
and home were also among the benefits that had come to
the district through the agricultural mission.

Various practical measures directed toward the building
up of the rural community could profitably be considered
by the mission. A study might prove useful of the rôle of the
mission station as a market centre and the possibility of
linking it with a system of markets for the district along
with other stations, administrative posts and chiefs' villages. Those commodities, now imported by the mission
from other districts, that could be supplied locally should
be discovered and the people encouraged to produce them.
The mission, in co-operation with Government, could also
help in organising district fairs where the people could
exhibit their farm produce and live-stock, and have an
opportunity to see what other Natives have accomplished.
In this way, new ideas, methods and implements could be
studied and demonstrated, and Native agricultural leadership stimulated.

The importance of good roads in the development of the
countryside, and the personal and communal advantages
to be derived from them, could be taught in the mission
schools by maps and diagrams illustrating how local and
territorial life are linked up socially and are dependent
commercially upon transport facilities. The villagers
could be encouraged to widen the footpaths between
their villages and to enlarge paths feeding existing highways into two-track routes suitable for hand-carts and
trucks. Small models of different modes of transportation
suited to highways could be built by the students and
shown to parents and friends on exhibition days. The
mission has an opportunity to demonstrate the road-
building art on its own grounds and the approaches to its
stations.

The possibilities of creating co-operative credit and
marketing societies could-profitably be explored. Father
Bernard Huss, formerly the Principal of St. Francis Native
Training College at Mariannhill, Natal, has had notable

success in developing co-operative activities among tribes of the South-East Coast.[1] Other African Native co-operative movements that would repay examination are those of the Gold Coast (Gold Coast Co-operative Societies Ordinance, 1931) with 270 experimental groups in 1932, of which 206 had sold cacao, and the Farmers' Associations of Nigeria also for the sale of cacao.

The co-operative principle has special significance for Bantu rural life, as it makes its adjustments to the inroads of individualism and the pressure of commerce and industry. It enables the Native to meet the new economic strains with a solidarity where as an individual he is helpless. It further embodies a social interdependence for which the Native is prepared by his communal inheritance. It will therefore both serve to help him retain his social solidarity and, as a medium for the interplay of progressive and traditional thought, will gradually transmute the conservatism of tribal sanctions into an onward-moving force.

"The Co-operative Movement is perhaps the most potentially fruitful single development for real cultural expansion that has been started among the Native people of South Africa up to the present time. The moral sanctions implicit in the co-operative principles are natural to the Native mind which has hitherto known no essential cleavage between the spiritual and the material world. Every major action of the Native had its spiritual significance. Co-operation is a discipline but one like in kind, if developing in application and in degree, to that of the Native's tribal past."[2]

The Native co-operative society provides a natural centre for promoting social activities and the gaining of general knowledge by groups and individuals. The Mariann-

---

[1] This movement dates from 1926. At the end of 1931 there were 35 societies with 3300 members and deposits amounting to £10,000. The funds are derived entirely from Native sources and no State loans have been utilised.

[2] D. R. O. Thomas, "Adult Education for the Native in South Africa", *Journal of Adult Education*, April 1933, vol. vi. No. 2.

hill Training School provides "social courses" for farmers and school teachers. Instruction is given in practical farming, simple economics, social psychology and domestic science. The responsibility for these co-operatives rests upon the people themselves. This encourages the integration of new knowledge and individual advancement with communal life and welfare. The gatherings of the co-operatives provide a meeting point for tribal interests such as dancing, the exchange of farming experience and a discussion of community problems.

Mr. C. F. Strickland well points to the danger of the pace at which changes in African social structure are taking place, and the fine adaptation of the co-operative society as a clearing-house in which the more progressive Natives may of their own initiative adjust the shock of sudden change to Bantu life. He says: 'If a rapid advance must be dared by Africa without . . . a historical preparation, it is essential that there be no violent divorce between past traditions and the new life, no uprooting of the growing plant from the ground in which its strength is stored. . . . Yet new social bonds are urgently necessary to reinforce, in some cases to replace those which fall apart as minds and interests expand. . . . Action which was instinctive or enforced by custom must become conscious. The spirit of communal obligation must yield to a rational desire for the public good and to a perception that it is identical with the advantage even of the most progressive and economic-minded individual. . . . A synthesis of Western and Native cultures has to be achieved which will retain the precious heritage of the past, while absorbing the wealth, material and ideal, which pours in from the modern world. Without dislodging the conservative from his social fortress it must enlarge its circuit to give a place also to the educated and critical man, holding him in the midst of his community to contribute toward and interpret its new morality and understanding."[1]

[1] C. F. Strickland, *Co-operation for Africa*, pp. 33-34. Oxford University Press, 1933.

From this argument it is seen that the co-operative principle as applied to the Native African goes far beyond the function of a mechanism for economic solidarity, and may prove to be one of the most effective means of achieving the education of the adult Bantu.

The co-operative plan could in time be used in a joint ownership of machines for production and transport, such as hand cultivators, carts and motor-lorries, that are beyond the resources of the individual. Groups of intelligent Natives could in time jointly operate their own motor-lorries for the hauling of produce to market, and avoid the prohibitive charges of the transport drivers. In the South African Union there are considerable numbers of Natives who own motor-cars and motor-bicycles and who have become skilled in the care of their engines and repair of broken parts. The mechanical skill necessary for the repair of intricate machinery is rare even in the case of European drivers of motor-cars, but there is reason to believe that the Black man will in due time learn this also from his White employer.

The obvious market for Native-grown crops is the Native himself. As already indicated, the Roan Antelope mine has followed the plan of buying the produce of the gardens of its own employees for feeding their labour force.[1] In 1931 about one-fifth of the garden-grown food purchases of this mine, aggregating twenty tons in weight, was raised by its Native employees. Under a consistent plan of fostering Native trade in the supply of Native-consumed commodities, this policy of the Roan Antelope mine could be widely extended on the copper belt.

The mission could effectively impress the importance of diversified crop-farming upon its people, with both immediate family needs and the increase of income in view. The limitations of subsistence farming and the economic weakness as well as the advantages of the cash crop system could be stressed in the schooling of the children and in contacts with villagers. Cases of Bantu who have success-

[1] Part II. Chapter V. pp. 74-75.

fully used the cash crop system, with names of the people and localities, and the nature of results, could be used with effect.

The mission school could profitably teach commercial geography and elementary economics. These subjects would include the relation of the minerals and other resources of Northern Rhodesia to the economic needs of the world, the commodities that Northern Rhodesia receives in exchange for its exports and the part that the Bantu people are playing in the international society. Through the school the children of the Territory might become familiar with the place of specialisation in the village, and a generation accustomed to the ideas of commerce, trade and diversified occupations in the community would in time come forward.

Each mission station, in so far as it has suitable land and trained personnel, should be feeling its way on the agricultural problems of its district. This is being well done by the Livingstonia Mission at Chitambo. This mission is demonstrating the raising of various grains that can be grown on local soil, is experimenting with fertilisers, comparing results obtained by their use with those obtained without fertiliser, arranging for competition in crop yields, and in many ways is encouraging modern methods of farming.

Where missions are well situated in relation to water, the demonstration of irrigation may be of value. Mbereshi Mission of the London Missionary Society was built on a ridge jutting out into a plain bounding it on either side. Water had to be carried up from the valley with such difficulty that its liberal use was out of the question. The station was dry and parched through much of the year. A member of the mission, with an elementary knowledge of surveying, discovered that the river in the valley below the mission, at a distance of nine miles from Mbereshi, was higher than the mission site, and he conceived the plan of building a water furrow. With the help of a force of Natives, in the course of three months he led an unfailing stream of mountain water to Mbereshi. The water has brought great benefits to the mission and its large group of Native dependents. Little streams running in many directions have created a place of beauty and prosperity, with orange groves, shade trees, fruits, flowers and vegetables. The water is used for a bathing-pool for the children's clinic, is led to outlying Native gardens and live-stock runs, and has lowered the average temperature of the station by three degrees. This furrow was built without previous irrigation experience and with the use of Native tools and methods. The channel through the ridge bounding the river was blasted by pouring cold water upon the heated rock surface.

The Native system of agriculture, with its tree-lopping and burning to produce ash fertiliser, results in the necessity of a periodic removal of villages and gives a semi-nomadic character to Northern Rhodesia society. This has a profound bearing on the development of the Christian community. The expectation of moving the village every five to eight years discourages the building of comfortable homes and the making of permanent improvements such as fruit orchards, hedges and shade trees. Few men will go to the labour of building a house of sun-dried brick with doors, windows and fireplaces under these conditions. Such a community is satisfied with the crudest type of school and church buildings. No roads will be developed. The idea of a permanent home as a place to which a man belongs, in which he takes pride, and for which he will sacrifice, cannot take root under these conditions. And with its absence some of the deepest values that make for character, community morale and social well-being are lost. To attempt to build a Christian community under such conditions is to make bricks without straw. A frequent and disheartening sight in Northern Rhodesia was the skeleton poles and rotting thatch of an abandoned village standing amongst the hacked remnants of the forest.[1] This method of farm-

_____

[1] The Government of Southern Rhodesia has made great progress towards the stabilisation of Native farming through the use of Native

ing may practically isolate a mission from the population. A mission visited by the Commission, which was originally built in a populous region, in twelve years had been virtually deserted by the villagers who moved farther and farther away, as the forest was burned, in search of wood for their ash fertiliser. This agricultural problem directly conditions the establishment of an enduring Church and can be solved only by skilled agriculturists. Plans should be made for community building on the basis of a permanent occupation, not only of the soil, but of a definite piece of land. Such permanent agriculture involves the fundamental question of soil conservation and the maintenance of soil fertility. What is equally important, it requires an attitude of mind in which the soil is looked upon as a trust whose productive powers must be kept intact for future generations.

If each mission were equipped with a trained specialist free to devote to it his whole energies and to experiment with soils, crops and fertilisers, in co-operation with Government experts and other mission specialists, in the course of time progress would be made toward stabilising the life of rural Rhodesia.

In discussing this subject it must be kept clearly in mind that agriculture is not only a method of making a living but a way of life. Further, that it is a way of life in which non-material values bulk quite as heavily as the material benefits to be gained thereby. There is a place in agriculture for pride in achievement, the release of the creative instincts, a sense of service in providing the primary needs of society, the development of orderliness, responsibility and the dignity of labour. All these things are quite as important as economic results.[1]

The attitude of the missionary toward agriculture and the worth of rural life is reflected definitely upon the mind of the Native. It is not sufficient that the missionary feel

Agricultural Demonstrators. Longer contact with European farmers too has influenced the people in the direction of permanent land occupation.

[1] Quoted from Dr. John Reisner, Agricultural Mission Foundation, 719 Fourth Avenue, New York.

that the future of the African is linked with the land, and that therefore some agricultural work should be undertaken by the mission school. A rural bias in the school is not so important as that the teacher shall be "rural-minded" and that his personal interest and attitude toward rural life shall be passed on to the student. The situation calls for a whole body of missionaries who believe in agriculture and as evangelists, teachers or agriculturists will dignify it and actively aid in building a community whose roots are in the soil.[1]

The experience of the United States in building up a landed Negro population through education and demonstration is one that could profitably be studied by the missionary who is faced with the task of creating a stable rural Christian community in Africa. The Phelps Stokes Fund of New York City has assisted more than two hundred missionaries, and others interested in African development, in studying Negro education and community activities in America.[2]

Through its handicraft training, missions could make invaluable experiments in stimulating Native production for the supply of Native needs. It may be questioned whether some of the energy that missions are now directing to the training of skilled joiners and cabinetmakers could not with advantage be turned to a study of the simple needs, equipment and tools of the Native village with a view to the training of artisans prepared to supply Native rather than European needs. Some years ago, in North China, the Chinese secretary of the Mass Education Movement conducted a series of agricultural experiments in a typical local "Hsien" or county.[3] Planting, seed selection, poultry-raising, ploughing, irrigation and farming implements were all made subjects of scientific

---

[1] In this connection a study of the principles embodied in the life and work of Jean Frederick Oberlin could well be a part of the preparation of every African missionary.

[2] The Phelps Stokes Fund, 101 Park Avenue, New York.

[3] Ting Hsien, Hopei Province. For a description of this rural educational work vide *Rural Education at Ting Hsien*, James Y. C. Yen, Pacific Affairs, Dec. 1932, vol. v. No. 12, pp 1067-69. Honolulu.

study. The principle of utilising and improving the traditional methods of the Chinese farmer was accepted. After experimenting with the man-power water-wheel of the paddy-fields, a wheel was produced which utilised the same principle as its predecessor but was capable of a double lifting capacity and required the labour of but one man instead of two. This result was gained by the use of a few elementary laws of physics and engineering. While it is too early to report the acceptance of the new wheel by the Chinese farmer, the principle illustrated is sound and capable of wide application. Here is a field for experimentation in Central Africa. The encouragement of the use of the Native hand-axe as a chisel has already been mentioned.[1] Mr. J. R. Fell, Director of the Government Jeanes School at Mazabuka, urges the introduction of the hand cultivator as being a simple machine, operated by one or two persons, but capable of extending the scope of land preparation five or six times as contrasted with the Native hoe. Furthermore, it is within Native power to buy and is easily kept in repair. The hand-cart might be added to the output of the mission shop, and the craft of the wheelwright included in its training.[2]

The Commission was impressed with the close relation between good craftsmanship and religion as illustrated in the technical training of African mission schools. For the primitive Native the character value of precision in using tools and in the designing, measurement and finish of tasks of carpentry, building and machine-work is hard to overestimate. Equally important are lessons of honesty with materials, fulfilment of contracts duly met in point of specifications and time. These are fundamentals on which the morale of a Christian community rests, and these can be effectively taught through the technical training of the mission.

African governments are blamed by some for the com-

[1] Part II. Chapter VI. p. 109.

[2] The work of such mission industrial schools as Tiger Kloof in the Union of South Africa and Morgenster in Southern Rhodesia offer examples of training adapted to the needs of Native society.

pulsion which drives men out from their villages to earn
tax money, but it is also possible to recognise the somewhat
similar rôle of missions in placing the equivalent of a
cultural tax on the people. This is the obligation to pay for
the expensive life to which the mission has introduced
them, including education, clothing, books, support of
churches and the many things which they have come to
appreciate through contact with the mission.

The Commission questioned many Natives working in
hotels, shops and offices on the railway line and the copper
belt in the effort to discover the reasons for their absence
from home. Several men stated that they were working
to pay for the education of their children in mission schools.
Although the payment of the poll tax is compelled by law
and that of the "cultural tax" is impelled by voluntary
choice, the mission cannot wholly escape the criticism that
it also is pushing out its people to enable them to pay the
price of the Christian order of society. It is impossible
wholly to separate the two processes. Missions are dependent upon Government for a political stability in which
they can create the Christian order. Moreover, a part of the
poll tax is put into the hands of missionaries for educating
the Native.

Since the Christian way of life has brought to the Native
new cultural necessities, a higher standard of living and
new economic burdens, missions cannot but interest themselves in the problem of building an economic framework
of society which will help him to attain these new standards.
There is an intrinsic lack in a Christianity that widens
horizons, creates new visions and stimulates desires, but
fails to make its influence effective in assisting men to
achieve these ideals. At this point the missions of the
Union of South Africa are in a weak position. For one
hundred years they have been preparing the Bantu for
participation in a Christian order of society. The Bantu in
the Union finds, however, that society is organised against
him except on the lowest scale of social and economic
activity. The result is a growing disillusionment, bitterness

and a discouragement amounting to apathy. There is also a resentment at the Christian teachers who have trained the Black man for this higher scale of life but can do so little to help him to achieve it.

Christian missions in Northern Rhodesia are in a favourable position in respect to this problem: the Government of the Territory is giving them strong practical support and actively supplementing their efforts for Native welfare. The absence of a large White population, and especially the White unskilled labouring group in Northern Rhodesia, reduces the fear of Black competition which is a fertile source of opposition to Bantu progress in the Union of South Africa. Consequently there does not yet exist a powerful White public opinion hostile to the interests of the Native.

A basic question for Rhodesian missions is, "Can Christianity find congenial soil and growth on the economic scale in which the Native social unit is at home?" Can the African Church thrive on the basis of the African village, African hut, African farming and African economy? How far must the Christian way of life wean the African away from the heart of Africa and create detached, semi-Europeanised groups with new tastes and needs, dependent on an alien culture and economy?

Can missions serve to buffer the shock of economic and cultural change and slow down rather than quicken the pace of these forces? The answers to these questions can be found only after patient and skilled study of all the factors. If missions will pay the price of such study, with both the religious and secular education of the people so largely in their hands, they may be able to turn the scale in the balance of forces that are struggling for the soul of Africa.

CHAPTER XXI

GOVERNMENT AND MISSIONS

THE statement is familiar to students of missions that religion is not concerned with politics and that missions should take a neutral attitude toward the administration of the territories in which they are working. However, in a social order which is undergoing a complete reintegration, the decision to keep aloof from questions of public concern may possibly in itself be an act with political consequences of the highest importance. A policy of inaction or neutrality toward a fluid and dynamic human situation may involve a mission in serious responsibility for results of a political character.

Missions are supplying the warp to the woof of administration in Northern Rhodesia. The co-operation and understanding obtaining between the missions and Administration has established a degree of harmony in carrying out far-reaching projects that should yield valuable results. The missions of the Territory have, with few exceptions, accepted the Government scheme of education and are adjusting their courses to it. A large majority of mission schools are supervised and subsidised by Government. Government offices are supplied with mission-trained Native clerks, interpreters and assistants; the members of the staffs of Government Normal and Jeanes schools are (almost without exception) graduates of mission schools. The director of the Government Jeanes School at Mazabuka, established to give practical training to the teachers of the Territory, is a man with many years of missionary experience. The Governor of the Protectorate and the Department heads have been attendants at the

Biennial General Missionary Conferences and have taken a valued part in the discussions.[1]

The programmes of missions and Government for the advancement of the people through education have every reason mutually to support each other, although the fundamental drive of each, in the nature of the case, differs. It is natural that each should feel the other to be a source both of strength and irritation. Each is using the other in a sense for its own purposes, yet with the united aim of securing the soundest development of the Native. This affords sufficient common ground for a workable relationship. It is of the highest importance that both missions and Government clearly understand the plans and aims of the other, and that the implications and limitations entailed by these plans be fully grasped. The unilateral nature of official policies makes it easier for missions to accomplish this than for Government. For missions are dealing with but one Government, while the Administration deals with nineteen mission societies which embrace a wide divergence of policies.

It would seem obligatory upon every missionary, before taking up residence in Northern Rhodesia, to acquaint himself thoroughly with the nature of the Government, the history of its occupation of the Territory, those Orders-in-Council or Legislative Acts which created it, and the scope of its limitations and responsibilities. The missionary should understand the obligations which the Government has undertaken with respect to the Native people, and its position in regard to Native laws and practices. He should understand the civil rights and duties of the people, including land laws and reserves and their financial requirements and taxes. He should be acquainted with the official position as to social observances and superstitions, an area where Government policy and mission teaching are sometimes at variance, as in the question of plural wives. The educational aims, policies and requirements of Government

[1] See published Reports of the General Missionary Conference of Northern Rhodesia (Lovedale Press).

should be understood, together with its economic policy with respect to labour, agriculture, industry, trade and transportation. The missionary should know the laws governing the freedom and personal rights of the people, including criminal procedure for non-payment of taxes and other misdemeanours. Of the highest importance is the missionary's grasp of the principles of Indirect Rule and its implications for his work. In short, since the mission shares responsibility for shaping the new moral, mental and social life of the people, it is important for him to master the nature and working of the framework into which this new life must be fitted. This whole subject is of such importance that it demands first-hand study by the new missionary rather than the second-hand interpretation of older associates.

The need of missionary understanding of Government policies has been reinforced by the entrance of industrialism into the Territory and the rapid dislocation of Native life that has accompanied it. The problems of Native society before the appearance of the copper-mines were difficult enough for missionary and Government: the industrial development of the last decades has increased the difficulty of the position, for it has brought a new set of influences into operation.[1]

It is important that the missionary be familiar with this group of subjects because of his unusual opportunity to help his people in adjusting themselves to and finding their place in the new order. An obligation rests upon him to help them to understand the laws and the reasons for official policies. The Bantu easily misunderstands the reasons for Native Reserves, why certain actions constitute crime, the difference between civil and criminal offences, the duties of subjects of the Territory and the position and duties of administrative officials. These are all matters of vital concern to him. Further, the value of Government and the significance of the poll tax and how it directly benefits the Native may well be explained. These questions

[1] See Part II. Chapter V., also Part V. Chapter XVIII.

should be taught by the mission school as elementary
civics. They could profitably be included in informal discussions with the older people. In these ways, in time, the
underlying principles of government would be grasped by
the people and a sense of fair play and the reasonable-
ness of the social and administrative order would be
gained.

The contrast between Bantu law and English law is seen
in the different social orientation of the two systems. Bantu
law is built upon the communal principle of the solidarity
of the group, with the tribal family as a unit; English law,
on the other hand, in a large measure centres upon the
rights and responsibilities of the individual. The Bantu
individual measure of worth is the extent to which the
person contributes to the solidarity of his tribal unit;
Anglo-Saxon criterion of society's worth, however, is the
degree to which the community can produce strong, successful individuals. These concepts are far apart and partly
explain the Native's confusion when faced with English
laws. That life, liberty, suffering and chastity are individual
matters and that goods may be personal property are new
ideas to the Native. The right of a Government to impose
European laws upon a people of a different mentality and
social structure may fairly be questioned and is not assumed in this report. To the credit of the British Government, it must be said that it recognises the incongruity and
injustice of the complete application of English law to
African Native groups. The policy of Indirect Rule now in
force in one form or another in several of the territories
under British control is a witness to this recognition. While
it cannot be assumed that the original Christian conception
of society was individualistic, nor that a Christian community cannot thrive on the communal basis, it is true that
the concepts inherent in the White man's law are difficult
to grasp without a knowledge of those implicit in his religion. As the Black man comes to understand the force of
Jesus' teachings relating to the supreme value of the person
and his responsibility to God, he will find more explicable

the laws that support the individualistic conception of society.

It would be difficult to overstate the importance of the missionary's understanding of the Government's policy of Indirect Rule, and its bearings upon the Christian movement in the Territory.[1] The recent policy of placing upon Chiefs as the leaders of their people the responsibility for administering Native society in its social, civil and domestic affairs carries a deep significance for the Christian Church in Northern Rhodesia. There are ethical principles involved in the system of Indirect Rule of the highest value. These cannot be ignored by the missionary, but should be defined and where possible harmonised with the sanctions of Christian teaching. Among these principles are the responsibility of the Chief for the well-being of his tribe, his obligation to carry himself as an example to his people and to enforce the law, maintain order, guard public health and safety, and to exercise his powers as an ethical trust. On the other hand, these duties of the Chief find their counterpart in the reciprocal duties of the people—in conducting themselves with sobriety, honesty and loyalty to the established order. The system appeals to the best instincts in both leaders and people. The fact that some of these instincts have been unused for a generation through the decline of the Chieftainship is an incentive for the missionary to see what can be accomplished with this new moral challenge that has come to Native society.

Indirect Rule requires an understanding of tribal organisation, customary law, the duties and prerogatives of the Chief and his powers in relation to the commoner. If the missionary is teaching different moral sanctions from those required by customary law, as in relation to polygamy or *lobola*, it is essential for him to know the bearing of the Christian teaching upon the status and kinship obligations of the believer, exactly wherein it conflicts with Native sanctions, the extent to which the mission can uphold a Christian Native in flouting tribal law, and the conse-

[1] See Part IV. Chapter XIV.

quences of such action for the Native in relation to his group. The effect of encouraging a Christian to break tribal law upon the status of the Chief and the missions' relations with him should also be considered. Many of the missions which were in the field before the establishment of European government have been notable for their respect and consideration for the Chiefs of their territories. Outstanding in this regard is the record of the French missionary, François Coillard, and his dealings with Paramount Lewanika of the Barotse nation.[1]

It will not be entirely easy for those missions which have entered the Territory during the period of the decline of the Chieftainship to acquire the attitude toward the office and its occupant which the policy of Indirect Rule demands. In cases where long familiarity with the vices and senility of a local Chief has bred a certain contempt and neglect of recognition, such a change may seem as unreal as it is difficult. The new relationship of Chiefs to their people acquired from Indirect Rule is one which needs the earnest study of every mission. The influence upon his pupils and Church members of the missionary's attitude toward Native customs and sanctions can hardly be over-estimated. The reception of the Lunda tribe Paramount Chief, Kasembe, by a mission station in Northern Rhodesia on the occasion of the visit of the Commission in 1932 made a favourable impression on all present. The buffoonery and savage ceremonial of the Chief and his court contrasted strangely with the serious courtesy with which the missionaries and hundreds of Native Christians and school pupils received him.

There is an obligation upon the modern mission to develop a new respect, not alone for the incumbent of the Chief's office, but for the office itself. The dilemma of the decrepit and unworthy Chief is a passing phase which time and experience tend to remedy. The dilemma is not alone the missionary's but is shared by the Native Christian. A missionary in the Union of South Africa described this dilemma:

---

[1] *Vide* Édouard Favre, *François Coillard*. Société des Missions Évangéliques, Paris, 1922.

"The humblest mission pupil is conscious of the fact that he knows more than his Chief about the world he lives in. How can he fundamentally respect him?" It would appear that a way out of the dilemma is to extol the office and its potential right to respect.

The importance of the Chieftainship in the life of the people should be upheld by the mission in their contacts with pupils, teachers, Church elders and members. Chiefs could be invited to visit the mission schools for exhibitions of handicrafts, games, singing and drama. Boy-scout and girl-guide troops could demonstrate for them. Chiefs could be encouraged to inspect mission hospitals, day clinics, technical training and agricultural enterprises. In these ways the meaning of education and its practical relation to the welfare of the people would be made intelligible. In the class-room, with the elucidation of Indirect Rule and its importance for guarding the solidarity and traditions of the tribe, should be explained the functions of British administration and the relation of Indirect Rule to it.

The missionary should not forget that his religious teaching tends to undermine the prestige of the Chief. In Bantu tribal organisation the Chief is not only the political and military head but their religious head as well. This gave him a powerful hold upon his tribe. The coming of European government and religion therefore is a double threat to the authority of the Chieftainship, which in practice has brought the office near to extinction. The missionary may well be sensitive to the inroads that his coming has made upon the solidarity of the tribe and welcome the reinstatement of the Chief with much of his former secular authority.

The Chief's Council[1] offers a possible channel for the play of Christian public opinion upon tribal legislation and practice. This body is open to the appointment of men of influence. Its functions should be understood by the Christian community, and membership in it looked upon as an opportunity for rendering public service.

[1] See Part IV. Chapter XIV.

The advent of Indirect Rule makes specially significant the opportunity of missions to develop sound Native public opinion as a basis for a Christian order of society. With both the religious training and secular education of the young in their hands, the position of missions in this regard is very strong. By these means, as the second and third generations of Christians come forward, ideas will take root, points of view will become established, new customs will spread. Gradually through a number of generations the seeds of Christian culture, supported by a growing public opinion, will germinate into customary law and a Christian society will be born. The process is exemplified in Basutoland[1] where the Christian Church has been growing for one hundred years. At Morija, a mission of the Paris Evangelical Society, we were privileged to be present at an open-air commemoration service of the Reformation attended by a thousand Christian Basutos. The gathering of soberly dressed men and women, some walking, some riding on horses which they picketed to the fence around the church, resembled a Negro congregation in the Southern States or peasants of Switzerland or Brittany coming in for a church festival. Among these Basuto communities, whose Paramount Chief Griffith is a Christian, polygamy is to-day an exception and the use of *lobola* has declined. About 30 per cent of the people are members of Christian churches and an equal proportion of the children are enrolled in mission schools. These results are not only a witness to the success of Christian missions, but also to the factor of time in Christianising community public opinion.

The cultivation through a period of years of the families of the Chief and his leading councillors is a type of mission strategy which could well be used in Northern Rhodesia. The Chief and his family are the stronghold of heathen practices and conservatism among Bantu tribes, and a

[1] A British protectorate, comprising 11,708 square miles, formed in 1884, and situated between the Orange Free State, the Transvaal, Natal and the Eastern Cape Province.   Population, 500,000.

definite policy of cultivation might in the end yield tangible results for the Christian community. In this way the leading people could be won to a better understanding of the nature of mission activity and its relation to tribal interests. There would also be the possible eventuality of the conversion of a Chief or of one of the councillors eligible to the office of Chief, and with it the penetration of the inner circle of heathen leadership by Christianity. Finally, through the schooling of the children of the Chief's family circle, Christianity might eventually find its way to the leadership of a tribe. This has already happened in Bechuanaland and in Basutoland, both protectorates being ruled by Christian Paramounts. A most interesting case of a Bantu tribe accepting a Christian Chief is that of the Western Pondos on the eastern borders of the Transkei.[1] Victor Poto, son of the hereditary Chief of the Pondos, was educated as a boy in a Wesleyan mission school where he became a Christian. As a young man he attended Fort Hare College. On the death of his father, Victor was called home from college to succeed him. A dramatic struggle then began between the Christian Chief and his councillors over his non-acceptance of plural marriage, tribal beer-drinks and other customary practices in which a Bantu Chief is supposed to lead. Though not without lapses, Victor Poto has followed his convictions and is living a Christian life at the head of a nation of whom a majority are still heathen. The Pondos have had Christianity among them for three generations and about 25 per cent of the people are believers.

This is not the place to discuss the problem of special schools for Chiefs' sons as contrasted with their education with commoners. We believe it, however, timely for missions, acting in collaboration with the Government of the Territory, to exert definite efforts in the direction of educating the children of Chiefs, and in the case of matri-

[1] The Transkeian territories comprise a district of 18,000 square miles in the Eastern Cape Province adjoining Natal. It is occupied chiefly by Native reserves with a population (1921) of 900,000.

lineal tribes the children of those families of influence from which the future leaders of their people will be chosen.

There is a marked contrast in the relations between missions and Government in Northern Rhodesia and the adjoining Belgian Congo. The causes are not difficult to find. The Protestant missionaries in the Belgian Congo, with few exceptions, are aliens and representatives of Anglo-Saxon nations and culture. The Roman Catholic Church, which is exceedingly powerful in the colony, looks upon each Protestant mission and school as a challenge to its supremacy, and the Government is apt to regard them as obstacles to the cultural solidarity of the country. This attitude is reflected in the discrimination shown by the Union Minière against Protestant work, by the denial by the Government to Protestant schools of the subsidies given to the Roman Catholic orders, by the refusal of recognition of graduates of Protestant schools and in many other ways. If an improvement is to be effected in the position of Protestant missions, it is necessary that they should realise the difficulties which their presence creates for the administration, and that their missionaries should be equipped intellectually and culturally to understand and appreciate the point of view of the Government. This involves, among other things, a competent mastery of the French language, a knowledge of Belgian colonial policies and laws, and an understanding of the official and social conventions which are current in Belgian life. These qualifications are especially important for those Protestant leaders who represent so large a number of missions in the Katanga copper-field.

The religious discrimination which exists in the Katanga is not found in the adjoining British territory. Here, although more than half the missionary body are Roman Catholics and of alien nationality, they are accorded the same freedom of residence and work and the same assistance as the Protestants. It is important to note that a very large proportion of the Roman Catholic missionaries in Northern Rhodesia use the English language. They also take an active part in the biennial General Missionary Conference and show in general a spirit of co-operation and comity with the Protestants.[1]

The chief and the only serious criticism of government by Northern Rhodesia missionaries was in regard to education. It was stated that Native education was not adequately supported; that the proportion of official funds spent on Native services is not commensurate with the taxes paid by the Natives nor with the expenditure on the small European population; that European residents escaped with relatively light taxation and that, instead of putting money into new Government schools, larger support ought to be given to the mission schools which are already operating and eager to do the work. Officials were among the first to admit the inadequacy of educational appropriations to meet Native needs. This applies not only to the support of mission schools but to almost every department of administration. The explanation, if not the justification, of the present state of affairs lies in the difficulty of providing administrative services for an immense primitive territory with a scanty and impoverished population and the consequent lack of taxable resources. The Biennial Missionary Council, which is attended not only by the missionaries but by the Government officials, serves as an excellent clearing-house for the discussion of these and other problems which are of common interest to missionaries and officials.

The missionary, through his intimate contact with the people, is in a favourable position for observing the effect of Government measures on Native life, and may often with advantage call the attention of the Administrator to possible undesirable effects of such measures as well as to breaches of the law and the miscarriage of justice. Before taking any such action, however, the missionary should be sure of the accuracy of his facts, should be fully informed of the laws relating to the matter in question, and should

[1] *Vide* published Reports of the General Missionary Conference of Northern Rhodesia (Lovedale Press).

endeavour to understand the difficulty which confronts the official in administering them. The missionary should never appeal to outside public opinion for the righting of what he considers to be a public wrong until he has first brought the matter privately to the attention of the responsible authorities and exhausted every means of inducing them to set matters right.

The co-operation and sympathy which exists between Missions and Administration in Northern Rhodesia is fine and real, but it could be considerably increased. The missionary may with profit consider the strength of his position, the complete freedom of activity, the influence through education that has been put into his hands by Government, and the degree of unity in aim between himself and the Administration. If he feels irritation at requirements placed upon his schools, he may well remember that the Government has the responsibility of education for an immense territory, that it is dealing with many different missions, and that the educational advancement of the people can best come upon the basis of a unified system. The missionary has every reason to look upon the Administrator as a friend and ally. He should lose no opportunity to call upon him and to counsel with him with utmost frankness on the many aspects of Native problems which they meet in common. He may well be aware that, if there are occasions when official requirements are a burden and an inconvenience for him, there are also aspects of the work of missions that try the patience of the Administrator. The missionary should bear in mind that the Administrator is the representative of the Government but that he also is a human being with social needs and susceptibilities, and that friendship forms a solid basis upon which an understanding of difficulties and a solution of mutual problems may be reached.

CHAPTER XXII

THE CHURCH AND THE COPPER BELT

HOWEVER urgent may be the demand for Christian Social Service and education on the copper belt, the spiritual task of missions is and must continue to be the central task.

Economic and political forces will shape the Native's outer world, but the incomparable task of the missionary is to communicate to him the forces and values that will vitalise, rationalise and control the new life he has entered.

The Church must relate its message to the morale of the new community. It must assist the Native to grasp a reasonable moral order, to become adjusted to a suitable scheme of things and an understandable set of values. It must help him to find a place for himself in the new society and to understand its sanctions, controls and progressive view.

In this new society the Native must be assisted to fit his past, find his present and plan his future. In it he must discover his responsibilities, privileges, satisfactions and obligations. The new life must provide him with a reasoned hope and ambition and help him to conserve his old respect for himself and for others. A new scheme of living must be substituted for the old, one that is built on a personal relationship to God as Father, but a scheme so far as possible built on the old. The new life for the African must have its controls, rational or irrational, superstitious or otherwise, to take the place of what he has lost.

The Christian religion can give these things to him. The Christian missionary must supply them, and he and what he represents are the only influence that can. In these ways the missionary will recreate the African's world for him and build a whole new order based on the Native's new conception of God and of himself.

The copper belts of Central Africa illustrate the moral and social confusion which attends the sudden meeting of widely contrasted cultures. Under these circumstances a marginal region, or moral "no-man's land", develops in which the controls and sanctions of both cultures are weakened and the vices and licence of both reinforce one another.

In the coming of the West to the Far East, although many individuals were completely broken from their *milieu,* the bulk of the people stood within the social fabric and moral controls of their society and were comparatively untouched by the sudden shock of foreign influence. This is not the case in Central Africa. Here alien influences are working both from within and without to undermine a primitive social fabric which is peculiarly susceptible to them. New communities of Africans are forming outside of the Bantu social structure and within the European framework. These new communities are powerfully affecting the whole of Native society. The Native is in a dark wood. The old trail is lost and the new not yet found. Under these circumstances it is not surprising that he breaks the moral codes of both orders of society—the old which he has left behind and the new which he does not yet understand.

The African Native must be equipped with stronger religious convictions and moral controls if he is to meet successfully the social and economic influences of the copper belt. The new wine of alien life requires new bottles or it will burst the old containers.

The situation demands not only a religion of a tougher fibre but one that is more comprehensive than a "European" or an "American Christianity". To identify the religion that comes to Africa from Europe with European civilisation is to involve the Native in confusion and unreality and to delay the growth of an indigenous African Church. Though the difficulty involved is immense, the missionary must struggle to dissociate his message and the Christian way of life from his own culture and help the African to make it his very own. It must have a quality suited to the Black man's needs and temptations wherever he may be, otherwise he will find it easy to live the Christian way on the mission station, but a totally different thing to do this in his distant village or in the pagan European household or office of the copper belt.

The mission tends to create the whole of the Christian Native's world. There are associated with its central spiritual task a bewildering medley of activities—economic, cultural and administrative—which are all building the new Christian society. These many activities easily confuse the motives to which the Church appeals, and endanger the quality and depth of its religion. The mission in the bush is a large employer of labour—for land-clearing, road work, house-building, transportation, cultivation, domestic service and many other tasks. As many as two or three hundred workers, together with their families, may be supported in this way.

From these workers converts are baptized, and at length a church and schools appear among the villages that grow beside the mission. The mission is often the chief source of ready money in a large district and is a market for food supplies and other commodities. It is also a centre of education and of new standards of food, shelter, clothing and various possessions. All of these things give to the mission a prestige and attraction that make a multiple appeal to the Native.

Under these conditions there is peril that the Native may confuse Christianity with material things and worldly prosperity. He has no relative standards by which to measure the mission. The sacrifice of the missionary, his meagre salary and simple living, are lost upon him.

The coming of a powerful industrial movement into such a situation, offering the people higher wages and living standards, may prove to be a blessing to the Church. It is a test of the sincerity of hundreds of Christians. It is

a shock to the prestige of the mission. It prunes it of many
material attractions and allows its spiritual values to take
their pre-eminent position. It may also purge the mission
of not a few unworthy hangers-on. In the end, it is probable
that the contact of the Bantu with higher economic standards, the competition of outside opportunity and the
realism of material civilisation will produce a stronger
Native Church than would be possible under the old
conditions.

Missions may well regard the strong controls of Native
society as allies in the worker's adjustment to his new surroundings. A step toward this end would be to keep promi-
nently before him his village ties and obligations and the
fact that these have a first claim upon him, and that he
must fulfil the expectations of his kin and Chief. Villages
should plan to keep in touch with their people on the
copper belt by regular visits of headmen, teachers and
evangelists who would find their tribesmen and establish
links with the home communities.

Every possible means should be used to foster the contacts and lines of communication between the recruitment areas and the mines. Both the missionary at the mine
and in the rural district could arrange for a letter-writing
service, through which the worker and his distant family
would be encouraged to write to one another.

The system in use on the Katanga field by which Christians departing for the copper belt are given a letter to the
new church should be adopted by all missions in recruitment areas. A constant effort should be made through
evangelists and village teachers to discover the people who
are going to the copper mines and to send their names and
destinations to the Christian workers there with the request that an effort be made to find and help them. The
departure of village people to the copper belt could well
be made the occasion of a special farewell in which the
travellers would not only be fêted but made to feel the
importance and difficulties of the step they were taking,
and the responsibilities to family, tribe and Church which

it involves..At the same time sound advice could be given and a sense of mission imparted. In these ways a worker would not slip unnoticed out of a community but would go away knowing that the eyes and expectations of many were upon him and that he had both a kinship and Christian status to uphold. It should be impressed also upon the worker that his going to the outer world is an opportunity to learn all possible that he can apply usefully on his return for the benefit of his people.

The Christian men at the mine could form tribal and inter-village associations for the purpose of promoting mutual aid and morale. The Christian miners should see in the new arrivals a chance for service in welcoming them, and helping them to be aware of the presence of fellow-Christians, the Church and other helpful influences.

Rural missionaries and evangelists should periodically visit the mines. In this way the Christians from their districts could be personally encouraged and made to feel that their absence was a matter of concern to the home church and community. By these visits mission workers would acquaint themselves with conditions at the mines, the peculiar problems and temptations of their people, and ways to deal with these problems both there and at home. On the other hand, the missionary of the copper belt should spend time in the recruitment areas observing the conditions from which the mine workers have come, becoming acquainted with the people in their homes and learning the difficulties caused by the absence of the men. Finally, through these visits the mission would better understand the full meaning of the industrial movement in the life of the Territory and its relation to its own programme for the development of the people.

In these ways the Church on the copper belt would integrate with the Church in the rural area, and a unified plan could be carried out for strengthening the Christian society of the Territory.

An implication of the new order for missions is the obligation to create a new and attractive content for Native society. Between Government and Church a large part of those social, recreational and emotional activities that form the normal fabric of Bantu life have been proscribed. And with them much of the joy and zest of life has gone. Government has outlawed intertribal wars, inter-village raids, ritual murders and acts of revenge. The practices of the witch-doctor are banned and restrictions are placed on the hunting of big game. Missions, on the other hand, have banned polygamy, and with few exceptions have condemned beer-drinks, dancing, drumming, the bride-price and the initiation rites that play so large a part in the life of the Bantu boy and girl. What has Christianity put in the place of these activities?

Unless missions address themselves to this problem they will discover that a vacuum has been formed in Bantu life and that Nature has violent ways of filling the vacuum.

In parts of the Union of South Africa, by reason of this negative policy, the Church is rapidly losing its Native young people. Three reasons are held as responsible: the boredom of a Christian community whose youth find little to interest them and happily occupy their time; the proximity of heathen villages where Native rites and social practices are in full swing and exert a powerful pull upon the Christian youth; and the new liberty to which Bantu young people are exposed in the towns, where their moral standards become confused and they are easily led into excesses. Wherever the African is coming out from his society into a European environment, the force of Jesus' parable is seen, where the man from whom a devil had been cast and was empty, swept and garnished, soon found himself inhabited by seven other unclean spirits more wicked than the first.[1]

If Rhodesian missions forestall this trend by vigorous and suitable action, the experience of the Union of South Africa need not be duplicated in the North.

It is futile to ban heathen social activities unless sub-

[1] Matthew xii. 43-45.

stitutes of equal interest take their place. If outlets for recreational and emotional instincts are not provided in the new society, the Native will go where they are provided or will devise his own. The sports day of a Christian village in Northern Rhodesia revealed a strange mixture of Native and European modes and the lack of adequate channels for expression. Many of the players had learned football at the mines. Some wore faded blazers, shorts and shoes, others were in Native garb and played barefoot. The umpire was a mission evangelist. He carried a large Bible, as badge of authority, and held it aloft as the signal for opening play. Between quarters the players stood in line and sang hymns or beat on drums while heathen dances were interspersed.

We were told that the winning team was sometimes greeted by the spectators singing "The Son of God goes forth to war", while the defeated side would be consoled with "Art thou weary, art thou languid, art thou sore distressed?" etc.

This poverty in the social life of the Native Christian community requires a new emphasis in the missionary programme of Central Africa. It is a fascinating field for exploration and experimentation. Pioneers are needed who are also prophets and community craftsmen who are artists. Such leaders must be thoroughly aware of the social and recreational values of Native life. They must know the instincts and abilities of the people in drama, rhythm, dances, story-telling, Nature-lore games and tests of strength and skill. They should be trained in the technique of community planning, rural betterment and social and recreational programmes, that has developed in America and Europe. These should be distinctly related to the surroundings and interests of the Native and should be made to fit into the whole scheme of evangelism, education and rural or urban activities that is directed to the building of the Christian community. The test of success of such a programme must be the degree to which it undergirds the Native village or urban life and finds its roots in the basic interests of Bantu society, and at the same time forms a basis for the progressive and harmonious growth of the community according to the Christian ideal.

The Bantu have certain artistic gifts and emotional qualities that may be enlisted as powerful allies in rebuilding, directing and enriching the social and recreational life of the Christian society.

Among these a few only may be mentioned here.

In the Native's love of rhythm, music and dancing is a key to his self-expression. Life is a series of rhythms to him; whether fighting, playing, paddling, marching, working or dramatising, each has its wave-length, its cadence and song. This powerful dynamo must be discovered, thoroughly understood and harnessed to the task of vitalising and making joyous the new order of society.

The dramatic powers of the Bantu are another of those mainsprings of Native life that must be capitalised by the Church. The Native is a born actor. He dramatises every experience of life. His powers of imagination, of projecting himself into the unseen and imaginary situation, are unusual. Here is an almost virgin field to be used in the service of Christ, awaiting the missionary of dramatic insight and skill.

Of much value will be competitive games and sports, trials of strength, skill and endurance, related to the traditional life in which hunting and combat took such central parts. Some of the old weapons, such as the spear, may still be used in athletic contests. Distance running and walking contests could be promoted. The old motives must be discovered, redirected and used in much the same way as mortal combat has been sublimated into athletic sports in civilised life. Thus inter-village and intertribal matches will eventually take the place of tribal and village raids.

The field of organised out-of-door life is finely suited to the needs of the new society. Here the Bantu boy and girl are traditionally at home. The Scout and Guide movements are finely suited to the instincts of Native youth, as is indicated by the experience of the Pathfinders, Wayfarers and Pioneers of the South African Union.

The field of Native preparation of youth for manhood and womanhood as embodied in the so-called "initiation schools" still awaits the exploration of the missionary gifted with insight, imagination, patience and courage. Possibly no other area of Native social life has such possibilities of adaptation and utilisation for the Christian order as this.

The training of the boys and girls in agriculture, horticulture and the care of poultry, bees and small live-stock would help to stabilise and enrich the rural community and prepare young people for a useful part in it, for these activities lie close to Native experience.

Discussion groups and debates on matters related to village life as well as world affairs could be supplemented by educational talks illustrated with cinema and lantern slides, by competitive gardening, baby-nurture groups, health and sanitation contests, cooking classes, sewing classes and the providing of simple village libraries for those who can read. Many other community activities could all in time be introduced as Native proclivities and interest were revealed.

Parallel with the work of keeping the worker conscious of his home relationships is the outstanding responsibility of missions to work for his Christianisation and to nurture the Church of the copper belt.

The special conditions which prevail in these districts give a peculiar point to this responsibility. The workers are concentrated upon a comparatively limited area. They represent the flower of the Bantu tribes. They are entirely accessible to mission work, and detached from tribal influence and controls. They are subjected to unusual moral and social strains. They come from nearly all the tribes and districts of the Territory, to which for the most part they return. They also form the advance guard of the future urban centres of population of the Protectorate.

We have seen that two developments of great importance
have taken place in the Christian work on the copper
belts: first, the pooling of the ministry of different missions
under the supervision of one society—in Katanga; and
second, the growth of an indigenous, self-supporting Native
Church, uniting the Christians of many Churches on the
Rhodesian copper-field. These two trends, one initiated
by the missions and the other by the Christian Natives,
are the lines upon which the Commission consider that the
religious work in these areas should expand. Both developments are sound, are suited to the special needs of the situation, and have progressed far enough to serve as a safe
index for shaping future plans. This belief was supported
by the widely expressed satisfaction with the success of
united mission work on both copper-fields which was
voiced to the Commission during its visitation of mission
stations in the recruitment districts of Northern Rhodesia
and Katanga.

The Commission strongly endorses the principle of the
uniting of the interests of the various Churches in this
region under the direction of one society. Considerations
which support the policy of pooling Christian effort are:
the presence of Christians of from fifteen to twenty different
churches with the comparatively small number of believers
belonging to most of these Churches; the confusion certain
to arise among the Christians in this small area from the
presence of numerous Churches; the insistence by the
management of the great mines upon the largest possible
measure of Church unity as a basis for granting facilities
for religious work in the locations; and, finally, the great
economy to be effected through the placing of the religious
activities of the copper belt under united direction.

However, the principle of the pooling of mission work
on the copper belt of Northern Rhodesia is limited in its
possible application by the presence of three Church com-
munions, the Roman Catholic, the Anglican and the
Protestant Free Churches.

Co-operation of this nature on the part of the Roman

Catholic Church is, at present, manifestly out of the question.

The Universities Mission to Central Africa (Anglican) consider that their Church discipline, liturgy, services and catechumen training differ so widely from those of the Free Churches as to make it out of the question for their believers to be served other than by a representative of the Anglican Church. The inadequacy of the six-months contract period at the mines for preparing for confirmation was given as a reason why this Church does not consider the stay of the worker at the mines to be a significant evangelistic opportunity.

Thus in practice the possible area of united mission effort is reduced to the Protestant Free Church Mission Societies, of which there are fourteen at work in Northern Rhodesia.

A second obstacle to a complete union of Christian work on the copper belt is the diversity of languages in use among the workers. Among the thirty or more languages spoken at the mines the two groups which predominate are the Chibemba and Chinyanja. A majority of the workers speak these or closely allied dialects. It is natural that missions whose work is entirely among people who use one of these language groups should feel the inadequacy of a Christian ministry for their people when carried on through the media of a different tongue.[1] However, this difficulty has been partly met in Katanga by the use of interpretation into various languages in the Church services.

The Commission believe it to be of the highest importance that the work of the Protestant Free Churches on the copper belt be united under the direction of one missionary society. While it is obvious that the recommendations

[1] On the Katanga copper belt, a form of "Swahili" known as "Kingwana" is steadily becoming the lingua franca of the mines. It is accepted as the standard language by Government, mines, and Protestant and Roman Catholic missions. This language seems destined to dominate the southern half of the Belgian Congo. Statement by Dr. John M. Springer, Jadotville, Katanga, March 16, 1933.

of the Commission cannot extend to the details of a plan for inter-mission co-operation, it is clear that certain general conditions would need to be met. First, the society to take charge should be one which has had long and intimate contacts with the mines through the people of its district.

The society which assumes this responsibility should have sufficient strength to take the initiative in meeting the growing needs of the copper-field.

The Union Native Church fostered during the last eight years by the South African Baptist Mission should be built upon and incorporated in any plan for united work.

The activities of the directing society on the copper belt should not be considered an extension of its work alone, but treated as a truly inter-mission movement in which all Protestant believers may find a spiritual home.

An inter-mission and Church Council for the supervision of the Christian work of the copper belt and towns of the railway zone should be created by the Northern Rhodesia General Missions Conference, which would represent all the Churches and missionary societies having interests in these areas.

The duties of such a council would be to study the whole problem of the mines area and town location in relation to the Christian work of the Territory; make recommendations in regard to policies, programmes and personnel, and act as a liaison between the religious bodies and the mines.

The Council's work should include in its scope the interests of all groups of Natives in the area, the religious needs of the European communities, and the problem of race relations between White and Black groups.

It is reasonable to expect that a united religious programme on the copper belt would receive support from those societies whose interests were served through a pooling of the cost of maintenance.

An alternative policy of missionary occupation of the mines area calls for a division of responsibility to be made upon the basis of the two dominant language groups represented at the mines. Under this plan the field would be divided between two societies, each being made responsible for the shepherding of the Christians of their language group irrespective of where they might be working.

A minority opinion in the Commission strongly favoured the assignment of a missionary to each large mine, with the expectation that in this way intensive personal work could be accomplished in a mine and its community which would hardly be possible were one missionary to supervise the religious work in a half-dozen mines.

Such representative and specialised service as has been outlined would demand of the personnel unusual spiritual and cultural gifts and a preparation suited to the peculiar needs of the field.

A further implication of the copper belt for the religious work of missions is the need of giving larger responsibility to Native Church leaders. At the mines and along the railway belt the Native finds that Bantu are being given increasing scope and opportunity for using their abilities. They are working side by side with White men and often carry the heavier end of the task. With increasing success they are being put in charge of groups of their own people in mines and shops.[1] They are learning with great rapidity the ways of the European. The Native returns from the mines with a new self-confidence and sense of his own capacity and with an urge to express it in the Church life, and he is often restless and dissatisfied under the old mission tutelage. We were told of the craving of evangelists, pastors and teachers for more of a share in shaping mission policies and for the confidence and comradeship of the missionary.

At the mines the Bantu discovers the multiple divisions of the Christian Church. To most Native Christians Church distinctions mean comparatively little. They are drawn

[1] The Natives studying to qualify for blasting certificates at Nkana mine are trained by Native foremen.

At the Roan Antelope mine the first-aid squads are in charge of Native leaders, who in turn work under the supervision of a White director.

together in a fellowship of faith which leaps across barriers of tribe and creed.

The heathen Native draws various realistic conclusions from these Church divisions. He observes that all are alike in urging gifts of money from members; that a number of Church workers gain a livelihood without physical toil—and he concludes that the Church business must be a profitable line.

The Native also notices that the status of an evangelist is one of honour; that he is accorded certain privileges and respect by mines and Government. He consequently argues that if it is good for the White man to operate many different Churches, why should he not do the same?

The activity of as many as thirty sectarian chapels standing side by side in front of the compounds of some of the Rand mines has stimulated the forming of Native separatist Churches in the Union of South Africa. In 1932 the Union Government officially registered three hundred different Native sectarian Churches, a witness to the weak strategy of duplicating Western theological distinctions among the Bantu.[1]

Northern Rhodesia has tried to forestall this trend by the Native Schools Ordinance of 1927, which forbids teaching and preaching by persons not authorised by Government or a recognised missionary of a religious society.[2]

In spite of its weaknesses, one hopeful aspect of this separatist trend is that it shows that the Bantu is able to take religious leadership and command a following of his people. Though many of the new sects are due to the restiveness of Native pastors when disciplined for moral breakdown or mishandling of funds, the withholding of responsibility from Native leaders by missions is also a contributory cause of their growth.

There is an important analogy for the religious work of missions in the use by Government agricultural departments of Native demonstrators. The Government of

---

[1] See Appendix E.
[2] Northern Rhodesia *Annual Report upon Native Education, 1931*, p. 9.

Southern Rhodesia, for example, has found that Native, rather than European, farm demonstrators are successful in introducing modern agricultural methods among the Bantu. The Native demonstrator understands the conditions which an innovation in traditional methods of farming must overcome. He knows the psychology of the people and the reasoning most likely to impress them. Moreover, the fact that a Black man is able to secure unprecedented results through strange methods is the most powerful argument that can be brought to bear. It puts the possibility of securing similar results within the reach of the Native. The work of the twenty-three Native demonstrators on the staff of the Agricultural Division of the Southern Rhodesian Government is steadily changing the farming methods of the Territory.[1]

There lies in this policy the ultimate hope of the Christian Church in Africa. Eventually the African must be transformed by a Christian witness and social order that is made intelligible to him through the African. Many of the missions of Northern Rhodesia are working on this principle in the training of Native priests, evangelists and pastors. In some cases encouraging progress has been made, but at best it is a slow process to create a Christian priesthood from a heathen population. The factor of time is needed for the bringing forward of a second and third generation of Christians as a natural source of Christian leadership.

A second promising step in the same direction is the appointment of the Bantu missionary to the Bantu—the use of the product of a stabilised Christian Native society in the Christianising of Central Africa.

Potential missionaries are emerging from such South African institutions as Lovedale, Morija, Amanzimtoti and Fort Hare. The training and allocation for service of carefully selected Native men and women in the European and American missions among the less advanced peoples of

[1] Vide *Southern Rhodesia Report of Director of Native Development for 1931*, pp. 14-15.

the North might, in time, prove to be an invaluable supplement to the work of the White missionaries. The practice of medicine, hygiene, nursing, social welfare, agricultural and industrial work, teaching and preaching, could all be eventually performed by Bantu missionaries working under the Foreign Mission Boards or the Mission Societies of South Africa. The cost in training, transportation and maintenance of the Bantu missionary would be modest as contrasted with that of the missionary from Europe or America. But far outweighing the material advantages would be those of the cultural and spiritual sphere, and the harnessing of the latent spiritual and racial energy of the coming generation of Bantu Christian youth to the stupendous task of Christianising their continent. We realise many of the difficulties in the way of putting such a plan into practical operation, but after a hundred years of missions in South Africa it is not too early to expect results from it. In fact the policy of the Bantu missionary to the Bantu has been in use for many years in South Africa. Basuto missionary evangelists have worked with excellent results in the Zambesi Mission of the Paris Evangelical Society. An officer of this society estimates that one-half of these Basuto missionaries to the Barotse people have succeeded in their work—a creditable record for any group of missionaries. The American Board Mission in Natal also reports a successful though less extensive use of Zulu missionaries in their Southern Rhodesia field at Mount Silinda.

A wider application of the same policy would be the appointment of highly qualified American Negro missionaries to African missions.

The transformation in Native community life brought about by the Negro missionaries of the American Congregational Board at Galangue, Angola, has been referred to, and could well be studied in relation to the whole strategy of Christian missions in Africa.

In many parts of Africa a certain amount of prejudice and fear connected with the presence of advanced American

Negroes would have to be considered in the use of this policy, but this would doubtless yield, as has been the case in Portuguese West Africa, to the tact and skill of properly selected missionaries.

The Commission wishes to record its conviction that the missionary should understand and endeavour to utilise the fundamental values, customs and concepts of Bantu life. This conviction has been deepened by observing the principle in successful action in a few of the mission centres visited. We are aware of some of the difficulties and pitfalls that lie in this field, and that not a few experienced missionaries consider Bantu culture barren as a source of enrichment of the Christian Church.

Church history reveals the Christian Society as emerging in various ages and cultures from the soil of the people and expressing itself through their peculiar genius and institutions. This was the case with the Germanic, Celtic and Slavic churches; we see it to-day in the growth of an indigenous Church in China, India and Japan. Eastern and Western Christians have unconsciously incorporated racial points of view, social forms, superstitions and customs into their belief and practice. Western missionaries may well be sensitive to the implications of this fact, and be generous in recognising the same principles in the growth of the Bantu Church that have attended the development of their own national Churches.

There is danger that the religious and social values of Native life will be overwhelmed in the Native's surrender to the alleged superiority of the White man's civilisation and that the wheat of Bantu life will be lost with the chaff.

The Native African too often has to fight his struggle for Christian status and belief upon ground and with weapons, rules and standards which have all been determined by the missionary. Under these conditions the Native catechumen is heavily handicapped in his effort to find himself and identify his newly won status with his Bantu inheritance.

We believe that the African Christian Church cannot

be built upon alien concepts alone, but must add to its foundations some of those inherited institutions and values that have made the people what' they have become. The fact that among these institutions and values some are out of harmony with European concepts of life and morality, and emphasise elements destructive of the Christian ideal, does not absolve the missionary from the obligation to search for their inner significance, try to discover elements of permanent value and see if these will not serve to bulwark the new Christian social order.

The communal sense and kinship obligations, the religious nature of all the major experiences of life, the immanence and reality of the unseen world, the fundamental respect for oneself and for others, the sacrificial element in human relationships, the essential unity and rhythm of the life of the tribe, the responsibility of preparing youth for the duties of citizenship and adult life, these are some of the materials that cannot be lightly thrown aside in the task of building the new structure of Christian society.

We believe that the abandoning of such potential values by the Church would not only delay the Christianisation of Africa and prove an irreparable loss to the African, but that the wider world community would also share in this loss.

Thus Religion and Anthropology meet on the mission field. Whatever estimate the Anthropologist may have of missions, there can be no question of the importance of the Anthropological sense and method for the missionary. The modern missionary who ignores the inheritance of Native society is much in the position of the physician who prescribes for a patient without a knowledge of the functioning of the circulatory, alimentary and nervous systems.

The emergence of the industrialised African constitutes a new necessity for understanding the mainsprings of action of both the urban and rural Bantu and the forces that have fashioned them. Only in this way can there be found types of Christian education and practice and Christian institutions that will serve to both stabilise and advance the life of the people.

CHAPTER XXIII

IN this final chapter will be summarised the chief recommendations arising from the study presented in this report. The data on which they are based have been variously approached in the foregoing sections. For convenience of presentation and to show their implications for missions they have been grouped in six divisions, viz. Social Welfare and Missions, Economics and Missions, Government and Missions, Education, Religious Work, and Missionary Personnel and Preparation.

These recommendations represent either the unanimous or the majority opinion of the Commission. Individual members are not to be regarded as responsible for all the recommendations, but where there was a strongly dissenting minority this is indicated. For the detailed recommendations for religious work the editor must bear the chief responsibility.

I. SOCIAL WELFARE AND MISSIONS

1. The profound social changes which the copper belt is causing in the structure of Bantu society constitute an obligation and a necessity on the part of missions to consider the problem of social welfare as an important field for study and for cultivation.

2. While recognising that the social welfare needs of the Natives employed by the mines are primarily the responsibility of the mines themselves, missions should be thoroughly acquainted with and sensitive to these needs, alert to ways of meeting them, and ready to co-operate with the mines in measures for coping with them.[1]

[1] Chapter XVIII. p. 311.

3. With this in view the missionary who ministers to the Natives on the copper belt should be equipped with training in social welfare, recreation, social hygiene and community planning, and be prepared to understand the bearing of the social needs of the people upon the growth of the Church both at the mines and in the rural areas, and to plan his work with the problem as a whole in view.

4. The Commission wishes to record its opinion that, in spite of certain grave dangers with which it is attended, the presence of the worker's wife at the mines under prevailing conditions in Northern Rhodesia and Katanga creates a sounder physical, social and moral environment and is productive of lesser evils in Native society than the compound system of employment of men unaccompanied by their families.[1]

5. It is recommended that, in view of the grave problems of unemployment which may arise if Natives stabilised at the mines lose contact wholly with their villages, missions both in the rural areas and at the mines should endeavour to assist the workers to maintain communication and contact with their original homes.

6. While recognising that important steps in welfare work have already been taken, and further recognising the difficulty of completely developing this field in the opening phase of operating the mines, the Commission records its earnest hope and belief that such responsible and progressive corporations as the Rhokana and Rhodesia Selection Trusts will, in the near future, place the welfare work for their Native employees upon as adequate a basis in organisation, equipment and leadership as any of the other departments of the industry.

7. With this in view, the Commission desires to point to the need in each mine location of the services of a highly skilled welfare officer, equipped with training and experience in the science of social welfare, with facility in the use of a Native language, with experience in handling Natives and with a genuine interest in their welfare.[2]

[1] Chapter XVIII. pp. 307-9.   [2] Chapter XVIII. pp. 305-6.

8. Further, that the presence of women and children at the mines creates special problems of social adjustment and hygiene which can only be met by the employment of a skilled woman worker on the staff of the mine.[1]

9. Missions are in a favourable position to stress the urgency of creating a larger body of health workers and nurses in the Protectorate, the importance of establishing a training centre for Native physicians and medical assistants and the universal need of hygienic teaching among the people.

10. They could also effectively stress the necessity of taking a regular census of the population in order that population trends, health and economic problems might be clearly seen and dealt with.

11. The Commission considers that the town location of the copper belt and railway line as centres of the future urban population of the Territory present special social needs for whose ministry the Christian mission has a peculiar responsibility.[2]

12. In supplementing the social welfare activities of Government and municipal councils for Natives of town locations, the mission is urged to enlist voluntary aid from the European residents in the form of teachers of day and night schools, sports and recreation leaders, Boy Scout masters, clinic and medical advisers, home visitors and domestic science instructors.[3]

13. The missions of the Territory are urged to consider the tribal sanctions and kinship obligations of the mines worker as allies in maintaining his morale in the new surroundings, and to do all possible to encourage frequent contact between him and his rural home.[4]

14. The Commission wish to call attention to the poverty of the social life of a Native community which is cut off from its rural and tribal environment. It considers a major task of the Church to be to enrich this social life, to organise it in wholesome channels, and to strive to create a new

[1] Chapter XVIII. p. 309. [2] Chapter XVIII. pp. 312-14.
[3] Chapter XVIII. p. 314. [4] Chapter XXII. p. 361.

network of Native interests which will serve as a foundation for urban Native society.[1]

15. We recommend that missionaries allocated to the copper belt and railway zone consider as an important part of their responsibility the creating of a better understanding between the Natives and the Europeans. With this in view, mission and Church leaders are urged to clarify race attitudes by the use of education carried on through the Press, pulpit and personal contacts, which would take fully into account the realistic as well as the ethical factors of the problem and would aim to reduce the fear of the Black man and to secure an estimate of him on the basis of individual quality and achievement rather than on the basis of his racial group alone.

16. While recognising the limitations of drawing an analogy between conditions in the Northern Territories and the Union of South Africa, the Commission wish to call attention to the success of the Inter-racial Councils of the Union in serving as clearing-houses for the discussion of matters of friction or of common interest between the two races and urge an early experimentation with this plan in the urban communities of Northern Rhodesia.

II. Economics and Missions

17. In view of the drawing out by the mines and other industries of large numbers of people from the rural areas and the consequent weakening of tribal life, missions are urged to exert their influence in and shape their activities toward rural stabilisation and the strengthening of the economic foundations of Native society.[2]

18. Missions are urged to—

   (a) Study the implications of the economic influences and changes at work in the Territory.

   (b) Help the people to meet these changes wisely.

   (c) Try to control the direction and speed of these changes.

[1] Chapter XXII. pp. 364-5.   [2] Chapters XI., XII., XX.

19. Missions are urged to study how the essentials and standards of the Christian way of living can be disentangled from the inessentials and peculiar standards which have grown around them during 1900 years of European civilisation, and how they can be readapted to the present social and economic needs of an African people.[1]

Such a study would require the re-thinking and adaptation to African life of the principles of Christian social and economic ethics.

20. It is recommended that missions carefully consider the central place of agriculture in the life of the Native community and the various implications to be drawn therefrom. With rural stabilisation in view it is urged that the values and the dignity of rural life and its activities be given a central place in the preaching, services and festivals of the Church, in the teaching of the schools and in the attitude and spirit of the mission personnel.[2]

21. In view of the disruptive effect of the semi-nomadic method of Native agriculture upon stable community and Church life, missions in co-operation with Government are urged to consider the problem of permanent community building—through rotation of crops, use of fertilisers, soil conservation, and the encouragement of better homes and permanent village improvements.[3]

22. So long as Government is not in a position to adequately undertake a comprehensive scheme for improving Native agriculture, missions are urged (a) to undertake agricultural experimentation and demonstration under their own trained leadership, but with as close as possible Government co-operation.

(b) To encourage and demonstrate diversified farming.

(c) To assist the growth of market centres for the sale of cash crops.

(d) To teach and exemplify the importance of improved means of transport through good roads and wheeled vehicles.

[1] Chapter XX. p. 331.   [2] Chapter XX. pp. 333-4.
[3] Chapter XX. pp. 340-41.

(e) To assist the organising of agricultural and industrial fairs, for the exhibition of produce, live-stock and handicrafts and the spread of new ideas and methods.

(f) To demonstrate where needed the values of irrigation in relation to an all-year cultivation.

23. Missions in co-operation with mines and Government should study the possibilities of supplementing the present training and experience of the Native employed on the copper belt in such a way as to increase his economic power on returning to rural life.

24. The attention of missions is called to the need for technical instruction to emphasise the training of Natives to serve Native needs, through the study of the Natives' tastes and designs in tools, implements and furniture, together with the adaptation of such designs directed to their improvement and a more adequate meeting of Native requirements.[1]

25. The attention of missions is called to their responsibility for assisting the Native to achieve the higher level of life to which they have introduced him. Contact with Christian missions involves the Native in, what is for him, an expensive way of living, for it raises the standards of education, housing and living conditions that he desires for himself and for his family.

26. With rural stabilisation in mind the Commission wish to draw attention to the value of a general supervision of labour recruitment throughout the Protectorate which would protect certain areas from an excessive draining of their man-power and the resulting demoralisation of social, economic and tribal life.

27. Missionaries are urged to use their influence against the two-price system of trading in vogue in trading centres, which discriminates against the Native buyer.[2]

28. The influence of missions should be used in favour of the introduction into the currency of the Territory of a smaller unit of exchange than the threepence piece. The use

---

[1] Chapter XX. pp. 342-3.   [2] Chapter V. p. 73.

of pennies and farthings would provide a basis of exchange suited to the economic power of the Native and would both increase the volume of Native trade and make possible for the Bantu a wider use of European foodstuffs and general merchandise.[1]

29. The importance of the co-operative movement is urged as embodying a principle natural to the instincts and social organisation of the Native and as providing a medium for strengthening his economic solidarity and of adjusting his ideas and values to the changing order of society.[2]

III. GOVERNMENT AND MISSIONS

30. Bearing in mind the close relationship existing between missions and Government in Northern Rhodesia and the degree to which they are co-operating for Native advancement, it is strongly recommended that every missionary, before going to the field, thoroughly acquaint himself with the history of the administration in the Territory, the structure of government and the laws and procedure under which administration is carried out.[3]

31. Since one result of the system of Indirect Rule is to revive much of heathen custom and practice in the tribe, missionaries have an obligation to try to fully understand its principles and programme together with the implications of Indirect Rule for their approach, teaching and position in relation to tribal life.[4]

32. With the purpose of creating sympathy with Christianity in the public opinion of the tribe, missions are urged to cultivate the friendship and intelligent co-operation of the families of influence, particularly those from which the counsellors of the Chief are chosen and the circle from within which the succession to the Chieftainship will be selected.[5]

33. While recognising the difficulties inherent in the

[1] Chapter V. p. 73; Chapter XI. p. 201.   [2] Chapter XX. pp. 335-8.
[3] Chapter XXI. pp. 347-8.
[4] Chapter XIV.; Chapter XXI. pp. 350-53.
[5] Chapter XV.; Chapter XXI. pp. 353-4.

system of matrilineal succession to the Chieftainship, the strategy of educating the children of Chiefs and influential families in the tribe is emphasised as a step toward securing a Christian and enlightened tribal leadership. At this point it is recommended that missions co-operate closely with administration.[1]

34. It is recommended that the missionary utilise more fully his opportunity of consultation with the administrative official in order that he may discuss with him mutual problems, keep him fully informed of mission activities, and so far as possible establish a harmony and understanding on matters of Native policy.[2]

35. In view of the great importance of the Native locations of the towns as sources of Native public opinion and as centres of the future urban population of the Territory, missions are urged in their work for such communities to do all possible to develop an intelligent Native leadership and sound public opinion as a preparation for whatever measures of self-government may in due time be instituted.[3]

36. It is recommended that the missionary should not forget the opportunity which is his to observe the effect of governmental law upon Native society and to call to the attention of Administration any miscarriage of justice, or ill effects of established law upon Native life, that comes under his notice.

The missionary, however, before acting in such cases, should be in a position to verify his facts, should bear in mind the peculiar difficulties of Government in administering the law, and should give every opportunity for the correction of abuses before making public criticisms.[4]

IV. RELIGIOUS WORK

37. The Commission unite in the conviction that the spiritual task of missions among the workers of the copper belt is the central and primary task.

[1] Chapter XXI. pp. 353-4.   [2] Chapter XXI. p. 357.
[3] Chapter XV. pp. 273-4.   [4] Chapter XXI. pp. 356-7.

A new spiritual world must be built for the Native—
one that is not cut off from his past and that is able to help
him in his adjustments to the new world he has entered.[1]

38. Missions are urged to address themselves to the task
of inculcating a Christian faith that evokes a greater depth
of moral conviction and loyalty to principle—a faith that
will hold the Native Christian when subjected to the new
and tremendous moral strains of the copper belt. His position is rendered all the more perilous by the absence of his
own social and moral controls and by his sudden introduction to a pagan European society.

39. Missions are urged to develop all possible contacts
and communication between the Church on the copper
belt and the Church of the rural areas. Regular and reciprocal visitation of one another's fields by rural and
mines missionaries and evangelists, the encouragement of
mutual help among the men at the mines and of letter-
writing between village and mine, and the introduction of
Christian workers by letter to the Church of the copper
belt with a previous notification of their coming, are
measures that are strongly recommended.[2]

40. In view of the barrenness of Christian Native social
life due to the general banning of heathen social and recreational activities, missions are earnestly advised to
address themselves to the task of enriching the content of
Church and Christian community life.[3]

41. It is recommended that, in view of the growing
responsibilities and opportunities for leadership and self-
expression which enterprising Natives are experiencing on
the copper belt, missions accord their returning workers a
larger degree of responsibility and leadership in the affairs
of Church and school.[4]

42. Bearing in mind the potential nature of the copper
belt through the assembling of Natives from nearly every
part of the Territory, it is recommended that missions

[1] Chapter XXII. pp. 358-9.
[2] Chapter XXII. pp. 361-2; Chapter XXIII. section 11.
[3] Chapter XXII. pp. 363-6; Chapter XXIII. section 12.
[4] Chapter XXII. p. 370.

look upon this area as a major missionary field and extend their efforts and concentrate their attention upon it.[1]

43. The Commission believe it to be of the highest importance that the missionary work of the Protestant Free Church societies on the copper belt be united under the care of one missionary society. In carrying out this policy, however, certain conditions would require to be met—

(1) First, it would be essential that the society to take charge should be one which has had long and intimate contacts with the mines.

(2) It should have sufficient strength in personnel and backing to meet the possible expanding needs of the area.

(3) A Union Native Church, interdenominational in organisation, spirit and practice, should be developed from the start: a Church in which all Protestant believers should find a spiritual home and fellowship. Stated in other words, the work of the directing society upon the copper belt should not be considered an extension of the Church work of that society but a truly inter-Church movement.

(4) The Union Native Church organisation fostered for the last eight years by the South African Baptist Church should be built upon and incorporated in the union plan.

(5) An inter-Church council or board for the direction of the Christian occupation of the copper belt should be created by the Northern Rhodesia General Missionary Conference. Representatives of all Churches and missionary societies having interest in the work of the mines area, including the Anglicans and Roman Catholics, should be invited to serve upon this council.

The duties of this council would be to study the whole question of the copper belt in relation to the Christian work of the Territory: make recommenda-

[1] Chapter XXII. pp. 358-61.

tions to missions, Government and mines, based on such study, in regard to policies, programmes and appointment and allocation of personnel: receive and act upon plans or proposals from any Church or society desiring to extend its work to the mines area: and act as a responsible liaison agent between the missionary body and the mines in relation to questions of Church or mission occupation.

The scope of the council's responsibilities should include the religious work for both Europeans and Natives.

44. The expenses of maintenance of a united mission work on the copper belt should be pooled by those mission societies having special interests in this area.

45. A modification of the above plan which received the approval of three of the six members of the Commission calls for a division of mission responsibility to be made upon the basis of the two dominant language groups represented at the mines. Under this plan the field would be divided between two societies, each being made responsible for the shepherding of the Christians of their language group, irrespective of where they might be working.

46. In view of the very large number of language divisions and dialects in use among the tribes of Northern Rhodesia, the Commission urges the importance of a comprehensive linguistic study being undertaken, aimed at the determination of one or more standard language media for the assistance of educational and religious work and the cultural growth and solidarity of the Territory.

47. A minority opinion in the Commission strongly favoured the assignment of a missionary to each large mine, with the expectation that in this way intensive personal work could be accomplished in a mine and its community which would hardly be possible were one missionary to supervise the religious work in a half-dozen mines.

48. The Commission considers the Christian opportunity of the urban Native locations to be one of no less import-

ance than that of the mines. The principle already outlined of uniting the mission work for Natives in these town locations is urged.[1]

49. The whole Native population of the mining centres, including township dwellers, household servants, police and store employees, as well as mines workers, should be included in the field of the mission.

50. The problem of race relations and the attaining of a better understanding between White and Black should be included in the task of all the missions and Churches of the Protectorate and be given a major emphasis in their teaching and preaching.[2]

51. The Commission calls attention to the unusual demands that such responsible united Mission work as outlined make upon the personnel appointed to the field, and recommends that only missionaries and pastors of exceptional spiritual, cultural and professional gifts and training be selected for such posts.[3]

52. The Commission considers that the social, physical, educational and religious activities for industrial workers, carried on by the Young Men's Christian Association in Western countries, is with certain adaptations well suited to conditions in the mines in Southern Africa, and since the Young Men's Christian Association represents the great body of evangelical Christian Churches in the world it is eminently fitted to undertake a united Christian social welfare programme for the mine-workers.

V. EDUCATION

53. The Commission wish to record their conviction that the only hope of progress for the people of these territories is through Christian education; that this is the sole means of bridging the gulf which separates the outlook of the Bantu tribe from that of the modern world

---

[1] Chapter V. pp. 78-87; Chapter XVIII. pp. 312-15.
[2] Chapter XXIII. section 15.
[3] Chapter I. pp. 2-10.

to which it is being progressively introduced, and that
education is the foundation of the structure of Christian
society that missions are building in Africa.

54. It is strongly recommended that the mission societies
of the Territory study together the goal towards which
their education is directed, define its purpose and visualise
the results which they are aiming to achieve. If such study
is to be of ultimate value, the co-operation of the Government must be secured and a joint programme be devised
that serves to achieve the ends in view.

55. The Commission desires to call the attention of
Government, mines and missions to the significance of the
stay of the worker at the mines as an opportunity of education not only of the individual but of the whole Territory through the return of the worker to the rural area.
With this in mind, it recommends the missions to use their
influence to secure action on the part of Government and
mines to establish schools for children and adults upon
mine locations suited to the task of adjusting the people of
the Territory to the new order of life that they are entering.
With this in view, the Commission calls attention to the need
of a larger service wage in the mines which would provide
for the organisation of the workers' spare time for constructive ends, such as adult education, etc. It further
urges the missions to hold themselves in readiness to assist
in such educational work as may be desired.[1]

56. The Commission expresses its earnest belief in the
necessity of strengthening education for girls in Central
Africa both in its volume and quality. The enlightening
opportunity of service on the copper belt or railway zone
experienced by a large proportion of Native men is denied
the women.

Since the Bantu women are the guardians of tradition
and conservatism, the progress of the Territory can only be
achieved by the equal enlightenment of the sexes. Missionary societies are urged to consider the bearing of this situation upon their strategy and policies for the Christianising

[1] Chapter VI. pp. 105-12; Chapter XIX.; Chapter XXIII. section 23.

of the Bantu and to shape their programme in expansion of
work, appropriation of funds and appointment of personnel
with it in mind.[1]

57. Missions are recommended to study the problem of
adapting their school training to the needs of the various
communities they serve. With this principle in mind, attention is directed to the differing outlook and requirements
of three types of communities. First, the isolated rural
villages whose contacts with the outer world are meagre
and whose interests are essentially rural in character.
Second, the detached and semi-detribalised Native groups
of the mine and town locations which are receiving the full
shock of alien and industrialising influences. And finally,
the communities in transition between the rural and urban
types. These are villages which are in close contact with
missions, trading stations, Government posts and European settlements, whose people are constantly passing
backward and forward between the rural and urban environments.[2]

58. It is recommended that in work for every type of
community the central educational emphasis of missions
should be directed toward preparing Bantu youth to serve
the needs of Bantu rather than European society.

59. With the aim of rural stabilisation in mind, the
Commission recommends that the syllabus for mission
schools should be so drawn as to dignify farming as a voca-
tion and give a central place to those subjects that will
prepare the pupil to be a useful member of the rural community.[3]

60. The Commission wishes to record its belief in the
excellent adaptation of the Jeanes School system for preparing teachers to serve the various educational needs of
the rural Bantu community.

61. The importance of a simplified system of adult education for both the urban and rural Natives is urged by the

[1] Chapter XIX. pp. 326-9.
[2] Chapter XIX. pp. 316-26; Chapter XXIII. section 24.
[3] Chapter XX. pp. 332-43; Chapter XXIII. section 20.

Commission. It is recommended in this connection that the experience of the Mass Education Movement of China and of the Soviet's training of illiterate Russian peasants be studied and adapted to African conditions.[1]

62. Two methods of visualised teaching are recommended for adult education: first, the picture poster, which is the basis of the remarkable adult education of the Soviets and has also been used by the Union Minière of Katanga; and second, the cinema. Missions are urged to experiment with both of these methods, and to be alert to co-operate with one another, with Government and mines in any programme that may be devised for the use of these or other educational devices that are adapted to the enlightenment of the adult Native.[2]

63. Missions are recommended to form an inter-mission standing committee on education in the Territory, for the purpose of studying the aims, policies and methods of African education, for co-ordinating and standardising the education of the various societies, and for closer integration and harmony with the educational aims and methods of Government, municipalities and mines.

64. In view of the steadily rising standards of African schools and the acceptance by mission societies of large educational responsibilities and subsidies from Government, the Commission wishes to urge the necessity of sending to their mission schools in Central Africa only men and women who have had special training and are highly qualified teachers.

VI. MISSIONARY PERSONNEL AND PREPARATION

65. The Commission wish to call the attention of the mission societies to the changing conditions on the mission field of Central Africa, with the need of taking these changed conditions and their demands upon mission personnel into careful consideration in selecting and training their appointees. Among these new factors may be mentioned

[1] Chapter XIX. pp. 322-3.   [2] Chapter XIX. pp. 323-6.

the growth of urbanised communities detached from their tribal surroundings, the movement of population to the copper belt, the growing independence, knowledge and ambition of the Native, the promulgation of the Government policy of Indirect Rule, the enlarged educational responsibilities of missions, the opportunity to assist the Native in handicrafts, in farming and in rural stabilisation, the growth of a critical and active European population, the close relationship existing between missionary and Administrator, the necessity of understanding and utilising the fundamental concepts and values of Native life, and the multiplication of missions in the Territory.[1]

66. Particularly does the Commission point to the need of selecting candidates who are prepared in the field of social welfare activities, community planning and betterment, both urban and rural, who will meet the requirements of the new social groupings that are appearing as a result of the opening of the copper belt.[2]

67. Of basic importance is the equipping of men and women with experience and ability in the agricultural field and the upbuilding of the life of the rural community.

68. It is recommended that every new missionary going to Central Africa be encouraged to read in Anthropology to the extent of securing an insight into the nature of those tribal customs, kinship obligations, rituals, beliefs and ceremonies which limit and condition to so great an extent the spiritual and social attitudes of the Bantu and his freedom to accept the Christian way of life.

69. In view of the successful experience of various missionary societies with the employment of trained Bantu mission workers in the Rhodesias and other parts of Africa, and bearing in mind the peculiar suitability and effective approach of the Christian African as a missionary to the less advanced members of his race, the Commission commend the strategy of this policy as a means of Christianising Africa, and recommend that the experience gained in

[1] Chapter I. pp. 5-10.   [2] Chapter XVIII. pp. 305-7.

this field be made a subject of careful study by the missionary societies.

The Commission question whether the same policy could not be usefully extended to include highly qualified American Negroes who could be trained and appointed to African fields by the American, European and South African missionary societies.

70. In view of the co-operation established between Government and missions in bringing about the general advancement of the Native, the missionary is urged to acquaint himself thoroughly with the nature of Government, its policies of Native development, the laws by which the Territory is administered, and the policy of Indirect Rule with its implications for the missionary programme.

It is further recommended that every missionary under appointment to the Territory be required to pass an examination in the above subjects, and that to facilitate such a procedure the Administration prepare a syllabus on these subjects for the use of the missionary societies.

71. It is urged that, in addition to his specialised training for the mission field, the missionary should have at least an introductory course in the following: Anthropology, Tropical Agriculture, Phonetics, Tropical Medicine, Native Customary Law, Social Welfare and Recreation, and that women missionaries in addition to Anthropology, Tropical Medicine and Social Welfare and Phonetics, should have training in Nursing and Domestic Science.

72. It is recommended that in addition to the usual equipment of Theological, Biblical and ecclesiastical training, the personnel of each major Rhodesian mission should include men and women who have had special training in the following subjects:—

Anthropology, Agriculture, Rural Community Planning, Land Economy, Civil Engineering, Medicine, Social Welfare and Recreation, Drama, Music and Folk Dancing, Phonetics, Sociology, Native Customary Law, Science of Teacher Training, Domestic Science and Hygiene, Colonial Administration and Common Law.

73. Missionary societies operating in Northern Rhodesia are urged to consider the timeliness of planning together and with Government for securing the occasional services for the Territory of first-rate experts in the fields of Economics, Anthropology and Sociology, who would be available to devote considerable periods to the problems of the Territory as a whole, and whose advice would be at the disposal of all the major interests represented in the Protectorate.

74. The Commission recommend that the missionary societies make arrangements with universities and colleges which offer special courses preparing for service in tropical Africa. In this way prospective missionaries to Northern Rhodesia and missionaries who are at home on furlough might be enabled to attend the lectures for Colonial Service Probationers already provided by the Universities of Cambridge and Oxford, and share the training given to selected candidates for the Colonial Service in such subjects as Phonetics, Primitive Thought and Religion, African Sociology, African Customary Law, Ethnology of East Africa, Culture Contacts, Material Culture, Economics, Tropical Hygiene, First Aid, Agriculture, Geography, History, etc.

75. It is recommended that, in view of the widening scope of missionary service and increasing demands for missionary specialists, the mission societies take steps toward securing the co-operation of missionary training colleges in providing courses and training facilities suited to the more adequate preparation of the missionary for his task.

APPENDIX A

PARIS EVANGELICAL MISSION

Established[1] 1885

La Société des Missions Évangéliques de Paris,
102 Boulevard Arago, Paris, XIV.

Livingstone	Address P.O. Box 53, Livingstone
Sesheke	Address P.O. Sesheke
Lealui	Address P.O. Mongu
Lukona	Address P.O. Mongu
Mabumbu	Address P.O. Mongu
Sefula	Address P.O. Mongu

LONDON MISSIONARY SOCIETY

Established 1887

48 Broadway, Westminster, London, S.W.1.

Mbereshi	Address P.O. Kawambwa
Kafulwe	Address P.O. Kawambwa
Mpolokoso	Address P.O. Mpolokoso
Kambole	Address P.O. Abercorn
Kawimbe	Address P.O. Abercorn
Senga Hill	Address P.O. Abercorn

[1] This refers in each case to the date at which work was started in Northern Rhodesia.

395

METHODIST MISSION
(Union of Primitive and Wesleyan Methodist Missions)
Established 1893

24 Bishopsgate, London, E.C.2.

Broken Hill   Address P.O. Box 3, Broken Hill

Nanzhila   Address P.O. Namwala, via Livingstone

Kanchindu   Address P.O. Choma

Namantombwa and Nambala   Address P.O. Mumbwa

Kasenga   Address P.O. Namwala, via Livingstone

Kafue Native Training Institute   Address P.O. Kafue

Kafue Mission   Address P.O. Kafue

Chipembi   Address P.O. Chisamba

LIVINGSTONIA MISSION
Established 1895

Church of Scotland Foreign Mission, 121 George Street,
Edinburgh.

Mwenzo   Address P.O. Isoka

Lubwa   Address P.O. Chinsali

Chitambo   Address P.O. Serenji

WHITE FATHERS' MISSION
Established 1895

Vicariate of Bangweulu

Chilubula   Address P.O. Kasama

Kayambi   Address P.O. Kasama

Chilonga   Address P.O. Mpika

Chilubi   Address P.O. Luwingu

Ngumbo   Address P.O. Fort Rosebery

Chibote	Address P.O. Kawambwa
Ipusukilo	Address P.O. Luwingu
Kapatu	Address P.O. Kasama
Malole	Address P.O. Kasama
Rosa	Address P.O. Kasama
Lubushi	Address P.O. Kasama
Lufubu	Address P.O. Kawambwa

CHRISTIAN MISSIONS IN MANY LANDS

Established 1897

1 Widcombe Crescent, Bath, England.

Kalene Hill	Address P.O. Mwinilunga
Kamapanda	Address P.O. Mwinilunga
Chavuma	Address P.O. Mongu
Chitokoloki	Address P.O. Mongu
Kalundu	Address P.O. Fort Rosebery
Johnston Falls	Address P.O. Fort Rosebery
Fort Rosebery	Address P.O. Fort Rosebery
Mubende	Address P.O. Kawambwa
Kawama	Address P.O. Kawambwa

DUTCH REFORMED CHURCH

Established 1898

Sending van die N.G. Kerk, O.V.S., Bus 399, Bloemfontein.

Madzimoyo	Address P.O. Fort Jameson
Fort Jameson	Address P.O. Fort Jameson
Nyanji	Address P.O. Fort Jameson
Tamanda	Address P.O. Fort Jameson
Magwero	Address P.O. Fort Jameson

Derika   Address P.O. Fort Jameson
Kamoto   Address P.O. Fort Jameson
Nsadzu   Address P.O. Fort Jameson
Merwe   Address P.O. Petauke
Hofmeyr   Address P.O. Petauke
Broken Hill   Address P.O. Broken Hill

JESUIT FATHERS' MISSION
Established 1905

Apostolic Prefecture of Broken Hill

Broken Hill   Address P.O. Broken Hill
Chikuni   Address P.O. Mission Siding
Chingombe   Address P.O. Mkushi
Kasisi   Address P.O. Lusaka
Katondwe   Address P.O. Feira
Kapoche   Address P.O. Feira

FRANCISCAN FATHERS' MISSION

Bwana M'Kubwa   Address P.O. Bwana M'Kubwa
Luanshya   Address P.O. Luanshya

CAPUCHIN FATHERS' MISSION

Livingstone   Address P.O. Livingstone

SOUTH AFRICAN BAPTIST MISSION
Established 1905

Rev. J. Edgar Ennals, D.D., Bompas Road, Dunkeld,
Johannesburg.

Ndola   Address P.O. Box 10, Ndola
Kafulafuta   Address P.O. Luanshya

SEVENTH DAY ADVENTIST MISSION
Established 1905

Choma	Address P.O. Choma
Rusangu	Address P.O. Mission Siding
Musofu	Address Private Bag, P.O. Ndola
Liumba Hill	Address P.O. Mongu
Chimpempe	Address P.O. Kawambwa
Mwami	Address P.O. Box 47, Fort Jameson

BRETHREN IN CHRIST MISSION
Established 1906

Rev. C. N. Hostetter, Washington Boro, Penna., U.S.A.

Macha	Address P.O. Choma
Sikalongo	Address P.O. Choma

UNIVERSITIES' MISSION TO CENTRAL AFRICA
Established 1910 [1]

Central Africa House, Wood Street, Westminster, London.

Livingstone	Address Church House, Livingstone
Mapanza	Address P.O. Choma
Msoro	Address P.O. Fort Jameson
Chipili	Address P.O. Fort Rosebery
Fiwila	Address P.O. Mkushi
Fort Jameson	Address P.O. Fort Jameson
Broken Hill	Address Church House, Broken Hill
Ndola	Address Church House, Ndola

[1] The Church work of the Universities' Mission at Livingstone, Broken Hill, Fort Jameson and Ndola is primarily for the European population of these centres, which for this reason are not listed among the stations of this mission upon the mission map.

SOUTH AFRICA GENERAL MISSION
Established 1911

P.O. Box 988, Cape Town.

Mukinge Hill	Address P.O. Kasempa
Mutanda Bridge	Address P.O. Kasempa
Luampa	Address P.O. Mongu
Kaba Hill	Address P.O. Mongu

CHURCH OF CHRIST MISSION
Established 1923

Sinde	Address P.O. Livingstone
Kabanga	Address P.O. Kalomo

THE SALVATION ARMY
Established 1927

P.O. Box 14, Salisbury, S. Rhodesia.

Ibwemunyama	Address P.O. Mazabuka

SCANDINAVIAN BAPTIST MISSION
Established 1931

Mpongwe	Address P.O. Luanshya

APPENDIX B

I. FIRST the kit of a married recruit from the Chinsali district of Northern Rhodesia. He had been working underground for twelve months at a wage of 30s. to 35s. a month and had on his person, in addition to his pack of goods, 30s. in cash. The fact should be mentioned that he had already paid taxes for last year, and this may account for the purse being small. Though married, his status wife had never left her Native kraal. On the mines he had lived in married quarters with a woman inherited from one of his kinsmen after the latter had returned to the Native village (and had passed her on to someone else by a *sub-rosa* arrangement as common as it is difficult of detection).

1 imitation leather suitcase	1 pr. puttees
8 women's dresses	1 sheet
3 women's head-cloths	1 towel
1 woman's slip	1 handkerchief
6 men's shirts	3 second-hand blankets
3 prs. men's shorts	1 steamer rug
5 prs. men's trousers	6 lengths of print (24 yds.)
(khaki, black, grey)	1 umbrella
3 singlets	6 bracelets
1 pr. new tennis shoes	1 enamel mug
2 sweaters	3 wash dishes
1 cardigan	2 mirrors
2 prs. men's socks	1 comb
3 men's ties	1 Gillette safety razor
1 sun helmet	1 shaving stick
1 cap	1 bottle toilet water

[1] The sampling method of selection has been used. We have listed the articles of the first kit examined, which belonged to a married man whose family had remained in his Native kraal; second, the kit of the first unmarried man; third, that of the first married man with a family. Variation between kits shows a wide range. There were two bicycles and a gramophone, but no sewing-machine in any of the baggage lists.

1 bottle perfume   1 pr. scissors
2 boxes blanco   1 box safety pins
1 toothbrush   8 bars soap
2 notebooks, 2 pencils, 2 pens 1 bottle salt

II. The second kit is that of an unmarried recruit—a keen-eyed, alert youngster of twenty or twenty-two years. He had been in a machine shop on the surface for fourteen months at a wage of 20s. a month and had in cash on his person £3:10s. He was apologetic about the paucity of articles as he compared his opened bundles with the more ambitious array in the kits of others, but justified himself by saying he had paid the taxes of his two kinsmen as well as his own.

1 composition suitcase   1 belt
3 blankets   1 singlet
2 coats, 1 vest   1 pr. women's knickers
1 hat, 1 cap   3 bars of soap
1 luggage strap   1 pencil
6 prs. of denim trousers   8 boxes of matches
5 shirts

III. The third kit is that of an underground worker, his wife, a boy of three and a young baby carried on the back of the mother. Inquiry disclosed that a girl of six had been left with his wife's mother in the home kraal. His work-card showed that he had been an underground helper for twelve months, received 30s. to 35s. a month and had in cash on his person £7. It was his second year of service at the mines. The pack was divided, the wife carrying the smaller bundle.

Wife's bundle (tied in a large coloured table-cloth)

5 children's hats   1 cloth dress
1 child's jersey   2 sweaters
3 child's print dresses 1 cap
3 women's head-cloths 8 two-yard lengths of blue
   (rayon)   print
1 sateen skirt   1 pr. silk stockings
5 women's blouses

Husband's bundle (in a large dilapidated tin trunk to which
           bundles of kitchen-ware were tied)

3 blankets   3 saucepans
3 meal screens   2 large enamel dishes

2 small enamel dishes
3 enamel mugs
11 enamel deep plates
2 baskets
4 bracelets
1 pr. ladies' shoes
10 boxes of matches

2 four-yard pieces of coloured
  print
1 jar of vaseline
1 box of Native medicines
1 mirror
10 bars of soap

APPENDIX C

Topics to be kept in mind in writing Life-History

NAME, address, place born, tribal group, present job or position.

1. The earliest memories you have of childhood; treatment by, or relations with, your parents, sisters, brothers, etc.

   Elements in your early education—prohibitions, taboos, ancient tales and tribal beliefs imparted by parents or old men or women.

   Your relations to your father and mother. Do you remember having had a different, closer, more intimate, emotional attachment for one than for the other? Did this attachment become transferred later to another member of the family or an outside person?

2. When did you first realise that there were differences in sex as between male and female? What information was given you on sex matters by family or friends? What were your earliest sex experiences? (This information, as all other, will be treated with the strictest confidence.)

   Your earliest wrong-doing. Was it punished or undetected? What was the effect on you of the knowledge of guilt, the shame of detection or the satisfaction from escape?

   Give description of taboos or prohibitions which surrounded you and which limited your freedom before the age of puberty (say 12 years). Were you prohibited from eating certain foods?

   The first trial or punishment of a member of your village for breaking tribal laws or taboos. Give the impression made upon you.

3. Attendance at heathen school for initiation into manhood. Give description of initiation ceremonies in detail. Did you anticipate them with pleasure or otherwise? How were you expected to behave after initiation? . . . toward your father, brothers, mother and sisters?

404

4. Your duties in the kraal. Daily tasks. What did you want most to do? What did you get most enjoyment from doing?

5. Any occasional or continuous bad feeling between members of your family or members of the village. How did you regard the authority of the headmen, the chief, the white Government and its officials?

6. Had you a totem or tribal mark? If so, what was the nature of the mark? After initiation did you take a new name? How was it chosen? Did your father on his marriage come to live in the village of your mother, or did your mother go to live in your father's village? Whose authority in your family was supreme—father's or mother's? What restrictions were placed upon your marriage? Could you marry your mother's sister, or her daughter, or your father's sister, or her daughter? If you are married, describe your courtship, marriage rites and payments, ceremonies attending the birth of first child.

7. Describe the medicine-man and his methods. In what connection did you first come into contact with him? How did you regard him? Incidents reported to you of his powers. Did you distrust him? If so, on what grounds?

8. Describe your first contact with white men and the impression made upon you by: trader, hunter, Government official, missionary. Which of these white men did you find most approachable and sympathetic?
Traditions your group had with reference to the white man. Did your experience actually bear out these traditions? How did your group feel about the coming of the white man's civilisation?
Inducements which brought you into fuller contact with the white man: economic, educational ambition, interest in his ways, glamour of the new life, interest in religion.

9. Points at which your education has been a disappointment to you. How far in your observation have the practices of the white man borne out his Christian teachings? By what incidents did you discover his weaknesses, faults, unfairness, impatience and lack of understanding? How far and in what direction have your sex concepts been changed by contact with the white man's civilisation?

10. Any work done in the mines; its advantages or disadvantages. How far did it change your attitudes toward your

tribal and kinship groups? Any overseas experience and the effect of the wider contacts upon your outlook on life.

11. Describe changes in your ambitions as you passed through periods of childhood, adolescence, young manhood into maturity. How far could these ambitions have been fulfilled without working directly for the white man? Would native traditions and usages have thwarted such ambitions had you remained in the native kraal? At what points do your relations with the white man interfere with your realisation of a perfectly free and well-rounded life?

APPENDIX D

THE Signatory Powers exercising sovereign rights or authority in African territories will continue to watch over the preservation of the Native populations and to supervise the improvement of the conditions of their moral and material well-being. They will, in particular, endeavour to secure the complete suppression of slavery in all its forms and of the slave trade by land and sea.

They will protect and favour, without distinction of nationality or of religion, the religious, scientific or charitable institutions and undertakings created and organised by the nationals of the other Signatory Powers and of States, Members of the League of Nations, which may adhere to the present Convention, which aim at leading the Natives in the path of progress and civilisation. Scientific missions, their property and their collections, shall likewise be the objects of special solicitude.

Freedom of conscience and the free exercise of all forms of religion are expressly guaranteed to all nationals of the Signatory Powers and to those under the jurisdiction of States, Members of the League of Nations, which may become parties to the present Convention. Similarly, missionaries shall have the right to enter into, and to travel and reside in, African territory with a view to prosecuting their calling.

The application of the provisions of the two preceding paragraphs shall be subject only to such restrictions as may be necessary for the maintenance of public security and order, or as may result from the enforcement of the constitutional law of any of the Powers exercising authority in African territories.

(The Powers signatory to this Convention were:

The British Empire, including the Dominion of Canada, the Commonwealth of Australia, the Union of South Africa, the Dominion of New Zealand, and India; United States of America; Belgium; France; Italy; Japan; and Portugal.)

407

APPENDIX E

African Native Catholic Church.
African Faith Mission.
African Catholic Bantu Church.
African Methodist Episcopal Church.
African Methodist Church of South Africa.
African Baptist Sinoia Church.
African Zulu Methodist Church.
African Zion Baptist Church.
African Native Church.
African Lutheran Church.
African Mission Home Church.
African Holy Catholic Church.
African Holy Baptist Church of South Africa.
African Seventh Day Adventists.
African Christian Christ Church.
African Seventh Church of God.
African Pentecostal Baptist Church.
African Pentecostal Faith Mission.
African Catholic Church of South Africa.
African Christian Catholic Baptist.
African Reform Church.
African Christian Apostolic Church (2 churches).
African Mission Society.
African Seventh Church of God Laodicean Mission.
African Free Catholic Church.
African Free Bapedi Church.
African National Baptist Church Association.
African Orthodox Apostolic Church.
African Presbyterian Bafolisi Church.
African Evangelistic Band.
African Native Mission Church.
African Native Free Church.
African Christian Church.
African Empumulanga Mission.

African Congregational Church.
African Province Church.
African Independent Baptist Church.
African Independent Apostle Church.
African United Church.
African United Ethiopian Church.
African Ethiopian National Church.
African Bethel Mission.
African Congress Catholic Church.
African United Brethren Church of St. Moravian.
Africa Church.
African United Zulu Congregational Church.
African Mission Catholic Church.
African Christian Apostolic Church in Zion.
African Christian Missionary Church.
African National (Bethel) Baptist Church.
African Baptist Mission Church.
African United Gaza Church.
African Pentecostal Mission.
African Catholic Episcopal Church.
African Sabbath Mission Church.
African Seventh Day Zulu Chaka Church of Christ.
African Mission Church.
African Native Methodist Church.
African Bakgatla National Church.
African Native Apostolic Church.
African Free Congregational Church.
African Independent Mission Church.
African Orthodox Church.
African Congregational Methodist Church.
African Catholic Church of Gaza.
African Catholic Mission.
African Holy Messenger Church in Zion.
African Cathedral Episcopal Church.
African Baptist Church in Zion.
African Baptist Sinoia Apostolic Church Beira.
African Pentecostal Church.
African Ethiopian Church.
African Province Ethiopian Catholic Church.
African Independent Ethiopian Church.
African Christian Baptist Church of South Africa.
African Bavenda Church.
Afrikaanse Natieve Evangelie Kerk.
Allmount Mount of Olives Baptist Church.

American Ethiopian Church.
American Christian Church.
Ama Yoyopiya.
Amakushe.
Assemblies of God Church.
Afro-Athlican Constructive Gaathly.
Apostle Church of the Full Bible of South Africa.
Apostle Church in Zion.
Apostles and Christian Brethren Church.
Abyssinian Baptist Church.
Algemene Volks Kerk.
Apostolic Church Messenger in Zion.
Apostolic Faith Church.
Apostolic Faith Assembly.
Apostolic Heaven Church in Zion.
Apostolic South African Zulu Church.
Apostolic Baptist Church in Zion.
Apostolic Zion Church.
Apostolic Church in Zion.
Apostolic Church of Zion in South Africa.
Apostolic Association of South Africa.
Apostoles Brethren Church.
Apostolic Faith Assembly.
Apostolic Holy Messenger Church in Zion.
Apostolic Holy Zion Mission in South Africa.
Apostolic Assembly Faith Church of South Africa.
Apostolic Church in Zion of the New Jerusalem Mission in
    Basutoland.
Apostolic Messenger Light World Church in Zion.
Apostolic Jerusalem Church in Sabbath.
Apostolic Church in Zion Amen.
Apostolic United African Church of South Africa.
Bethel Church.
Brethren Mission Church.
Bechuan Methodist Church.
Bechuana Methodist Church in Zion.
Bethel Apostolic Baptist Church.
Bethesda Zion Apostolic Church of Africa.
Basuto Redemption Episcopal.
Berean Bible Readers' Society.
Bantu Ngcqika-Wtsikana Church.
Bantu Baptist Church.
Bantu Presbyterian Church of South Africa.
Baptist Church of the Seventh Day Adventists of Africa.

Baptist of the Seventh Day Adventists.
Bible Standard Church of America.
Catholic African Union.
Christian Apostolic Heaven Church in Zion.
Christian Catholic Apostolic Church in Zion.
Christian Bavenda Church of South Africa.
Christian Brethren.
Christian Evangelical Mission Church.
Christian United Church.
Christian Catholic Church in Zion.
Christian Catholic Apostolic Holy Spirit Church in Zion.
Christian Congregational Baptist Mission.
Christian Apostolic Church of South Africa.
Christian Apostolic Church in Zion.
Christian Bethlehem Church.
Christian Church.
Christian Church Mission of South Africa.
Christian Church of South Africa.
Christian Apostolic Zulu Churches of Zion.
Chaka Zulu Church.
Church of God and Saints of Christ.
Church of Christ.
Church of the Holy Kingdom of Christ the Saviour.
Church of Africa Mission Homes.
Church of Christ for the Union of the Bantu.
Church of Christ South Africa.
Church of Israel.
Church of God.
Church of the Nazarenes.
Church of the Prophets.
Church of the Christian Evangelist.
Mission Church of Israel.
Church of the Holy Ghost.
Congregational Union African Church.
Congregational Church of Christ.
Congregational Gaza Church.
Die Namakwa Independente Kerk van Zuid Afrika.
Ethiopia Church Lamentation of South Africa.
Ethiopian Catholic Church in Zion.
Ethiopian African Church of Zion in South Africa.
Ethiopian Church.
Ethiopian Catholic Church of South Africa.
Ethiopian Baptist Church of South Africa.
Ethiopian Mission of South Africa.

Ethiopian Church of Basutoland.
Ethiopian Methodist Church of Africa.
Ethiopian Church of God the Society of Paradise.
Ethiopian Orthodox Catholic Church.
Ethiopian Messenger Catholic Church in South Africa.
Epifania African Church.
East African Gaza Church.
Episcopal Egreja Luzo Africana Church.
Ethiopia Church of Abyssinia.
East Heathlon Church.
Evangelist Catholic Church.
East Star Baptist Church of Portuguese East Africa.
Empumalanga Gospel Church.
Free Methodist Episcopal Church.
Full Gospel Church.
Filadelfia Church of Africa.
First Catholic Apostolic Church Jerusalem in Zion of South
    Africa.
First Church of God Asia in Efese Church in South Africa.
First Native Church of Christ.
Gospel Messenger Church.
Griqua Independent Church.
Gazaland Zimbabque Ethiopian Church.
General Convention Church of New Jerusalem.
Gaza Mission Church.
Gaza Church.
General Church of the New Jerusalem Mission of South
    Africa.
Heaven Apostolic Jerusalem Church in Zion.
Holy Catholic Episcopal Church.
Heaven Twelfth Apostle Church in Zion.
Holy National Church of South Africa.
Home Natives Co-operative Society.
Hephzibah Faith Mission Association.
Holy Missionary Evangelist Church.
Holy Apostolic Church.
Holy Catholic Apostolic Church in Zion.
Holy Trinity Church of God.
Holy Apostolic Church in Zion.
Holy Sabbath Church.
International Missionary Alliance.
International Holiness Church.
International Baptist Church of God.
International Foursquare Gospel.

Independent Church of South Africa.
Independent Native Presbyterian Church.
Independent and United National Church.
Independent Methodist Church of Africa.
Inter-Communion Church of South Africa.
Independent Ethiopian Congress Mission.
Independent Presbyterian Church.
Independent or Congregational Church.
Jerusalem Christian Church in Zion of South Africa.
King of Salom Melchizedek Church.
Kush Nineveh Church.
Kush Apostolic Church.
Lutheran Bapedi Church.
Lott Carey Baptist Mission of South Africa.
Magana National Church Association.
Methodist Episcopal Church.
Methodist African Church.
Metropolitan Church Association.
Mayen Church.
Modern Mission.
Mount Zion A.M.E. Church.
New Apostolic Church.
Nazarenes (or Shembites).
Native African Christian Church.
Native Congregational Church.
Native Congress Catholic Church.
Native Catholic Episcopalian Church.
Native Denomination Church of South Africa.
Native Modern Religious Society of East Africa.
Native Nation Union Church.
National Native Apostolic Church.
National Protestant Church in Zion.
National Swazi Native Apostolic Church of Africa.
National Church of Ethiopia in South Africa.
National Baptist Church of South Africa.
National Convention Church of the New Jerusalem.
National African Church of Salom.
National Church of God Apostolic in Jerusalem Church.
South African Gaza Mission.
Seventh Day Baptist Church.
Seventh Day Baptist Church of London.
Seventh Church of God.
St. Philip's Ethiopian Church of South Africa.
St. Peter's Apostolic Church.

Spade Reen Gemeentes van Suid Afrika.
Star Baptist Church.
Tembu Catholic Church of South Africa.
Transvaal Basuto Church.
Transvaal Basuto Lutheran Church.
The Supreme Apostolic Church of South Africa.
The True (Truth) Zion Church of God.
United African Apostolic Church.
United Bantu Lutheran Church.
United Free Independent Church.
United Ethiopian Catholic Church of Africa.
United National Catholic Church of Zion.
United National Congress Church.
United National Church in Africa.
United Church of the Brethren in Zion.
United African Missionary Society.
United Churches of Christ.
United Independent National Church of God.
Universal Church of Christ.
Union Apostolic Church of South Africa.
Uhlanga or Church of the Race.
Ukukanye Mission.
Universal National Christian Union.
Unto the Church of God Apostolic Jerusalem in Zion.
Volks Kerk van Zuid Afrika.
Vula Zingene Yehova e-Zion.
Watch Tower Movement.
Zion Brethren Mission Apostolic Church in South Africa.
Zion Gospel African Church.
Zion Revelation Apostolic Church of South Africa.
Zion Apóstolic Faith Mission.
Zion Apostolic Gaza Church of South Africa.
Zion Apostolic in Jerusalem Church.
Zion Apostolic New Jerusalem in South Africa Church.
Zion Christian Church.
Zion Mission African Apostolic Church.
Zion City Apostolic Paulus Church in South Africa.
Zion Holy Church Nation of South Africa.
Zulu Congregational Church.
Zulu or African Ethiopian Church.
Zulu Ethiopian Church.

INDEX